Too Global to Fail

DIRECTIONS IN DEVELOPMENT
Environment and Sustainable Development

Too Global to Fail

The World Bank at the Intersection of National and Global Public Policy in 2025

J. Warren Evans and Robin Davies, Editors

WORLD BANK GROUP

Contents

Boxes

Figures

Tables

Foreword

What will the world look like in 2025? Too Global to Fail was commissioned by the World Bank Group in an effort to answer this challenging question. By examining some of the challenges ahead, it identifies how the international community must adapt to effectively reduce poverty and secure sustainable growth.

In an increasingly interconnected and complex world, communities at all scales rely more and more on global public goods—from reduction of carbon emissions to combat climate change, to food security and vaccines. This book paints a picture of a landscape where everything is changing and the availability of global public goods is challenged by threats like climate change that could stifle poverty reduction efforts and slow economic growth.

The science is clear: By the 2030s, the world will be 2 degrees warmer. Climate change will bring resource scarcity, more frequent and severe storms and droughts, more widespread disease, and disrupted food and energy supplies. Billions of people will be affected, and the poor will suffer the most.

The impacts of climate change are compounded by rapidly growing urbanization—with two thirds of the global population expected to live in cities by 2050. This shift to living densely will not only put more people and assets at risk but also drive increases in the consumption of natural resources and the production of harmful wastes. To produce enough food to nutritiously feed the 9 billion people who will inhabit our planet by 2050, farmers will need to produce as much food as they have over the past 8,000 years.

Clearly, the magnitude of the challenges calls for a commensurate response. This entails an approach to development assistance that integrates local country-level needs with global concerns. Too often these two dimensions are seen to be in opposition.

The World Bank Group has two ambitious and quantifiable goals: ending extreme poverty and boosting shared prosperity by 2030 in a sustainable way. Recognizing climate change as the ultimate threat intensifier, we have committed to screen all our projects in the most vulnerable countries for climate and disaster risks. This is part of an effort to ensure global issues are considered in the design of country-level interventions and that local knowledge feeds into the global development debate.

To see a video of Vice President Rachel Kyte introducing this study: http://youtu.be/Qu_4uwayqWs

It is this ability to address national needs in the context of global trends that gives the World Bank Group a unique advantage as it brings public and private partners together to provide global public goods and meet long term challenges.

Rachel Kyte
Vice President and Special Envoy
for Climate Change
World Bank Group

Preface

This volume is about environment-related and other global public goods in the context of the global development process, and about the role of international organizations, particularly the World Bank, in supplying such goods. At the present time, and for the foreseeable future, there is a distinction between developing and developed countries. We work in development and our concern is the sustainability, in the long term, of development. It is our belief that global sustainability depends crucially upon the provision of certain global public goods, and that the prevailing approach to development and development assistance does not sufficiently recognize this fact.

The global public goods with which we are concerned are enablers of sustained poverty reduction, human well-being, and economic growth in all countries and regions, but particularly in developing countries. They are global public assets, to which correspond some major global public liabilities—the medium- and long-term risks posed by the degradation of ecosystems and the services they provide; the depletion of common-pool resources; pandemics; and instability in global markets for food, energy, and finance.

The rapid acceleration of urbanization will, under business as usual, drive corresponding surges in the consumption of natural resources and the production of harmful wastes. When one also factors in the growing effects of the great exacerbator, climate change, global risk profiles move into largely uncharted territory. While the impacts of climate change are difficult to predict with any certainty in particular locations, the world will experience, with unchecked carbon emissions, even greater resource shortages, more frequent and severe storms and droughts, more widespread disease, the disruption of food and energy supplies, and perhaps in some cases climate-related inter- or intrastate conflict.

In the face of these daunting global risks, we are now witnessing major changes in the international order which are tending to revive interest in global public goods. We are seeing the emergence of development financing on a substantial scale from newer official donors who do not subscribe to Organisation for Economic Co-operation and Development norms, together with a decline in aid from traditional sources. We are seeing shifts in the geography of global poverty and, as a result, the potential withering away of the client base of some multilateral development banks' concessional financing arms. And we are seeing climate change become ever more significant as a call on international public

---

To see Vice President Rachel Kyte discuss global public goods provisions: http://youtu.be/1hgkOiVQTa8

financing—with expectations that developed countries will mobilize as much as $100 billion per annum for climate-related international action by 2020. In light of these developments, some commentators are calling for a transformation of traditional official development assistance to focus much more intensively, or even exclusively, on global challenges: to become what might be termed "global public finance."[1]

Against the above backdrop, the present volume aims to increase understanding of, and explore options to address, the barriers that the World Bank and other development financing institutions face as they search for an appropriate balance between what one would hope were two complementary aims: meeting the poverty reduction and economic growth needs of developing countries, and supporting effective action on global development challenges.

Listening to Youth

In the course of preparing some of the chapters which compose this volume, there were many opportunities to engage young staff of the World Bank Group, and of several other academic institutions and development agencies. We sought their opinions and potential solutions to the kinds of global challenges that they, in their working lives, will continue to face as this century unfolds. Several chapters include short, relevant essays by young Bank staff members expressing a youth view on the topic of concern.

The greatest concern, across all the youth responses featured, was the specter of inaction: the fear that nothing would be done, or else that too little would be done, too slowly. An urgency lacking in the arena of multilateral diplomacy and international development assistance came through very clearly in the expressed concerns of young professionals. From a wide range of sectoral backgrounds, they all voiced a similar conviction that changes are needed in the way in which the multilateral "system" addresses global challenges.

Young professionals were concerned particularly that organizational silos and fragmentation of effort would inhibit working at the scale necessary to deal meaningfully with global challenges. The appetite for working collaboratively within partnerships is strong. Young staff who have seen it work well in some World Bank–led programs to date were optimistic that it could render the kind of solutions needed, at the scale required.[2]

Most encouraging was the fact that the youngest cohort of professionals does not consider development and environmental sustainability to be mutually exclusive, neither conceptually nor in practice. In fact, the opposite is the case: The view is that one cannot exist without the other—that development is only possible if we stop regarding environmental sustainability as an unaffordable luxury and realise that its demise will create a world in which even the necessities are unaffordable.

Young staff gave much prominence to innovative forms of financing, with an emphasis on mobilizing both private financing and "grassroots" financing. The concept of vulnerability loomed very large too, whether in connection with climate-related impacts, natural disasters, or the effects of increasingly dense urbanization.

Finally, young professionals called for the multilateral world to look to the private sector not just for finance but for real partnership. They saw the relevance of private sector incentive structures for inducing behavioral change. They saw also the increasing emphasis in some quarters of the private sector on social entrepreneurship[3] and impact investing—a shift beyond the profit motive and also beyond mere corporate social responsibility.

Chapter Summaries

Following an Introduction by the coeditors, 10 essays are arranged in three sections. In the first section are three pieces dealing with the overall context for the discussion; in the second are three pieces dealing with financing and related issues; and in the third are four pieces dealing broadly with matters of strategy and delivery. The volume closes with some concluding observations by the coeditors.

Chapter 1: Introduction
J. Warren Evans and Robin Davies explain, and place in historical perspective, the concerns that led them to prepare this volume, and they set out its structure and main points.

Part 1: The Future of Global Public Goods

Chapter 2: Global Public Goods and International Development
Scott Barrett sets out the distinctive features of global public goods and gives a contemporary perspective on their relevance for international development. He argues the World Bank can and should play a strategic role in ensuring that the provision of global public goods contributes to meeting its principal aim of reducing poverty. The supply of global public goods is, he says, a "patch-work." The Bank should develop a coherent strategy for their provision for the next quarter century, with a focus on policies and projects that complement the Bank's core business of country lending and increase the returns on more traditional development projects. It should build strong and mutually beneficial relationships with a wide range of organizations for this purpose, and existing sources of funding should be consolidated and supplemented in order to implement the new strategy.

Chapter 3: Environmental Sustainability as a Development Issue:
The Evolution of an Idea
J. Warren Evans[3] provides a brisk review of the evolution of what began as an environmental agenda in developing countries from the late 1970s, and subsequently evolved into what is now recognized as the sustainable development agenda. He explains how this agenda was taken up by the World Bank following the publication of the report of the Brundtland Commission in 1987,

and how the Bank's policy framework and organizational arrangements have developed since that time.

Chapter 4: The Future Is Now: Scenarios to 2025 and Beyond

J. Warren Evans surveys global scenarios for the period from 2025 to 2050, particularly as they relate to the supply of internationally shared public goods. He examines population and economic development projections, highlights growing pressures on common-pool resources, summarizes the likely impacts of an increase in the global average temperature of between two and four degrees above pre-industrial levels, explores resource-scarcity scenarios and discusses the potential impacts of technological progress. He underlines that the development policies and actions pursued by countries today, often with World Bank support, will have long-lasting effects on the future of the global commons as well as on their own future national prosperity. He argues that the policies and programs of the World Bank are likely to require substantial transformation in order to reflect the realities of a resource-constrained, warming world, and help guide it toward a more sustainable future.

Part 2: Financing Global Public Goods

Chapter 5: Something's Gotta Give: Aid and the Financing of Global Public Goods

Robin Davies explores the use of international aid for global public goods. He identifies a growing disconnect between what traditional donors say about their aid and what they do with it. The notion of aid as a transfer to poor countries in support of national development strategies is at the center of their concept of aid effectiveness. But in fact they increasingly use aid for the provision of a variety of global public goods including, most notably and recently, climate change mitigation. He argues there are limits on the extent to which this trend can continue along present rails, grounded in the prevailing aid effectiveness doctrine, diplomatic considerations, and moral concerns. The use of aid for global public goods is, or soon will be, grinding against these limits, which friction is likely to generate heat.

Chapter 6: Aiding Global Public Policy: Rethinking Rationales and Roles

Robin Davies argues that, in the absence of continued aid volume growth and new sources of financing for global public goods, the tensions described in the previous chapter must, sooner or later, be resolved by reconceiving the rationale for aid. He proposes a relatively conservative modification of it, which carries implications for resource allocation, delivery mechanisms, the institutional and global governance of the relevant financial flows, and the measurement of those flows. He elaborates on the implications for the World Bank and other multilateral development banks, calling for the development of strategic, linked institutional frameworks for financing global public policy; the determined pursuit of global goals through country operations as well as global programs; a shift to the use of more flexible financing packages to create incentives for deviations from business as usual; and the establishment of a Global Financing Facility to finance global public policy through existing institutions.

Chapter 7: Financing Global Public Goods at Scale

Kenneth Lay starts from the premise that public credit alone cannot meet the world's greatest challenges. He explores options for accessing global savings—the large and extensively institutionalized pools of public and private sector savings that have accumulated in many countries since World War II. Noting that much of the work being done to address key global challenges is local, relatively small scale, and idiosyncratic, he argues that the fundamental question is how to enable the relevant assets to be pooled and securitized, with any required application of public credit enhancement occurring in the most efficient manner to reach investment grade. He argues there is a need for broad international agreement on a limited number of high-priority activities that would benefit from pooling and securitization, such as urban conversion to LED street lighting, distributed generation of renewable energy, and multi-peril/multi-party catastrophe risk insurance. For each high-priority area, a vehicle should be created to act as issuer of the fixed-income instruments created from the aggregated and securitized projects, on the model of the International Finance Facility for Immunization.

Part 3: Strategic Directions for the Provision of Global Public Goods

Chapter 8: Emerging Economies, Emerging Development Partners

J. Warren Evans, Laura Tlaiye, Tae Yong Jung, and Esther Choi discuss the rapidly changing roles of emerging economies in the provision of global public goods, with an eye to implications for the World Bank. In her case study of Brazil, Laura Tlaiye explores how Brazil's growing share of and connectedness to the world economy might translate into growing influence among other developing countries, notably in Latin America and Africa, and how Brazil might engage in the supply of global public goods. She suggests the extent of that engagement will depend upon how far Brazil has been able to satisfy domestic concerns, or find areas of convergence between those and global concerns.

In their case study of the Democratic People's Republic of Korea, Tae Yong Jung and Esther Choi examine the processes and mechanisms through which Korea addresses global public goods, especially in relation to climate change and related sustainability challenges. They conclude that, as the host country of international organizations and agencies such as Global Green Growth Institute, the Green Climate Fund and the World Bank regional office focusing on advancing strategies for sustainable development, Korea has significant potential to become a regional and global hub for addressing global public goods.

Both case studies stress the importance of ongoing World Bank engagement with emerging economies as clients in order to support joint knowledge-sharing engagements with third parties. Evans concludes there is a remarkable opportunity now for the World Bank to tap into the resources and capacities of the emerging economies for the benefit of poorer countries and the world as a whole.

Chapter 9: Shifting Priorities: Re-envisioning World Bank Partnerships for Transformational Impact

Warren Evans, Isabel Nicholson, Lelei TuiSamoa LeLaulu, and Alison Wescott bring together perspectives on the potential for innovative, multistakeholder coalitions to contribute solutions to global problems. They review the experience of the World Bank's participation in, and leadership of, global and regional partnership programs, finding that the results have been mixed. They provide case studies of the Critical Ecosystem Partnerships Fund, Global Tiger Initiative and Global Partnership on Oceans highlighting areas where the Bank's traditional modus operandi required adjustment to lead new forms of partnership. They stress the importance of structuring partnerships so as to meet the five key conditions of "collective impact," namely a common agenda, shared measurement, mutually reinforcing activities, continuous communication and backbone support.

Chapter 10: Urban Sustainable Development: Re-envisioning the City of 2025

Drawing on extensive discussions with both low-income and professional youth in Bangkok, Manila, Tokyo, and Washington, D.C., Julianne Baker Gallegos and Sintana Vergara consider in detail what makes a sustainable city, what are the forces that threaten it, and how the World Bank might promote measures to ensure that cities act to both conserve the global commons and promote human health. They argue multilateral institutions like the World Bank are uniquely qualified to "nudge" urban consumption patterns and thus influence the state of the global commons. They can do this by effectively valuing natural resources as a source of wealth and heritage; helping to protect natural resources, even before they are threatened; and facilitating networked action by major cities to shift toward more sustainable patterns of production and consumption.

Chapter 11: Managing Transitions to Sustainable Provision of Global Public Goods

Derk Loorbach, Roebin Lijnis Huffenreuter, Niki Frantzeskaki, and Jan Rotmans of the Dutch Research Institute for Transitions provide their perspective on the management of the transitions which must be negotiated in order to achieve global sustainability and related institutional changes. They detail the key features of their specific approach to transition management, with particular reference to the governance of sustainability transitions, and make suggestions for its implementation in a global context. They call for the development of generic guiding governance principles for sustainability transitions; the establishment of open-source pool of knowledge, experts, and instruments; the building of a "world map of transition" to provide deeper insight into transition dynamics in different areas; and the provision of funding and other support for transition management processes.

Part 4: The Final Stretch: High Road or Low?

Chapter 12: Conclusion

Robin Davies and J. Warren Evans conclude that the World Bank and other international organizations have a central role to play in addressing long-term global challenges such as climate change and food security, but that these institutions must transform themselves and their partnerships if they are to be fit for purpose. Given the likelihood that ODA will continue to decline, and global challenges worsen, international organizations need to adopt a far more determined and strategic approach to the delivery of global public goods. Without effective action, many of the development gains of the last decades may be lost.

Notes

1. Sumner and Mallett (2012); Birdsall and Leo (2011); Severino and Ray (2009).
2. To see Green Belt Movement Leader Wanjira Maathai discuss future leaders: http://youtu.be/9IsaFP15qQ0
3. With inputs from Esther Choi, Eun Joo Yi, and Udayan Tripathi.

Acknowledgments

The authors are grateful to the numerous individuals that contributed in a variety of ways to the conceptual and substantive development of this book. Inger Andersen, as Vice President of Sustainable Development, was instrumental in getting the work off the ground. Rachel Kyte in that same role also supported the study in many ways; most important was her substantive guidance and vision. The Government of the Netherlands provided financial support—Ms. Kitty van der Heijden, Ambassador for Sustainable Development and Director of the Department of Climate, Energy, Environment and Water in the Ministry of Foreign Affairs, was particularly supportive and participated in a number of consultations on the issues addressed in the book.

Marianne Fay, Chief Economist for the World Bank Susrtainable Development Network provided valued oversight for the study. Peer reviews of the draft by Concepcion Aisa-Otin, Patricia Bliss-Guest, Mark Cackler, and Patricia Zurita were very helpful in shaping the final direction of the book. The Rockefeller Foundation provided a unique opportunity to research and write sections of the book while a resident at the Rockefeller Center in Bellagio.

Several young staff in the Bank provided one-pagers expressing their view on long-term challenges they will face in the coming decades. The authors give sincere thanks to Inka Schomer, Climate Investment Funds; Kevin McCall, Climate Policy and Finance team; Nasser Brahim, Climate Investment Funds; Benedikt Signer, Global Facility for Disaster Reduction and Recovery; Jun Rentschler, Sustainable Development Network Chief Economists Office; Mark Hirschboeck, World Bank Institute; Anna Lerner, Latin America and Caribbean; Lorraine Sugar, Task-force to Catalyze Climate Action; and Timothy Bouley, Global Partnership for Oceans.

More than 30 brainstorming workshops with more than 300 participants were convened to discuss issues and solutions discussed in the book. The authors express thanks to all of the participants for their valued inputs. Several consultations were held in the World Bank with the Africa Region Environment and Natural Resources Management team led by Idah Pswarayi-Ridihough; Treasury staff led by Heike Reichelt; young staff organized by Julianne Baker Gallegos and Sintana Vergara; and seasoned sustainable development advocates Patricia

To see all videos from co-authors of *Too Global to Fail:* https://www.youtube.com/playlist?list=PLDCQOIA RPxDEGDTJvjfkojdUsQSr-d2os

Bliss-Guest, Julia Bucknell, Dan Hoornweg, Charles di Leva, Jeffrey Lewis, Judith Moore, Neeraj Prasad, Jae So, and Xueman Wang.

External consultations were organized at the Institute for Global Environmental Strategies in Tokyo led by Hideyuki Mori; the Asian Development Bank in Manila led by Nessim Ahmad; the USAID Asian Adaptation program led by Brad Philips; University House at the Australian National University (with a selection of people from the Pacific island countries and Pacific regional organisations); the Development Policy Centre within the Crawford School of Public Policy at the Australian National University (which organized a public event on the role of multilateral organizations in providing global public goods); a meeting of representatives of low-income communities in Manila organized by Lessandra Berbano; private sector representatives in Seoul organized by SungWoo Kim, Tae Yong Jung, and Esther Choi; Department for International Development in London; AusAID in Canberra; two sessions at the Dutch Ministry of Foreign Affairs in The Hague—one with young professionals and one with a more senior team organized by Kitty van der Heijden; Danish Ministry of Foreign Affairs organized by Eva Grambye; Center for Global Development in Washington, DC, organized by Michele de Nevers; and a joint discussion with the Overseas Development Institute and the Organisation for Economic Co-operation and Development in London.

Esther Choi, Isabel Nicholson, Udayan Tripathi, and Eun Joo Yi provided the support needed to carry out the study—from research assistance to information technology and web management and dozens of tasks in between. This group of young professionals also engaged many of their counterparts across the globe to seek their views and inputs. They were the backbone of the study and a real pleasure to work with.

About the Contributors

J. Warren Evans is an independent adviser to international development organizations, governments, and the private sector on sustainable development, particularly on environment and climate change. He retired from the World Bank in August 2013 after serving as a senior adviser at the Sustainable Development Network and Director of the Environment Department. During this time, he led a team responsible for establishing several innovative environment and climate finance mechanisms including the Climate Investment Funds, and served as an advisor for the design of the Green Climate Fund. Before joining the World Bank in 2003, Mr. Evans spent 25 years working on environment and development issues across Asia including 15 years at the Asian Development Bank.

Robin Davies is the associate director of the Development Policy Centre at the Crawford School of Public Policy, Australian National University. His research focuses on multilateral development policy, development financing, and aid effectiveness. He previously held various positions in the senior executive service of the Australian Agency for International Development, both in Australia and overseas. Mr. Davies was Australia's representative on the G20 Development Working Group from its establishment in 2010. He played an active role in shaping the Seoul Development Consensus for Shared Growth and subsequent work on "growth with resilience." He oversaw the development of a series of climate change initiatives in the period 2007–10, and he contributed to the design of the Climate Investment Funds. He has represented Australia on the Organisation for Economic Co-operation and Development, Development Assistance Committee and the boards of the World Food Programme and the International Fund for Agricultural Development, and he managed Australia's aid program in Indonesia from 2003 to 2006.

Scott Barrett is a leading scholar on transnational and global challenges, ranging from climate change to disease eradication. His research focuses on how institutions like norms, customary law, resolutions, and treaties can be used to promote international cooperation. He has advised a number of international organizations, including the United Nations, the World Bank, the Organisation for Economic Co-operation and Development, the European Commission, and the International Task Force on Global Public Goods. He was previously a lead author of the Intergovernmental Panel on Climate Change and a member of the Academic Panel to the Department of Environment in the United Kingdom. Dr. Barrett previously taught at The Johns Hopkins University School of Advanced International Studies in Washington, DC, where he also directed the International Policy program. Before that, he was on the faculty of the London Business School. He has also been a visiting scholar at Yale. He is a research fellow with the Beijer Institute (Stockholm, Sweden), CESifo (Munich, Germany), and the Kiel Institute for the World Economics (Kiel, Germany).

Kenneth Lay is a senior managing director of The Rock Creek Group, a firm in Washington, DC, that manages approximately $7 billion for about 50 major pension and sovereign wealth funds, endowments, and foundations. Until December 2010, Mr. Lay served as the Vice President and Treasurer of the World Bank, where he and his colleagues financed the World Bank and other clients for roughly $15–30 billion annually in international debt markets. He also invested more than $115 billion for the World Bank and for member country central banks, sovereign wealth funds and pension funds, the International Monetary Fund, and others. Earlier in his career, Mr. Lay headed the World Bank's financial sector practice, where he developed with International Monetary Fund colleagues the Financial Sector Assessment Program that now is the principal mechanism for monitoring and oversight of countries' financial systems. He was the World Bank's country director for countries in Latin America and Southeastern Europe and, previously at the World Bank Treasury, he conceived and executed the first global bond, now the principal vehicle for sovereign financing in international markets. Before joining the World Bank, Mr. Lay was an enforcement lawyer at the Securities and Exchange Commission. He holds the Chartered Financial Analyst designation and is a member of the California Bar.

Julianne Baker Gallegos is a junior professional associate focusing on the relation between cities and climate change at the World Bank's Urban and Resilience Management Unit. She is originally from Costa Rica, where she studied biology and specialized in climate change impacts on coastal ecosystems. She became interested in the urban environment while obtaining her master's degree in environmental management from Yale University. Julianne's graduate research focused on climate change adaptation policy and practice and disaster risk in a periurban community located in the outskirts of Bogotá, Colombia. She has worked in the field in Latin America, Southern and Eastern Africa, and East Asia and has collaborated with several international and local nongovernmental organizations as well as with organizations such as the Red Cross/Red Crescent and United Nations Development Programme.

Sintana Vergara is a junior professional associate in the World Bank's Urban and Resilience Management Unit. She has a bachelor of science in environmental engineering from Cornell University; a master of science in environmental engineering from the University of California, Berkeley; and a doctorate in energy and resources from the University of California, Berkeley. She has worked with local nongovernmental organizations on small-scale water treatment in Bangladesh, India, and Mexico, and on solid waste management in Colombia. Her dissertation explored the climate mitigation benefits of reuse as a waste management strategy for cities. She focused on the environmental trade-offs from informal recycling in Bogotá, Colombia, where her research was funded by a Fulbright Fellowship. At the World Bank, she has focused on assessment and improvement of solid waste management in cities.

Derk Loorbach is the director of the Dutch Research Institute for Transitions and associate professor at the Faculty of Social Science, both at Erasmus University, Rotterdam, The Netherlands. He was among the first researchers to develop the concept and approach of transition management. He has been involved in numerous scientific and policy projects in different areas and is frequently invited for lectures and debates, both nationally and internationally. At present, the focus of his research is on urban transitions and the possibilities for urban transition management.

Roebin Lijnis Huffenreuter is a doctoral candidate at Erasmus University, carrying out research at the Dutch Research Institute for Transitions on financial-economic transitions and sustainability, particularly the trade-offs among financial-economic efficiency, ecological effectiveness, and social inclusiveness in societal systems.

Niki Frantzeskaki completed her PhD in 2011 at Delft University of Technology, the Netherlands, on the subject of "Dynamics of Societal Transitions: Driving Forces and Feedback Loops." Since April 2010, she has been working with the Dutch Research Institute for Transitions. From November 2011 until June 2012, Niki was a visiting scholar at Monash University, Melbourne, Australia, working in the Monash Water for Liveability Centre. Her research interests include sustainability transitions, socialecological systems, and their governance.

Jan Rotmans is a socially engaged scientist with more than 200 publications in the field of climate change and global change modeling, sustainable development and transitions, and system innovations. In September 2004, he founded the Dutch Research Institute for Transitions and became full professor in transitions and transition management at Erasmus University Rotterdam. In addition to his scientific work, he also co-founded Urgenda in 2007, a new type of nongovernmental organization that aims to accelerate transitions to a sustainable future in the Netherlands.

Lelei TuiSamoa LeLaulu is a development entrepreneur who works at the confluences of climate change, communication, sustainable tourism, food security, civil society, and renewable energy. He is a special advisor to the World Bank for Oceans, a member of the Advisory Panel for Business and Sustainability of the International Finance Corporation, and a member of the High-Level

Expert Group reviewing the 10-year strategies of the Asian Development Bank. He is also chairman of the Foundation of the Peoples of the South Pacific, the Earth Council Alliance, and the Leadership Council of The George Washington University School of Business Department of Hospitality and Tourism Management. Born in Samoa, Mr. LeLaulu's United Nations service included organizing and promoting the series of global conferences and summits in the 1990s, which fed into the United Nations (UN) Millennium Development Goals. He was on the UN Reform Team, which gave the organization its first major overhaul, secretary of the Task Force to Re-Orient UN Public Information, and served for a decade as chairman of the Committee for the Security and Independence of the International Civil Service.

Alison Wescott is currently the advisor for institutional effectiveness at Africa Lead, a project funded by the United States Agency for International Development to support Africa's agricultural transformation. She is a specialist in leadership and management. Her advisory work and research interests include institutional assessment, strategic planning, implementation of policy change and reform, capacity development, and management for development results. Before joining Africa Lead, Ms. Wescott spent 7 years working with the World Bank. For World Bank Institute, she coauthored and coordinated a path-breaking study on the role of leadership in achieving development results in fragile states. From 2011 to 2013, she worked with the Global Tiger Initiative, where she played a key role in the design and delivery of a new program on leadership for results in conservation. Ms. Wescott has spent nearly 15 years based in Africa, Asia, and the Pacific.

Laura Tlaiye is the sustainability advisor in the World Bank Treasury. She has worked on environment and climate change issues for the past 20 years in various capacities. In her current role, she provides technical and strategic insights on financial products addressing sustainability, such as green bonds, forest bonds, and other financial services linked to climate change and the environment. She is part of the team that selects the portfolio of projects that are supported by World Bank green bonds. Her more recent assignments, before joining the World Bank Treasury, were as sector manager for Environment and Water and for the Environment Department.

Tae Yong Jung is a professor at the Korea Development Institute School of Public Policy and Management. Before his current position, he held various positions in the Asian Development Bank, the Global Green Growth Institute, the World Bank, and the Institute for Global Environmental Strategies of Japan. He has been involved in many international activities and researches related to climate change issues, including the Intergovernmental Panel on Climate Change and the UN High-Level Panel on Global Sustainability. His research interest is how to implement the concept of sustainable development taking into account climate factors in developing countries.

Esther Choi is currently a doctoral student at the University of California Berkeley's Department of Environmental Science, Policy, and Management, exploring the intersection between international environmental governance and climate finance. Before returning to the University of California Berkeley, Esther worked as a consultant at the World Bank's Sustainable Development Network and as a program officer at the Global Green Growth Institute.

Isabel Nicholson is a communications associate for RARE's new Fish Forever program. She received a master's degree in international development from American University where she focused on cross-sectoral partnerships within the sustainable development field. In addition to working as a consultant to the World Bank's Sustainable Development Network, she worked for the World Wildlife Fund, where she analyzed the organization's partnership practice in support of her graduate thesis. She has also worked for GoodWeave International to build a monitoring and evaluation system, as a Middle East field representative for GlobalGiving, and as an analyst for a Colorado policy think tank.

Eun Joo Yi is a senior operations officer for the new World Bank Korea Green Growth Trust Fund. Previously she consulted for the World Bank Sustainable Development Network on resource scarcity and conflict issues and the International Finance Corporation Advisory Services on global resource efficiency and clean energy. Ms. Yi has worked with a Norwegian engineering firm, an international secretariat working with the U.S. Environmental Protection Agency and the State Department, as well as Pfizer, Inc.

Udayan Tripathi is a junior professional associate at the World Bank working to support and advance the work of the Climate Change Group Vice Presidency especially in efforts to adapt to and mitigate climate change. He is the principal associate in the preparation of the present study.

Abbreviations

CEPF	Critical Ecosystems Partnership Fund
CGIAR	Consultative Group for International Agricultural Research
CIF	Climate Investment Fund
CSO	civil society organization
DAC	Development Assistance Committee
DEEP	Development Experience Exchange Program
DfID	Department for International Development
EACP	East Asia Climate Partnership
FCPF	Forest Carbon Partnership Facility
GCF	Green Climate Fund
GDP	gross domestic product
GEF	Global Environment Facility
GHG	greenhouse gas
GNI	gross national income
GPG	global public good
GPO	Global Partnership for Oceans
GRPP	Global and Regional Partnership Programs
GTI	Global Tiger Initiative
GTRP	Global Tiger Recovery Program
HGFI	high-grade fixed income
HPA	high-priority activities
IBAMA	Institute of Environment and Renewable Natural Resources
IBD	international business district
IBRD	International Bank for Reconstruction and Development
IDA	International Development Association
IEG	Independent Evaluation Group
IFFIm	International Finance Facility for Immunisation
IMF	International Monetary Fund
IT	information technology

KEIC	Korea Export Industrial Corporation
KSP	Knowledge Sharing Program
MDB	multilateral development bank
MDF	municipal development fund
MFI	multilateral finance institutions
MLP	multilevel perspective
MPT	modern portfolio theory
NGO	nongovernmental organizations
OECD	Organisation for Economic Co-operation and Development
SDF	subregional development funds
SIDS	Small Island Developing States
SMC	small and medium cities
SME	small and medium enterprises
SOC	social overhead capital
TRIPS	Trade-Related Aspects of Intellectual Property Rights
UNEP	United Nations Environment Programme
UNFCCC	United Nations Framework Convention on Climate Change
UNIFAD	United Nation's International Fund for Agricultural Development
WBG	World Bank Group
WTO	World Trade Organization

CHAPTER 1

Introduction

J. Warren Evans and Robin Davies

This book is about global public goods (GPGs), particularly those related to the environment, in the context of the global development process. We, the co-editors of this volume, are concerned with the long-term sustainability of development, as the distinction between developing and developed countries is expected to continue for the foreseeable future. We contend that global sustainability depends on—indeed, consists of—the provision of certain GPGs, and that the prevailing approach to development assistance does not sufficiently recognize this fact.

While we came to the decision to produce this book from different backgrounds, both of us have worked as development practitioners for many years, and we both are concerned that today's form of bilateral and multilateral development assistance might not adapt rapidly enough to the changing world to help all countries achieve lasting development. The last 35 years have witnessed a number of dramatic shifts, both in the conception of development and in the nature of international development assistance.

Perhaps the most important shift has been the transition from a largely donor-driven process to a more balanced donor-recipient collaboration and, in many cases, a recipient-driven process. This shift is reflected in the development assistance norms now accepted by Organisation for Economic Co-operation and Development (OECD) donors, as codified in the 2005 Paris Declaration on Aid Effectiveness and the 2008 Accra Agenda for Action:

> It is now the norm for aid recipients to forge their own national development strategies with their parliaments and electorates (ownership); for donors to support these strategies (alignment) and work to streamline their efforts in-country (harmonization); for development policies to be directed to achieving clear goals and for progress towards these goals to be monitored (results); and for donors and recipients alike to be jointly responsible for achieving these goals (mutual accountability). (OECD 2013, 1)

Though grounded in a concern for aid effectiveness, these development assistance norms reinforce governments' view that their first priorities should be national priorities, concerning the economic and social conditions of their citizens in an immediate and often urgent way, and over which they have a high degree of control. And in recognition of this shift, international development agencies have reoriented their efforts toward supporting the national development priorities of developing country governments. Country ownership and leadership of externally supported development assistance programs is now a central tenet of aid policy, if not always faithfully reflected in aid practice.

The strength of this accord between donors and recipients on how aid should be used is understandable, but at the same time a little surprising in that it has in effect reduced attention and action on addressing some of the critical, long-term regional and global challenges. Developing countries' problems, and their solutions, do not all lie within their borders. Many of their most serious challenges—climate change; water scarcity; communicable disease; volatility in international food, fuel, and financial markets; and the depletion of common-pool resources, such as fisheries—affect entire regions, sometimes the whole world, and generally require international cooperation if they are to be met.

Clearly such regional and globally focused bilateral and multilateral cooperation does not sit comfortably with the development assistance norms that currently give priority to supporting recipient-driven locally focused objectives. A new focus on global problems often benefits developing countries disproportionately, but not exclusively, such that the case for supporting it with aid funds intended for developing countries' poverty reduction is not clear-cut. To compound the problem, many global challenges are seen as remote: their most serious impacts are perceived to be in the relatively distant future or in other places, or the probability of achieving the degree of cooperation necessary to address them is perceived to be vanishingly small. Hence these remote-seeming challenges tend to be assigned lower priority than more immediate ones, even where the latter are harbingers of the former.

Nevertheless, the norms have so far prevailed. International development assistance is still used predominantly to help countries deal with today's crises, provide a basic level of national public goods, and, in the right circumstances, generate enough growth to move countries up the economic ladder. Its contributions to the provision of GPGs, while larger than many assume and growing substantially, are still insufficient and also largely invisible in donors' aid narratives.

Certainly some challenges that are international in scope but extremely pressing have elicited an effective response, for example, the HIV/AIDS pandemic. Other challenges that have longer term impacts but can be addressed through relatively straightforward cooperation measures have also been dealt with effectively, such as the challenge of atmospheric ozone depletion. But long-term global challenges involving complex cooperation efforts are, on the whole, low priorities for both national governments and the international development agencies that support them. Climate change, the greatest challenge of all, is, at best, somewhere in the middle of the spectrum: although significant efforts have been made, they do not even begin to approach the scale of action needed to adequately mitigate greenhouse gas (GHG) emissions or to build resilience to the unavoidable impacts of global warming.

Another important shift in perspective, somewhat in tension with recipient-driven aid, took place in the late 1980s with the recognition—articulated forcefully in the report of the Brundtland Commission (UN 1987)—that development, and the positive impacts of development assistance, could be made much more durable if environmental and social factors were adequately addressed as an integral part of the planning and implementation of development programs. This was accompanied by a growing recognition that the balance of resources for development needed to be adjusted in favor of spending with explicit social and environmental objectives.

The 1992 Rio conference—the "Earth Summit"—and consequent international agreements brought countries together to tackle global environmental challenges with a general understanding that rich countries would help poor countries cover the incremental costs of protecting the global environmental commons UNEP 1992. The establishment of the Multilateral Fund for the Implementation of the Montreal Protocol and, soon afterward, the much larger Global Environment Facility (GEF) at the World Bank set the stage for the use of international public financing for development to support global environmental objectives.

This sustainability "turn" led in the first instance to the adoption of social and environmental safeguard policies by many developing countries and by multilateral development banks (MDBs). At the MDBs, this largely reflected a donor agenda. However, many developing countries, particularly those that were rapidly industrializing, had already adopted environmental safeguard frameworks at the national level by the early to mid-1980s. The MDBs' environmental safeguards were largely consistent with these, and thus not all that contentious.[1]

After the Earth Summit, however, the concept of sustainability could no longer be confined to the realm of safeguard policies. The World Bank established a vice presidency for environmentally sustainable development in 1993, and the policy and institutional framework for the Bank's engagement in sustainable development has been evolving since that time. These actions included strengthening the Bank's interest in GPGs, when the Bank's Development Committee adopted *Global Public Goods: A Framework for the Role of the World Bank* (World Bank 2007),[2] and the Development Committee's adoption of the *Development and Climate Change: A Strategic Framework for the World Bank Group* (World Bank 2008b). The Bank recently approved a new environment strategy, Green, Clean, and Resilient World for All (World Bank 2012b) that will guide its work on environmentally sustainable development for the next decade. The Bank, together with a number of partners, has also recently launched the Green Growth Knowledge Platform, consistent with the Bank's strategy in *Inclusive Green Growth: The Pathway to Sustainable Development* (World Bank 2012a), to enhance efforts and address major knowledge gaps in green growth theory and practice, as well as to help countries design and implement policies to move toward a green economy.

These developments within the World Bank form part of the context for this study. Equally important, though, are the ongoing discussions—emerging from the Rio+20 conference (UN 2012)—on a new set of global sustainable development goals for the post-2015 era, as well as the rapidly unfolding changes in the international development landscape. The significance of those changes might prove to be quite profound.

We are now seeing the emergence of financing on a substantial scale from new donors that do not subscribe to the OECD norms mentioned earlier, while at the same time aid from traditional sources is flattening. This is happening in conjunction with striking shifts in the geography of global poverty and, as a result, the potential withering of the client base of some MDBs' concessional financing arms. At the same time, we are seeing the growth of climate change financing as a major new call on international public financing—with expectations that developed countries will mobilize as much as $100 billion per annum for this purpose by 2020.

In light of these developments, some commentators are calling for a transformation of official development assistance to focus more intensively or even exclusively on global issues and to become "global public finance" that facilitates resource mobilization and generates results appropriate to current and future international development needs, particularly for GPGs (Birdsall and Leo 2011; Severino and Ray 2009; Sumner and Mallett 2012).

Against this backdrop, the purpose of this study is to understand and explore options to address the barriers that the World Bank and other development financing institutions face when they seek an appropriate balance between meeting the poverty reduction and economic growth needs of developing countries and supporting effective action on global development challenges.

Several major reviews by the World Bank's Independent Evaluation Group (IEG) in 2008 (World Bank 2008a) and 2011 (IEG 2011a, 2011b)—examining the Bank's work on climate change and other global issues—have already recommended a rationalization of the Bank's engagement in addressing global challenges that, among other issues, takes account of the relevance of those challenges to sustained economic development and the Bank's capacity to deliver adequate resources for it. The IEG also points to a disconnect between the Bank's country and global priorities.

Our interest here, however, is in arriving at actionable recommendations for policy and structural change—change that will see the Bank achieve a much greater impact on systemic global challenges without abandoning its fundamental role as a source of development finance for sovereign governments and change that will spill over to other development financing institutions in the way that most successful innovations at the World Bank do.

We stress that it is important to recognize that different GPGs are provided in different ways. Some require coordinated efforts by all countries (for example, polio eradication); some require only the efforts of major actors (climate change mitigation); some require collaboration between particular actors (river basin management); and a few require just one successful effort (vaccine discovery). It might seem that what is common to these cases—except for a few of the "one successful effort" public goods[3]—is international cooperation. But in fact the provision of certain GPGs requires not so much international cooperation as international mediation from an organization like the World Bank, which can provide incentives across multiple countries whose net effect is to provide a global public good in a significant quantity.

The implication of this new view of GPGs is that an organization like the World Bank need not completely change its fundamental operating model to have a greater impact on global challenges. Perhaps it would need to do so if it were to take on disease eradication or drug discovery and development, but those are GPGs of a kind, we believe, that the Bank and similar institutions are not well placed to provide.

We stress also that it would be a mistake to see the prevailing OECD development assistance norms as somehow misguided. Aid provided in accordance with those norms has achieved a very great deal indeed. Many developing countries have made tremendous progress in reducing poverty and achieving rapid rates of economic growth as measured by GDP. The number of people living in extreme poverty fell from about 1.9 billion three decades ago to about 1.2 billion in 2010, despite a 59 percent increase in the developing world's population (World Bank 2013). Impressive progress has been made in areas such as educational enrollment, access to improved water sources, and the control of HIV/AIDS, tuberculosis, and malaria.

Country-oriented official development assistance from multilateral and bilateral sources, and nonconcessional financing too, has played a significant role in achieving many of today's success stories, not only through public sector reforms and investments but also by direct invesment in private sector development. Institutions like the World Bank responded to the Paris Agreement no less fully than bilateral agencies, by decentralizing and transforming their country operations to make them much more country led and country owned.

Our concern, rather, is that the GPGs agenda, particularly the global environmental agenda, has not fared as well as the national poverty reduction and economic growth agendas and that the latter two, in the long run, depend upon the former two. The quality and productivity of the global natural environment is generally on a downward trajectory. Although small battles are being won all the time, the war is not. One has only to consider the findings of the Millennium Ecosystem Assessment (WRI 2005), multiple "state of the environment" reports, and contemporary scientific findings regarding the state of the oceans, as well as, of course, the climate. The downward trajectory is evident in many rich, middle-income, and poor countries.

The international community of sovereign states has occasionally shown that it can collectively deal with global threats. The Montreal Protocol on ozone-depleting substances (World Bank 2012c) is the best such example of successful collective action, if somewhat overworked. But the same community has not been able to agree on effective action to address the most serious long-term threat—climate change—and has not been very successful in reducing the degradation of shared ecosystems, biodiversity loss, and fisheries depletion.

Looking ahead to 2025 and beyond—and taking into account the changes in the environment for development financing that can reasonably be expected over the coming 10–15 years—we believe the Bank and similar organizations need to carefully consider a number of fundamental policy and operational changes if they are to maintain their impact and relevance at the global and regional levels and even at the country level.

The first key question is whether the country-ownership model is even compatible with global sustainability. Experience shows that recipient countries will seek to capture as much donor financing as possible for their national development priorities, and they are generally only willing to agree to allocating funds for regional and global action if those funds are perceived to be additional to their share of aid, however the latter might be determined. Under decentralization, World Bank staff are much closer to their clients, but they therefore might be more prone to adopt shorter term outlooks if these happen to be their clients' outlooks.

A second key question is whether the political will exists to make the provision of GPGs an explicit and central objective of official development assistance—especially in the face of objections from those who believe aid should be solely concerned with the eradication of poverty through national or community-level interventions. Without this, it is conceivable that as a result of inadequate action on global and regional public bads, and particularly on climate change, a number of developing countries could experience a dramatic reversal of the progress made over the last several decades. Paradoxically, this would have the effect of replenishing the client base of the MDBs' concessional arms and reducing pressure on those financing mechanisms to take preventive action on global public bads.

A third key question concerns the mobilization and use of resources for the World Bank's work to support the provision of GPGs. The Bank is a major player on many regional and global issues, but its work at these levels is usually enabled by donor contributions, most often in the form of grants targeted for a particular purpose. The bulk of the Bank's work on climate change has been made possible by its access to the GEF (in its early years), various carbon funds, and more recently the Climate Investment Funds. If the World Bank had not had such additional funds, to what extent would it have been able to take a leadership role? Is it wise to hope that such discretionary funding will be available in the future for addressing global and regional issues that can undermine the development impacts of the World Bank's day-to-day country-level work? And is grant-based financing ever going to leverage the large-scale private investment required to achieve meaningful impacts on global warming?

The chapters that follow in Part 1 discuss these questions from conceptual, policy, financing, and organizational governance perspectives. Part 2 paints a picture of how two dynamic countries, Brazil and Republic of Korea, and also many of the world's major cities, are dealing with sustainability challenges and thereby contributing to the provision of GPGs. Part 3 presents some ideas for moving forward, focusing on the future role and management of official development assistance, the role of MDBs in mobilizing private investment with global public benefits, the role of global coalitions in effecting global change, and the management of major transition processes. Part 4 crystallizes our recommendations for change.

Our most general contention is that international development assistance needs to undergo a major transition, such that it takes as an explicit and principal objective the provision of GPGs important for development. The World Bank can play a leadership role in this transition, working within new kinds of coalitions but not abandoning the fundamentals of its operating model. Some of the most important GPGs are provided through the separate and cumulative actions of multiple countries, so the challenge for the Bank is to find ways of investing strategically and sharing knowledge across countries, while keeping faith with their national development strategies, so as to achieve maximum global impacts. The World Bank can also play a unique role in stimulating the private provision of GPGs through risk sharing and market creation.

Box 1.1 What Young Development Professionals Think About Collaborative Consumption

Lorraine Sugar, Task-force to Catalyze Climate Action

My generation is different. We have inherited a huge, global mess from our parents and grandparents, and now it is our job to clean it up.

My family members and mentors are quick to remind me that every generation shares this sentiment. Whether it was about Vietnam or women's rights, there is a track record of young people bearing the load of global issues and fighting tirelessly for change. I believe that climate change is the defining issue of my generation: it is our fight to finish. If we are ever going to avoid a 4 degree world, we are the last hope. My generation will make up the last cohort of leaders that could possibly get its act together in time to avoid the worst of the worst that climate change will bring.

What makes my generation different? Millennials, as we are called, are often accused of being self-centered and individualistic (Generation "Me," so to speak). But it is so much more than that. We have distinctly different ideals of work and life, particularly focused on intrinsic values and civic responsibility. We are globally plugged-in. Our networks and communities span across borders, and we are consuming differently than generations before us, particularly young people in cities. We are going to drive change, one community at a time.

Personal Consumption and Choice

The message is clear: The lifecycles of all the goods we buy and other items we consume have emissions implications that extend beyond our borders, as well as beyond our awareness. With a growing consumer base in China and India, one could imagine a broadening and reorienting in a way that reflects shifting global economies and powers.

Cities are at the epicenter of this conundrum. By 2050, 75 percent of the global population will live in cities. Currently, activities in cities are responsible for 70 percent of global greenhouse gas emissions. While cities are where people consume the most, they are also where change happens. Cities are drivers of social movements—not just their governments, but the *people* in cities.

The role of the individual as an actor in solving the climate change problem is enormous. For a person who wants to live sustainably, the implications can make your head explode. I find myself constantly grappling with this dilemma. How can I make choices that will somehow contribute to driving the systems I participate in on a day-to-day basis towards sustainability? For example, do I choose to use a mug for my coffee—which has energy and water imbedded in its production, transport, and decomposition—or a paper cup, which will decompose in a landfill immediately after I finish using it? I know my peers are also asking these kinds of questions and feeling confused. And, to be perfectly honest, often my lifestyle feels like it is soaked in hypocrisy, especially when I take long-haul flights (known to produce a lot of emissions) to help clients grapple with climate change issues (even though the World Bank offsets mission travel).

The Shift to Collaborative Consumption

Even with all these uncertainties and pending questions, here is why I am hopeful: My generation is leading the charge to move from from individual consumption toward collaborative consumption, particularly in cities. We are using bike-sharing and car-sharing programs, shared work spaces, and platforms to support trends for buying and selling used goods. We are using technology to foster networks and make connections, and business and entrepreneurship are growing as vehicles to implement social change. We are even putting our money where our mouth is: crowdfunding and other collaborating fundraising methods are changing the way we support issues we care about. There is a renewed focus on community and the power of the crowd for generating knowledge, raising funds, and driving change.

In 2025, the world will look very different than it does today. Climate change will bring more extreme weather events. There will be a shortage of water and other resources, as well as general limitations of global public goods for a growing population. The pressures faced will be crippling. The way we manage and navigate such a future will depend on the strength and social fabrics of our communities. This is where the attributes of the millennial generation will thrive. We will create solutions, collaborate, and consume in consort with our local and global communities. I strongly believe that all the characteristics that bring millennials criticism now–the short attention spans, Facebook, texting and obsession with personal experience—will make our generation equipped to live sustainably in ways the world has not seen before. We will redefine the very models of consumption and negotiation that got us into this mess in the first place.

Notes

1. Social safeguard policies, such as those related to resettlement, presented greater challenges due to a lack of consistency with some developing countries' policies.

2. The term "global public goods," for convenience, is taken to include regional public goods—which tend naturally to loom larger in the sights of regional development banks and other regional organizations. The present study follows this convention, without implying that regional public goods are of secondary importance. It could prove to be the case that even global institutions' efforts are on the whole most cost-effectively directed toward the delivery of regional public goods.

3. Even some of the GPGs will involve collaboration between multiple actors across borders if the requisite knowledge and infrastructure is not concentrated in one country. However, international cooperation is in such cases only a practical necessity rather than an inherent part of the solution.

References

Birdsall, Nancy, and Benjamin Leo. 2011. "Find Me the Money: Financing Climate and Other Global Public Goods." Working Paper 248, Center for Global Development, Washington, DC.

IEG (Independent Evaluation Group). 2011a. *The World Bank's Involvement in Global and Regional Partnership Programs: An Independent Assessment.* Washington, DC: World Bank.

———. 2011b. *Trust Fund Support for Development.* Washington, DC: World Bank.

OECD (Organisation for Economic Co-operation and Development). 2013. "The Paris Declaration on Aid Effectiveness (2005) and the Accra Agenda for Action (2008)." Paris. http://www.oecd.org/dac/effectiveness/parisdeclarationandaccraagendaforaction.htm.

Severino, Jean-Michel, and Olivier Ray. 2009. "The End of ODA: Death and Rebirth of Global Public Policy." Working Paper 167, Center for Global Development, Washington, DC.

Sumner, Andy, and Richard Mallett. 2012. *The Future of Foreign Aid: Development Cooperation and the New Geography of Global Poverty.* Basingstoke, U.K.: Palgrave MacMillan.

UN (United Nations). 1987. *Report of the World Commission on Environment and Development: Our Common Future* (Brundtland Report). New York. http://www.un-documents.net/our-common-future.pdf.

———. 2012. "The Future We Want: Outcome Document from United Nations Conference on Sustainable Development." Rio+20 conference, Rio de Janeiro, June.

UNEP (United Nations Environment Programme). 1992. "Rio 1992: 1992 Declaration on Environment and Development." Report of the United Nations Conference on the Human Environment, Stockholm, June 5–16.

WRI (World Resources Institute). 2005. *Ecosystems and Human Well-Being: Biodiversity Synthesis.* Millennium Ecosystem Assessment. Washington, DC: WRI.

World Bank. 2007. *Global Public Goods: A Framework for the Role of the World Bank.* DC2007-0020. Washington, DC: World Bank.

———. 2008a. "Shared Global Challenges, Lessons from the Bank's Experience." In part 2 of the *2008 Annual Review of Development Effectiveness.* Washington, DC: World Bank.

———. 2008b. *Development and Climate Change: A Strategic Framework for the World Bank Group*. Washington, DC: World Bank.

———. 2012a. *Inclusive Green Growth: The Pathway to Sustainable Development*. Washington, DC: World Bank.

———. 2012b. *Toward a Green, Clean, and Resilient World for All: A World Bank Group Environment Strategy 2012–2022*. Washington, DC: World Bank.

———. 2012c. *The World Bank–Montreal Protocol Partnership: Promoting Ozone Smart, Climate-Balanced Development*. Washington, DC: World Bank.

———. 2013. *The State of the Poor: Where Are the Poor and Where Are They Poorest?* Washington, DC: World Bank. http://www.innpdf.com/ebooklist/the-world-bank-us -billion.html.

The Future of Global Public Goods

CHAPTER 2

Global Public Goods and International Development

Scott Barrett

Public goods have two key features: first, no party within the jurisdiction in which the public good is supplied can be excluded from benefiting from its provision; second, each party's consumption of a public good does not diminish the amount of the good available to other parties. The first feature is especially important because it creates an incentive for parties to "free ride," and thus affects whether public goods are provided in the first place.

At the domestic level, the "parties" referred to are citizens and other "legal persons," including firms, and the incentives to free ride are overcome by government being given the authority to pass laws that are binding on all members of a society. These include the power to tax so as to finance the supply of public goods. At the international level, the parties are states, but because there is no world government, the provision of transnational public goods is much more difficult.

Local and national public goods have long been known to be critical for development. Transnational public goods have more often been neglected, but public goods on all these levels are important (see box 2.1).

Security from war, violence, and crime are examples of public goods that are essential to the wellbeing of any society, in addition to being prerequisites for economic development. Institutions such as the rule of law, property rights, and contract enforcement, when made available and applied consistently and impartially without discrimination, are similarly essential in order for markets to flourish. The provision of all these public goods is a central responsibility of government, the essence of "good governance." Other public goods (uncongested roads, for example, facilitate trade) add to what markets can provide or reduce the harm caused by unregulated markets (pollution, for example). They are all important for development, some as means and some as ends.

However, development economists have routinely neglected regional, international, and global public goods, despite the contributions they make to development.[1] For example, the eradication of smallpox, possibly the greatest

---

To see Scott Barrett discuss the history of global public goods in international development: http://youtu.be/JTlfq8qtuyk

Box 2.1 A Taxonomy of Public Goods

Public goods are goods that benefit everyone within a jurisdiction. They have the properties that (1) no party within the jurisdiction can be excluded from benefiting from their provision and (2) each party's enjoyment of the good does not diminish others' enjoyment.

Local public goods are supplied within a locality, usually situated within a single state. Examples are flood and crime control and sanitation.

Domestic or national public goods are supplied more broadly within a state. Examples are national defense and malaria elimination.

Regional public goods are supplied and enjoyed within a region. An example is the elimination of polio and measles in the Americas.

International public goods are supplied and enjoyed by a subset of countries scattered throughout the world. Examples are **the eradication of Guinea worm and prevention of the emergence of drug-resistant malaria.**

Global public goods benefit every country, irrespective of which ones provide them. Examples are the eradication of smallpox, nonuse of nuclear weapons, and protection of the ozone layer.

public investment in human history, saved millions of lives and removed the need to vaccinate people, freeing up resources to be spent on other good causes. It could not have been achieved by a single state acting independently; its provision depended on the cooperation of all states (see box 2.2).

The neglect of transnational public goods may be because development is perceived as occurring at the level of the state or country.[2] From a domestic perspective, vaccination is important, but eradication is unimaginable. By definition, its achievement must be global.

State, Regional, and Global Development

There is good reason to focus on development at the country level. The state is a legal entity to which other states may lend money (bilaterally or multilaterally) with the prospect that the recipient cannot easily avoid its obligation to repay. In addition, a state's government is the organization most able to create the conditions for development (including the provision of national public goods)—an important consideration for grant financing as well as lending.

So the question isn't whether a focus on country-level development is appropriate and necessary. The question is whether this focus is enough.

The central message of this chapter is that the prospects for a state's development depend on also recognizing the connections between the state and its region, as well as between the state and the wider world. Each state's development depends in part on the supply of regional, international, and global public goods.

Box 2.2 Smallpox Eradication

Estimates of the benefits and costs of smallpox eradication are shown in table B.2.2.1. The benefits reflect avoided vaccination and infection costs. These are annual estimates. Assuming that the annual savings would be realized forever, and discounting future benefits at 3 percent, the present value benefit of eradication would be about US$47.3 billion in 1967 dollars. The costs shown in the table are the additional costs over and above routine vaccination necessary to achieve eradication. Taking this cost to be a one-time expenditure, the benefit-to-cost ratio is 159:1 if all costs are included and 483:1 if international finance only is counted. The latter is the money given by industrialized countries to finance smallpox elimination programs in developing countries. By any standard, these are extraordinary numbers.

Table B2.2.1 Benefits and Costs of Smallpox Eradication

Benefits and costs	Amount 1967 US$ (millions)
Annual benefit to India	722
Annual benefit to all developing countries	1,070
Annual benefit to the United States	150
Annual benefit to all industrialized countries	350
Total annual benefit	1,420
Total international expenditure on eradication	98
Total national expenditure by endemic countries	200
Combined total expenditure on eradication	298
Benefit-to-cost ratio	
International expenditure	483:1
Combined total expenditure	159:1

Source: Fenner et al.1988: 1364–66. Benefit-cost ratio is found by dividing annual benefit by 0.03 (that is, a 3% discount rate), and dividing that number by the one-time expenditure estimate.

It would clearly be irresponsible today to support development projects that would be unlikely to pay off in a world in which climate change is expected. Therefore development must reflect needs for climate change "adaptation." But adaptation is only necessary because of a failure by all countries collectively to limit greenhouse gas (GHG) concentrations—a global public good. It is inconsistent for development to focus on the former need while neglecting the latter. However, a country can only control its adaptation, whereas it can't, all by itself, control climate change. To do that requires global collective action.

Often regional public goods can be at least as effective a means for achieving development as local public goods.[3] Indeed, one acknowledged development success story is unusual for having been designed as a regional initiative from its inception—the effort to control river blindness, a parasitic disease transmitted to humans by the bite of a blackfly. As the World Bank's webpage says, "One of the great success stories in the history of the World Bank has been its role in the control of *onchocerciasis*, commonly known as river blindness" (World Bank 2003). And yet this success remains something of an exception. The Bank has declined to participate actively in similar efforts. For example, as reported in an article published in *Science* in 1987, the Bank was reluctant to participate in the effort to eradicate rinderpest, a cattle disease:

> From the start of discussions on the rinderpest campaign, the World Bank has questioned the form and objectives of the effort. The bank was not a potential donor to [the Pan-African Rinderpest Campaign], which does not fit the Bank rule that it make loans only for specific development projects.... Poul Sihm of the Bank's technical staff says that bank objections centered on the weakness of the African veterinary services and inaccessibility of areas where there was civil strife.... He says that the Bank is still arguing that "you can't eradicate rinderpest as distinct from controlling it." (Walsh 1987: 1291)

Fortunately, the United Nations Food and Agriculture Organization stepped in to provide financing as well as technical support to combat rinderpest. In May 2011 the World Organization for Animal Health declared the disease eradicated (Mariner et al. 2012).

By succeeding, the effort to eradicate rinderpest proved the World Bank wrong, at least as far as its technical assessment of the feasibility of eradication. But we only know that the World Bank was wrong because other organizations stepped in to help. Of course, it might be argued that the World Bank's reluctance to participate was of no consequence, given that these other organizations stepped in to the breach. However, the Bank did not step aside because it felt its involvement was unnecessary; it stepped aside because it felt that the effort could not succeed. Moreover, only the World Bank has a responsibility for understanding the significance of an achievement like this for development. Rather than see eradication as being impossible because of the weakness of African veterinary services, the Bank might have looked at the eradication effort as an opportunity for improving these services, just as efforts to eradicate human diseases like smallpox provided a platform for a successful, expanded program for immunization and as the current effort to eradicate polio is piggybacking on this effort to provide vitamin A supplements, deworming tablets, and other health services. Rather than look at civil strife as an impediment to eradication, the Bank might have looked to as the need to help reduce civil strife because of the complementary relationship to the eradication effort and development in general.[4]

It is hard to see the contrast between the experiences with river blindness and rinderpest and not ask whether the Bank could achieve more by integrating global and regional public goods considerations into its overall strategy. How many opportunities like rinderpest have been missed for lack of World Bank support?

This chapter provides further evidence of inconsistency in the World Bank's record, considering cases in which it has helped to supply transnational public goods and others where it has not. The Bank should be more consistent.

The provision of transnational public goods should form part of a coherent strategy for development. In particular, the Bank should reorient its lending and other activities. Country-level development should be reinforced and viewed in the context of regional, international, and global development.

Public Goods and Development

From the perspective of development, the provision of transnational public goods has five important features. First, rich countries can have a strong incentive to finance the provision of global public goods and to ensure that their provision succeeds. Multilateral development assistance (especially grants and highly concessional loans), by contrast, relies more on motives of charity and compassion than self-interest, with the focus sometimes being on the amount of resources provided (as in the 0.7 percent gross national income target for aid) rather than the impact of that expenditure on poverty alleviation.[5] While this feature of global public goods is to the advantage of developing countries, it also means that rich countries determine which global public goods are provided. Rich countries often set the agenda. Here, the World Bank can play a useful role in underscoring the implications of the supply of global public goods for international development.

Second, this incentive to supply a global public good can be muted when rich countries can substitute a local public good for the global public good. For example, when a rich country can eliminate an infectious disease within its own borders through mass immunization, it will not benefit directly from the control of this disease outside its borders. (Disease eradication, discussed later in this chapter, is an exceptional situation.) Similarly, if rich countries found it relatively easy to adapt to climate change, they would have a reduced incentive to limit their emissions. Indeed, if collective action to limit emissions is difficult for whatever reason, the most able countries may choose to invest domestically to limit their exposure to a global public bad, rather than to invest globally to increase provision of a global public good. This would be to the detriment of the world's poorest countries, and could accentuate existing inequalities. It's important that the World Bank, a multilateral institution, convey the message to its members that global issues are best addressed globally.

Third, some kinds of global public good can only be supplied with the active and effective involvement of developing countries. For example, polio will never be eradicated so long as there continues to exist a refuge for polioviruses in the border region shared by Afghanistan and Pakistan. Similarly, a world free of international terrorism and piracy depends on all states being able to exercise sovereignty throughout their territory, including their territorial and adjacent waters. It is in the collective interests of all countries that none fails, which explains why the richest countries have invested substantially in "state-building."

The World Bank has played a valuable role in this effort, particularly in managing the multidonor State- and Peace-Building Fund.[6] However, ensuring that a state "succeeds" rather than "fails" is difficult and requires an "internal" imperative for stability rather than an externally imposed arrangement for order. Moreover, preventing failure is itself a global public good, vulnerable to free riding. And, here again there can be incentives for states to substitute alternatives. For example, states have individual incentives to protect their own vessels from attack by pirates, rather than to address the root cause of the piracy—a lack of governance in Somalia.

Fourth, in some cases, the benefit of supplying a global public good depends on the supply of a local public good. For example, the global public good of the knowledge of how to immunize against a disease only offers a benefit to poor countries if the vaccine embodying this knowledge is widely distributed within the population, stimulating herd immunity. Development thus increases the total returns to supplying a global public good, just as the returns on investments in development increase with the supply of global public goods. Development and the supply of global public goods are often complementary, therefore they should be considered together.

Fifth, a transnational public good that uniquely benefits the poorest countries will require either collective action by these countries or an orientation of development assistance toward the provision of these goods. Public goods of this type will be regional or international in nature. Examples include a tsunami warning system for the Indian Ocean and the eradication of Guinea worm, another tropical disease. Opportunities for development on this scale are often overlooked. Poor countries generally lack a history of close collaboration, and a country-focused orientation of development may miss opportunities. Many of the constraints on development occur regionally and internationally, not domestically.

Complementarities, noted earlier, are especially important for the provision of regional and international public goods. If each developing country lacks the domestic public good that makes provision of the global public good valuable, the collective incentive to supply a regional or international public good will fail to materialize. For example, a tsunami warning system is only helpful if warnings issued by a regional system can be communicated quickly to the people at risk (Barrett 2007). The World Bank, in partnership with regional development banks and other international organizations, can ensure coordination between within-country development and regional and international development.

To sum up, global public goods and development are intimately related. Development and the supply of global public goods should be determined jointly, not separately.

Global Public Goods and Sovereignty

The concept of sovereignty is important for development. Aid conditionality strikes a nerve, but corruption can undermine the best intentions. The provision of regional and global public goods raises even more issues related to sovereignty. To supply these goods, countries must work together, meaning that their mutual dependence must be acknowledged. There must also be trust among them.

As noted, the provision of public goods on all levels can be undermined by free rider incentives. States as institutions are accorded special powers by their citizens, including the power to tax in order to supply public goods like infrastructure and the power to regulate to reduce pollution. Extreme examples of this authority include conscription for national defense and mandatory vaccination and quarantine for the control of infectious diseases. The ability of a government to exercise political authority over its population and within its territory is called domestic sovereignty.[7] Domestic sovereignty is a necessary, though not sufficient, condition for growth and development.

States may also possess international legal sovereignty, a condition that confers international recognition upon the state. It also implies certain rights and responsibilities, such as the right to non-intervention and the responsibility not to harm other states. Membership in the World Bank is limited to states with international legal sovereignty. Taiwan, China, for example, is not a member. Failed states possess international legal sovereignty, but they lack domestic sovereignty, and for that reason, they are perhaps the greatest challenge for development.

"Westphalian sovereignty" refers to a state's ability to control its government, people, and resources, to the exclusion of outside influence.[8] State failure is sometimes an invitation for foreign intervention—with obvious consequences for Westphalian sovereignty. In the poorest states, foreign influence is common; aid conditionality is routine though not always successful.

Misuse of domestic sovereignty can also be an invitation for intervention. States that fail to fulfill their international responsibilities risk losing their Westphalian sovereignty. An emerging norm recognizes a state's responsibility to protect its citizens, meaning that it must prevent egregious violations of human dignity on a massive scale (genocide being perhaps the most extreme example). Should a state fail to fulfill these obligations, the norm further stipulates that other states then become responsible to intervene. This is a shift from the traditional concept of sovereignty, which recognized a state's right to non-intervention.

If this emerging norm, the responsibility to protect, were applied consistently, it would provide a new global public good—protection of populations everywhere from mass atrocities and ethnic cleansing, with the main vehicle for provision not being intervention but the (credible) threat of intervention deterring behavior in contravention of the right to protect. However, the norm has not been applied consistently. It was invoked recently to protect large parts of the Libyan population from attacks by the government of longtime leader Muammar Gaddafi, but has not been invoked to protect Syrians from attacks by the government forces under the command of President Bashar al-Assad. There are numerous reasons for this. One is the lack of political consensus, but another has been the reluctance by key countries to intervene in the Syrian Arab Republic (thus revealing that the threat to intervene is lacking credibility in this instance).

Finally, interdependence sovereignty refers to the state's ability to control the movement of people, capital, and goods (marketed and nonmarketed) across its borders. The provision of transnational public goods always implies a lack of interdependence sovereignty. It can also lead to an erosion of Westphalian sovereignty.

States of all kinds (weak and strong) routinely enter into agreements that constrain their freedom to act. The European Union (EU), for example, makes many (though not all) of its decisions by qualified majority voting—decisions that are binding even upon member states that oppose them. The effect of this was dramatically evident in the recent euro crisis. Another example, which involves the supply of a global public good, is the Montreal Protocol, a remarkable treaty that has halted destruction of the ozone layer and that is expected to allow the ozone hole to recover. Adjustments in agreed reductions in the production and consumption of substances controlled by this treaty may be adopted by a two-thirds majority of the parties present and voting, representing a majority of developing country parties and a majority of industrialized country parties. So far, the treaty has been adjusted five times. Of course, states can exercise their international legal sovereignty by withdrawing from either of these arrangements. However, the consequences of withdrawal can be extreme—trade restrictions would be imposed in the case of the Montreal Protocol; system-wide bank runs would result in the case of the EU. The more important difference between these situations is that some countries today regret having joined the EU in the first place, whereas support for Montreal remains strong.

Interdependence sovereignty is fundamental to the supply of global public goods. Every state is only partly responsible for the accumulation of chlorine in the atmosphere, but all states will be affected by the ozone depletion caused by this environmental change. Countries cannot insulate themselves from this interdependence, but by cooperating, by ceding some of their Westphalian sovereignty, they can improve the supply of this vital global public good. That, of course, is precisely what the Montreal Protocol did.

Global Public Goods for Development

Transnational public goods can be classified by the underlying incentive structure (Barrett 2007) or by topic area. This chapter covers four important topics relevant to international development, in each case explaining how the underlying incentive structure helps or hinders supply. The topics are knowledge, climate change, emerging infectious diseases, and transnational fisheries.

Knowledge for Development

According to the *World Development Report 1998/99: Knowledge for Development* (World Bank 1998), knowledge, not capital, is the key to sustained economic growth and improvements in human well-being.

While not a pure public good, knowledge does have public good attributes (Stiglitz 1999). One person's use of codified knowledge does not reduce the amount available to others, but exclusion is possible by means of conventions like patents and copyrights. Whether exclusion is exercised is a social choice.

Efficiency is shaped by both the production and distribution of knowledge. One without the other is of little use. Both are necessary, but it can be difficult to design an incentive system that achieves both objectives simultaneously. The essential problem is financing (see box 2.3): knowledge is costly to produce, and yet after it has been produced, and the costs of producing it have decreased, efficiency demands that the fruits of this effort be made available at near-zero cost (the cost of disseminating knowledge).

There are four different approaches to getting around this problem. First, knowledge can be produced directly, by a state in isolation or by a collective of states. Second, knowledge production can be subsidized, an example being tax credits to corporations. Third, producers of specific, discrete pieces of knowledge can be awarded prizes—perhaps the most famous example from history being the discovery of a way to determine longitude (Sobel 1995). Finally, rights to the use of knowledge can be privatized, for example, by patents and copyrights. In this case, however, intellectual property must be coupled with policies for the (second-best) efficient distribution of the products embodying the new knowledge—in

---

Box 2.3 The Case for Financing Knowledge for Development

The incentives to produce knowledge that is of unique value to the world's poorest countries have historically been weak, partly because of small country markets and partly because of inadequate patent protection. Harmonization of intellectual property rules worldwide— mainly as a result of the World Trade Organization's Agreement on Trade-Related Aspects of Intellectual Property Rights, but also because of stronger rules negotiated in various preferential trade agreements and other agreements under the World Intellectual Property Organization—will ensure patent protection with time and eventually overcome the problem of market size. However, the incentives to invest in R&D that promises to benefit only the world's poorest countries will also be limited by low purchasing power. There is clearly a case for grant financing of R&D for development.

When knowledge is itself an input in the supply of another public good, the case for grant financing is especially great. For example, use of a vaccine creates an "externality." A person who is vaccinated helps to break the chain of transmission, reducing the chances that others will become infected. This means that the social value of a new technology exceeds the private value. It also means the social value of the knowledge needed to develop the technology exceeds the private value.

Note, however, that this externality provides a rationale for government purchases of vaccine, and therein lies another problem. If governments are the sole buyers, they can negotiate lower prices. Low prices are good from the perspective of distribution, but bad from the perspective of innovation: low prices reduce the returns to R&D. Indeed, the role of government in purchasing vaccines is one reason the development and production of vaccines is unsatisfactory, even in rich countries (see, for example, Offit 2005). Grant financing of the R&D is one way to avoid this problem. Price commitments are another.

---

particular, price discrimination through market segmentation—as has been exploited by the Medicines for Malaria Venture, a public-private partnership promoting the development and distribution of new, effective, and affordable antimalarial drugs.

The first three approaches typically rely on knowledge being financed by the state or a group of states out of general tax revenues. (Private philanthropists, such as the X Prize Foundation, have also funded prizes.) Intellectual property systems, by contrast, allow these costs to be financed entirely by the market. This distinction is important because only the first three approaches allow the fruits of research and development (R&D) to be made available to the public at near-zero cost. Under the intellectual property system, this only happens after the life of the property right has ended.

Each approach has strengths and weaknesses (David 1993). The first two approaches create "push incentives" for R&D, relying on the state or a group of states to pay for the inputs to knowledge creation. However, these approaches have the obvious problem of having to pay for failure as well as success. They also require monitoring to ensure that the money provided is well spent. But they have advantages, too. Government laboratories often produce research that will be procured directly by government—of special importance when the R&D is vital to national security. Push incentives are especially needed to fund basic research, which, because of its broad nature, cannot be patented.

Prizes and the intellectual property right system are functionally different. Prizes create "pull incentives" for R&D—that is, they reward success. A problem with these approaches is that they offer "winner takes all" rewards and so encourage excessive R&D (Dasgupta and Stiglitz 1980). Too much effort may be devoted to capturing the rents to knowledge creation—a common problem. Prizes have another handicap: they can only reward targeted discoveries and achievements. The social returns to this approach thus depend on the choice of target. Patents, by contrast, promote a wider array of innovation. But patents have other drawbacks. They create incentives for those who possess knowledge to keep what they know secret until it can be patented (in contrast to the rush by scientists to publish their latest discoveries). As noted by David (1993), this creates problems of duplication and delay—a potentially serious cost. The proliferation of patents—on, say fragments of genes—can also frustrate the R&D process by allowing each owner of an upstream patent "to set up another tollbooth on the road to product development, adding to the cost and slowing the pace of downstream biomedical innovation" (Heller and Eisenberg 1998: 699).[9]

Finally, of course, the patent system makes the owners of the rights to knowledge state-approved monopolists for the term of the rights (typically, 20 years in the case of patents globally). The problem here is that monopolists will charge a price in excess of marginal cost, and this is inefficient. As explained previously, once the knowledge has been produced, it should be distributed at marginal cost—a price near zero. The intellectual property rights system thus creates incentives for knowledge to be produced, but at the cost of discouraging its efficient distribution.

It is essential to note, however, that the distribution of knowledge at a near-zero price is not the only means for achieving efficiency. In theory, perfect price discrimination will achieve the same result. This would involve every potential user of knowledge being charged his or her marginal willingness to pay. From the perspective of allocative efficiency, the result would be the same as if the knowledge were made available for free because all users willing to pay a positive price, however small, would be able to purchase the knowledge.

It will help to distinguish between innovation that benefits all countries and innovation that uniquely benefits the poorest countries. In the former case, the market in rich countries will usually be enough to stimulate R&D investment with the promise of market returns. Extending patent protection to poor countries is not needed for efficiency and could be injurious to human welfare.

This problem attracted worldwide attention when patent-holding pharmaceutical companies attempted to block the production and distribution of life-saving antiretrovirals in poor countries, where the HIV/AIDS crisis has produced millions of orphans. The interests of the companies were protected by the Trade-Related Aspects of Intellectual Property Rights (TRIPS) agreement, which threatened the legitimacy of the World Trade Organization (WTO), which sets and enforces the rules for multilateral trade. As Maskus and Reichman (2004: 307) put it, "if nothing had been done to address the plight of millions dying of AIDS because of TRIPS patent rights, then the WTO would have contributed to the greatest health tragedy in history."

Fortunately, something was done. TRIPS allowed governments to make limited exceptions to patent rights in "national emergencies." The WTO's Doha Ministerial Conference held in November 2001 made these exceptions clearer and ensured that TRIPS positively supported public health by promoting access to existing medicines as well as by creating incentives for the development of new medicines. An agreement reached in 2003 went further still, allowing members to import cheap generics made in foreign markets under compulsory licensing arrangements. The effect of both changes has been to segment the market, allowing the same drugs to be sold at higher prices in the industrialized countries and at lower prices in the developing countries. It is important to emphasize that this pricing is not only equitable but efficient. And there is no reason why application of this form of pricing should be limited to "essential medicines."

A recent example illustrates this. On May 10, 2013, a story was published on the front page of the *New York Times*, "Cancer Vaccines Get a Price Cut in Poor Nations." The story explains that a cervical cancer vaccine, which costs $130 per dose in the United States (three doses are needed for protection), will be made available for less than $5 per dose in poor countries. The high price in rich countries is the reward for doing the R&D. The low price in poor countries should cover manufacturing costs and no more. This is an efficient outcome, but it depends on a "gray market" being prevented, so that the vaccine sold in poor countries is not shipped back to rich countries—that is, it requires separating rather than integrating markets.

Agricultural Research

For more than 35 years, the World Bank has worked with the Consultative Group on International Agricultural Research (CGIAR), the organization credited with developing modern crop varieties for developing countries, spurring the so-called Green Revolution (see box 2.4). These were varieties that devoted more of their energy to producing grain and that responded more favorably to fertilizer. The first discoveries were made at international research institutes based in Mexico (the International Center for Wheat and Maize Improvement) and the Philippines (the International Rice Research Institute). Since then, the network of such institutes has expanded. Today, the CGIAR comprises 15 collaborative centers.[10]

Box 2.4 The Green Revolution

What was the real contribution of international research to improvement in agricultural productivity? It is impossible to know for sure. If international research had not been undertaken, national programs would likely have expanded—though by how much cannot be known precisely because this "counterfactual" is unobservable. A recent study, however, suggests that the Green Revolution would have been muted were it not for international agricultural research. The results are shown in table B2.4.1.

Table B2.4.1 Effect of International Agricultural Research

	Change from counterfactual (%)	
	Developed countries	Developing countries
Crop yields	−1.4 to −2.5	8.1 to 8.9
Cropped area	−1.6 to −1.9	−1.6 to −1.9
Crop production	−1.0 to −1.7	6.5 to 7.3
Crop prices	−18 to −21	−18 to −21
Change in imports	NA	−6 to −9
Children malnourished	NA	−2.0 to −2.2
Calorie consumption per capita	NA	4.5 to 5.0

Source: Evenson and Gollin 2003.
Note: NA = not applicable

Without international research, crop prices would have been higher, stimulating an increase in crop yields in developed countries as farmers increased use of inputs like fertilizers. It also would have increased the area planted everywhere. Consumers everywhere would have been worse off, but the effect on developing countries would have been greatest: caloric intake per capita would have fallen, and the proportion of children malnourished would have increased.

Was the investment worth the cost? A recent study (Raitzer 2003) found that the aggregate investment in international agricultural research—about $7 billion from 1960 to 2001—yielded the world a benefit-cost ratio in the range of 2:1 to 17:1.

The popular view of the Green Revolution is that it consisted of a one-time burst in productivity, realized in the 1960s and 1970s. Recent analysis suggests that its effects were more long-lasting. The early successes that are so well known initiated a process of continuous improvements, with each new increment in knowledge creating yet another improvement. The existing stock of knowledge is an important input into the creation of more knowledge. Indeed, Evenson and Gollin (2003) show that productivity gains from the modern varieties were larger in the 1980s and 1990s than in the previous two decades. As shown in box 2.4, this investment in research has yielded a benefit more than twice the cost.[11]

Tropical Medicine

No institution like the CGIAR exists for doing research into the diseases that predominately or uniquely affect developing countries. Although R&D in the so-called neglected diseases has increased, coverage has been uneven. A recent survey found that HIV, tuberculosis, and malaria accounted for 125 million disability-adjusted life years (DALYs) in developing countries and received almost 80 percent of total R&D funding. In contrast, pneumonia and diarrheal diseases accounted for 165 million DALYs and received less than 6 percent of total funding. Similarly, helminth infections (including river blindness) account for 20 times the disease burden as dengue fever, but receive half as much R&D funding (Moran et al. 2009).

In addition, it may pay to consider tropical diseases as a group, especially if evidence can be found for their creating a poverty trap (Bonds et al. 2010). The poverty trap consists of multiple equilibria. Start from a situation in which people are poor, and disease is a fact of life. Because of illness from infection, these people are unable to earn a decent income. Because of their poverty, they are unable to fight off infection. They are trapped. By this view, to enable development it may be necessary to control a broad range of diseases for a sustained period of time, long enough to allow incomes to rise and people to be liberated from their poverty trap.

Clearly, the priorities of the current funders may not match those for development. The World Bank should collaborate—with the World Health Organization (WHO), the United Nations Development Programme, and perhaps other organizations—in developing an overall framework for deciding on these priorities.

An accident from history illustrates the kind of benefit that could come from R&D focused on development. In 1978 a researcher at pharmaceutical giant Merck & Co. discovered that the drug he had developed to treat worms in horses was also effective in controlling onchocerciasis in humans. Clinical trials financed by Merck and the WHO demonstrated that one dose a year of the drug, Mectizan®, or ivermectin, could relieve symptoms of the disease for a year. Thus this discovery provided a new tool for fighting this disease, allowing the effort begun in West Africa to be extended to Eastern and Central Africa, regions where aerial spraying was either ineffective or excessively costly. This new program, covering 19 additional countries, was initiated in 1995. The knowledge that ivermectin can help fight a human disease is another public good, but the discovery was made almost by accident and certainly did not result from a deliberate effort to help people burdened by onchocerciasis. Initiatives like the Medicines for Malaria Venture, which the World Bank supports, are a new and better model for development.

Energy

What developing countries need most are new technologies that suit their special circumstances. The absence of a landline infrastructure, for example, made mobile phones especially valuable in developing countries. Statistical analysis shows that adding 10 more phones per 100 people in developing countries can increase growth in GDP per capita by 0.6 percent (Waverman, Meschi, and Fuss 2005).

Similarly, many poor countries have little in the way of an electricity grid, especially in rural areas, making distributed electricity generation of particular value to these countries. Since rich countries would gain less from distributed energy, they have little incentive to innovate in this area. However, rich countries would gain if renewable sources of distributed generation displaced investment in fossil fuel generation in developing countries—a reason for grant financing of R&D for distributed energy.

Correa (2009) notes that the CGIAR could provide a model for climate change mitigation and adaptation research. Similarly, Jones, Downie, and Purvis (2011) have proposed creating the Consultative Group on Low Emissions Development. Their proposal is for a network of "solution centers," the purpose of which would be to "help nations tailor sector- and region-specific best-practice policies to local circumstances" (Jones, Downie, and Purvis 2011: 11). The CGIAR is also noted in the *World Development Report 2010: Development and Climate Change* (World Bank 2009), although its full relevance was not explored. A cluster of research centers akin to the CGIAR—on solar power, wind energy, carbon capture and storage, and so on—may have merit; certainly, the notion needs to be developed in detail.[12]

Climate Change and Development

Climate change will arguably be the greatest challenge for development this century. Economic activity depends on the climate in both obvious and surprising ways. Agriculture, discussed later in this section, is highly sensitive to climate, but so is labor. In a study of 28 countries in the Caribbean, Hsiang (2010) finds that output in nonagricultural sectors is more sensitive to climate than agriculture—which is consistent with studies of the effect of thermal stress on productivity but has been ignored by earlier studies of the costs of climate change.

Of course, adaptation to climate change will reduce damages, but adaptation itself has implications for climate change. For example, one way to reduce heat stress is by using air conditioning. But this requires energy, and if the energy used to power air conditioners is produced using fossil fuels, adaptation to climate change will in turn aggravate the underlying problem. More generally, the best way to adapt to climate change is for the economy to develop. Higher incomes will make adaptation more affordable. Just as important, the institutions needed for development (property rights, the rule of law, and so on) will also facilitate adaptation. However, development will increase emissions unless the traditional correspondence between fossil fuel use and national income is broken.

It is for this reason that efforts to reduce greenhouse gas emissions (GHG) emissions and to adapt to climate change must be considered jointly. In the context of development, emissions growth is largely a problem involving the fast-growing, large, emerging economies like China and India. Vulnerability, by contrast, is greatest for the small, poor developing countries, including small island developing states and countries prone to cyclones and droughts.

Reduction of GHG Emissions

> It's enough to give you whiplash. Last month, the World Bank put out a devastating new report on why 4°C of global warming "simply must not be allowed to occur." This month, the Bank is considering whether to provide financing for a new coal-fired power plant in Mongolia. (Sheppard 2012)

The World Bank faces a challenge in deciding whether to finance investments like coal-fired power plants: Should the Bank finance such investments, ignoring the implications for global climate change? Should it refuse to finance them? Should such investments only be financed if they can be justified by use of a value representing the "cost of carbon"? If so, what cost value should be used?

These are awkward questions. If a zero value is used, investments like coal plants will appear more favorable, and the Bank will be supporting investments that harm the world and that could make future development much more difficult. If a high value is used, investments like coal will appear less favorable, but if the country needing the energy is forced to turn to a more expensive alternative, its development will be compromised—unless the country is compensated for the difference in cost.

Of course there is also the added problem that if the World Bank adopts a hard line on such investments, countries in need of energy investment may turn to other sources of finance. Their borrowing costs would rise, but switching lenders may prove the cheaper alternative overall. In this case, the World Bank would fail in its role in facilitating investment for development, without helping to reduce emissions significantly.

The World Bank would not be in this bind if an effective global regime existed for limiting GHGs that set a global "price" on carbon, either a market price (if countries were obligated to impose a carbon tax or there existed a market in emission entitlements) or a shadow price (if emissions were constrained by regulations and technical standards). But thus far world governments have not even proposed an approach that works in supplying the global public good of emission reductions. In particular, their efforts have so far failed to overcome the basic free rider problem. When a country cuts back on its emissions, the biggest share of the benefit goes to other countries. Each country therefore has an incentive to abate less (emit more) than is collectively desirable, with the consequence that the world as a whole abates too little (emits too much) relative to the outcome in which all countries cooperate fully. To overcome free riding incentives, agreed emission reductions must be enforced (Barrett 2007).

The Bank has tried to fill the vacuum created by this failure. Its Partnership for Market Readiness, involving more than 30 countries, provides a clearinghouse for the exchange of ideas and experience in domestic emissions trading schemes, carbon offsets, and carbon taxes. The Bank also manages a number of "carbon funds," such as the Prototype Carbon Fund and the Carbon Fund for Europe.

Carbon funds could be a vehicle for compensating developing countries for investing in alternatives to coal.[13] Firms constrained by the EU emissions trading scheme can purchase certified emission reductions (CERs), or carbon credits, for investments in developing countries under the Kyoto Protocol's clean development mechanism (CDM). However, this vehicle is imperfect. Currently, the price of permits traded in the scheme is very low, due to a high allocation of allowances, weak demand due to the recession, and complementary policies favoring investment in renewable energy (see box 2.5). Reliance on this value alone will have virtually no effect.

One important issue is whether the price of carbon used to evaluate such investments should reflect the damage caused to the world or the damage caused to a country, making the investment (self-inflicted damage). The latter value should certainly be included; to ignore this value would mean making investments that could be harmful to the country in the long run. However, for the smallest, poorest countries, this value will be very small. Very large, fast-growing, and climate-sensitive developing countries, like China and India, will have much larger values. According to Nordhaus (2011), the social cost of carbon to these countries is about $3 and $2/tCO$_2$, respectively. These values are low relative to the global social cost of carbon (which Nordhaus calculates to be about $12/tCO$_2$), but they are greater than the current price of CER—the global market price for an investment offset.

The case for using a global value is particularly strong when all other countries use the same global value, for in this way every country would benefit from the practice.[14] However, even in this situation, equity considerations may favor compensation to the poorest countries. (After all, these countries are not to blame for today's high level of atmospheric concentrations.) Moreover, rich countries have an incentive to pay compensation. To see this, note that Nordhaus (2011) calculates that the social cost of carbon for the United States and the EU is about $1/tCO$_2$ each, with the value for all high-income countries being about $3/tCO$_2$.

The problem is that while these countries have a collective incentive to compensate, so as to ensure emissions are reduced, they also have an individual incentive to free ride.

Coal plants are lumpy investments. So the question is whether the decision to build a coal plant or a low-carbon alternative will be different whether the investments are evaluated using the global social cost of carbon or the value

Box 2.5 The Cost of Carbon

There are two main ways to calculate the "cost of carbon": by calculating actual price and by estimating the social cost of carbon.

Actual price

In most of the world, there is no "carbon market," making the actual price of carbon zero. That said, Europe has the most well developed carbon market in the world; its current spot price is shown in table B2.5.1. It is important to note, however, that the price of carbon allowances has fluctuated dramatically. In 2006 the price peaked at more than €30/tCO_2. The price of "offsets" certified emission reductions under the EU emissions trading scheme is heavily discounted; it is currently barely above zero. Table B2.5.1 also shows two different carbon tax values. However, note that the Swedish carbon tax exempts electricity generation and is discounted for industry; it is not a "pure" carbon tax.

Social cost

This is an accounting estimate of the damage to the world due to increasing CO_2 emissions by one ton. Because damage will depend on the concentration of greenhouse gases now and into the future, this value will vary with the CO_2 concentration trajectory (being higher for higher concentrations); it will also change over time (generally increasing due to concentrations increasing). The official values shown in table B2.5.1 are all estimates of the social cost of carbon today. Note how the values calculated by Stern and Nordhaus (2011) vary with the scenario. If nothing is done to limit concentrations, they will keep on rising, greatly increasing the social cost of carbon. If international cooperation succeeds in limiting concentrations, the social cost of carbon will be lower.

Table B2.5.1 Various Estimates of the Cost of Carbon

	$/$tCO_2$
Actual prices	
EU ETS allowance price	5
EU CER price	0.40
British Columbia's carbon tax	30
Sweden's carbon tax	150
Official values	
World Bank estimate for "genuine savings"	20
U.S. government	21
U.K. government	39
Academic estimates	
Stern (based on business as usual)	85
Nordhaus (based on business as usual)	12
Stern (based on limiting concentrations to 550 ppmv)	30
Nordhaus (based on limiting temperature change to 2°C)	27

Source: EU values from Point Carbon (Thompson Reuters 2013 accessed July 8, 2013); carbon tax values from Carbon Tax Center (CTC 2013, accessed July 8, 2013); World Bank estimate from World Bank Environmental Economics (accessed July 8, 2013); U.S. government value from Greenstone, Kopits, and Wolverton 2013; U.K. government estimate from Price, Thornton, and Nelson 2007. Stern values were also taken from Price, Thornton, and Nelson 2007, but are in 2000 values. Nordhaus estimates are from Nordhaus 2011.
Note: tCO_2 = tonne of CO_2; ppmv = parts per million (by) volume; ETS = emissions trading scheme; CER = Certified Emission Reduction.

appropriate for the individual country (this value being perhaps some combination of its own social cost of carbon and the offset price available in the market place). Hamilton and Stöver (2012) show that the investment decision will only be affected if the switching price—the price of carbon that makes the country indifferent between investing in the coal plant and investing in the best low-carbon alternative—lies between these two values. This analysis provides a measure of the compensation needed to ensure that the investment project that is best for the world goes forward and that the developing country is made no worse off as a consequence.

The Free Rider Problem

The issue then comes down to whether the free rider problem can be addressed. A proposed solution is as follows. Let the compensation needed to "tip" the investment toward the low-carbon alternative be denoted C, and let N denote the members of the World Bank that are willing to fund the difference. These might be the countries listed in Annex I of the United Nations Framework Convention on Climate Change (UNFCCC), the so-called industrialized country parties. $N = \{1,2,\ldots,n\}$. Suppose that $\sum_{i \in N} B_i = B > C$, where B_i denotes the benefit country i receives from the reduction in emissions associated with choosing the low-carbon alternative instead of the coal plant. Then it will pay the members collectively to ensure that the low-carbon facility is built instead of the coal plant. In other words, a deal can be done, making all the parties better off. To ensure the amount C is paid, the Bank should create a new facility whose members would establish a total budget, chosen to ensure that all projects that meet the above test are funded, and budget shares (perhaps calculated in proportion to these countries' World Bank shares).[15]

This proposed solution is actually similar to an existing arrangement—financing of compliance with the Montreal Protocol by developing countries. When this agreement was amended in 1990 to compensate developing countries for the incremental costs of their compliance, a multilateral fund was created. The work of the fund is undertaken by four implementing agencies, all overseen by an executive committee representing the parties to the treaty and comprising an equal number of representatives from developed and developing countries.[16] As one of these implementing agencies, the Bank disburses almost half of the fund's total budget, specializing in funding for large-scale investment projects. The World Bank also disburses funds through its Global Environment Facility GEF to finance compliance by the economies in transition. In total, more than $3 billion has been disbursed so far.[17]

The difference between the situations is that the Montreal Protocol is an effective treaty, but there is no equivalent treaty for climate change. The so-called Durban Platform for Enhanced Action is meant to lead to a new climate treaty by 2015, to be implemented by 2020, but even if this effort succeeds, the deadline is six years away. However, as explained in the next section, the new Green Climate Fund, which is part of the multilateral climate regime with the

World Bank serving as interim trustee, creates a new opportunity for funding—an opportunity that can integrate mitigation and adaptation assistance.

Climate Change Adaptation

Failure to supply the global public good of reductions in emissions of GHGs will increase the need for, and the returns to, adaptation. Clearly, every long-term investment made from now on must be shown to pay off in a world in which the climate is expected to change.

The key question is who should pay for the investments needed because of climate change. This is an equity issue. The poorest and smallest developing countries are very likely to be the most vulnerable to climate change, even though they have contributed the least to the problem.

The rich countries have accepted the responsibility to assist developing countries with adaptation. In the 2009 Copenhagen Accord, they affirmed a "collective commitment … to provide new and additional resources, including … through international institutions, approaching USD 30 billion for the period 2010–2012 with balanced allocation between adaptation and mitigation." In addition, "in the context of meaningful mitigation actions and transparency on implementation," developed countries committed "to a goal of mobilizing jointly USD 100 billion dollars a year by 2020 to address the needs of developing countries." These obligations were formalized at the Conference of the Parties to the Framework Convention in Cancun in 2010, leading to the establishment of the Green Climate Fund (see below).

However, acceptance of the principle of assistance does not guarantee that the rich countries will contribute or that the investments they make will pay off. One problem is that their commitment is a collective one; no country is individually responsible for contributing a particular amount. A second problem is that the incentives for developed countries to contribute are weak; the obligations are voluntary and there is no means for enforcing them. To be sure, rich countries have a collective incentive, in addition to a moral obligation, to fund adaptation. For example, there is strong evidence that global climate may be associated with civil conflict (Hsiang, Meng, and Cane 2011), with implications for regional stability and geopolitics. However, preventing such disruptions would itself be a global public good, vulnerable to free riding.

Adaptation and Development. Yet another problem is that it isn't clear what "adaptation" is. What should be financed? Adaptation involves choices that are made in anticipation of, or in reaction to, climate change—all taken for the purpose of reducing the damage (and increase the benefits, if any) caused by climate change. The World Bank report *Economics of Adaptation to Climate Change* (World Bank 2010a) puts a dollar value on the investments that can be identified as being needed because of climate change—mainly local and regional public goods, such as dikes, sea walls, levees, and paved roads. This value "between 2010 and 2050 for adapting to an approximately 2°C warmer world by 2050 will be in the range of $70 billion to $100 billion a year." This is about the same amount of money given as foreign aid (World Bank 2010a: xix). Note, however, that based on current projections, the world is almost certain to surpass 2°C, and damages are expected to be nonlinear in mean global temperature. That is, the damage caused by going from 3°C to 4°C is expected to be much greater than the damage caused by going from 2°C to 3°C.

Construction of local public goods like dikes and seawalls are obvious examples of adaptation; but as the World Bank report readily acknowledges, adaptation will require much more than this, and take much less obvious forms. In particular, it isn't clear if adaptation is different from development. This is assessed as follows. A global study of the effects of climate change on agriculture through 2080 found that production overall would fall about 3 percent from baseline.[18] This is a very small change in an expected future level about 70 years from now—so small as to be indistinguishable from zero.[19] In other words, in a world with free trade, climate change will increase output in some places and decrease it in others, perhaps having little effect on output overall. In a world with free trade, to a first approximation, this implies little overall effect on prices. However, the same study shows that production potential in individual countries—all of them developing countries—could fall by a third or more. For the poorest countries that rely on agriculture for a large share of their income, this would amount to a devastating loss in income and therefore purchasing power. Future development would blunt this effect, by reducing agriculture as a share of national income.

In addition, much of the adaptation will need to be done by the private sector, and the incentive for the private sector to make long-term investments depends on the provision of basic national public goods like the rule of law, property rights arrangements, infrastructure, macroeconomic stability, freedom from conflict, and so on—the same national public goods that are needed for "ordinary" development.

So, if adaptation finance is to be "additional," there needs to be a baseline from which change is determined. There first needs to be a baseline for climate, which is hard to determine empirically, given natural variability and uncertainties. But there also needs to be a baseline for development, which is perhaps even more uncertain. Consider an example: Intuitively, a warmer world should increase the geographic extent of malaria; there is some evidence that higher temperatures may have increased malaria transmission in the African highlands (Patz et al. 2005). However, over the last century, the overall spatial extent of malaria has shrunk dramatically, thanks to improvements in control and increases in investment in environmental measures, bed nets, antimalarials, and so forth. As noted by Gething et al. (2010: 342), "Predictions of an intensification of malaria in a warmer world, based on extrapolated empirical relationships or biological mechanisms, must be set against a context of a century of warming that has seen marked global declines in the disease and a substantial weakening of the global correlation between malaria endemicity and climate." In short, any new finance must be additional to the efforts being made already to control malaria, which are more than keeping pace with climate change.

What is really needed, therefore, is more development, in addition to some specific adaptation investments.

World Bank Funding Adaptation Efforts

The World Bank already has a little experience funding adaptation projects through vehicles like the Global Environment Facility. However, the more important mechanisms will be associated directly with the multilateral climate agreements. These are the Adaptation Fund and especially the Green Climate Fund.

The World Bank is trustee to the Adaptation Fund, which was established under the Kyoto Protocol and is financed by a 2 percent levy on CDM transactions. This is a novel approach to finance, but it is seriously flawed for several reasons. First, by increasing the price of CDM transactions, the mechanism will depress uptake of emission offsets—precisely opposite the effect desired. Second, the total amount of money raised is related to the volume of CDM transactions, which is completely unrelated to the need for adaptation assistance. The two values have nothing to do with each other and should not be linked. Third, as explained previously, the price of CDM transactions has been volatile. Currently the price is very low, and yet the need for adaptation assistance has increased rather than fallen. Finally, the CDM has come under scrutiny, particularly for funding projects that produce "phantom" emission reductions. The EU has recently restricted the range of investments for which it is willing to assign credit. For all these reasons, the Adaptation Fund is an unreliable source of finance.

The Green Climate Fund, an operating entity of the UNFCCC, is different, and could possibly become the leading source of adaptation assistance in the future. Managed by a board representing both developed and developing countries, the Green Climate Fund has yet to determine which organization will act as trustee. The World Bank is currently fulfilling this role on an interim basis, but has been given very little authority; it can do little more than transfer funds on instruction of the board or a designated secretariat. The Bank should be made the permanent trustee. The amount of money proposed—an undetermined fraction of a total collective pledge of $100 billion per year by 2020—could be huge, potentially as large as the World Bank currently disburses in a given year. No other organization has the ability and experience to manage this amount of finance.

The World Bank should also be more directly involved in the formation of the Green Climate Fund's policies and in its eventual implementation. Adaptation can't be conceived of as being completely distinct from development; at the very least, efforts in both areas must be highly integrated and coordinated. The same is true of investments for reducing emissions, as the returns on these will depend on investments in complementary infrastructure and on energy pricing and other policies. Establishment of the Green Climate Fund creates an opportunity to reimagine the role of the World Bank in supplying global public goods, just as greater involvement by the World Bank in the formation of the fund will increase the chances of this new institution being successful in the long run. Indeed, greater involvement by the World Bank in the early stages will enhance the Green Climate Fund's credibility with donors, encouraging them to contribute more. This is crucial. If too little money is contributed, the Green Climate Fund will achieve very little, irrespective of how it is managed.

Infectious Disease and Development

The news is full of reports from China of new cases of an influenza virus—human infections of influenza A (H7N9)—that has so far circulated in birds but that could possibly mutate to allow person-to-person transmission. Indeed, this virus could become a pandemic. Regardless of whether this particular strain develops in this way, however, new forms of influenza can be expected and they can emerge at any time (see box 2.6). The emergence of new infectious diseases is a threat to everyone on the planet.

Other types of emerging infectious disease also take the world completely by surprise. Examples in recent years include HIV/AIDS, bovine spongiform encephalopathy (BSE), and, severe acute respiratory syndrome (SARS). These are well-known cases, but more than 300 infectious diseases are known to have emerged since around 1940 (Jones et al. 2008). More unexpected new diseases will surely strike in the future.

Addressing both kinds of emerging infectious disease—the ones we know about and the ones not yet known—involves the supply of five different kinds of global public good: preparedness, prevention, surveillance, reporting, and response.

Preparedness

Investments made in advance of an outbreak can help reduce impacts. These investments can be generic, such as planning for hospital "surge" capacity. They can also be specific, such as the stockpiling of antivirals in anticipation of a possible future influenza pandemic.

Antivirals protect people exposed to the virus, especially if taken before symptoms first appear. They also slow spread of the disease. According to modeling efforts discussed below, under the right conditions, judicious use of antivirals can stop a virus in its tracks. Even if the intervention only slows spread of disease, it can be of benefit, as it takes time to develop, produce, and distribute vaccine for a new influenza virus.

However, stockpiling is costly. Not only must the drugs be purchased, they must also be distributed with great care. Unplanned distribution will not do. The drugs would almost certainly need to be rationed. In particular, they would need to be targeted to the most vulnerable people and distributed optimally for purposes of containment. To be effective as a prophylaxis, antivirals would also have to be administered quickly (Longini et al. 2004). Finally, there is no guarantee that the drugs will work. Indeed, no one ever knows if they will work unless and until they are used.

The benefits of stopping or slowing spread of an emerging infectious disease are global. Rich countries have an incentive to stockpile unilaterally, irrespective

Box 2.6 Influenza Pandemics

Seasonal influenza follows a fairly predictable pattern, making it possible for a vaccine to be reformulated every year, based on scientists' best guess for how the virus will evolve over the course of the year. It takes many months to produce normal stocks of vaccine and to ready them for distribution. In some years, the predictions about virus evolution work well, and the vaccine is effective. In other years, an unanticipated strain may appear and come to dominate, making the vaccine relatively ineffective.

Pandemic influenza is different. These viruses emerge infrequently—three emerged in the previous century, and one so far in this century—when a virus passes from animals to humans and mutates to become transmissible person to person. Vaccines based on existing and expected strains offer little if any protection against these new strains. New vaccines can be formulated, once samples of the virus are available, but production and distribution take time—usually about 6–8 months.

Two aspects of pandemic influenza virus are crucial: transmissibility and virulence. A key parameter in epidemiology is the basic reproductive number for a pathogen. This is the average number of secondary infections that result when a single infected individual is inserted into a population in which everyone is susceptible. A value greater than one is needed for a disease to spread; higher values result in greater spread. Virulence can be represented by the case fatality ratio—the ratio of deaths to cases showing symptoms. Table B2.6.1 compares two different pandemics: the most deadly one in history: the 1918–19 "Spanish flu" and the 2009 H1N1 pandemic. The basic reproductive number is much higher for the 1918–19 pandemic, indicating that this virus spread relatively easily. More worrisome, the case fatality rate is many times higher.

Table B2.6.1 A Comparison of Two Pandemics

Pandemic	Basic reproductive number/ source	Case fatality ratio
1918–19 Spanish flu	2.9–3.9 Mills, Robins, and Lipsitch 2004	2.5% Taubenberger and Morens 2006
2009 H1N1 influenza	1.3–1.7 Yang et al. 2010	0.05% Presanis et al. 2009

of the global benefits; and some rich countries, like the United States and United Kingdom, have accumulated stocks. However, poor countries lack the incentive to stockpile.[20] Furthermore, in the event of an outbreak, rich countries with stocks are likely to want to hold on to them for reasons of national security, rather than donate them to contain a global threat. That is the reason the WHO maintains its own stockpile.

Epidemiological modeling suggests that under the right circumstances, a stockpile of about 3 million treatment courses should suffice to stop an epidemic

(Enserink 2005)—an amount that happens to equal the number of courses donated to the WHO by Roche, the manufacturer of Tamiflu (WHO 2005). However, extinguishing an outbreak is a tricky business. To succeed, a prophylactic course of antiviral medicine must be given to the contacts of every suspected flu patient and must be coupled with other measures, like school closings, quarantines, and travel restrictions. Crucially, all these measures will only be effective if the basic reproductive number for the disease is no greater than about 1.8 (Enserink 2005), and some variants are more prone to spread than this (see box 2.6). Moreover, action would need to be swift; antivirals would need to be distributed within about two weeks of the first cases, meaning that surveillance would have to be very effective. In addition, the contacts of infected individuals would need to be reached within about two days of a patient showing symptoms—requiring a responsive and effective health system. A weakness in any part of the chain would endanger the entire enterprise.

Prevention

Medical and public health services cannot prevent outbreaks of every potential emerging disease, but they can reduce the likelihood of some diseases emerging and spreading. The best way to do this is to address the conditions that give rise to outbreaks in the first place—conditions like poor sanitation, nutrition, and food safety. As noted in the introduction to this chapter, the provision of international public goods and development must often be determined jointly.

In some cases, specific remedies are needed. This is especially true of resistant strains, which are similar to emerging diseases in that they can render our existing tools for defense impotent. Resistance can be prevented or at least made much less likely by improved use of drugs—influenza antiviral treatments, antibiotics, and antimalarials are all prone to becoming resistant—and vector control methods. Such measures are weakest-link global public goods. All else being equal, a disease is more likely to emerge in the country that undertakes the least effort to guard against an outbreak. This makes each country's policies for drug use and animal husbandry of interest to every other country. In particular, minimum standards should be set and applied globally.

The history of antimalarials explains the problem. Chloroquine, introduced in 1946, has probably saved millions of lives. It was once the best malaria treatment. However, drug resistance emerged independently in Colombia and on the Cambodia-Thailand border in the late 1950s, spreading to Africa in the 1970s. By the 1990s, Chloroquine was ineffective throughout much of Africa, where malaria results in much greater mortality. Resistance to another drug, sulphadoxine-pyrimethamine, also emerged in western Cambodia and led to a similar situation. Fortunately, new artemisinin-based drugs, coupled with widespread use of insecticide-treated bed nets, have reduced the burden of malaria throughout Asia and Africa. However, resistance to artemisinin combination therapies (ACTs) emerged in western Cambodia in the mid-2000s and is appearing in new strains today (Miotto et al. 2013), threatening to repeat the earlier mistakes. Resistance is emerging because most treatments are distributed through the private sector using monotherapy versions of the drug that are prone to resistance. Another problem may be the use of substandard and counterfeited drugs. Precisely why emergence is occurring in western Cambodia is not entirely understood (Dondorp et al. 2010). However, it is of great importance that resistance be stopped in its tracks. If it were to spread to Africa, millions of lives would be threatened. Currently no back up antimalarial is available.

One approach to limiting the emergence and spread of resistance is the Affordable Medicines Facility–malaria (AMFm), a mechanism for subsidizing ACTs so that they can help eliminate of chloroquine and the artemisinin monotherapies. A pilot effort was funded by the Global Fund to Fight AIDS, Tuberculosis, and Malaria, but the Global Fund later decided to integrate AMFm into its standard model, which is country-driven. The Global Fund would support subsidies for combination therapies, but only if individual countries requested the funds for this purpose. The problem with this model of funding is that it ignores the incentive problem. Resistance involves huge global externalities.

In addition, global standards are needed for drugs—for their production (artemisinin monotherapies should be banned) and distribution (which should be limited, thereby requiring rapid diagnostic testing). Other approaches can also help, such as temporal cycling of different combination drugs. Finally, a case can be made for trying to eliminate malaria in the Cambodia-Thailand area where resistance has emerged before (Dondorp et al. 2010). This may be the best investment for assisting Africa.

Surveillance

No state can defend itself against an infectious disease without first knowing that the disease exists, where it circulates, and how it is transmitted. Disease surveillance identifies new outbreaks, allowing measures to be taken to reduce spread. Surveillance everywhere is of value, but the global returns to investment will be highest in the countries in which surveillance is weakest. Most reports of emerging infectious diseases come from developed countries; almost one-third of reports worldwide have come from the United States. The reason isn't that these countries are especially vulnerable to outbreaks. The main reason is that developed countries have stronger surveillance systems. For example, while the 2009 H1N1 pandemic influenza, discussed in box 2.6, was first detected in the United States, it had been circulating for months before that in Mexico.

Careful analysis of the data shows that after adjusting for differences in reporting, emerging infectious diseases are correlated with human population densities. In addition, most emerging infectious diseases have zoonotic origins, with the bigger problem being wildlife rather than domestic animals (Jones et al. 2008). The returns to investments in surveillance are thus likely to be greatest in the areas in which people agglomerate and come into contact with animals. Jones et al. (2008) identify "hot spots" for emergence, among them Central America and tropical Africa and South Asia. These should be the target areas for global investments in surveillance.[21]

The International Health Regulations—the only legally binding international agreement on infectious diseases—oblige countries to report "events that may constitute a public health emergency of international concern," but do little to address the real weaknesses in the system. Its revisions to date require that states "develop, strengthen and maintain … the capacity to detect, assess, notify and report" and "respond promptly and effectively to public health threats and public health emergencies of international concern." But they do not offer the poorest countries financial assistance for bringing their surveillance systems up to a level sufficient to meet global demand. To be sure, the revisions state, "WHO shall assist States Parties, upon request, to develop, strengthen and maintain" surveillance capacity. However, the resources of the WHO are limited, and the revisions do not say what this assistance would consist of, how it would be determined, and, most important, how it would be financed.

Reporting

Surveillance is a public good only if the information obtained is reported. The failure to report helped to allow the SARS outbreak to become a pandemic.[22] Fortunately, the incentives to report have improved as a result of the SARS experience, which led to an important revision in the International Health Regulations. The reason the United States identified H1N1 in 2009 before Mexico did was not because Mexico had identified the virus and failed to report it. The reason was that Mexico had not understood that the infections observed there were due to a new disease strain.

A study by HealthMap, a prominent aggregator of disease outbreak information, found "a clear bias towards increased reporting from countries with higher numbers of media outlets, more developed public health resources, and greater availability of electronic communication infrastructure" (Brownstein et al. 2008: 1021). In other words, there is a strong correlation of reporting with development. As noted by Michaud (2010), the HealthMap study found not a single report from countries like the Democratic Republic of Congo and the Central African Republic, but more than 4,000 from the United States and more than 700 from China.

Response

Response can include attempts to extinguish an epidemic where it first emerges, such as by the tried-and-true measures of quarantine. It can also include defensive responses, such as restrictions on the movements of people and trade. In the longer run, of course, it would also include the development of new treatments and vaccines.

The International Health Regulations say that at "the request of a State Party, WHO shall collaborate in the response to public health risks and other events by providing technical guidance and assistance and by assessing the effectiveness of the control measures in place, including the mobilization of international teams of experts for on-site assistance, when necessary." Sovereignty could be a problem here, but poor countries have an incentive to accept assistance that is offered. The bigger problem is with the timing of the assistance. As noted earlier, there will be a tendency for rich countries to hold on to their stocks of antivirals in the event of the emergence of a new strain of pandemic influenza. Similarly, rich countries have incentives to immunize their own population to protect against imported infections. Taking the 2009 H1N1 epidemic as a case study, the WHO requested that vaccine manufacturers donate at least 10 percent of their production to poor countries or otherwise make their vaccines available to poor countries at a reduced price. As noted previously, efficiency demands price discrimination. Eventually, vaccine was given, but that occurred mainly when the disease seemed less of a threat. As noted in a *New York Times* article, "countries that can afford vaccines save themselves first, and, when the worst has passed, transfer their leftovers to the poor" (McNeil 2010: A-11).

The inequity of distribution was exposed when in 2006 Indonesia refused to share its flu samples—sharing is a long established practice—for purposes of either global surveillance or product development. This created a huge vulnerability worldwide, as Indonesia is a hotspot for influenza virus. The standoff was resolved when the World Health Assembly adopted a resolution requiring "the timely sharing of viruses and specimems," while at the same time guaranteeing "transparent, fair and equitable sharing of the benefits arising from the generation of information, diagnostics, medicines, vaccines and other technologies" (WHA 2007).

The most important implication of this summary of infectious disease and development is that reductions in the threat of emerging infectious diseases require efforts on all five fronts. Failure in any one effort reduces the returns to each of the others. The rich countries have powerful incentives to supply all five; poor countries do not. They need assistance, and it is in the collective interests of the rich countries to provide assistance.

Fisheries Management for Development

A report by the World Bank and the Food and Agriculture Organization (2008) estimates that overfishing reduces the net benefits to be derived from the world's ocean fisheries by $50 billion a year—a colossal waste.

Conservation of fish stocks is not a global public good. Public goods are non-rivalrous, and as every fisherman knows, fishing is exceedingly rivalrous; consumption of a fish stock by any country reduces the amounts that others can catch. Public goods are also non-excludable, but in the case of fish stocks, exclusion is feasible. Just as laws can make knowledge a private good, they can also "nationalize" the seas. Indeed, the greatest change in property rights perhaps occurred in the 1970s when the territorial sea was increased from three to 12 miles, and exclusive economic zones extending up to 200 miles were created. This change in the property right system brought the majority of the ocean's fisheries resources within national jurisdiction. However, there are still gaps. The biggest problems today are with high seas fisheries, and especially fisheries that overlap different jurisdictions, including highly migratory fisheries, like those involving tuna. Management of these fisheries is similar to provision of a transnational public good. It requires international cooperation. In particular, it requires every country being willing to limit its harvest. As noted in an earlier World Bank (2004b: 3) study,

> Weak governance is the main underlying cause of overfishing. The common access nature of the fishery resources; technical and enforcement difficulties in controlling the levels of the catch; and the migratory character of the fish resources and the resulting supranational institutional requirements for effective control all provide great challenges to the governance structure, which many international, regional, and national institutions have not been able to meet.

The UN Fish Stocks Treaty requires that coastal states and states fishing on the high seas cooperate by becoming members of a regional fisheries management organization (RFMO). To become a member, a state must have a "real interest" in the fisheries concerned. The Fish Stocks agreement, which applies only to parties (currently 78), goes farther than the Law of the Sea. Its aim, essentially, is to turn "open access" into "common property" by limiting the right to fish to those states that belong to a RFMO. Non-members are to be excluded. The aim is to transform "unregulated" fishing into "illegal" fishing.

A key issue is how a "real interest" is interpreted. If it is interpreted broadly, membership in a RFMO could include every country. In this case, the problem would come full circle, with common property management by a very large number of countries being indistinguishable from "open access." Even if this provision were interpreted narrowly, membership of an RFMO could be so large as to render the enforcement provisions of the agreement weak.

Ocean Fisheries Management

These new property rights arrangements and new management organizations are the two instruments for managing ocean fisheries. Neither is adequate. To improve on the current situation, more radical change is needed.

The fisheries economics literature proposes two different visions for the future. Munro (2007) believes that the problem lies with the right of "new" countries to enter a fishery. He advocates restricting membership to "charter members." If a "real interest" is interpreted too broadly, he fears, the number of parties sharing a common property resource will be excessive. Limit membership, he believes, and these agreements can be more effective. Hannesson (2011) in contrast thinks that the enforcement capabilities of regional fishery management organizations will be limited even in the absence of the so-called new member problem. To Hannesson, the solution is to extend coastal state jurisdiction.

As a practical matter, it seems that a combination of approaches will be tried by fishing states in the future. In the Atlantic, Indian, and Pacific Oceans, an extension of property rights will not help very much. In these regions, the best approach will be to strengthen the enforcement capabilities of their respective RFMOs through combinations of observer schemes, port state measures, and trade restrictions.

An interesting exception is the central and western Pacific Ocean. Scattered throughout this ocean are islands belonging to a number of Pacific island states. When these countries claimed their exclusive economic zones, including their archipelagic waters, a huge portion of this vital tuna fishery came under their control. At first, eight of these countries, comprising the larger share of the fishery, developed their own collective organization for managing about half the fishery. Later, they joined the other coastal states and distant water fishing nations in establishing a regional organization, the Central and Western Pacific Fisheries Commission. Perhaps the most innovative approach tried so far is a vessel day scheme for restricting effort (see box 2.7).

In 2011, the eight states that signed the Nauru Agreement effectively closed areas of the high seas surrounded by their exclusive economic zones. Legally, they could not deny access. However, they were able to limit the distribution of licenses to countries that refrained from fishing in these high seas waters. It would not do for the World Bank to become directly involved in these arrangements, but the Bank can help build capacity for improved fisheries management by developing countries.

Box 2.7 Managing Tuna in the Central and Western Pacific

About half the world's tuna harvest is taken from the Central and Western Pacific region. One recent estimate suggests that bigeye harvests are currently about one-third over the maximum sustained yield. However, stocks of skipjack and yellowfin tuna are not overexploited (ISSF 2013).

In the 1970s, distant water fleets began fishing for tuna in these waters. They were unregulated and paid no fees. The Law of the Sea treaty changed this: It allowed the coastal states to declare rights to fish within their exclusive economic zones. It therefore also allowed them to charge for access. Since the ocean in this region is dotted with small islands, these claims to an exclusive economic zone, including archipelagic waters, make this fishery a common property resource.

This zone system offers a potential for improvement over open access, but there is still a collective action problem. Collectively, all the states in the region have an incentive to limit access and restrict harvests so as to build up the stocks and increase the economic value of the entire fishery. Individually, each of the coastal states has an incentive to increase access, for the costs of doing so would be spread among all the members of the collective.

In the early 1980s, eight countries—the Federated States of Micronesia, Kiribati, the Marshall Islands, Nauru, Palau, Papua New Guinea, the Solomon Islands, and Tuvalu—formed a subregional alliance with the Nauru Agreement. The aim was to negotiate as a group, setting harmonized terms and conditions for access by foreign fleets. In the early 2000s, in response to the requirements of the Law of the Sea treaty and the United Nations Fish Stocks Agreement, all the Pacific island states and the distant water nations formed the Western and Central

box continues next page

Box 2.7 Managing Tuna in the Central and Western Pacific *(continued)*

Pacific Fisheries Commission, a regional fisheries management organization (RFMO). Decisions by the commission are by consensus, which means that the parties to the Nauru Agreement do not have full control over all decisions. However, the commission is useful to these countries as well, particularly in helping them to monitor and enforce the total allowed catch and catch allocation (Havice and Campling 2010).

The parties to the Nauru Agreement developed a vessel day scheme to manage their resource, and the commission later built on this approach. While a total allowable catch is normally preferred, participation in a fishery is much easier to monitor than catches. The allocation applies to the whole of the area controlled by the parties to the Nauru Agreement; each party is compensated according to the time vessels spend in its waters. For all its limitations, the vessel day scheme has significantly increased returns to the developing country coastal states (Havice 2013).

Collective management is a complex enterprise. To negotiate it successfully, each party must understand its own interests and the collective interests of all parties. The Bank could help in developing these analyses. The process also requires regular meetings to help establish trust. But being able to negotiate effectively is costly. According to Havice and Campling (2010, 104), "Pacific island countries struggle with the Commission policy making process, including: the costs associated with attending meetings, engaging in multiple negotiating issues, and diplomatic coordination to develop regional positions among a range of island states. The effect is that Pacific island countries are unable to fully participate in [Central and Western Pacific Fisheries] Commission negotiations." Making matters worse, Japan, a major distant water nation, has funded the participation in commission negotiations of some Pacific island states, but only the ones with which Japan has bilateral access agreements (Havice and Campling 2010). Clearly, it would be better if funding for these states' participation in the commission came from an objective source—again, a possible role for the Bank.

The World Bank's Role in Promoting Global Public Goods

When the World Bank was founded almost 70 years ago, the world was a very different place than it is today. The Bank's original mission was to help rebuild Europe after World War II. Not long after it was created, however, its mission changed. The Bank's focus became lending money to the world's poor countries, to aid their development. Over a decade ago, the Bank became interested in global public goods and made supplying global public goods a strategic theme. But the Bank's involvement in partnerships and regional and global programs has been uneven, with some great achievements, like river blindness control, and some missed opportunities, like rinderpest eradication. Should the Bank be transformed more radically? Should it become "a global institution addressing the global challenges of the future through global collective action"? (Birdsall and Subramanian 2007).

There is no single institution responsible for supplying global public goods; instead, there are many. The Global Polio Eradication Initiative is run by the WHO, though with outside funding and currently under the watchful eye of an independent review board. The global effort to address climate change is being coordinated under an umbrella agreement, the UNFCCC. The environmental impacts of international maritime transport are being addressed by agreements negotiated by the members of the International Maritime Organization. The list is long. The point is that different global public goods raise different issues, require different technical expertise, and are of special interest to different collections of countries. It would be impractical for the World Bank to take on a role like the one proposed by Birdsall and Subramanian (2007). Moreover, there is also no obvious need. Many of these organizations work very effectively to supply global public goods.

However, leaving these matters entirely to other organizations would also be a mistake. The World Bank can and should play a role in ensuring that the provision of global public goods contributes to meeting its principal aim of reducing poverty. The Bank should also get involved when existing arrangements fail, as they have in the case of climate change. Finally, the World Bank should play a strategic role in looking for connections among the different global public goods and its own development agenda. The supply of global public goods is a patchwork. The Bank can and should develop a coherent strategy for their provision.

Any change needs also to build upon rather than replace the Bank's traditional competency in country-based development. Birdsall and Subramanian (2007: 5) state,

> The Bank should as quickly as possible oversee a major effort to see how global warming can be addressed (building upon the existing Global Environment Facility), including, for example, monitoring and surveillance of any agreed reductions by countries; and how R&D for new technologies for poor countries can be substantially increased.

The global effort to address climate change has been unsuccessful, but it is not for lack of trying. No effort in world history has attracted as much diplomatic attention as climate change, and it is difficult to see why countries would be willing to turn this issue over to the World Bank or why the Bank would be more successful in orchestrating global collective action than the countries themselves. Nor is it obvious why the World Bank should be given the authority to monitor compliance with an agreement to limit emissions. At the same time, as explained above, the World Bank cannot stand aside simply because the global effort has failed. It should resist financing investments that it knows will be harmful to global development in the long run. As noted previously, it should devise an arrangement whereby its members finance the amount needed to favor a "green" alternative.[23] By doing this, the World Bank can ensure that its own investments are consistent with the aim of supplying the global public good of climate change emission reductions—an essential condition for long-run development. As explained previously, a case can also be made for why the World Bank should support the creation of a CGIAR-like organization for energy. Certainly, the proposal merits further study.

In the area of climate change adaptation, the Bank can potentially play a larger role. The best protection from climate change is development. But climate change also threatens development. Clearly, every investment made must be shown to pay off in a future in which the climate may be very different. In addition, financing needs to change. The rich countries have acknowledged a responsibility to assist developing countries with adaptation. The Bank, along with other organizations, including the board of the Green Climate Fund, should ensure that these funds are made available and invested wisely.

These are just a few examples. Others discussed in this chapter include investment in tropical medicine research, infectious disease surveillance, and the development of collective institutions for the management of global common property resources. The Bank can and should do more in all of these areas. The aim here has not been to be comprehensive, but a comprehensive review is needed and should be undertaken by Bank staff. The focus of the review should be on establishing priorities for the supply global public goods for development. So far, the Bank's involvement in this area has been ad hoc, often done in reaction to a crisis or inspired by outside parties. The Bank's involvement should be more strategic. More ideas need to be generated internally. The focus should be on policies and projects that complement the Bank's core business of country lending. The aim should be for the supply of global public goods to increase the returns on more traditional development projects.

This review should also identify key partners in this effort, such as the World Health Organization, in the area of infectious disease control. Success will depend on building strong and mutually beneficial relationships with a wide range of organizations.

To play a fuller role, the Bank needs resources dedicated for the purpose. To this point, the Bank has relied on trust funds and short-term pilot schemes; overall, funding has been inadequate. Existing sources of funding should be consolidated into a Global Public Goods Fund and tied to the new strategic focus, but additional resources will be needed to implement the new strategy. In addition to identifying priority areas for investment, the major strategic review should include budgets for each area and consistent criteria for allocating resources across the different investment areas. Perhaps the most important single piece in this new portfolio will be climate change. The funding mechanism showing the greatest promise in this area is the Green Climate Fund. The role that the Bank will play in this effort is still to be determined, but it is obvious that the Bank has unique experience in allocating very large sums of money, that the distinction between development and climate adaptation is unavoidably blurred, and that investments for emission reductions need to be compatible with general development aspirations. Now would seem a propitious time to consider jointly the arrangements for the Green Climate Fund and the strategic orientation of the World Bank over the next quarter century.

Box 2.8 What Young Development Professionals Think About Sustainability in Development

Inka Schomer, Climate Investment Funds

Talking about sustainability is always bittersweet for me. It conjures up thoughts on how much progress has been made in the multiple fora of the international environment agenda and the incredible challenges that lie ahead for my generation. The amount of innovation in sustainability, seen in initiatives ranging from sustainable stock exchanges to ambitious carbon neutrality goals in the Maldives, are in one way or another a product of major events in sustainable development, climate change, and biodiversity of the past 3 decades. Yet it is still hard to sleep peacefully while being aware of the serious risks of not transforming our multiple human systems.

When the World Bank was created in 1945, its institutional focus was on rebuilding countries after the shattering impacts of World War II. Since then, the World Bank has been slowly integrating environmental policies and practices in to its operations. However, environmental concerns are still not seen as a primary focus in the task of development and poverty reduction. Which brings up the question: How do we move beyond a current reality where much of the meaningful and impactful work on sustainability is done on the sidelines of business as usual? How do we shift out of a "neurosis" that enables us to repeatedly do the same thing and expect different results?

In beginning to unpack these questions, it is pivotal to first think about the end goal we would like to work toward. To start this, we will have to redefine institutional focuses and envisage another reality beyond the one we have right now. Instead of tracking the devastating climate and natural resource scenarios, more attention needs to be paid to investing resources and time to the global scenarios that would be aspirational, ambitious, and meaningful to the multiple stakeholders that are part of the ecological economies that are most affected. Unless we transition to a dialogue and a means of communicating that resonate with people, we are not going to progress. We need to stop churning out report after report on impacts and start demonstrating what low-carbon resilient economies will look like. We need to learn; we need to fail and try to implement the alternatives to the norm.

Many studies on behavioral norms have indicated that a purely doom-and-gloom approach to communication does not elicit positive responses from people. Individuals respond best to chilling facts on climatic change when combined with suggestions and solutions to shift us out of current trends. These types of conversations will also be incredibly important for the client countries who often already face tough choices on earmarking scarce resources for development needs and are unaware of alternative development pathways. It is in situations like these where the World Bank could be very impactful. I look forward to the day when I come to work knowing that I am part of an institution that does not treat development needs and environmental concerns as mutually exclusive.

Notes

1. In a paper titled "Public Goods and Economic Development," Besley and Ghatak (2006) do not even mention international and global public goods.

2. These terms are used interchangeably here, but note that there can be a distinction. For example, formally, England is a country; the United Kingdom is a state.

3. Birdsall (2006) makes the same argument.

4. The case for addressing conflict in order to enable development is made by Collier et al. (2003).

5. By contrast, bilateral aid is sometimes aimed more at furthering the economic and political interests of the donor.

6. Donations include contributions from the World Bank and the governments of Australia, Denmark, the Netherlands, Norway, Sweden, and Germany. Funds have been disbursed to Tunisia, Libya, and Somalia, in addition to the countries affected by the conflict in Syria. See the *State- and Peace-Building Fund Annual Report 2012* (World Bank 2012).

7. The classification of sovereignty presented here draws from Krasner (1999).

8. The term derives from the Peace of Westphalia treaties that were signed in 1648 to end the Thirty Years War and the Eighty Years War, which recognized for the first time the exclusive sovereignty of each party to its territory and population.

9. Heller and Eisenberg call this the "anticommons."

10. For a recent detailed and updated review of the CGIAR, see World Band 2004a.

11. Though smaller than the benefit-cost ratio for other global public goods, like smallpox eradication, the nature of the estimate also differs. The economic returns to agricultural research were calculated for the full effort, not only those parts that turned out to be successful. (A cost benefit analysis of all eradication programs would appear less attractive than the one for smallpox alone; the expensive malaria eradication effort, for example, failed to achieve its goals.) Certainly, when compared with most public investments made at the domestic level, the benefit-cost ratio for international agricultural research is very attractive. For the CGIAR's own claims of success, see CGIAR (2011).

12. Countries already collaborate on specific energy research endeavors, for example, the ITER project on nuclear fusion, which is "big science" research. Parties to the agreement include China, the European Union, India, Japan, the Russian Federation, the Republic of Korea, and the United States.

13. A complementary idea is to reduce emissions from deforestation and to increase carbon removal from the atmosphere by the enhancement of foreign carbon stocks. This is the objective of the Forest Carbon Partnership Facility, for which the World Bank serves as trustee.

14. It should be noted that all countries in total would benefit from the practice; lump sum transfers may be needed to ensure that every country benefits individually from the practice.

15. The logic of linking payments to the value C is explained in chapter 13 of Barrett (2003). Should contributions to such a facility be linked to emissions trading programs? The author states, "I caution against this. I see nothing wrong with the European Union deciding to link its emissions trading program to this facility, allowing its members to obtain credits (as they currently get through the UN clean

development mechanism for their contributions, but I don't think the facility should link contributions to any trading programs, for contributions would then fluctuate with vagaries of those markets."

16. The others are the United Nations Environment Programme, the United Nations Development Programme, and the United Nations Industrial Development Organisation; see Multilateral Fund 2011a.

17. Multilateral Fund 2011b. See "About Us."

18. Cline 2007: 71, table 5.8; this estimate includes carbon fertilization.

19. Losses to agriculture could be much greater overall than indicated here. Making use of fine-scale weather data for the United States and flexible regression models, Schlenker and Roberts (2009: 15594) show that the effect of temperature on yields is nonlinear and non-monotonic. In particular, they find that "yields increase with temperatures up to 29°C for corn, 30°C for soybeans, and 32°C for cotton but that temperatures above these thresholds are very harmful." Depending on the climate scenario used, they find that yields will fall from 30 to more than 80 percent before the end of the century. This is to be compared with Cline's (2007) estimate for the United States showing an 8 percent increase in yields!

20. See Carrasco et al. (2011), who estimate that stockpiles of antivirals are cost-effective for countries accounting for no more than about one-half the world's population.

21. Other issues include linking existing surveillance networks, like the Program for Monitoring Emerging Diseases (ProMED), the Global Outbreak Alert and Response Network (GOARN), and the Global Public Health Intelligence Network (GPHIN); developing syndromic surveillance capabilities (for example, looking out for sudden increases in the number of people staying home from work and school, rather than direct clinical evidence of disease); and developing new technologies for detection, such as for improved diagnostics.

22. Surveillance of markets in wild animal species in China may have detected the SARS pathogen earlier; see Kuiken et al. (2005).

23. Such new arrangements should reflect the lessons learned from earlier efforts, including the Clean Technology Fund.

References

Barrett, S. 2003. *Environment and Statecraft: The Strategy of Environmental Treaty-Making.* Oxford, U.K.: Oxford University Press.

———. 2007. *Why Cooperate? The Incentive to Supply Global Public Goods.* Oxford, U.K.: Oxford University Press.

Besley, T., and M. Ghatak. 2006. "Public Goods and Economic Development." In *Understanding Poverty*, edited by A. Banerjee, R. Benabou, and D. Mookherjee. Oxford, U.K.: Oxford University Press.

Birdsall, N. 2006. "Overcoming Smallness: The Challenge of Underfunded Regionalism." In *The New Public Finance: Responding to Global Challenges*, edited by I. Kaul and P. Conceicao. Oxford, U.K.: Oxford University Press.

Birdsall, N., and A. Subramanian. 2007. *From World Bank to World Development Cooperative.* Center for Global Development, Washington, DC. http://www.cgdev .org/sites/default/files/14625_file_WorldDevCooperative.pdf.

Bonds, M. H., D. C. Keenan, P. Rohani, and J. D. Sachs. 2010. "Poverty Trap Formed by the Ecology of Infectious Diseases." *Proceedings of the Royal Society B* 277 (1685): 1185–92.

Brownstein, J. S., C. C. Freifield, B. Y. Reis, and K. D. Mandl. 2008. "Surveillance Sans Frontieres: Internet-Based Emerging Infectious Disease Intelligence and HealthMap Project." *PLoS Medicine* 5 (7): e151.

Carrasco, L. R., V. J. Lee, M. I. Chen, D. B. Matchar, J. P. Thompson, and A. R. Cook. 2011. "Strategies for Antiviral Stockpiling for Future Influenza Pandemics: A Global Epidemic—Economic Perspective" *Journal of the Royal Society Interface* 8: 1307–13.

CGIAR (Consultative Group on International Agricultural Research). 2011. "The CGIAR at 40 and Beyond: Impacts That Matter for the Poor and the Planet." CGIAR Fund Office, Washington, DC.

Cline, W. 2007. *Global Warming and Agriculture: Impact Estimates by Country*. Washington, DC: Peterson Institute for International Economics.

Collier, P., V. L. Elliott, H. Hegre, A. Hoeffler, M. Reynal-Querol, and N. Sambanis. 2003. *Breaking the Conflict Trap: Civil War and Development Policy*. Oxford, U.K.: Oxford University Press.

Correa, C. M. 2009. "Fostering the Development and Diffusion of Technologies for Climate Change: Lessons from the CGIAR Model." Policy Brief No. 6, International Centre for Trade and Sustainable Development, Geneva, Switzerland.

CTC (Carbon Tax Center). 2013. "Where Carbon Is Taxed." CTC, New York. http://www.carbontax.org/progress/where-carbon-is-taxed/.

Dasgupta, P., and J. E. Stiglitz.1980. "Industrial Structure and the Nature of Innovative Activity." *Economic Journal* 90: 266–93.

David, P. A. 1993. "Intellectual Property Institutions and the Panda's Thumb: Patents, Copyrights, and Trade Secrets in Economic Theory and History." In *Global Dimensions of Intellectual Property Rights in Science and Technology*, edited by M. B. Wallerstein, M. E. Mogee, and R. A. Schoen, 19–61. Washington, DC: National Academies Press.

Dondorp, A. M., S. Yeung, L. White, C. Nguon, N. P. J. Day, D. Socheat, and L. von Seidlein. 2010. "Artemisinin Resistance: Current Status and Scenarios for Containment." *Nature Reviews Microbiology* 8: 272–80.

Enserink, M. 2005. "Drugs, Quarantine Might Stop a Pandemic Before It Starts." *Science* 309: 870–71.

Evenson, R. E., and D. Gollin. 2003. "Assessing the Impact of the Green Revolution, 1960 to 2000." *Science* 300: 758–62.

Fenner, F., D. A. Henderson, I. Arita, Z. Jezek, and I. D. Ladnyi. 1988. *Smallpox and Its Eradication*. Geneva, Switzerland: World Health Organization.

Gething, P. W., D. L. Smith, A. P. Patil, A. J. Tatem, R. W. Snow, and S. I. Hay. 2010. "Climate Change and the Global Malaria Recession." *Nature* 465: 342–46.

Greenstone, M., E. Kopits, and A. Wolverton. 2013. "Developing a Social Cost of Carbon for U.S. Regulatory Analysis: A Methodology and Interpretation." *Review of Environmental Economics and Policy* 7 (1): 23–46.

Hamilton, K., and J. Stöver. 2012. "Economic Analysis of Projects in a Greenhouse World." World Bank Policy Research Working Paper 6117, World Bank, Washington, DC. http://elibrary.worldbank.org/docserver/download/6117.pdf?expires=1367778781&id=id&accname=guest&checksum=2FCB1A89F2D63348DD3276B8971E549A.

Hannesson, R. 2011. "Game Theory and Fisheries." *Annual Review of Resource Economics* 3: 181–202.

Havice, E. 2013. "Rights-Based Management in the Western and Central Pacific Ocean Tuna Fishery: Economic and Environmental Change under the Vessel Day Scheme." *Marine Policy* 42: 259–67.

Havice, E., and L. Campling. 2010. "Shifting Tides in the Western and Central Pacific Ocean Tuna Fishery: The Political Economy of Regulation and Industry Responses." *Global Environmental Politics* 10 (1): 89–114.

Heller, M. A., and R. S. Eisenberg. 1998. "Can Patents Deter Innovation? The Anticommons in Biomedical Research." *Science*, 280: 698–701.

Hsiang, S. M. 2010. "Temperatures and Cyclones Strongly Associated with Economic Production in the Caribbean and Central America." *Proceedings of the National Academy of Sciences of the USA* 107 (35): 15367–72.

Hsiang, S. M., K. C. Meng, and M. A. Cane. 2011. "Civil Conflicts Are Associated with the Global Climate." *Nature* 476: 438–41.

ISSF (International Seafood Sustainability Foundation). 2013. "ISSF Stock Status Ratings–2013: Status of the World Fisheries for Tuna." ISSF Technical Report 2013-04, ISSF, Washington, DC. http://iss-foundation.org/wp-content/uploads/downloads/2013/05/Status-of-the-World-Fisheries-for-Tuna-201304.pdf.

Jones, A., C. Downie, and N. Purvis. 2011. "A Proposal for a Consultative Group for Low Emissions Development." Resources for the Future Discussion Paper 11–25, Resources for the Future, Washington, DC.

Jones, K. E., N. G. Patel, M. A. Levy, A. Storeygard, D. Balk, J. L. Gittleman, and P. Daszak. 2008. "Global Trends in Emerging Infectious Diseases." *Nature* 451: 990–94.

Krasner, S. D. 1999. *Sovereignty: Organized Hypocrisy*. Princeton, NJ: Princeton University Press.

Kuiken, T., F. A. Leighton, R. A. M. Fouchier, J. W. LeDuc, J. S. M. Peiris, A. Schudel, K. Stöhr, and A. D. M. E. Osterhaus. 2005. "Pathogen Surveillance in Animals." *Science* 309: 1680–81.

Longini, I. M., M. E. Halloran, A. Nizam, and Y. Yang. 2004. "Containing Pandemic Influenza with Antiviral Agents." *American Journal of Epidemiology* 159 (7): 623–33.

Mariner, J. C., J. A. House, C. A. Mebus, A. E. Sollod, D. Chibeu, B. A. Jones, P. L. Roeder, B. Admassu, and G. G. M. van't Klooster. 2012. "Rinderpest Eradication: Appropriate Technology and Social Innovations." *Science* 337: 1309–12.

Maskus, K. E., and J. H. Reichman. 2004. "The Globalization of Private Knowledge Goods and the Privatization of Global Public Goods." *Journal of International Economic Law* 7 (2): 279–320.

McNeil, D. G., Jr. 2010. "Progress Is Slow on Moving Surplus Swine Flu Vaccine to Countries That Need It." *New York Times*. February 2. http://www.nytimes.com/2010/02/02/health/02flu.html.

Michaud, J. 2010. "Governance Implications of Emerging Infectious Disease Surveillance and Response as Global Public Goods." *Global Health Governance* 3 (2): 1–16. http://www.ghgj.org.

Mills, C. E., J. M. Robins, and M. Lipsitch. 2004. "Transmissibility of 1918 Pandemic Influenza." *Nature* 432: 904–06.

Miotto, O., J. Almagro-Garcia, M. Manske, B. MacInnis, S. Campino, K. A. Rockett, C. Amaratunga, P. Lim, S. Suon, S. Sreng, J. M. Anderson, S. Duong, C. Nguon,

C. M. Chuor, D. Saunders, Y. Se, C. Lon, M. M. Fukuda, L. Amenga-Etego, A. V. O. Hodgson, V. Asoala, M. Imwong, S. Takala-Harrison, F. Nosten, and X.-Z. Su. 2013. "Multiple Populations of Artemisinin-Resistant *Plasmodium Falciparum* in Cambodia." *Nature Genetics* 45: 648–755.

Moran, M., J. Guzman, A.-L. Ropars, A. McDonald, N. Jameson, B. Omune, S. Ryan, and L. Wu. 2009. "Neglected Disease Research and Development: How Much Are We Really Spending?" *PLoS Medicine* 6 (2): e1000030. doi:10.1371/journal.pmed. 1000030.

Multilateral Fund. 2011a. "Multilateral Fund for the Implementation of the Montreal Protocol." http://www.multilateralfund.org/aboutMLF/Implementingagencies /default.aspx.

Multilateral Fund. 2011b. http://www.multilateralfund.org/default.aspx.

Munro, G. R. 2007. "Internationally Shared Fish Stocks, the High Seas, and Property Rights in Fisheries." *Marine Resource Economics* 22: 425–43.

Nordhaus, W. D. 2011. "Estimates of the Social Cost of Carbon: Background and Results from the RICE-2011 Model." Cowles Foundation Discussion Paper 1826, Yale University, New Haven, CT.

Offit, P. A. 2005. "Why Are Pharmaceutical Companies Gradually Abandoning Vaccines?" *Health Affairs* (May/June): 622–30.

Patz, J. A., D. Campbell-Lendrum, T. Holloway, and J. A. Foley. 2005. "Impact of Regional Climate Change on Human Health." *Nature* 438: 310–17.

Presanis, A. M., D. De Angelis, The New York City Swine Flu Investigation Team, A. Hagy, C. Reed, S. Riley, B. S. Cooper, L. Finelli, P. Biedrzycki, and M. Lipsitch. 2009. "The Severity of Pandemic H1N1 Influenza in the United States, from April to July. 2009: A Bayesian Analysis." *PLoS Medicine* 6 (12): e1000207. doi:10.1371/journal .pmed.1000207.

Price, R., S. Thornton, and S. Nelson. 2007. "The Social Cost of Carbon and the Shadow Price of Carbon: What They Are, and How to Use them in Economic Appraisal in the UK." Department of Environment, Food, and Rural Affairs, London, U.K. http://archive.defra.gov.uk/evidence/series/documents/shadowpriceofcarbondec -0712.pdf.

Raitzer, D. A. 2003. "Benefit-Cost Meta-Analysis of Investment in the International Agricultural Research Centres of the CGIAR." Prepared for the CGIAR Standing Panel on Impact Assessment, Science Council Secretariat, Food and Agricultural Organization of the United Nations.

Schlenker, W., and M. J. Roberts. 2009. "Nonlinear Temperature Effects Indicate Severe Damages to U.S. Crop Yields Under Climate Change." *Proceedings of the National Academy of Sciences of the USA* 100 (37): 15594–98.

Sheppard, K. 2012. "The World Bank's Climate Hypocrisy." *The Guardian*, December 14. http://www.guardian.co.uk/environment/2012/dec/14/worldbank-climate-change.

Sobel, D. 1995. *Longitude: The True Story of a Lone Genius Who Solved the Greatest Scientific Problem of His Time*. London: Fourth Estate.

Stern, 2011. "The Economics of Climate Change." UK: London.

Stiglitz, J. E. 1999. "Knowledge as a Global Public Good." In *Global Public Goods: International Cooperation in the 21st Century*, edited by I. Kaul, I. Grunberg, and M. A. Stern, 308–25. New York: Oxford University Press.

Taubenberger, J. K., and D. M. Morens. 2006. "1918 Influenza: The Mother of All Pandemics." *Emerging Infectious Diseases* 12(1): 15–22. http://dx.doi.org/10.3201/eid1209.050979.

Thomson Reuters. 2013. "Thomson Reuters Point Carbon." Thompson Reuters, Oslo. http://www.pointcarbon.com/news/euets/.

United Nations Framework Convention for Climate Change. 1992. http://unfccc.int/files/essential_background/background_publications_htmlpdf/application/pdf/conveng.pdf.

Walsh, J. 1987. "War on Cattle Disease Divides the Troops." *Science* 237: 1289–91.

Waverman, L, M. Meschi, and M. Fuss. 2005. "The Impact of Telecoms on Economic Growth in Developing Countries." In *Africa: The Impact of Mobile Phones*, Vodafone Policy Paper 2, pp. 10–23.

WHA (World Health Assembly). 2007. "Pandemic Influenza Preparedness: Sharing of Influenza Viruses and Access to Vaccines and Other Benefits." WHA60.28, WHA, Geneva, Switzerland.

WHO (World Health Organization). 2005. "Donation of Three Million Treatments of Oseltamivir to WHO Will Help Early Response to an Emerging Influenza Pandemic." WHO, Geneva, Switzerland. http://www.who.int/mediacentre/news/releases/2005/pr36/en/index.html.

World Bank. 1998. *World Development Report 1998/99: Knowledge for Development.* Washington, DC: World Bank.

———. 2003. "Pages from World Bank History: The Fight Against Riverblindness." World Bank Archives, Washington, DC. http://go.worldbank.org/CO9LM3GDZ0.

———. 2004a. *Addressing the Challenges of Globalization: An Independent Evaluation of the World Bank's Approach to Global Programs.* Independent Evaluation Group, Washington, DC.

———. 2004b. "Saving Fish and Fishers: Towards Sustainable and Equitable Governance of the Global Fishing Sector." Report 29090-GLB, World Bank, Washington, DC.

———. 2009. *World Development Report 2010: Development and Climate Change.* Washington, DC: World Bank.

———. 2010a. *Economics of Adaptation to Climate Change.* Washington, DC: World Bank.

———. 2012. *State- and Peace-Building Fund Annual Report 2012.* Global Center on Conflict, Security, and Development, World Bank, Washington, DC. http://siteresources.worldbank.org/EXTLICUS/Resources/511777-1240930480694/6069541-1362168066814/SPF-AnnualReport2012-final.pdf.

World Bank and Food and Agriculture Organization. 2008. *The Sunken Billions: Economic Justification for Fisheries Reform.* Washington, DC: World Bank.

Yang, Y., J. D. Sugimoto, M. E. Halloran, N. E. Basta, D. L. Chao, L. Matrajt, G. Potter, E. Kenah, and I. M. Longini, Jr. 2010. "The Transmissibility and Control of Pandemic Influenza A (H1N1) Virus." *Science* 326: 729–33.

CHAPTER 3

Environmental Sustainability as a Development Issue: The Evolution of an Idea

J. Warren Evans

By the late 1970s, most rapidly developing countries were in the process of conceiving national environmental policies. Most of these agendas evolved into broader sustainable development agendas and are now being transformed further to include a global agenda of cooperation for the greater public good. This chapter reviews that history and relates the evolution to directions the World Bank and other development assistance organizations may need to take in the next few years to be able to optimize benefits from global public goods (GPGs) to developing countries and help avoid or respond to future disruptions to sustainable development.

Evolution of the International Environmental Agenda

Starting in the early 1970s, with assistance from bilateral aid programs and the United Nations Environment Programme (UNEP), numerous industrializing and urbanizing countries passed environmental laws, pollution controls, and environmental impact assessment (EIA) regulations, and they set up institutions to promote and enforce such laws and regulations. Most developing countries modeled such national environmental policy after the U.S. and European systems.

As the focus on environment and development grew, there was also recognition in the late 1970s through the mid-1980s by "environment and development" practitioners—a new type of development practitioner whose objective was to integrate environmental management into the development process—that the new environment agencies had limited clout and that the sensible approach to changing the development process was not through strong regulations and enforcement, but by "infiltrating" the development process. For example, the EIA, a regulatory process developed in the early 1970s in some rich countries, was modified to serve as a planning tool to assist in the preparation of development projects (Lohani et al. 1997). The multilateral development banks (MDBs)

To see J. Warren Evans discuss the evolution of sustainability: http://youtu.be/i2sVRpRWVo0

established their own EIA policies and guidelines in the late 1980s, then broad-ened the EIA's planning tool objective of reducing adverse impacts to cover social development, indigenous peoples, and various "safeguards."

Over time, the MDBs translated the guidelines into a compliance-based, regu-latory mechanism applied to projects they funded. The MDBs also became a major source of technical assistance for environmental and other sectoral agen-cies to strengthen countries' ability to implement their national environmental policies and programs.[1]

By the early 1990s, and particularly following the 1992 Rio conference (United Nations Conference on Environment and Development, UNCED), the political and bureaucratic leadership of many developing countries began to understand the economic costs of the depletion and degradation of their natural resources and the unabated pollution within their respective national boundaries. By the mid-1990s "environmental lending" became a significant part of MDB operations.

Also, after the 1992 Rio conference, most countries started to take seriously the risks to the sustainability of their own socioeconomy that result from the actions of other countries. An international sustainability agenda emerged at about the same time that, with many industrializing developing countries making significant investments in environmental infrastructure and conservation as well as strengthening enforcement of their environmental regulations. Several coun-tries undertook subnational "economic-cum-environment" development plan-ning and programming exercises. Regional environmental organizations initiated multicountry environmental initiatives in various regions, examples being the South Pacific Regional Environment Programme (now the Secretariat of the Pacific Regional Environment Programme) and the UNEP Regional Seas Programme. Regional economic cooperatives, such as the Association of Southeast Asian Nations (ASEAN) and the Mekong River Commission, also took on regional environmental issues. The World Bank and regional development banks, such as the Asian Development Bank (ADB), together with UN organiza-tions and many bilateral assistance agencies, were deeply engaged in supporting and funding this process. For the first time, new long-term regional development partnerships, such as the Greater Mekong Subregion (GMS), included environ-mental sustainability as a core element of their development programs.

At the international level, rapid-growth countries and others, some richer and some poorer, agreed upon a number of environmental treaties to stop using globally harmful chemicals, reduce loss of biodiversity, protect shared water resources, and constrain global climate change. Many developing coun-tries put their most capable scientists, engineers, and ecologists to work on these global issues, and developing countries that were home to some of the world's most valuable and unique biodiversity took steps to conserve what was left. The Global Environment Facility (GEF) was established at the World Bank with financial contributions mostly from richer countries in order to assist developing countries meet their obligations or commitments to the global environmental commons.

With the financial crisis of 1997, a number of countries backed off from their national environmental investment programs and, in some cases, relaxed enforcement of environmental regulations. Shortly after this global crisis—though impacts were most severe in some Asian industrializing countries—the World Bank and many other organizations linked to official development assistance (ODA) agencies took steps to strengthen their focus and impact on recipient-driven poverty reduction.

World Bank Sustainable Development Institutional Framework

One of the most popular and enduring definitions of "sustainable development" comes from the 1987 report of the World Commission on Environment and Development (WCED), *Our Common Future*, commonly known as the Brundtland Report, after its chairman, Gro Harlem Brundtland (UN 1987). The notion of sustainable development—which "meets the needs of the present without compromising the ability of future generations to meet their own needs"—highlighted the need to address developmental and environmental imperatives and grabbed the attention of the international community.

Upon its creation in 1949, the World Bank focused on rebuilding Europe and jumpstarting exhausted economies after World War II. As former colonies gained independence, the focus on physical capital shifted to agriculture and rural development. The late 1960s and 1970s saw the emphasis shift to education and health, while in the 1980s economic reforms focusing on financial capital flows were initiated to help countries transition to industrializing nations (World Bank 2012a).

The Bank did not begin to focus on the environment until 1987, when it did so in response to some serious criticism by civil society organizations (CSOs) over the lack of attention to environmental impacts of many large-scale development projects funded by the Bank. In 1970 the Bank had created the Office of the Environmental Advisor which had little capacity and impact within and outside the Bank. Consequently, by the mid-1980s the Bank was lagging behind in implementing environmental policies and practices, and was again taken to task by environmental and social justice forces. This external criticism combined with suggestions from the Brundtland Report (UN 1987) prompted changes within the World Bank, whose initial response was to create the Environmental Department and establish its first set of environmental safeguard policies in 1989 (World Bank 2012a).

The 1990s brought the full array of environmental stresses into focus at the Bank, with the 1992 UNCED, the Earth Summit, in Rio de Janeiro capturing global attention. In addition, the voice and clout of civil society was growing and paying considerable attention to how the World Bank was dealing with environmental issues in its operations. This led to a new kind of partnership for the Bank, which began engaging CSOs alongside member countries (see box 3.1).

A major shift in broad World Bank priorities and objectives was initiated when a voluntarily implemented action plan to achieve sustainable development was

Box 3.1 Bank Nurtures Leadership in Joining with Civil Society Organizations

Reflections by J. Warren Evans

Over the last 25 years, the role of civil society organizations—CSOs, formerly lumped into the non-government organization (NGO) category—in the sustainable development process and their engagement with development assistance organizations have evolved.

When I was a young environmental specialist at the Asian Development Bank (ADB), most CSOs were from developed countries and focused on either environmental conservation issues or environmental advocacy, or both. The World Wildlife Fund, Nature Conservancy, Greenpeace, Friends of the Earth, International Rivers Network, and many other CSOs were interested in working with multilateral organizations to direct funding into conservation or away from projects they considered bad for the environment. This is obviously a gross generalization, but the early engagement with CSOs and multilateral development banks (MDBs) was largely either as partners or adversaries, with considerable distrust and lack of understanding on both sides. In 1990 I was asked to serve as NGO coordinator—the first such designation by ADB—for the ADB Annual Meeting in Hong Kong SAR. The NGOs were pretty well organized and had agreed on a set of priority issues they wanted to discuss with ADB senior management. Some of the senior management staff were keen to establish an open and honest dialogue on topics such as how ADB could promote integrated pest management through its agriculture operations. But others were unsure why they should give any time to the NGOs—after all, the client is the country—and a few others wanted to figure out how we could give them some grant money to make them less critical of us. But a number of agreements were reached, and as prospective partners, we were about to part company when an interview with NGO leaders revealed that they had concluded the ADB was not interested in environmental sustainability and should not be supported. When I asked my new NGO colleagues about their pronouncement, they explained that I did not understand—that they needed to be critical of us if they were to maintain their support base. As a result of this experience, we agreed on both sides that a much deeper and more meaningful collaboration was required, otherwise we would continue to have generally negative and unconstructive engagements, which was not in the best interests of developing countries or the environment. A formal working relationship with reasonably transparent communications evolved between ADB and the NGO community by the late 1990s.

The relationship between the World Bank and NGOs/CSOs started off rather coldly in the 1980s, when the Bank was severely criticized for a number of projects and programs that were causing or could cause severe adverse environmental and social impacts. That relationship heated up quickly when in 1992 at the Rio Earth Summit NGO Forum, the World Bank booth was burned down. Since then—with many years of constructive dialogue and partnerships and leadership from advocates for sustainable development, like the Bank Information Center—a considerable level of mutual trust has emerged. Further, with the emergence of developing country CSOs, many of them growing to national and international prominence from grassroots beginnings, the voice and impact of CSOs has

box continues next page

Box 3.1 Bank Nurtures Leadership in Joining with Civil Society Organizations *(continued)*

been substantially strengthened. International and bilateral assistance agencies and international CSO partners have been instrumental in many countries in promoting the growth of local CSOs; a good example is the Critical Ecosystem Partnership Fund, described in chapter 9.

The World Bank and similar international development organizations now recognize the importance of engaging with, listening to, and learning from, as well as partnering with CSOs of all types and at all levels. There is also a shifting momentum in many developing countries whereby national CSOs are asked to help in the development process. In many cases, it just takes one individual leader to stimulate a CSO-based movement—for example, the late Prof. Wangari Maathai in Kenya, who founded and expanded the Green Belt Movement (GBM), and Mechai Veravaidya, who impacted millions in Thailand and beyond through his family planning advocacy and Population and Community Development Foundation.

A strategic direction and challenge that the Bank should be considering is how to build on such leadership to extend highly effective but geographically limited programs to reach other countries and regions. To achieve this requires a strong focus and commitment to build CSO leadership. Any long-term effort to address GPGs will require not only national government leadership, but also national CSO leadership.

Wanjira Maathai, a board member of both the GBM and the Wangari Maathai Institute for Peace and Environment, has reflected on the potential for CSOs to help governments and international assistance agencies in the sustainable development process.

Note: To see a video from Green Belt Movement Leader Wanjira Maathai: http://youtu.be/wLWRVRWkdyk

---

initiated through the UN's Agenda 21, and the Bank committed to a roadmap to sustainability. The *World Development Report 1992: Development and the Environment* (World Bank 1992) called for major policy, program, and institutional shifts within the Bank to help countries achieve sustainable economic and human development by improving environmental conditions instead of degrading them.

In response to the recommendations of the 1992 *World Development Report* and the global push to broaden the environmental agenda to sustainable development, the Bank created the Vice Presidency for Environmentally and Socially Sustainable Development (ESSD) in 1993, and the policy and institutional framework for the Bank's engagement in sustainability further evolved. Within 14 years, environmental programs and partnerships amounted to 62 percent ($775 million) of total disbursements of the World Bank Group's portfolio of global programs and partnerships. It also became a significant proportion of country operations in lending and technical assistance.

After a lull following the 1998 financial crisis, environmental, and more broadly, sustainable development operations picked up by 2005 and have continued to form a significant part of the World Bank portfolio. By mid-2011, 87 percent of World Bank's Environmental and Natural Resources Management (ENRM) projects were being managed by non-environmental sectors, indicating a high level of success in mainstreaming the environmental agenda. From 2005 to 2010, ENRM activities accounted for about 9 percent of total new lending, with the largest lending operation a $400 million low-carbon development policy loan to Mexico.

In 2007, 14 years after the ESSD was created, two World Bank networks, ESSD and Infrastructure (INF), were integrated to form the Sustainable Development Network (SDN), comprising six "anchor" departments: agriculture and environmental services; climate policy and finance; sustainable energy; social development; transport, water, information and communicable technology; and disaster risk and urban development. SDN's purpose is to help develop new financial and knowledge products, manage partnerships, promote operational quality, and ensure that sector expertise contributes to data-driven and results-focused business associated with a $110 billion lending portfolio. As of 2012, close to 2,000 World Bank staff were associated with SDN.

Nonetheless, based on a 2007 review by the World Bank's Independent Evaluation Group, environmental objectives had yet to be fully integrated into Bank operations. The Independent Evaluation Group observed that although World Bank professionals in general were aware of the importance of environmental issues, they often saw them as a self-standing agenda and not as elemental to their core task of supporting development and poverty reduction. Similarly, awareness of the importance of environmental issues was still evolving in many Bank client countries. These countries often faced difficult choices in allocating scarce resources among pressing development needs, thus the environment often had a hard time competing with other goals.

Figure 3.1 presents a summary timeline of some of the major international meetings that have been instrumental in driving the evolution of the environment agenda to where it is today.

The World Bank and Environmental Global Public Goods

The World Bank has been actively and intentionally working on environment-related GPGs for the last 20 years since the Global Environment Facility was established in 1991. The GEF was established as a pilot program by the World Bank Group (WBG) to assist in the protection of the global environment, thereby promoting environmentally sound and sustainable economic development (IEG 2013). Under the pilot program, grants or concessional loans were to be provided to developing countries to help them implement programs to protect the global environment. Four areas were identified for the operations of the GEF: (a) protection of the ozone layer; (b) limiting emissions of greenhouse gases; (c) protection of biodiversity; and (d) protection of international waters.[2]

Following the Rio Earth Summit in 1992, the GEF was restructured in 1994 and became a permanent, separate institution, though legally still part of the World Bank. As part of the restructuring, the GEF was entrusted to become the financial mechanism for the Convention for Biological Diversity (CBD) and the United Nations Framework to Combat Climate Change (UNFCCC), and

Figure 3.1 Major International Conferences and Meetings on Sustainable Development, Climate Change, and Biodiversity

1972 UN Conference on the Human Environment (Stockholm)
Participants from 114 countries

1990 2nd World Climate Conference (Geneva)
First part comprised nongovernmental scientific sessions attended by 747 experts; second part was discussions among heads of government and ministers from 137 states

1948 IUCN 1st Meeting (Fontainebleau, France)
18 governments, 7 international organizations, and 107 national nature conservation organizations

1979 1st World Climate Conference (Geneva)
Organized by the World Meteorological Organization

1991 1st Environment for Europe Ministerial Conference (Prague)
Ministers from 34 countries

1992 UN Conference on Environment and Development (Earth Summit) (Rio de Janeiro)
35,000 participants from 172 governments with 108 heads of state or government, NGOs, and the media

1994 CSD 2 (New York)
More than 40 ministers

1994 CBD COP 1 (Nassau, Bahamas)

1993 2nd EfE Ministerial Conference (Lucerne)
Ministers from 45 cotries

1993 CSD 1 (New York)
Representatives from 53 member countries and others

1996 CSD 4 (New York)

1996 UNFCCC COP 2 (Geneva)
More than 1,500 participants

1996 IUCN 1st World Conservation Congress (Montreal)
3,000 participants

1996 CBD COP 3 (Buenos Aires)

1995 UNFCCC COP 1 (Berlin)
4,000 participants

1995 CSD 3 (New York)
Over 50 ministers

1995 3rd EfE Ministerial Conference (Sofia, Bulgaria)
Ministers from 49 countries

1995 CBD COP 2 (Jakarta)

1997 CSD 5 (New York)

1998 CSD 6 (New York)

1998 CBD COP 4 (Bratislava, Slovakia)
1,500 participants

1997 UNFCCC COP 3 (Kyoto)
125 ministers and more than 10,000 participants from 160 countries

1998 4th EfE Ministerial Conference (Buenos Aires)
52 UNECE member countries and 70 IGOs and NGOs

1998 UNFCCC COP 4 (Buenos Aires)
More than 5,000 participants from 170 governments

1999 CBD COP Extraordinary Meeting (Cartagena, Colombia)

1999 CSD 7 (New York)

1999 UNFCCC COP 5 (Bonn)
4,000 participants from 166 governments

figure continues next page

Figure 3.1 Major International Conferences and Meetings on Sustainable Development, Climate Change, and Biodiversity *(continued)*

2000 **CSD 8 (New York)**
47 ministers

2000 **CBD COP 5 (Nairobi, Kenya)**
1,500 participants from 156 governments and others

2001 **CSD 9 (New York)**
Over 500 participants

2001 **UNFCCC COP 6-bis (Bonn)**
4,600 participants from 181 governments and others

2000 **IUCN 2nd World Conservation Congress (Amman, Jordan)**
2,000 participants from 140 governments and others

2001 **UNFCCC COP 7 (Marrakesh)**
4,500 participants from 171 governments and others

2000 **UNFCCC COP 6 (The Hague)**
7,000 participants from 182 governments and others

2003 **CSD 11 (New York)**
About 40 ministers and government representatives and over 900 representatives from NGOs and other stakeholders

2002 **CBD COP 6 (The Hague)**
2,000 participants from 176 governments and others

2002 **World Summit on Sustainable Development (Johannesburg)**
22,000 participants from governments and others

2003 **5th EfE Ministerial Conference (Kiev, Ukraine)**
Ministers from 51 countries

2002 **CSD 10 (Johannesburg)**
Over 500 participants

2003 **UNFCCC COP 9 (Milan)**
5,000 participants from 181 parties and others

2002 **COP 8 (New Delhi)**
3,000 participants from 185 parties and others

2004 **CBD COP 7 (Kuala Lumpur, Malaysia)**
2,300 participants from 161 governments and others

2004 **CSD 12 (New York)**
80 ministers

2005 **CSD 13 (New York)**
About 40 ministers and government representatives and over 900 representatives from NGOs and other stakeholders

2004 **IUCN 3rd World Conservation Congress (Bangkok)**
4,800 participants

2005 **UNFCCC COP 11 (Montreal)**
9,000 participants

2004 **COP 10 (Buenos Aires)**
6,000 participants from 180 parties and others

figure continues next page

Figure 3.1   Major International Conferences and Meetings on Sustainable Development, Climate Change, and Biodiversity *(continued)*

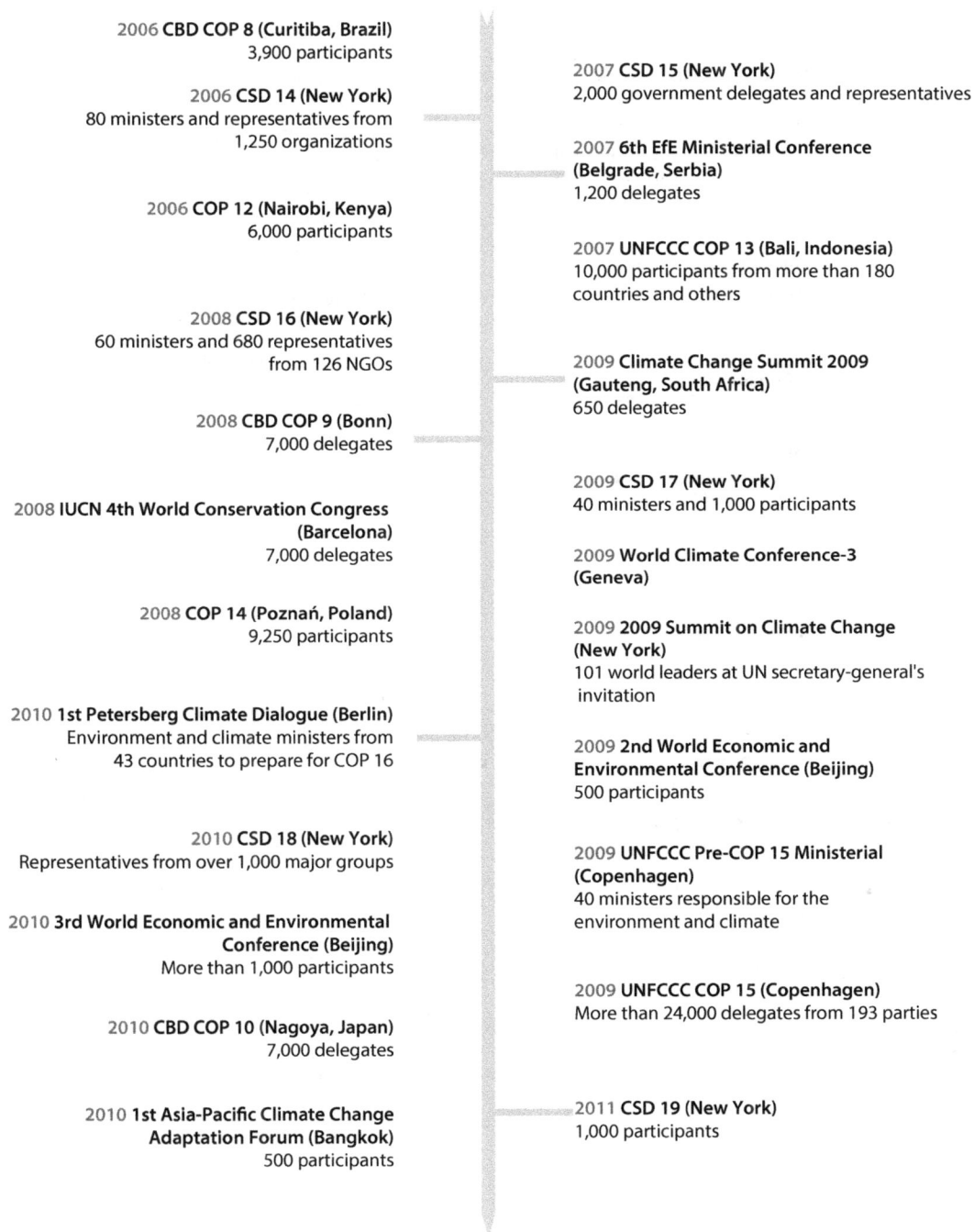

2006 **CBD COP 8 (Curitiba, Brazil)**
3,900 participants

2006 **CSD 14 (New York)**
80 ministers and representatives from
1,250 organizations

2006 **COP 12 (Nairobi, Kenya)**
6,000 participants

2008 **CSD 16 (New York)**
60 ministers and 680 representatives
from 126 NGOs

2008 **CBD COP 9 (Bonn)**
7,000 delegates

2008 **IUCN 4th World Conservation Congress
(Barcelona)**
7,000 delegates

2008 **COP 14 (Poznań, Poland)**
9,250 participants

2010 **1st Petersberg Climate Dialogue (Berlin)**
Environment and climate ministers from
43 countries to prepare for COP 16

2010 **CSD 18 (New York)**
Representatives from over 1,000 major groups

2010 **3rd World Economic and Environmental
Conference (Beijing)**
More than 1,000 participants

2010 **CBD COP 10 (Nagoya, Japan)**
7,000 delegates

2010 **1st Asia-Pacific Climate Change
Adaptation Forum (Bangkok)**
500 participants

2007 **CSD 15 (New York)**
2,000 government delegates and representatives

2007 **6th EfE Ministerial Conference
(Belgrade, Serbia)**
1,200 delegates

2007 **UNFCCC COP 13 (Bali, Indonesia)**
10,000 participants from more than 180
countries and others

2009 **Climate Change Summit 2009
(Gauteng, South Africa)**
650 delegates

2009 **CSD 17 (New York)**
40 ministers and 1,000 participants

2009 **World Climate Conference-3
(Geneva)**

2009 **2009 Summit on Climate Change
(New York)**
101 world leaders at UN secretary-general's
invitation

2009 **2nd World Economic and
Environmental Conference (Beijing)**
500 participants

2009 **UNFCCC Pre-COP 15 Ministerial
(Copenhagen)**
40 ministers responsible for the
environment and climate

2009 **UNFCCC COP 15 (Copenhagen)**
More than 24,000 delegates from 193 parties

2011 **CSD 19 (New York)**
1,000 participants

figure continues next page

Figure 3.1 Major International Conferences and Meetings on Sustainable Development, Climate Change, and Biodiversity *(continued)*

2010 **UNFCCC Pre-COP 16 Ministerial (Mexico City)**
Representatives from 42 countries

2010 **COP 16 (Cancún, Mexico)**
12,000 participants

2012 **OECD Environment Ministerial 2012 (Paris)**
34 OECD member countries and others

2012 **Global Green Growth Summit 2012 (Seoul)**
1,500 participants

2012 **2nd Asia-Pacific Climate Change Adaptation Forum (Bangkok)**
800 participants

2012 **UN Conference on Sustainable Development (Rio de Janeiro)**
50,000 participants

2012 **CSD 20 (Rio de Janeiro)**

2012 **3rd Petersberg Climate Dialogue (Berlin)**
Ministers from 31 countries

2012 **IUCN 5th World Conservation Congress (Jeju, Korea)**
11,000 participants

2012 **CBD COP 11 (Hyderabad, India)**
6,000 delegates

2012 **UNFCCC Pre-COP 18 Ministerial (Seoul)**
300 participants from 50 countries

2012 **5th World Economic and Environmental Conference (Beijing)**

2012 **1st OECD Forum on Green Growth and Sustainable Development (Paris)**
250 participants

2012 **UNFCCC COP 18 (Doha, Qatar)**
17,000 participants

2011 **4th World Economic and Environmental Conference (Qingdao, China)**
500 participants

2011 **Global Green Growth Summit 2011 (Seoul)**
1,000 participants

2011 **2nd Petersberg Climate Dialogue (Berlin)**
Ministers from 35 countries

2011 **UNFCCC Pre-COP 17 Ministerial (Stellenbosch, South Africa)**
Representatives from 42 parties

2011 **7th EfE Ministerial Conference (Astana, Kazakhstan)**
1,500 delegates

2011 **UNFCCC COP 17 (Durban, South Africa)**
12,500 participants

Note: CBD = Convention on Biological Diversity; COP = Conferences of the Parties; CSD = Commission on Sustainable Development; EfE = Environment for Europe; IGO = intergovernmental organization; IUCN = International Union for Conservation of Nature; NGO = nongovernmental organization; OECD = Organization for Economic Co-operation and Development; UNECE = UN Economic Commission for Europe.

subsequently the Stockholm Convention on Persistent Organic Pollutants, 2001, and the UN Convention to Combat Desertification, 2003. The GEF is now the largest public funder of projects to improve the global environment, bringing 182 countries in partnership with international institutions, CSOs, and the private sector to address global environmental issues while supporting national sustainable development initiatives.[3] GEF funding is primarily from donor countries as ODA.

Since 1991, the WBG mobilized more than $4.5 billion from the GEF to support more than 700 projects that address biodiversity conservation, climate change, international waters, and other concerns. After the GEF became a separate institution in 1994, the WBG served as the trustee of the GEF Trust Fund and provided administrative services.

The two environmental GPGs that have received the most attention from the World Bank are climate change and biodiversity. Biodiversity partnerships in which the World Bank has been a significant partner have focused on conservation, sustainable use, and benefit sharing.[4] An example of a success story in terms of sustained partnerships with substantial impact at the local, regional, and global levels is the Critical Ecosystem Partnership Fund (CEPF). This global program, further discussed in Chapter 9, provides funding and technical assistance to nongovernment organizations (NGOs) and private sector partners to protect vital ecosystems. A joint initiative of the GEF, the European Union, the government of Japan, L'Agence Française de Développement, Conservation International, European Union, and the World Bank, CEPF focuses on biodiversity hotspots, and since its establishment in 2000 has provided grants to support civil society in 21 of the 35 recognized global biodiversity hotpots, with conservation activities worth $12.9 million (World Bank 2013).

The first time the World Bank directly assessed its role in the supply of GPGs was in 2000. Four priorities—communicable diseases, environmental commons (climate change mitigation, adaptation, sustainability of exhaustible resources, partnerships), international financial architecture, participation of developing countries in the international trading system—have guided the Bank's involvement in GPGs (World Bank 2007a). In 2007, the Bank's Development Committee endorsed a long-term strategy for the financing and delivery of GPGs, implying that expanding the delivery of regional and global public goods was one of four building blocks for a future bank. However, the strategy generated some criticism in that the focus was mainly on the existing traditional lending operations of the WBG, with little indication of what is "new" in terms of mandate and related financing (Birdsall 2012).

A more recent environmental GPG initiative is the Global Partnership for founded in 2012 to raise $1.5 billion for the world's overfished, polluted, and warming oceans; double marine protected areas; and rebuild fish stocks. It is a coalition of governments, NGOs, scientists, and businesses committed to mobilizing at least $300 million in catalytic financing to leverage another $1.2 billion from businesses, NGOs, and other institutions.[5] At $1.6 billion in current investments, the WBG has one of the largest portfolios of ocean-related projects of any international development agency.[6] This new partnership could represent the future in terms of how partnerships are conceived and managed to tackle massive, complex, long-term GPG challenges. The new directions for collaboration and partnerships are discussed in detail in Chapter 9.

The largest-scale investment program undertaken by the World Bank (and perhaps the world) relating to a GPG is climate change. In 2010, 30 out of 34 country assistance and partnership strategies (CAS/CPS) emphasized climate action, and by 2012 all 130 CAS/CPS included climate change as a core area for World Bank support (World Bank 2012b). The growth of climate change-related activities has been impressive. In 2002, the environment portfolio of the WBG was about $14 billion, of which about $1.5 billion (11 percent) related to climate change (World Bank 2012b). Today climate change is the largest share of the environment portfolio. Almost $4.6 billion of 2012 lending, or twice the 2011 amount, supported adaptation and more than $7.1 billion for mitigation[7] (40 percent of 2012 lending is to contribute to mitigation and/or adaptation). Under the International Financial Institution Framework for a Harmonised Approach to Greenhouse Gas Accounting,[8] the WBG began conducting GHG accounting for energy and forestry in 2013 and in transport projects in 2014.[9]

The World Bank pioneered carbon finance with the $180 million Prototype Carbon Fund, established in 2000—the first global carbon fund to provide a framework for action and to demonstrate how greenhouse gas (GHG) reduction could contribute to sustainable development while lowering the costs of complying with the Kyoto Protocol. By the time the Kyoto Protocol came into effect in 2005, the World Bank was managing about $1.5 billion in carbon funds from developed country governments and private companies. The carbon fund portfolio grew to more than $2.5 billion by 2009. A diversification of World Bank carbon funds took place during the second half of the last decade to test the application of carbon markets in natural resource management (particularly forests), agro-ecosystems, and community development as well as conventional GHG emission reduction from energy generation and consumption and waste management. This resulted in major new development: for the first time a major conservation NGO, the Nature Conservancy, joined national governments and private companies as an investor in a carbon fund, the Forest Carbon Partnership Facility.

The Climate Investment Funds (CIFs), established in 2008, comprise the world's largest financing facility for climate action in developing countries. The CIFs are unique in that the facility, while managed by the World Bank, is a new kind of partnership involving the MDBs as a cooperative for decision-making support as well as implementation support. The CIFs consist of four funding windows to help developing countries pilot low-emissions and climate-resilient development. Donor country governments have pledges more than $7.5 billion for concessional loans and grants to 49 countries and private entities, leveraging about $43 billion in investment from other sources.[10]

Box 3.2 What Young Development Professionals Think About Multidisciplinary Partnerships

Timothy Bouley, Global Partnership for Oceans

Looking to the future, I envision partnership, not merely because our interconnected and globalized world demands it, but because the leaders of tomorrow will be trained in it. Transdisciplinary, multidisciplinary, cross-disciplinary, inter-disciplinary, inter-disciplinary: regardless of the flavor, the four terms represent a new and predominant underlying ethic in engagement. Multiple planes of thought coalesce around a collaborative common ground. Traditional understandings are transcended and new thinking forged as specialists work together to solve complex and multivariate problems.

As students of science, humanities, and art, we are still today trained with the rigor and expectation of expertise as previous generations. Yet we are increasingly expected to engage with our academic and professional kin in sophisticated, meaningful, and balanced ways. Students of all types are commonly brought together in universities through student groups and increasingly through integrated curricular exercises and programs. Business students are partnered with medical students to consider new biotechnologies, environmental students with lawyers to overlay legal frameworks upon understanding of natural ones, and diplomacy students with those studying climate science to help them conceive of their (and everyone's) imagined futures. Compounding this interpersonal collaborative training is the intrapersonal. Many students today pursuing higher education will study one subject as undergraduates before moving on to unrelated graduate study. The effect creates individuals with deeply-ingrained understandings of multiple spheres and enables them to function both as masters of specialized information and as bridgebuilders, capable of connecting disparate intellectual and practical disciplines.

In recent years, students with this kind of training have flooded the workforce. Coalition building and maintenance comes easily to us and feels more natural than working among subject-specific silos in small, walled offices. It is easy to imagine this new tendency will bleed beyond the confines of any given institution. The leaders of tomorrow will default to collaboration and flourish on deep-rooted connections in many sectors and diverse geographies of professional life, established throughout the (now requisite) years of formal training.

The next generation will still be diversely specialized, but with an inherent inclination toward collaboration and with the understanding that building consensus requires tact, patience, and understanding. As an institution with regions and sector work as different as the global population it serves, and existing in a context of lightening globalization, the World Bank will only serve to benefit from this new expertise, so long as institutional willingness and structures are ready and ripe to nurture it.

Notes

1. A useful summary of World Bank environmental safeguards can be found in World Bank. Independent Evaluation Group, 2010 *Safeguards and Sustainability Policies in a Changing World: An Independent Evaluation of World Bank Experience.* Washington DC.

2. http://www.thegef.org/gef/whatisgef.

3. The World Bank in a Changing World: Selected Essays, Volume 2. http://www.thegef.org/gef/whatisgef.

4. http://go.worldbank.org/CW40VKKJM0.

5. http://www.guardian.co.uk/environment/2012/feb/24/world-bank-coalition-marine-protection.

6. WB FAQ: Oceans <http://go.worldbank.org/YVGPTY4Q40>.

7. http://climatechange.worldbank.org/content/world-bank-lending-doubles-adaptation.

8. http://climatechange.worldbank.org/sites/default/files/IFI_Framework_for_Harmonized_Approach%20to_Greenhouse_Gas_Accounting.pdf.

9. Doha: keeping hope alive- http://blogs.worldbank.org/climatechange/doha-keeping-hope-alive-just.

10. Doha: keeping hope alive- http://blogs.worldbank.org/climatechange/doha-keeping-hope-alive-just.

References

Birdsall, N. 2012. "The World Bank and Climate Change: Forever a Big Fish in a Small Pond?" CGD Policy Paper 007, Center for Global Development, Washington, DC.

Independent Evaluation Group. 2013. "The World Bank Group's Partnership with the Global Environment Facility." World Bank, Washington, DC.

Lohani, B., J. W. Evans, H. Ludwig, R. R. Everitt, R. A. Carpenter, and S. L. Tu. 1997. *Environmental Impact Assessment for Developing Countries in Asia.* Asian Development Bank, Manila.

UN (United Nations). 1987. *Report of the World Commission on Environment and Development: Our Common Future* (The Brundtland Report). New York: United Nations.

World Bank. 1992. *World Development Report 1992: Development and the Environment.* World Bank, Washington, DC.

———. 2012a. *Environment Matters.* World Bank, Washington, DC. http://siteresources.worldbank.org/EXTENVMAT/Resources/3011350-1339798526004/Environment Matterswholebook.pdf.

———. 2012b. *Development and Climate Change: A Strategic Framework for the World Bank Group.* Completion Report fy09/11. World Bank, Washington, DC.

———. 2013 "World Bank Environment Overview." http://www.worldbank.org/en/topic/environment/overview.

CHAPTER 4

The Future Is Now: Scenarios to 2025 and Beyond

J. Warren Evans

Strategic thinking about the long-term possibilities for the World Bank and similar organizations to support sustainable wealth creation in developing countries, including securing their stake in global public goods (GPGs), requires some speculation on future possibilities. In addition, it is important to recognize that countries' development actions today, often with World Bank support, will have a long-lasting influence not only on those countries but also on the future of the global commons as well as their own well-being. The World Bank will likely need to change its policies regarding sustainability and GPGs—not the same but certainly interrelated—and the likely drivers of such change are:

- changes in population, economics, and demographics;
- changes in sources of development finance (discussed in chapter 4); and
- changes in access to natural resources and technology at the national, regional, and global levels.

Sir John Beddington, while England's chief scientific advisor, warned in 2012 that global challenges constitute a "perfect storm" in that by 2030 the world will need to produce around 50 percent more food and energy, together with 30 percent more fresh water, while mitigating and adapting to climate change (Beddington 2009; Population Institute 2010).

Leading up to the perfect storm, we can also expect a dramatic increase in wealth and consumption from a rapidly growing middle class, mostly in developing countries. Such economic growth would result in a substantial reduction in the number of countries currently eligible for International Development Association (IDA) support: one study projects that half of today's IDA countries will graduate by 2025, leaving IDA to support one-third the current population it serves (Moss and Leo 2011). In any case, IDA is likely to have a smaller, more fragile, and mostly African clientele. The next section examines key ingredients of the likely perfect storm and how this threat might affect the roles of the World Bank Group in the coming years.

To see Vice President Rachel Kyte discuss what's at risk from climate change: http://youtu.be/3dr9N5aj3owe

Population and Economic Growth Projections

The current global population of 7.2 billion will increase to 8.1 billion by 2025 and 9.6 billion by 2050. Most of the increase will occur in developing countries, increasing from 5.9 billion today to 8.2 billion in 2050 and with 70 percent of the population living in cities (Clay 2011). The world's 49 least developed countries are projected to double in population, from 900 million in 2013 to 1.8 billion in 2050 (UNDESA 2013). High-income countries, emerging East Asian nations, and transition economies of Europe and Central Asia are getting older while Sub-Saharan Africa and South Asia will remain relatively young.

Developing countries dominated global growth in gross domestic product (GDP) in the decade leading up to the 2008 economic crash. The crisis affected developing countries with dwindling capital flows, which made huge withdrawals of capital, leading to losses in equity markets and skyrocketing interest rates. Nevertheless, many developing country economies recovered more quickly than developed countries (IMF 2010). Similar to their share in world GDP, developing countries' share in world trade has also roughly doubled, from 14.6 percent in 1990 to 30.3 percent in 2010. Two-thirds of global investment over the last 10 years has originated in developing countries (World Bank 2013a).

The output of the global economy is projected to increase from $35 trillion in 2005 to $72 trillion (at constant market exchange rates and prices) by 2030 (NIC 2012). The long-term outlook projects world economic growth ranging around 2.6–3.0 percent per year, with the developing world growing at

Figure 4.1 Urban Population, Percentage of World Population and Total, Projections to 2050

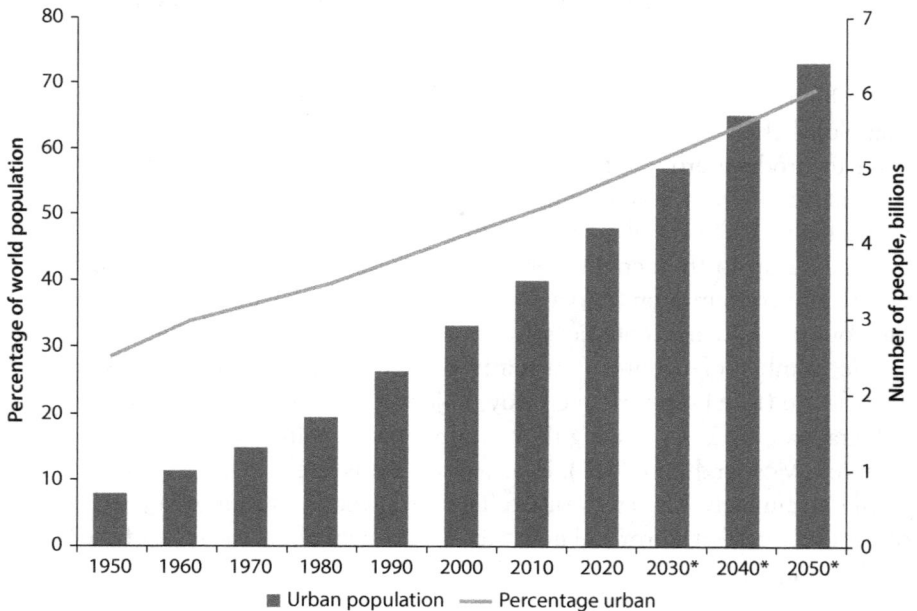

Source: UN Department of Economic and Social Affairs, Population Division.
* Medium Scenario, not high or low projection

4.8–5.5 percent over the same period. (See Figure 4.1 these scenarios do not attempt to take into account trends such as climate change or shocks such as financial crises (World Bank 2013a).

These population and urbanization trends as well as other demographic trends, such as population aging and changes in household size and composition, improved education and health, better governance systems, globalization, and information communications are enabling developing countries to continue to catch up with higher productivity levels in more advanced countries (World Bank 2013a). This progress is already contributing to changes in lifestyle, consumption patterns, and dietary preferences. About 600 million new consumers living in 440 cities in emerging markets will generate almost 50 percent of global GDP growth between 2010 and 2025 (McKinsey 2012). This increase in per capita disposable income will increase consumption of energy and water and generation of wastes. Demand for food is expected to rise by 35 percent and energy by 50 percent over the next 15–20 years (NIC 2012). Unless current policies and governance systems are transformed to support sustainability of such dramatic increases in consumption, adverse environmental and social impacts will reach new levels on already over stressed ecosystems and urban systems (World Bank 2007; Prins et al. 2011).

Natural Resource and Climate Scenarios

Many natural resource changes are expected to affect and be affected by development in the coming decades. The most commonly identified are climate, water, biodiversity, and landscapes and oceanscapes in terms of food productivity. Of course, these are not separate "resources" in the sense that the "health" of each impacts on the health of the others. But by far, climate change is the dominant "wooly mammoth in the room." This section draws on several recent environment-related scenario studies showing that the more we learn about climate change, the clearer it becomes that future productivity of ecosystems and water and land resources will be largely influenced by climate impacts. The combined effects of major global shifts from economic growth, climate change, and technological advances will be felt over the next decades in different places and with different results—but the greatest adverse impacts will be felt by developing countries that are less resilient to shocks and less able to manage and adapt (OECD 2008).

Biodiversity

At the opening plenary of the 2010 Convention for Biological Diversity Conference of Parties in Nagoya, Japan, then president of the World Bank Group Robert Zoellick said:

> You probably know of the World Bank Group as a development institution. So, you might wonder, why is the World Bank attending a conference on biodiversity? Our answer is clear: successful conservation of our natural resources, our

ecosystems, and our biodiversity is central to addressing all development challenges and to improving the lives of the poor. Biological resources provide livelihoods, sustenance, medicines, trade, tourism, industry, and more. Forests, grasslands, lakes, oceans, deserts, and other natural ecosystems provide a range of natural services that people have often taken for granted, even though they are vital to human welfare. I would add one more consideration: each of us—all of us—are stewards of other life on this planet. We should respect those lives. (Zoellick 2010)

The concerted international effort of many decades to protect and conserve biodiversity has had some notable successes. But while many battles have been won, yielding considerable benefits to humans in the form of ecosystem services, the war against ecosystem and biodiversity loss and degradation is being lost—quite miserably—because of the ever-growing pressures and demands on the globe's natural resource base and ecosystems. The first systematic global accounting of biodiversity, the four-year Millennium Ecosystem Assessment (UNEP 2005), concluded in 2005 that about 60 percent of ecosystem services studied were degraded or were being used unsustainably. The unsustainable consumption and degradation of ecosystems and their services—such as supply of clean, fresh water and pollination of crops—will worsen at least to 2050 as global population and GDP grow and the two key drivers of ecosystem degradation—climate change and excessive nutrient loading—become more severe.

Shortly after the Millennium Ecosystem Assessment was initiated, the signatory countries to the CBD agreed "to achieve by 2010 a significant reduction of the current rate of biodiversity loss at the global, regional and national level as a contribution to poverty alleviation and to the benefit of all life on Earth" (CBD 2002). While it would have been difficult to measure progress toward such a loosely defined target, that was not a problem because by 2010 the situation had dramatically worsened: there was not a net reduction, let alone a significant reduction, in the rate of biodiversity loss. In spite of 170 countries having formulated national biodiversity strategies and action plans, in 2010 the CBD Secretariat concluded that biodiversity was continuing to decline (CBD 2010). The five key causes of the decline—land-use change, overexploitation, pollution, invasive alien species, and climate change—are either constant or increasing in intensity and impact. Species assessed for extinction risk had on average moved closer to extinction, with nearly a quarter of plant species facing extinction. The abundance of vertebrate species continues to fall: nearly a third of species populations were lost on average between 1970 and 2006. While the rate of loss of forest ecosystems has declined, freshwater wetlands, salt marshes, coral reefs, and several other habitats are rapidly being degraded or lost.

Global Biodiversity Outlook 3 (CBD 2010) predicts continuing high levels of extinctions and loss of habitats for the foreseeable future. Scenarios for terrestrial ecosystems project that future species extinction rates could exceed recent rates of extinction by more than two orders of magnitude. Land-use change will continue to be the most critical short-term driver of terrestrial ecosystem loss and degradation, but climate change will soon impart severe impacts as well.

Tropical forests are expected to continue to be cleared for agricultural expansion, increasingly for biofuels. The aggregate loss of biodiversity and ecosystem services benefits associated with global loss of forests is estimated by the Organisation for Economic Co-operation and Development (OECD) to be $2–5 trillion per year (OECD 2012). Climate change will impact species' ranges, and several species will shift toward the poles. Examples of plausible scenarios include the following:

1. The dieback of the Amazon due to deforestation, fire, and climate change, resulting in, among many other frightening impacts, reductions and pattern shifts in regional rainfall that could compromise the sustainability of agriculture over large areas of South America and southern North America (CBD 2010; Vergara and Scholz 2011).
2. Cascading extinctions and ecosystem instabilities in island environments due to invasive alien species.

About a third of global freshwater biodiversity has already been lost, and this is expected to continue, particularly in Africa, Latin America, and parts of Asia. By 2070 fish extinctions will occur in about 30 percent of the world's rivers due to climate change and increasing water withdrawals (Pereira et al. 2010). Marine and coastal ecosystems will see some of the most dramatic changes, with reduced wild fish stocks, increased coastal dead zones due to increasing nutrient loads, and reduced coastal wetland and other coastal ecosystems to fringe habitats due to sea level rise and coastal development (such as infrastructure and aquaculture). *Global Biodiversity Outlook 3* (CBD 2010) considers the collapse of large marine predator species populations as a plausible scenario resulting from continued unsustainable exploitation.

OECD points to compelling evidence that once ecosystems' tipping points are reached, the irreversible consequences are rapid and potentially severe in terms of impacts on human populations. However, there is little consensus on how close we are to the accelerating loss of biodiversity and ecosystem services reaching tipping points and what happens when this does occur (CBD 2010; OECD 2012).

Water Resources

About 40 percent of the world's human population lives in or near internationally shared river basins, 200 of which are shared by more than two countries (NIC 2012). Agriculture, industry, and cities have overexploited and severely polluted many of the world's fresh surface and groundwater resources. More urbanites have no household connection to a water supply today than in 1990. Increased population and urbanization will increase consumption, further stressing river and lake basins and aquifers. Freshwater eutrophication caused by agricultural and urban runoff is increasing in all regions.

Agriculture accounts for about 70 percent of water use today, and about 45 percent more water will be needed to meet 2030 food production needs

(NIC 2012). By 2030 about half the world population will live in water-stressed areas most notably in North and Southern Africa and South and Central Asia, and about a third of all people will face water deficits exceeding 50 percent of needs. Total demand is expected to increase by about 40 percent by 2030 (WRG 2009; NIC 2012) and 55 percent by 2050 (OECD 2012). Most of the cumulative demand increase to 2050 will be for manufacturing, which will increase about 400 percent, while power generation will be up by 140 percent and domestic use by 130 percent (OECD 2012) (see figure 4.2).

Perhaps the most significant threat to agriculture and urban water supplies is the depletion of aquifers due to extraction rates far exceeding recharge rates

Figure 4.2 Distribution and Use of the Earth's Water, 2010

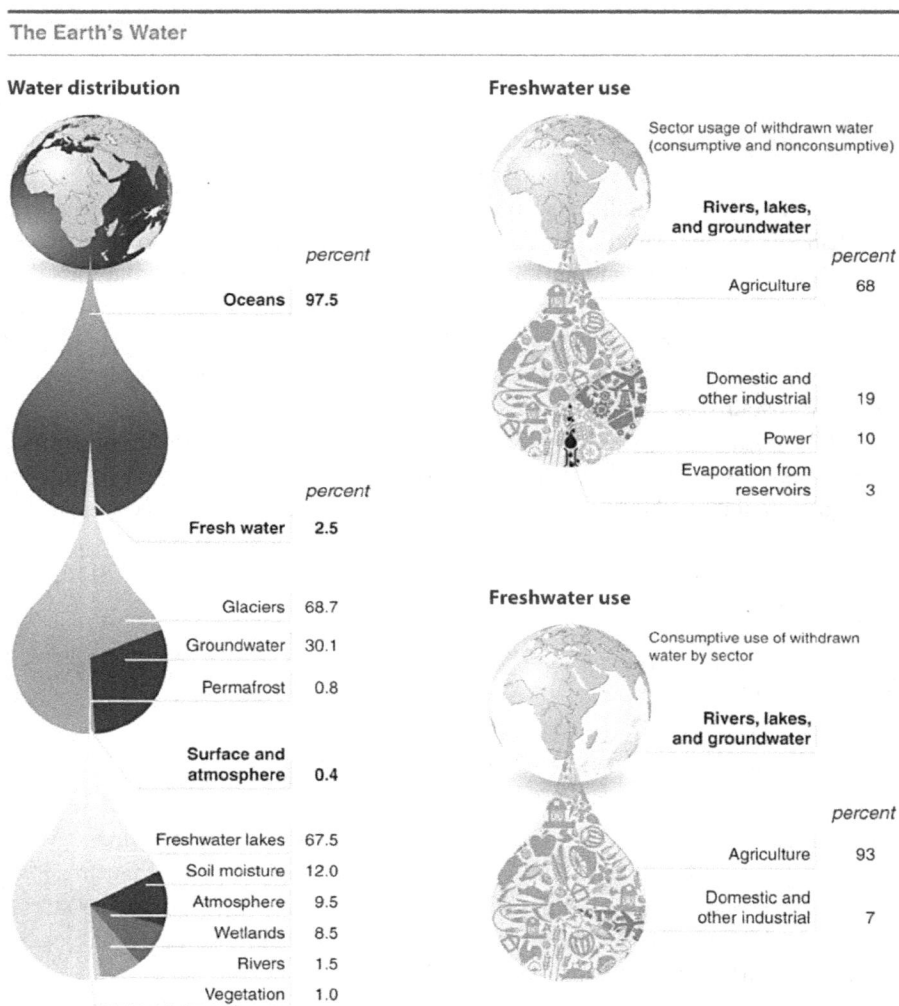

The Earth's Water

Water distribution

	percent
Oceans	97.5

	percent
Fresh water	2.5

Glaciers	68.7
Groundwater	30.1
Permafrost	0.8

| Surface and atmosphere | 0.4 |

Freshwater lakes	67.5
Soil moisture	12.0
Atmosphere	9.5
Wetlands	8.5
Rivers	1.5
Vegetation	1.0

Freshwater use

Sector usage of withdrawn water (consumptive and nonconsumptive)

Rivers, lakes, and groundwater

	percent
Agriculture	68
Domestic and other industrial	19
Power	10
Evaporation from reservoirs	3

Freshwater use

Consumptive use of withdrawn water by sector

Rivers, lakes, and groundwater

	percent
Agriculture	93
Domestic and other industrial	7

Sources: World Bank 2010; NIC 2012: ii.

(OECD 2012). Increased efficiency is also not providing a sustainable improvement in water use; since 1990 improvement was 1 percent across both rainfed and irrigated areas. This rate of improvement would account only for 20 percent of the supply-demand gap in 2030. River basins in India could face the severest deficit, with the Ganga, Krishna, and Indus facing the biggest absolute gap in water supply (WRG 2009).

Opportunities abound to improve water management and minimize freshwater pollution that would reduce the risks of future water shortages, multitude of adverse consequences. Technical improvements, like increasing supply and improving water productivity, could help, but would require $50–60 billion per year to close the resource availability gap. Additionally, rearranging economic activity to reduce water withdrawals would make a difference. However, current trajectories are heading in the opposite direction, and this is without reference to the climate impacts discussed next. Climate change is already having large-scale impacts on water resources and will increase in the near term (WRG 2009). Communities in water-stressed areas with limited resilience to weather shocks will be hardest hit, and the risk of conflict over access to scarce water supplies is already on the rise.

Oceans

The oceans are a remarkable GPG, but have generally been under- and misused, mainly because of the challenge of their sustainable use and management, and because their marine and coastal ecosystems and resources are extremely complex. They play a critical role in regulating the global climate, they feed and provide employment for a large segment of the global population, and they contribute billions to the global economy. It is estimated that 80 percent of all life on earth depends on healthy oceans and coasts. Two-thirds of the earth's population lives within 100 kilometers of the 620,000 kilometers of seacoastline. The value of marine and coastal goods and services was estimated to be about $20 trillion (in 1997), or about two-thirds of the value of the earth's biosphere. Fisheries were worth about $140 billion in 2002, offshore gas and oil about $132 billion in 1995, marine tourism about $161 billion in 1995, and trade and shipping $155 billion (Barange et al. 2011).

Until recently few holistic, at-scale efforts to address the challenges of managing the ocean resources had been made. The fledgling Global Partnership for Oceans (GPO), a recent initiative of the World Bank and partners, is attempting to get a handle on this complex challenge (see chapter 8 for more details). The initial 100-plus partners of the GPO agreed at Rio+ 20 in June 2012 on a Declaration for Healthy, Productive Oceans to Help Reduce Poverty, which notes, Despite global commitments made to date as well as the efforts of many organizations, governments, enterprises, and individuals, the oceans remain under severe threat from pollution, unsustainable harvesting of ocean resources, habitat destruction, ocean acidification, and climate change" (GPO 2012) (Hoegh-Guldberg, O. 2013).

The health of marine ecosystems has been in decline for decades. In 2008, several marine scientists got together to develop a global map of human impact on marine ecosystems (NCEAS 2008). They determined that there is no area unaffected by human influence and that about 41 percent of ocean area is strongly affected by multiple drivers—particularly commercial fishing, land-based pollution, and physical destruction of habitat (Halpern et al. 2008). The oceans have warmed substantially over the last 50 years, causing profound changes in marine ecosystems. Climate change, discussed in the next section, will most certainly overtake overfishing, coastal land-use change, and pollution as the greatest risk to the oceans. Nevertheless, overfishing, land-use, and pollution are much more manageable in the near term. The marine fish catch total was about 16.7 million tons (Mt) in 1950. By 2000 it was 84 Mt, and about 76 percent of the fish stocks were fully exploited or overexploited (Halpern et al. 2008).

About 3.5 million of the world's 18 million hectares of mangrove forests have been destroyed. The world has already lost 40 percent of its coral reefs; even the Great Barrier Reef, heavily protected from other impacts, such as pollution and overfishing, has lost more than 50 percent of its coral since the early 1980s and is currently losing coral at the rate of 2 percent per year. One of the tricky challenges with marine fisheries is that large areas of international waters are outside of any effective governance structure, and there has been no international decision on who should take responsibility for management. Figure 4.3, developed by GPO, provides a snapshot of many of the threats to the oceans.

The future of the health and productivity of the oceans will be affected by many policy decisions that are only indirectly linked to marine and coastal resource management policy-making. Energy policy will be a key factor—not only because future energy development will significantly impact greenhouse gas (GHG) emissions and climate risks, but it will also determine the extent to which offshore windfarms are developed, whether offshore oil and gas exploration and production will expand, and whether and where large volumes of oil and gas will be transported by ship.

In any case, the potential of the oceans to help meet food and job requirements in the future is huge. For the optimal yields of the ocean's benefits to humankind to be secured and sustained, emerging ocean-based industries—such as offshore wind, tidal, and wave energy; sea-bed mining; marine aquaculture; and marine biotechnology, along with existing industries, like tourism and fisheries—will need to be developed within a broader, more holistic resource management framework that achieves healthy oceans.

Climate Change

Climate change will continue to affect the global environmental commons just discussed—biodiversity, fresh water resources, and the oceans—which is not surprising because the inhabitability of coastal areas and cities, food production, health, global economy, and just about every other human need is linked to climate change. The extent of the impact and these resources ability to adapt

Figure 4.3 Stresses on Ocean Resources

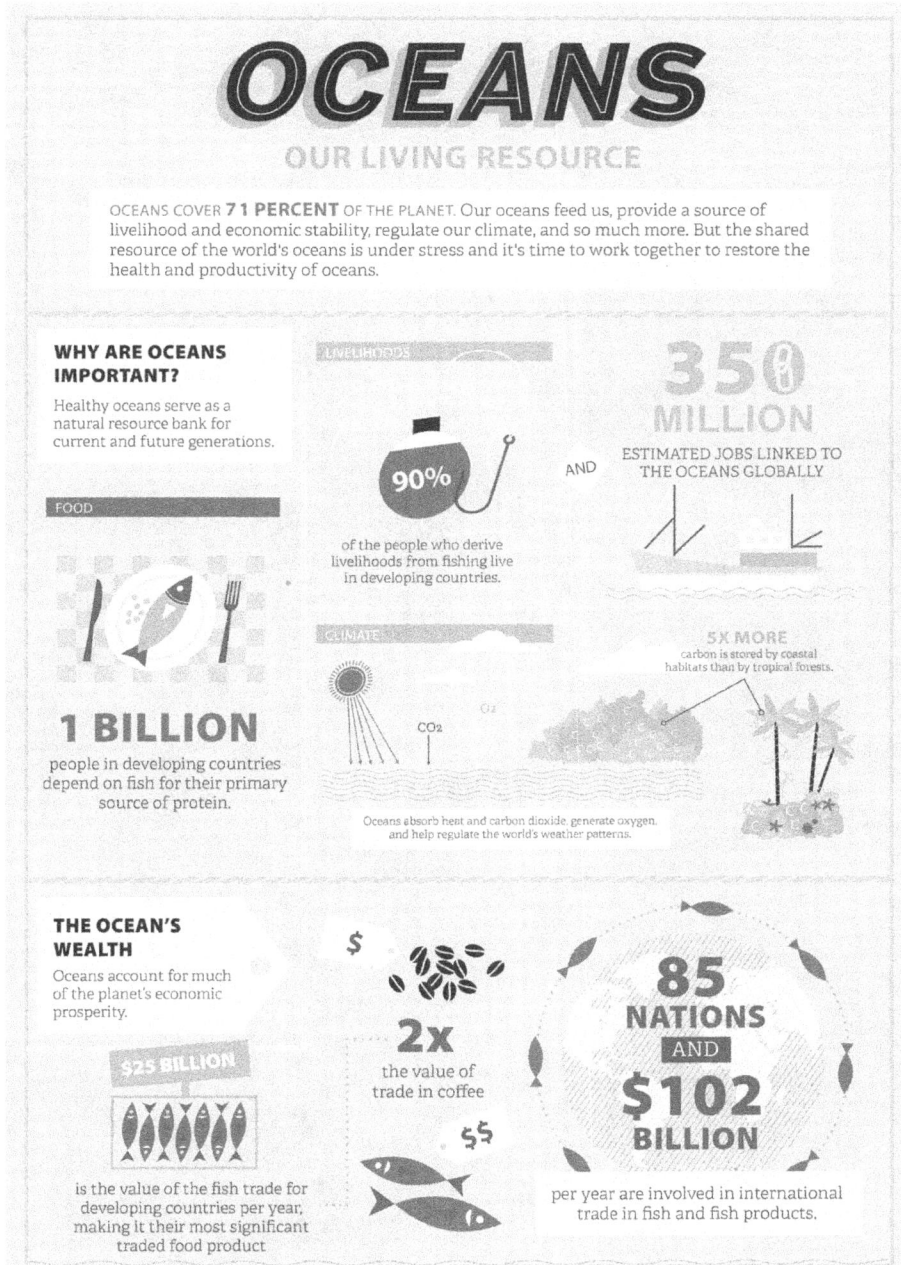

OCEANS
OUR LIVING RESOURCE

OCEANS COVER **71 PERCENT** OF THE PLANET. Our oceans feed us, provide a source of livelihood and economic stability, regulate our climate, and so much more. But the shared resource of the world's oceans is under stress and it's time to work together to restore the health and productivity of oceans.

WHY ARE OCEANS IMPORTANT?

Healthy oceans serve as a natural resource bank for current and future generations.

FOOD

1 BILLION

people in developing countries depend on fish for their primary source of protein.

LIVELIHOODS

90%

of the people who derive livelihoods from fishing live in developing countries.

AND

350 MILLION

ESTIMATED JOBS LINKED TO THE OCEANS GLOBALLY

CLIMATE

CO_2

O_2

5X MORE carbon is stored by coastal habitats than by tropical forests.

Oceans absorb heat and carbon dioxide, generate oxygen, and help regulate the world's weather patterns.

THE OCEAN'S WEALTH

Oceans account for much of the planet's economic prosperity.

$25 BILLION

is the value of the fish trade for developing countries per year, making it their most significant traded food product

$

2x

the value of trade in coffee

85 NATIONS
AND
$102 BILLION

per year are involved in international trade in fish and fish products.

figure continues next page

Too Global to Fail • http://dx.doi.org/10.1596/978-1-4648-0307-9

Figure 4.3 Stresses on Ocean Resources *(continued)*

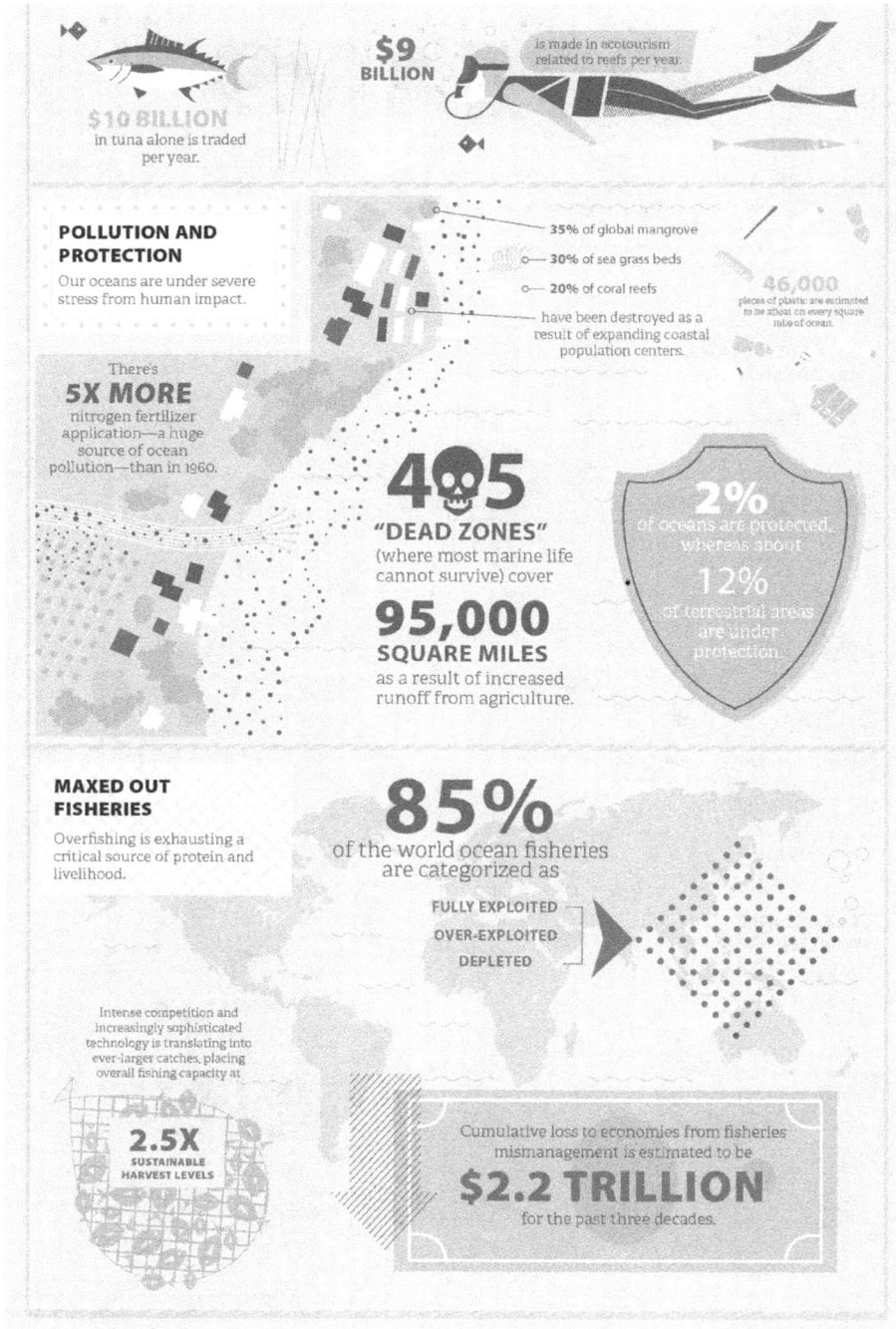

$10 BILLION
in tuna alone is traded
per year.

$9
BILLION

is made in ecotourism
related to reefs per year.

**POLLUTION AND
PROTECTION**

Our oceans are under severe
stress from human impact.

35% of global mangrove
30% of sea grass beds
20% of coral reefs
have been destroyed as a
result of expanding coastal
population centers.

46,000
pieces of plastic are estimated
to be afloat on every square
mile of ocean.

There's
5X MORE
nitrogen fertilizer
application—a huge
source of ocean
pollution—than in 1960.

405
"DEAD ZONES"
(where most marine life
cannot survive) cover

95,000
SQUARE MILES
as a result of increased
runoff from agriculture.

2%
of oceans are protected,
whereas about

12%
of terrestrial areas
are under
protection.

**MAXED OUT
FISHERIES**

Overfishing is exhausting a
critical source of protein and
livelihood.

85%
of the world ocean fisheries
are categorized as

FULLY EXPLOITED
OVER-EXPLOITED
DEPLETED

Intense competition and
increasingly sophisticated
technology is translating into
ever-larger catches, placing
overall fishing capacity at

2.5X
**SUSTAINABLE
HARVEST LEVELS**

Cumulative loss to economies from fisheries
mismanagement is estimated to be

$2.2 TRILLION
for the past three decades.

Source: Global Partnership for Oceans World Bank, 2013.

will depend on the level and pace of temperature rise. The temperature rise will largely depend on increases in the amount of human-generated GHG emissions (see Figure 4.4).

International governmental groups have been debating how to reduce the risks of disastrous climate change for the last 20 years with little resulting action, but with wishful proclamations, such as the decision in 2009 that the world would keep global warming below 2°C above pre-industrial levels. This is considered the point at which impacts, though dangerous and painful, are manageable and to which humans could adapted. The World Bank—recognizing the risks that climate change presents to the poorest countries and communities and the sustainability of its efforts to help developing countries alleviate poverty and generate sustainable wealth—has actively integrated climate finance (including pioneering carbon markets and establishing the multibillion dollar Climate Investment Funds) and analytical work into its operations. The Bank has committed significant resources (with financing from donor countries) to understanding linkages of climate to development. See most notably "Development and Climate Change: Strategic Framework for the World Bank Group" (World Bank 2008b), the *World Development Report 2010: Development and Climate Change* (World Bank 2009), and the *Economics of Adaptation to Climate Change* (World Bank 2010).

All of this work assumed that the Bank's developing country partners might face a world that is 2°C warmer by the turn of the century, about 80 years from now. However, lack of progress in international negotiations resulted in the Bank

Figure 4.4 Atmospheric CO_2 Concentrations at Mauna Loa, Hawaii, Observatory, 1960–2010

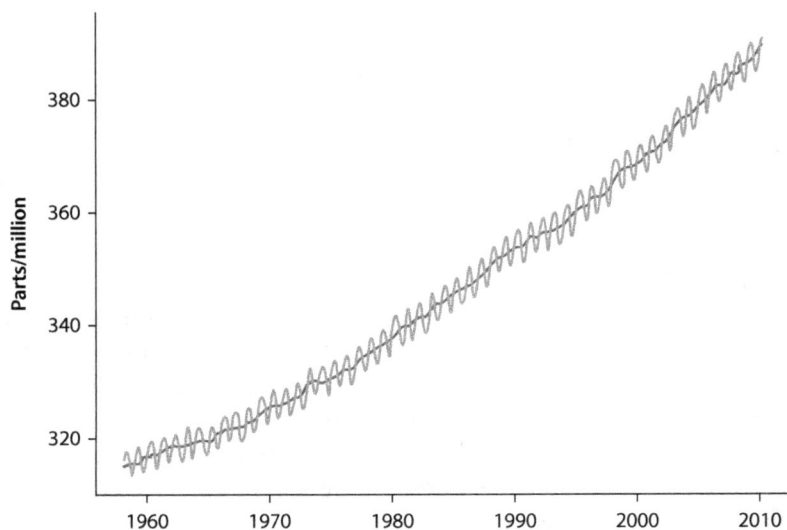

Source: Scripps Institution of Oceanography and NOAA (National Oceanic and Atmospheric Agency) Earth System Research Laboratory.

taking the risky step of conducting a reality check on the likelihood of this level of change. The resulting "Turn Down the Heat" reports (World Bank 2012b, 2013b) were instrumental in highlighting the real-world risks of devastating results from the current path. The current GHG emission trajectories could result in a "4 degree world" this century, the Bank projected. If countries meet their current commitments to reduce GHGs, then the world is likely to warm by more than 3°C, with a 20 percent chance of hitting 4°C by 2100.

What would a four-degrees-warmer world look like? Disastrous climate events since 2010 all occurred with global average temperatures at 0.8°C above pre-industrial levels. They were a preview of how dramatically human activity will irrevocably change the natural environment. A frustrating lack of immediate action and the poor progress of international agreement to reduce pollution have created conditions that make this century's global warming likely to be more than 4°C, with an outside chance of reaching 5°C at century's end. This would only be a milestone: the 22nd century is forecast to be even hotter, with even higher sea levels and much greater climate volatility across regions and weather patterns.

Some likely scenarios in different developing regions follow. Many of the earth's ecosystems and biodiversity will not be able to adapt to such dramatic change, thus much of the efforts of the last decades to conserve and protect biodiversity would be lost. Glacial melt, already affecting some vulnerable areas in the Andes and Himalayas, would reduce water availability for hundreds of millions of poor people. The current growth of emissions places the world oceans on a pathway to a crisis with planetary-scale implications. Many coastal and pelagic fish stocks will disappear, while others will be relocated thousands of kilometers away, raising major food security issues. Coral reefs will almost certainly disappear.

The first "Turn Down the Heat "report, while recognizing the great uncertainties in projecting impacts of a 4 degree world, includes the following sobering statement: "The projected impacts on water availability, ecosystems, agriculture, and human health could lead to large-scale displacement of populations and have adverse consequences for human security and economic and trade systems" (World Bank 2012b: xvii).

The expected effects of a four-degrees-warmer world on various different regions of the developing world are as follows.

Sub-Saharan Africa
Sub-Saharan Africa is particularly vulnerable because warming risks there are so severe that even containing the increase to 2°C this century does not preclude further warming increases. Even with the increase capped, the situation is volatile: regional food production will be threatened. Heat extremes that are historically unprecedented are projected over a wider area as warming grows from 2°C to 4°C. Undernourishment is a great concern, given that development gains of the last decades will likely be rolled back by climate impacts. It is projected that the current range of 15–65 percent undernourishment will shift to a range of 25–90 percent, varying by subregion in Sub-Saharan Africa.

The increased heat will put large stresses on local species and the vegetation of large parts of this region. Aridity is a cause for concern too; it is estimated that hyper-arid areas will increase by 10 percent in a 4 degree world. With a 3°C warming, it is estimated that savanna land will be one-seventh of its current size, significantly threatening various species—including grazing animals—for which this habitat is vital.

Heat extremes will be coupled with a sharp fall in annual rainfall, projected at one-third of current rainfall. Furthermore, large swaths of Southern and West Africa might lose 50–70 percent of their groundwater, increasing likelihood of drought. The lack of uniform impact of global climate change means Africa's Horn and northern East Africa will see increased rainfall during intense periods, giving rise to the possibility of dangerous flooding.

The impact on agriculture is projected to be damaging to maize and sorghum production, with the former dropping 40 percent, the latter also similarly threatened, especially so in the western Sahel and Southern Africa.

Southeast Asia

Southeast Asia suffers risks posed by sea level rise, ocean warming, and ocean acidification. Sudden-onset impacts as were seen in the last decade from tropical cyclones and rapidly increasing heat extremes are projected to increase.

Sea level rise is a real threat to the coastal areas of the region, with Bangkok, Ho Chi Minh, Jakarta, and Manila City all at great risk from a projected sea level rise 50 centimeters above current levels by midcentury, a full meter by 2090. Tropical cyclones will have associated extreme rainfall one-third stronger than previously before, reaching 50–80 millimeters per hour.

The region is also likely to suffer monthly heat extremes in a 2°C-hotter world that currently do not exist. These extremes are projected to cover 60–70 percent of land in the northern summer, with 30–40 percent of the extremes at unprecedented levels. With a 4°C warming, today's unprecedented summer heat peak levels would be normal, affecting nearly 90 percent of the region from June to August. New heat level peaks would increase in frequency.

Fisheries would suffer from a primary productivity drop of 20 percent by the end of the century. Particularly damaged would be fisheries in the Java Sea and the Gulf of Thailand, which would be affected by a combination of warming and decreased oxygen levels in the ocean. Southern Philippines fish stock could fall by 50 percent.

Coral reefs have suffered greatly over the past few decades from a rise in sea surface temperature. Frequently repetitive coral bleaching can devastate reefs and is projected to be highly likely as ocean warming increases. Annual bleaching as early as 2030 can be predicted with just under 1.5°C warming. Acidification will also threaten corals as chemical stress damages reefs.

The Mekong Delta in Vietnam today accounts for half of the country's agricultural production. Just a 30-centimeter rise in sea level, potentially occurring by 2040, could remove 12 percent of that crop production. In Vietnam, 41 percent of the urban population lives in informal settlements, particularly vulnerable to floods. Lack of drainage is dangerous, especially because damage to sanitation and water facilities carries severe health risks.

This level of sea rise is also threatening to major urban areas like metropolitan Bangkok. The city is projected to suffer flooding from extreme rainfall and sea level rise by the 2030s. With inadequate adaptation, under a 15-centimeter sea level rise, 40 percent of the city would be flooded. This could increase to 70 percent in the 2080s, with sea level rise increasing to 88 centimeters. This is under a projected 4°C increase. The impact will be amplified by the urban heat island effect and could result in devastatingly deadly heat spells.

South Asia

South Asia is projected to face significant water supply crises. Water for irrigation and hydropower production is threatened, as is water for cooling of thermal power production. The annual mean monsoon levels will increase by 10 percent, with a 15 percent increase in variability, making the monsoon stronger and less predictable.

The compounded risks of temperature, flooding, sea level rise, and cyclones will leave deltas and coastal urban agglomerations at risk. Bangladesh is acutely vulnerable to all these risks, and warming there will cause unusually hot summers with a substantial increase in mortality.

The region should have a 60 percent increase in crop production without climate change, but under just a 2°C rise the more likely scenario is food imports needing to double to meet caloric needs. Decreasing food availability in 2050 is projected to cause a 35 percent increase in childhood stunting as undernourishment worsens.

A cascading of impacts in South Asia is particularly worrisome because pressure in just one factor, such as decreased crop yield, can severely impact huge populations for generations. Malnutrition and stunting in childhood leads to health risks later in life. This kind of multiplier of impacts is dangerous because it is nonlinear: under a 2°C increase, 20 percent of the population is at risk from multiple stress impacts. Under a 4°C increase, it is projected to increase to 80 percent.

Some Indications of Progress

What is being done to avoid this disastrous future? The good news is that many countries and the European Union have taken serious action or commitments to do so. Two large emerging economies that are current and future major sources of GHG emissions, China and India, have each started implementing programs to shift growth trajectories that will substantially reduce their share of global emissions. Very recently U.S. President Barack Obama used executive authority to launch a major reduction in GHG emissions, pledging to double the amount of renewable electricity generation in the United States by 2020.

The bad news is that it has taken 20 years of failed negotiations to get to this point. The United Nations Framework Convention on Climate Change (UNFCCC) process has generated some positive outcomes—most notably, the Kyoto Protocol—but that is now more or less defunct. After 18 rounds of international talks involving some 153,000 participants and supported by another 100-plus international meetings (each with at least 200 participants), the world is facing a +4°C future. The international dialogue has been seriously flawed in many ways. Clearly there is limited accountability for producing results; international meetings on climate change jumped from an average of four per year for the 1992–2008 period to 12 per year for the 2009–2012 period (see figure 4.5). Representatives of governments that participate in the negotiations continue to have the same disagreements on issues that they have had for many years. At the same time, there has been little progress in providing an opportunity for real engagement with key stakeholders, such as private financiers who are expected to foot the multibillion dollar bill for the transition to a low-carbon future or with mayors and other leaders who are well placed to take action.

The authors are not advocating doing away with the existing international negotiating process—it is essential if a legally binding agreement is to be reached (theoretically by 2015, taking effect in 2020). But given the seriousness of the risks if a transformation does not occur, it is time to explore parallel actions by like-minded parties. Such parties may include national governments, but are not limited to these entities. Private sector players, mayors, civil society leaders, philanthropic organizations, multilateral development banks, and academic and research organizations need to come together to take climate action at scale. For example, about 70 percent of GHG emissions come from cities—cities that have massive urban infrastructure development needs. The priority of most urban

Figure 4.5 Major International Meetings on Climate Change, 1992–2012

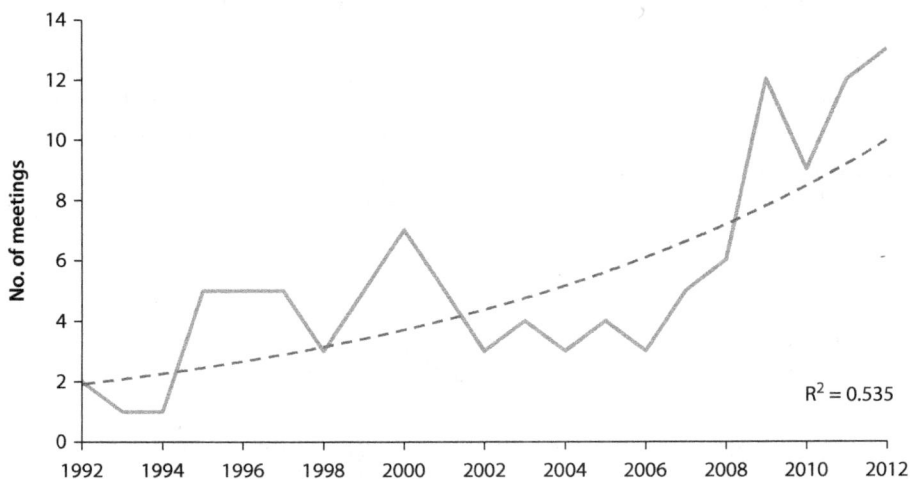

$R^2 = 0.535$

leaders is to meet such needs, but many have indicated a willingness to do so in a low-carbon way instead of locking into long-term high-carbon investments. But they need support to be able to meet their priorities through a low-carbon approach. The urban development challenge presents a unique opportunity for collective action to be undertaken that has tremendous development benefits and a measurable impact on atmospheric GHG concentrations (see part 4). Such collective action–oriented partnerships would require participation of all of the players mentioned, supported by a new type of governance that gives real voice to each stakeholder/partner.

Leadership on climate has come from a variety of like-minded parties, including heads of state, city mayors, corporations, civil society organizations, and countries. In some instances, countries have led; China's pilot carbon market aiming toward a networked carbon trading scheme covers Beijing, Guangzhou, Shanghai, and Tianjin. China is also evaluating a carbon cap, an instrument by which China pledges by 2025 to be polluting at just 50–55 percent of 2005 emissions. India has similarly committed to reducing its emissions per unit of GDP to 20–25 percent below 2005 levels by 2020.

Obama's Climate Action Plan is a strong step forward for the United States: carbon pollution from new and existing power plants will be limited, a regulatory duty the Environmental Protection Agency has been empowered with since 1970s Clean Air Act. An estimate from the National Resources Defense Council, the U.S. environmental action group, estimates a 26 percent reduction in emissions from this change. The plan also invests heavily in renewable energy sources and pledges to double American clean energy production by 2020. Energy efficiency is a third pillar of the plan, with a pledge to provide $250 million in grants for efficiency investments immediately.

The difficulties in passing climate change legislation through the U.S. Congress are well known; at the time this chapter was written, 109 representatives and senators continued to reject the idea that anthropomorphic climate change is real, making it virtually impossible to pass any climate legislation. Acknowledging this, President Obama's 2013 agenda was a presidential order requiring no congressional approval.

The Climate Action Plan also calls strongly on the private sector to reduce its emissions. General Electric and Wal-Mart have both made substantial voluntary pledges to reduce their net emissions, including how they select suppliers around the world. Action on climate change has come from a variety of other parties, many of which are not represented in the formal climate negotiations. This gap is problematic because, as leaders commonly say, action on climate requires action by everyone. The measures enacted by more than 1,000 American mayors and chief executive officers, among others, range from mitigation efforts to resilience planning and are ahead of national government plans. New York's $20 billion coastline defense plan followed the devastation of 2012's Hurricane Sandy, only some of which is supported by the federal government. The formal negotiations are greatly weakened by this inability to bring all interested parties to the table to strengthen the possibility of strong agreement and decisive action.

Too Global to Fail • http://dx.doi.org/10.1596/978-1-4648-0307-9

Drilling Down: The Resource Scarcity Dilemma

The discussions of future scenarios for population, urbanization, economic growth, and consumption; the growing demand for food, water and energy; and intensified resource stress on biodiversity, water, and oceans, in this volume collectively point toward an ever-elevating risk—increased resource scarcity and competition. Examining climate impacts under both a 2°C or 4°C world indicates a dramatically exacerbated resource scarcity challenge (Burke 2009). The issue is not simply depletion of resources, but also the likelihood of disruptions, volatile prices, and rising political tensions over resource access (Lee et al. 2012). From a development perspective, it is broadly agreed that this means resource scarcity is likely to affect the most vulnerable and least resilient communities and hinder efforts to reduce poverty. Beyond that, the three key resource scarcity responses that dominate a growing dialogue in response to the increased risks are conflict, migration, and trade.

The U.S. National Intelligence Council's *Global Trends 2030* (NIC 2012) concludes that increased demand for food, water, and energy—each demand linked to the others—will result in scarcities and be worsened by climate change. Taking into consideration key "game changers," such as global economy, governance, and regional instability, resource scarcity could play a role in increased intrastate and interstate conflict.[1] The NIC researchers see fragile states as being most susceptible and needing the most outside help,[2] but consider that even countries like China and India are vulnerable (NIC 2012). The most recent World Economic Forum *Global Risks* report, which has a 10-year outlook, sees unmanaged migration due to resource scarcities as one of the top 10 social risks (and again with linkages to a number of other risks, such as climate change, food shortage crises, and water supply crises) (World Economic Forum 2013).

The literature discussing resource scarcity and conflict and migration, including the 2010 *World Development Report* (WDR) on climate change (World Bank 2009) and the 2011 WDR on conflict, security, and development (World Bank 2011), and UN Secretary General's report on climate change and conflict (UN 2009) make it clear that no one agrees on the risks that resource scarcity presents in terms of conflict and migration, but few dispute that it plays a significant role.

It is generally agreed that a combination of factors can lead to conflict or migration and that resource scarcity can be central to or a driver leading to conflict or migration. The National Intelligence Council report states, "Many experts also have hypothesized that growing resource constraints combined with the possibility of increasing environmental degradation may be a tipping point for societies already struggling and lead to greater intra- or interstate conflict" (NIC 2012, 80). Afghanistan and the Republic of Yemen are examples of internal conflicts being waged along hydrological lines. In both, warlords have emerged whose basic job is to maintain control over a source of water (RFE/RL 2013). Insufficient natural resources like water and arable land in many countries cause them to risk intrastate conflict due to demographics or faltering governance institutions, or where tensions such as those in tribal, ethnic, religious, and national groups might be heightened (World Bank 2009, 2011; NIC 2012).

The relationship between resource scarcity and migration has been debated by various organizations, including the UN Security Council. A 2009 report by the UN secretary-general (UN 2009) identified involuntary migration, competition with other communities or groups over scarce resources, and an overburdening of local or national governance capacities as secondary results of climate impacts, such as water scarcity. People experiencing scarcity of critical resources, such as water and arable land, are forced to move to be able to survive, especially those in more vulnerable places, often in developing countries (UKGOFS 2011).

Use of the "environmental refugees" label (Black 2001; Ferris 2007) to describe such people has also been debated. It is often argued that migration is historically normal, and those migrating from places where there is limited access to food, livelihoods, or water are not environmental refugees, as these conditions are a function more of the local governance and political situation than environmental degradation due to climate change (Raleigh and Urdal 2007). While links to resource scarcity as a direct causal factor for conflict might not have been shown, what has been clear through analysis and observation is that socioeconomic conditions are associated with increasingly negative impacts on livelihood or access to critical resources. These dynamics are amplified by climate change in uncertain ways, in most cases also exacerbating existing stresses, such as poverty or inadequate infrastructure. Thomas Fingar, chairman of the National Intelligence Council, testified to the U.S. Congress that climate change will exacerbate poverty and increase social tensions, leading to internal instability and conflict and giving parts of the global population additional reasons to migrate (NIC 2012).

In a 2025 context, conditions may give people more reasons to migrate en masse, should the state of vital resources such as water and food result in loss of livelihood or inability to meet basic human needs. In a recent report, "Mali: Migration, Militias, Coups and Climate Change," the Center for Climate and Security examined the insecurities that may have contributed to conflicts in Mali. "This political and constitutional crisis sits atop an already extremely vulnerable situation—a volatile mix of climate change, drought, food shortages, migration and immobility, armed insurrection and heavy weapons proliferation that threaten to plunge the country into a state of instability not unlike Somalia" (Femia and Werrell 2012: 2).

In the nexus between climate change, migration, and conflict, another potential concern is for those who cannot afford to migrate or escape from a climate-related event and are in essence stuck. According to geographer Dave Thomas at Oxford University, "The people we should really be thinking about are...those who stay behind, who may wish to migrate but can't. They are trapped, they are the most vulnerable" (Femia and Werrell 2012: 4).

The impact of trade on resource scarcity and vice versa is also a growing area of concern. It is not a new issue—generally, increased investment, technology innovations, and markets have enabled adaption to resource scarcity–trade issues. But resource trade has hit new levels, increasing about 50 percent over the last 10 years. Much of this is for nonrenewable extractives, like minerals, oil, and gas, but trade in food crops, timber, fish, and oilseeds has also grown.

Future resource scarcity and trade challenges will be driven by the depletion of water resources; for example, a range of estimates have been made of how water shortages will affect agricultural production, and the resulting import requirements, in China. Results vary widely, but at current levels of water use efficiency, one estimate is that China's grain production will fall short of projected demand by 156 million metric tons (MMT) in 2025. It is also estimated that China will need to import more than 47 MMT of grain in 2025, rising to over 56 MMT if water prices are tripled. While China is unique in its huge demand, it is not unique in its future prospects for reduced crop yields due to water and arable land shortages. This is at a time that the world is only one or two bad harvests away from another global food crisis.

The Chatham House Resources Futures project (Lee et al. 2012) and the U.S. National Intelligence Council *Global Trends 2030* study (NIC 2012) both involved consultation and inputs from experts across the globe, and both studies view trade as a frontline for resource scarcity conflicts. This was demonstrated by export controls in a number of countries in 2008 and 2011 that were intended to control price escalation but ended up increasing food price hikes. Several major emerging economies that are key exporters of industrial raw materials have installed export restrictions. According to Lee and colleagues,

> Resource politics, not environmental preservation or sound economics, are set to dominate the global agenda and are already playing themselves out through trade disputes, climate negotiations, market manipulation strategies, aggressive industrial policies and the scramble to control frontier areas. The quest for resources will put ecologically sensitive areas under continuous pressure unless a cooperative approach is taken, not least in the Polar Regions, major forests and international fisheries. (Lee et al. 2012: viii)

Given the lack of progress thus far with international trade, climate, and biodiversity negotiations, new approaches for tackling these global issues by like-minded stakeholders that can deliver real change are warranted.

Technology: The Planet's Salvation?

The pace and innovativeness of technology development over the last several decades certainly should give hope to reversing or reducing the global risks to the globes' inhabitants—human and others—outlined earlier in this chapter. Recent publications that assess plausible scenarios of the future—the Rockefeller Foundation's "Scenarios for the Future of Technology and

International Development" (Rockefeller 2010), the National Intelligence Council's Global Trends 2030 (NIC 2012), Shell's "New Lens Scenarios" (Shell 2013), Al Gore's book *The Future* (Gore 2013)—all consider the possibilities that technology will help address the challenges described in this chapter and thereby reduce the risks of resource scarcity impacts, such as conflict and migration.

Former U.S. vice president Gore in particular balances the hope that technology may save the day against the risk that technology may exacerbate some global and regional challenges if not accompanied by improved governance and policy. He terms the future "Earth Inc."—a hyperconnected, tightly integrated, highly interactive, and technologically revolutionized economy. The hyperconnectivity will further speed up the application of new technologies and increase micro- and macro-inventiveness. In particular, Gore sees the accelerating technological advances as transforming the future role and consumption of resources, but whether this leads to greater sustainability is a large and open question (Gore 2013).

The NIC study foresees much of the future technological activity migrating toward the newly emerging BRIC (Brazil, Russia, India, China) countries over the next 10–15 years, increasing the competitiveness of their corporations. Risk capital will be a controlling element in the equation; if companies in these emerging economies have access to capital, then the growth of technological innovation in these countries will be rapid. The speed with which this transfer takes place will depend on political stability, well-functioning institutions, and public confidence that intellectual property will be protected (World Bank 2008a; NIC 2012). For many developing countries, the transfer will also depend on local investments in capabilities—knowledge and skill—to receive and absorb technologies (UN 2011). Connecting local technological needs to international technological opportunities is a key challenge for several developing countries. These countries have a tremendous opportunity to leapfrog technologies as one way of reducing the risk of resource scarcity and to improve access to and add value to their use of regional and global public goods. This is an important agenda for future financial and technical development assistance.

The NIC study identifies four technology arenas as shaping 2030 global socioeconomic and military developments: information technologies, automation and manufacturing technologies, resource technologies, and health technologies (NIC 2012). Gore predicts that today's advanced materials science will generate a molecular economy, particularly using nanotechnology, and that this will drive a third industrial revolution (Gore 2013). Both the NIC and Gore consider that technology will play a key role in improving the security of resources required to meet future food, water, and energy needs. These new technologies will include genetically modified crops, precision agriculture, improved water management technologies, and renewable energy (in particular, solar and non-food biomass).

Box 4.1 What Young Development Professionals Think About Collective Global Governance

Kevin McCall, Climate Policy and Finance, World Bank Group

The "perfect storm" brewing on the horizon reads straight out of the newest post-apocalyptic novel. Truth is indeed often stranger than fiction. Our problems are many, and they are urgent. Meanwhile, our options for solutions are politically or economically difficult and involve harsh trade-offs. So, what hope for the future?

To my mind, the best option for a collective solution to put the world on a sustainable development pathway is to amplify the nascent trends in good governance and strong regulation we are beginning to see at a global scale. We are getting, I believe, a first glimpse at the saplings of the future landscape of global governance. It differs from the collective action and solution agreed by 51 nation states in 1945 to establish the United Nations, involving a shift away from the state-centric model of reaching decision and crafting solutions. The discussion table has become much bigger, and seats a different set of decision makers. States are still at the table, but their ability to create and implement solutions depends more than ever on the other stakeholders at their side: organizations that connect citizens to their governments and industries that operate across borders and create the wealth that grows economies.

The positive influence of these civil society organizations and private sector actors on transparent, longer-term focused governance and regulation is increasingly apparent. Voluntary industry codes of conduct, while not the norm today, are becoming more common. The Equator Principles—a framework for assessing and managing environmental and social risk in investment projects—is adhered to by nearly 80 financial institutions, responsible for more than 70% of international project fnance debt in emerging markets. Certified "B Corporaations" stand out in the private sector landscape as providing not only profit to shareholders, but creating shared value in the communities and economies in which they operate. Impact Investment, with its "triple bottom line" of financial profits and social and environmental benefits is no longer a niche or boutique investment for philanthropic purposes, but has blossomed into a class of assets that is expected to hold about $500 billion across capital lines within the next five years.

These trends give me cautious optimism to think that a collective solution to boosting governance and mainstreaming regulation—driven by a broad-based coalition of the full range of stakeholders—is within our reach. Today we are only witnessing the saplings of this solution. To ensure that these take root and achieve collective solutions to collective problems within less than a generation, today's policy makers need to be able to adapt to a multidisciplinary, multiactor policy landscape. They need to understand that designing and implementing collective solutions requires non-traditional partnerships with new and relevant stakeholders. And most of all, they need to get their act together to agree and advance any collective solution within the next ten years while the possibility of altering our trajectory toward the "perfect storm" still exists.

Too Global to Fail • http://dx.doi.org/10.1596/978-1-4648-0307-9

Notes

1. More than 1.5 billion people live in countries affected by violent conflict.

2. Supporting fragile or conflict-affected states is a priority for the International Development Association (IDA), the poverty focused, soft-financing arm of the World Bank. Consideration of resource scarcity is highly relevant for strategic planning by poverty reduction/development institutions like the World Bank. By 2015 about 52 percent of the world's poor will live in fragile and conflict-affected situations. Currently 34 out of 36 countries and territories considered fragile, conflict-affected, or post-conflict are eligible for IDA support.

References

Barange, M., J. Field, R. Harris, E. Hoffman, I. Perry, and F. Warner, editors. 2011. *Marine Ecosystems and Global Change*. Oxford, U.K.: Oxford University Press.

Beddington, J. 2009. "Food, Energy, Water and the Climate: A Perfect Storm of Global Events?" Department for Business Innovation & Skills, United Kingdom. http://www.bis.gov.uk/assets/goscience/docs/p/perfect-storm-paper.pdf.

Black, R. 2001. "New Issues in Refugee Research: Environmental Refugees—Myth or Reality?" Working Paper 34, University of Sussex, England.

Burke, S. 2009. "National Security." Working paper, Center for New American Security, Washington, DC.

Clay, J. 2011. "Freeze the Footprint of Food." *Nature* 475: 287–89.

CBD (Convention on Biological Diversity). 2002. *Sixth Ordinary Meeting of the Conference of Parties Decision VI/26*. The Hague, Netherlands.

———. 2010. *Global Biological Diversity Outlook 3*. Montreal, Canada.

Femia, F., and C. E. Werrell. 2012. *Mali: Migration, Militias, Coups and Climate Change*. Washington, DC: Center for Climate and Security.

Ferris, E. 2007. *Making Sense of Climate Change, Natural Disasters, and Displacement: A Work in Progress*. Brookings-Bern Project on Internal Displacement. Washington, DC: Brookings Institute.

Gore, A. 2013. *The Future: Six Drivers of Global Change*. New York: Random House.

GPO (Global Partnership for Oceans). 2012. *Declaration for Healthy, Productive Oceans to Help Reduce Poverty*. Rio de Janeiro: GPO.

Halpern, B., S. Walbridge, K. Selkoe, C. Kappel, F. Micheli, C. D'Agrosa, J. Bruno, K. Casey, C. Ebert, H. Fox, R. Fujita, D. Heinemann, H. Lenihan, E. Madin, M. Perry, E. Selig, M. Spalding, R. Steneck, and R. Watson. 2008. "A Global Map of Human Impact on Marine Ecosystems." *Science* 319 (5865): 948–52. http://www.globalpartnershipforoceans.org.

Hoegh-Guldberg, O. 2013. "The Ocean and Climate Change." Briefing Note prepared for Global Partnership for Oceans. February 11.

IMF (International Monetary Fund). 2010. *World Economic Outlook*. Washington, DC: IMF.

Lee, B, F. Preston, J. Kooroshy, R. Bailey, and G. Lahn. 2012. "Resources Futures: A Chatham House Report." London: Chatham House Resources Futures Project. http://www.chathamhouse.org/publications/papers/view/187947.

McKinsey (McKinsey & Company). 2012. "Manufacturing the Future: The Next Era of Global Growth and Innovation." McKinsey Global Institute, New York. http://www.mckinsey.com/insights/manufacturing/the_future_of_manufacturing.

Moss, T., and B. Leo. 2011. "IDA at 65: Heading Toward Retirement at 65 or a Fragile Lease on Life?" Working Paper 246, Center for Global Development, Washington, DC.

NCEAS (National Center for Ecological Analysis and Synthesis). 2008. "A Global Map of Human Impacts to Marine Ecosystems." NCEAS, Santa Barbara, CA. Interactive map: http://www.nceas.ucsb.edu/globalmarine.

NIC (National Intelligence Council). 2012. *Global Trends 2030: Alternative Worlds*. NIC: Washington, DC.

OECD (Organisation for Economic Co-operation and Development). 2008. *Environmental Outlook to 2030*. Paris: OECD. http://www.oecd.org/env/indicators-modelling-outlooks/40200582.pdf.

———. 2012. *Environmental Outlook to 2050: The Consequences of Inaction*. Paris: OECD. http://www.oecd.org/environment/indicators-modelling-outlooks/oecdenvironmentaloutlookto2050theconsequencesofinaction.htm.

Pereira, H., P. Lendly, V. Proenca, R. Alkemade, J. Scharlemann, J. Fernandez-Manjarres, M. Araujo, P. Balvenera, R. Biggs, W. Cheung, L. Chin, I. H. Cooper, E. Gilman, S. Guenette, G. Hurtt, H. Huntington, G. Mace, T. Oberdorff, C. Revenga, P. Rodrigues, R. Scholes, U. Sumaila, and M. Walpole. 2010. "Scenarios for Global Biodiversity in the 21st Century." *Science* 330 (6010): 1496–501.

Population Institute. 2010. "2030: The Perfect Storm Scenario." Population Institute, Washington, DC. http://www.populationinstitute.org/external/files/reports/The_Perfect_Storm_Scenario_for_2030.pdf.

Prins, A., S. Slingerland, T. Manders, P. Lucas, H. Hilderink, and M. Kok. 2011. "Scarcity in a Sea of Plenty? Global Resource Scarcities and Policies in the European Union and the Netherlands." PBL Netherlands Environmental Assessment Agency, The Hague, The Netherlands. http://www.groupedebruges.eu/pdf/PBL_Scarcity_in_a_sea_of_plenty.pdf.

Raleigh, C. and H. Urdal. 2007. "Climate Change, Environmental Degradation and Armed Conflict." *Political Geography* 26: 674–94.

RFE/RL (Radio Free Europe/Radio Liberty). 2013. "Interview: Author [Brahma Chellaney] Discusses Asia's Water Woes." January 24.

Rockefeller (Rockefeller Foundation and Global Business Network). 2010. "Scenarios for the Future of Technology and International Development." Rockefeller Foundation, New York; Global Business Network, San Francisco.

Shell. 2013. "New Lens Scenarios: A Shift in Perspective for a World in Transition." Shell Oil Company, The Hague, Netherlands. http://s01.static-shell.com/content/dam/shell-new/local/corporate/Scenarios/Downloads/Scenarios_newdoc.pdf.

UKGOFS (UK Government Office for Science). 2011. *Migration and Global Environmental Change Future Challenges and Opportunities: Future Scenarios*. London: The UK Government Office for Science.

UN (United Nations). 2009. *Climate Change and Its Possible Security Implications: Report of the Secretary-General of the United Nations*. UN General Assembly, Sixty-fourth session, Item 114 of A/64/150. 2009. New York: United Nations.

———. 2011. "Technological Learning and Innovation Capacity: A Cross-Cutting Issue for Inclusive Development." UN System Task Team on the Post-2015 UN Development Agenda United Nations, New York.

UNDESA (United Nations Department of Economic and Social Affairs). 2013. *World Population Prospects: The 2012 Revision*. New York: United Nations. http://esa.un.org /wpp.

UNEP (United Nations Environment Programme and World Resources Institute). 2005. *Millennium Ecosystem Assessment Synthesis Report*. New York: United Nations. http:// www.unep.org/maweb/en/index.aspx.

Vergara, W., and S. Scholz. 2011. *Assessment of the Risk of Amazon Dieback*. Washington, DC: World Bank. License: CC BY 3.0 Unported. https://openknowledge.worldbank .org/handle/10986/2531.

2030 Water Resources Group (WRG). 2009. "Charting Our Water Future-Economic Framework to Inform Decision-Makers." 2030 Water Resources Group. http:// www.2030wrg.org/wp-content/uploads/2012/06/Charting_Our_Water _Future_Final.pdf.

World Bank. 2007. "Global Economic Prospects 2007: Managing the Next Wave of Globalization." World Bank, Washington, DC. http://go.worldbank.org /ZZC7M4RHK0.

———. 2008a. *Science, Technology, and Innovation: Capacity Building for Sustainable Growth and Poverty Reduction*, edited by A. Watkins and M. Ehst. Washington, DC: World Bank.

———. 2008b. "Development and Climate Change: Strategic Framework for the World Bank Group." World Bank, Washington, DC.

———. 2009. *World Development Report 2010: Development and Climate Change*. Washington, DC: World Bank.

———. 2010. *Economics of Adaptation to Climate Change: Synthesis Report*. Washington, DC: World Bank. http://documents.worldbank.org/curated/en/2010/01/16436675 /economics-adaptation-climate-change-synthesis-report.

———. 2011. *World Development Report 2011: Conflict, Security, and Development*. Washington, DC: World Bank.

———. 2012a. "Environment Matters." Washington, DC: World Bank. http://siteresources .worldbank.org/EXTENVMAT/Resources/3011350-1339798526004/Environment Matterswholebook.pdf.

———. 2012b. "Turn Down the Heat: Why a 4°C Warmer World Must Be Avoided." World Bank, Washington, DC. https://openknowledge.worldbank.org/handle/10986 /11860.

———. 2013a. *Global Development Horizons: Capital for the Future—Saving and Investment in an Interdependent World*. Washington, DC: World Bank.

———. 2013b. "Turn Down the Heat: Climate Extremes, Regional Impacts, and the Case For Resilience." Working paper, World Bank, Washington, DC.

World Economic Forum. 2013. *Global Risks 2013*. World Economic Forum, Geneva, Switzerland. http://www3.weforum.org/docs/WEF_GlobalRisks_Report_2013.pdf.

Zoellick, R. 2010. "Speech at Convention on Biological Diversity." Nagoya, Japan. http://www.worldbank.org/en/news/speech/2010/10/27/remarks-for-opening-plenary-of-the-high-level-segment-cop-10.

PART 2

Financing Global Public Goods

CHAPTER 5

Something's Gotta Give: Aid and the Financing of Global Public Goods

Robin Davies

There is one particularly striking disconnect between what traditional donors say about their aid and what they do with it. What these donors—the longstanding members of the Organisation for Economic Co-operation and Development's (OECD) Development Assistance Committee (DAC)—mostly say is that their aid is a transfer of resources to poor countries for the purpose of helping those countries meet their own national development objectives. This notion is part of the canonical concept of aid effectiveness, which has at its core the linked concepts of "ownership," meaning leadership of development programs by beneficiary countries, and "alignment," meaning alignment of those development programs with national priorities.

What traditional donors increasingly do, however, is use aid to help provide a variety of global public goods (GPGs). A large majority of their aid is still devoted to meeting the development objectives of individual poor countries. But a sizeable minority of it is rather quietly dedicated to GPGs, most notably and recently including climate change mitigation. About one-quarter of aid outflows from DAC donors, and one-half of aid outflows from multilateral organizations, is currently dedicated either to GPGs or to complementary national public goods that must be present if a country is to avail themselves of the benefits of GPGs. Sometimes this use of aid is prominent, as for example, in the case of investments in vaccines and immunization programs for neglected diseases that almost exclusively afflict poor countries. For the most part, though, it happens under the radar.

Even if a substantial proportion of global aid is spent on GPGs, the global aid pie—$127 billion in 2012, or 0.29 percent of the combined gross national income (GNI) of DAC members—is small in proportion to the scale of transnational problems, particularly that of climate change mitigation.[1] It is not controversial, therefore, to argue that the provision of more public financing for GPGs would be a good thing for the development of poor countries, particularly if such financing could be used in part to leverage private contributions toward the

To see Robin Davies discuss aid and the financing of global public goods: http://youtu.be/TQ07jAHgacg

provision of some GPGs. What is controversial is the argument that aid should be the source of such financing. However, the discussion that follows does not enter into normative questions about whether aid, as distinct from some other stream of international public finance, should be used for GPGs or whether aid for GPGs should be additional in some sense to existing aid. Nor is it argued that there should be a dramatic expansion in the share of aid that is used for GPGs, even though it is conceivable that the development benefits of such an expansion would, up to a certain level of substitution, outweigh the benefits foregone as a result of reductions in aid support for purely national priorities. For present purposes, it is simply taken as a fact that aid budgets are now, and are likely to remain, the source of almost all international public financing for GPGs.

The purpose of this chapter is simply to examine how aid is in fact being used for GPGs and to discuss how, in a changing context, something like the present level of investment in GPGs might be maintained. The approach is largely descriptive and analytical; the intention is to demonstrate that a tension between the two uses of aid just mentioned—GPGs and country priorities—might soon become much more acute owing to recent and rather dramatic changes in the global context in which aid is provided. Chapter 6 adopts a more normative perspective, arguing in broad terms that aid's rationale, and its multilateral delivery mechanisms, would need to be revisited in a certain way in order to resolve this tension.

The argument of this chapter is as follows. The first section specifies which GPGs are of principal interest from an international development perspective and briefly discusses how they are produced, which ones receive the most financing, and from what sources that financing is received. The second section looks at some long-term trends in the provision of aid financing for GPGs, based on an analysis of data from the OECD's Creditor Reporting System (CRS). The third section summarizes some relatively recent changes in the context for aid. The fourth section concludes that the use of aid for GPGs is, or soon will be, grinding against significant limits, and the friction is likely to generate heat. If so, donors may have to choose between two courses of action: realigning their aid with the standard narrative or changing the standard narrative. For a range of reasons, which are explored, the choice is not easily made.

Global Public Goods for Development

A public good is something that confers benefits on people without restriction or exhaustion, like a street light. A GPG is a public good whose benefits transcend national boundaries, like climate change mitigation or, to be more exact, whatever international arrangements deliver climate change mitigation. National public goods are generally provided by governments, since markets do not provide things that they cannot commodify. In the absence of a world government, international public goods are generally provided by cooperation between governments, usually supported by international organizations.

To be more specific, the term "global public goods" is here used to cover a class of products that provide sustained yields of shared benefits in areas of particular importance to developing countries. "Products" entails human action of some kind. "Sustained yields" means that the benefits in question are not finite and therefore not subject to long-run allocation decisions (though they might be rationed where production cannot keep pace with demand). "Shared benefits" means that no country for which the benefits are relevant is restricted in its access to them.

With its requirement that benefits be sustained and shared, the above notion of GPGs incorporates the characteristics of non-rivalry and non-excludability that feature in textbook definitions of "a pure public good." However, it allows that these characteristics might be contingent. For a product to be a GPG, it is sufficient that it be provided in such a way as to yield sustainable, shared benefits. Its publicness might therefore be the result of a policy choice (Kaul et al. 2003) rather than being intrinsic.

The most significant GPGs, in terms of their importance for development and their reliance on aid financing, fall under three broad outcome areas:

- infectious disease surveillance, control, and eradication;
- sustainable management of transboundary natural resources, such as the atmosphere, forest and marine ecosystems, fresh water and fisheries; and
- the production of knowledge for development, which both cuts across and extends beyond the above two areas.

Other GPGs are notable from a development perspective but tend to make smaller, less frequent, or sometimes questionable calls on aid budgets. Free and open trade and global financial stability are often also mentioned as GPGs, likewise peace and security. The World Bank's 2007 GPG policy framework, for example, gives prominence to trade and financial stability, along with GPGs relating to global health, the global environment, and knowledge (World Bank 2007). More recently, global food security is sometimes mentioned as a GPG and the aspirational concept of a global "social protection floor," advocated by the International Labour Organization, is articulated in ways that would tend to make it a GPG. In all these areas, there is no question that agreements or cooperation-related mechanisms with strong GPG characteristics can be identified, and also that they will be of substantial or primary relevance to developing countries. Other GPGs, such as global standards that facilitate the expansion of economically or socially important networks, might be of relatively less importance to developing countries.

GPGs can also be classified according to their mode of production, rather than by outcome area. In fact, from a financing perspective this is perhaps a more useful method of classification.[2] GPGs can be produced through singular, cumulative, or structured actions. Different financing and production strategies are required in each case. For example, singular GPGs might be produced by any one of a number of competing actors in response to financial incentives, such as prizes. Structured GPGs require careful management of, and financial and technical support for, the contributing actions of multiple parties, with strong institutional mediation. Cumulative GPGs, which present perhaps the greatest financing and strategic challenges, require at least tacit agreement on some kind of a common goal among the most significant actors, and often arrangements for the provision of financial benefits as incentives for participation by some parties, for example, through side payments or flexibility mechanisms pursuant to a multilateral or plurilateral agreement.

Figures 5.1 and 5.2 below show the major purposes for which cumulative bilateral and multilateral GPG funding has been used over ten years up to and

Figure 5.1 Bilateral GPG Funding, by Major Purpose, 2001–2011
millions of USD

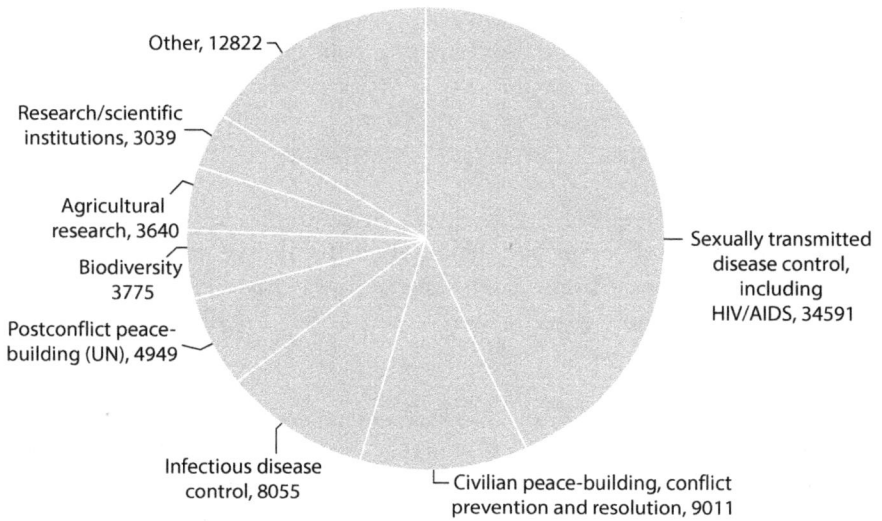

Source: Calculations based on OECD Creditor Reporting System data.

Figure 5.2 Multilateral GPG Funding by Major Purpose Period
millions of USD

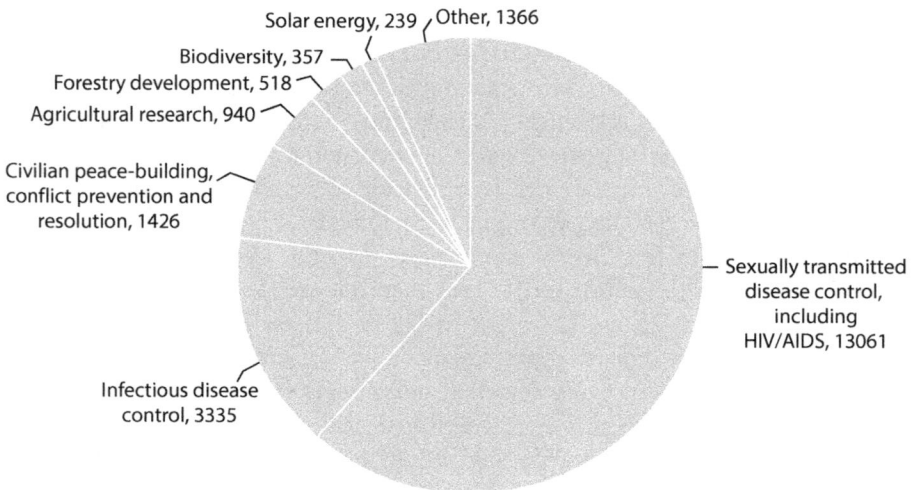

Source: Calculations based on OECD Creditor Reporting System data.

including 2011, the last year for which detailed comparative data are available. In interpreting these figures it is important to note that multilateral and bilateral totals cannot be added together. Bilateral totals reflect outflows from DAC donors, some of which are also inflows to multilateral funds and organizations. The latter funds or organizations will either convert those inflows into outflows, though not necessarily in the same calendar year, or simply consume them, as in the case of health and agricultural research organizations. In some cases multilateral funds and organizations also receive funding from private sources, or generate them internally, as in the case of the multilateral development banks. Thus bilateral and multilateral totals must be considered separately.

Bilateral outflows totaled around $80 billion over the decade and are dominated by financing for infectious disease control and peace-building. Multilateral outflows totaled around $20 billion and are dominated by financing for the same two purposes, but with an even greater share of the total—approaching two-thirds—allocated to infectious disease control.

Figures 5.3 and 5.4 below show the major sources from which cumulative bilateral and multilateral GPG funding has been received over the decade up to and including 2011. In reading figure 5.4 it should be noted that the OECD treats the Bill & Melinda Gates Foundation as a multilateral donor for statistical reporting purposes. However, the foundation passes much of its funding to traditional multilateral donors. Thus there is some double-counting in the figure below: some outflows from Gates will also, if in the same calendar year, appear as outflows from the multilateral organizations supported by Gates.

Figure 5.3 Bilateral GPG Funding by Major Source
millions of USD

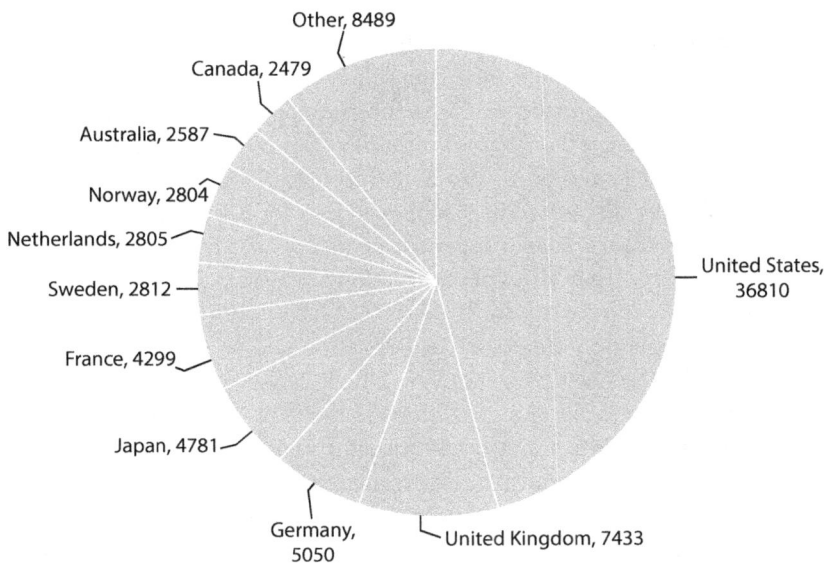

Source: Calculations based on OECD Creditor Reporting System data.

Figure 5.4 Multilateral GPG Funding by Major Source
millions of USD

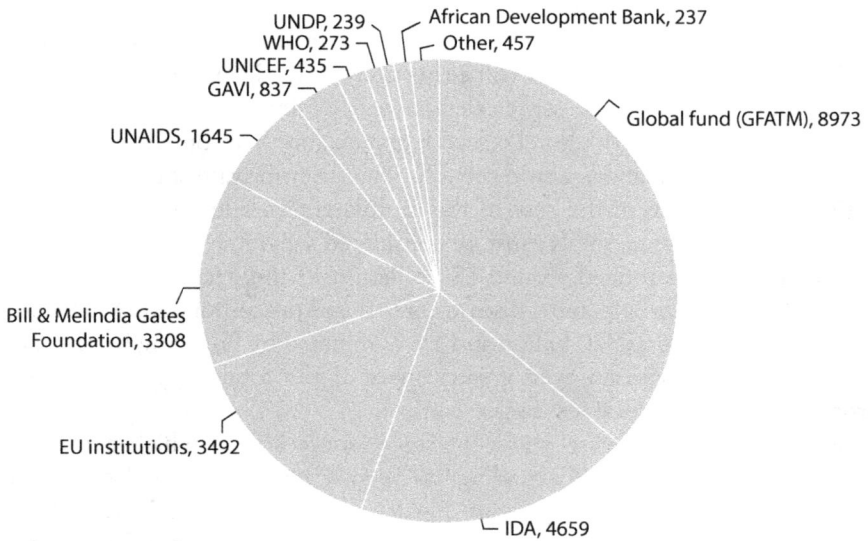

UNDP, 239 ⟍   ⌐ African Development Bank, 237
WHO, 273 ⌐ ⟍ ⟍ ⌐ Other, 457
UNICEF, 435 ⌐
GAVI, 837 ⌐
                              ⌐ Global fund (GFATM), 8973
UNAIDS, 1645 ⟍

Bill & Melindia Gates
Foundation, 3308 ⌐

EU institutions, 3492 ⌐

                              ⌐ IDA, 4659

Source: Calculations based on OECD Creditor Reporting System data.

While figure 5.3 illustrates that bilateral donors provide GPG funding roughly in accordance with their ranking on the DAC donor "league table," figure 5.4 illustrates the dominance of the Global Fund to Fight AIDS, Tuberculosis and Malaria (GFTATM)—established in January 2002, the first year of the decade under consideration—as a source of GPG financing.

A final observation to close this section is that the acuteness and scale of global challenges has spurred public and private providers of development finance to experiment with new, complex financing schemes during the last decade. These are aimed at securitizing future aid flows for immediate effect, tying financing to development outcomes rather than development inputs, and stimulating market-based private sector provision of products important for development, such as drugs for neglected diseases. Such schemes are not well understood outside expert circles, nor always unanimously supported within those circles.

It is not quite true that all experimentation with new financing instruments and approaches is related in some way to GPGs: some payment-by-results approaches are applied in areas such as education and water supply and sanitation. However, for the most part, innovative financing approaches are being used to achieve innovation, scale, and speed for the delivery of GPGs. It is also important to note that the increasing preference for complex financing approaches reinforces the centrality of multilateral organizations as agents for the delivery of GPGs. Arguably, only such organizations can aggregate and manage resources, and monitor results, in the way needed for the effective execution of these complex approaches.

A Trend Analysis

There is no systematic or regular consideration of the share and composition of aid allocated to GPGs, whether at the global level or by individual donor countries or by the multilateral institutions that spend a substantial proportion of this aid. This is rather surprising given the frequently expressed concern that aid for GPGs might be provided at the expense of aid for more local priorities. This likely displacement effect is occasionally remarked upon,[3] and it has been seen as a major risk in connection with developed countries' collective commitment to scale-up climate change financing between 2009 and—which had already resulted in the allocation of some 13 percent of all aid to climate-related activities by 2011 (OECD 2013).

In the period from about 1999 to 2004, when there was a notable spike in international interest in GPGs, several efforts were made to estimate the quantity of aid used in support of them. These efforts yielded quite divergent figures, ranging from 4 to 30 percent.[4] The divergence is explained by several factors.

First, the primary source of data, the OECD Development Assistance Committee's CRS, employs a coding system that is by no means useful for identifying aid in support of GPGs. Being itself an established and widely used global public good, the CRS is not easily modified, even to meet such pressing needs as determining the quantity of aid allocated to climate change mitigation. (The "Rio marker" system [OECD 2013], which now includes a climate change mitigation marker, is poorly applied by reporting agencies and allows only very rough quantification.)

Second, the various estimation efforts of the late 1990s and early 2000s took quite different views about what constitutes a GPG. For example, Raffer (1999) inexplicably includes all aid for water and sanitation. The differences might have been less if the CRS coding system were better suited to the task, but they probably also reflect quite different understandings of the concept of a GPG.

Third, only the World Bank, whose 2001 estimate is at the lower end of the spectrum, has attempted to make a clear distinction between core GPGs and complementary funding for related national public goods, the latter being necessary for the consumption of GPGs (World Bank 2001). Other estimates appear to include many national public goods without necessarily applying the latter restriction.

What all past estimation efforts have agreed on, regardless of their methodology and the exact time window in question, is that aid for GPGs increased dramatically through the 1990s into the early 2000s, perhaps roughly doubling as a share of total aid relative to the 1980s. And there are several reasons to expect that the growth of aid for GPGs would have further accelerated since the above estimations were made.

The main reason is that since the turn of the century, several major new GPG financing mechanisms have been established, including the GAVI Alliance (founded in 2000); the GAVI Alliance-related International Financing Facility for

Immunisation (2006); the Global Fund to Fight AIDS, Tuberculosis and Malaria (2002); and the Climate Investment Funds (2008). The GAVI Alliance, the Global Fund, and the Climate Investment Funds immediately became three of the five largest global programs in which the World Bank is involved, the others being the Global Environment Facility (GEF) and the Consultative Group on International Agricultural Research (CGIAR).

Many other, smaller mechanisms have also been created, such as

- the Critical Ecosystem Partnership Fund (2000);
- the Global Crop Diversity Trust (2004);
- a considerable number of health-sector product development partnerships, such as the Medicines for Malaria Venture (late 1999) and the Drugs for Neglected Diseases Initiative (2003);
- pilot "pull" mechanisms, such as the Pneumococcal AMC (Advance Market Commitment) vaccination initiative (2006) and the AgResults initiative (2012); and
- World Bank–led mechanisms, such as the Extractive Industries Transparency Initiative (2002) and the State- and Peace-Building Fund (2008).

As a rough indication of the scale of financing allocated to such mechanisms in recent years, it is useful to consider contributions to World Bank–managed trust funds with global and regional objectives. During the period 2002–10, donors contributed $57.5 billion to trust funds managed by the World Bank, of which around half was likely to have funded GPGs through large "financial intermediary" funds (IEG 2011a). In 2011 the World Bank was involved in 120 global and regional partnership programs with total spending of $7 billion (IEG 2011b).[5]

A second reason to expect growth in aid for GPGs is that philanthropic donors, most notably, the Bill & Melinda Gates Foundation, have also played an increasingly prominent role through the first decade of this century in funding GPGs through many of the above, and other, mechanisms. Recent annual reports show the Gates Foundation is spending well over $3 billion per annum (BMGF 2011). It is now providing more aid than all but the top dozen or so OECD DAC donor countries—with a very strong emphasis on funding for GPGs.

A third reason to expect growth in aid for GPGs is that all major donors made commitments at or following the United Nations Framework Convention on Climate Change (UNFCCC) conference in Copenhagen, in 2009, to provide collectively an average of $10 billion per annum over the three years, from 2010 to 2012, in "fast-start" financing for action on climate change in developing countries. A substantial majority of this has been allocated to climate change mitigation, a GPG.

Given the appearance of the new multilateral financing mechanisms listed above, the growth in foundation financing for GPGs, and the known growth of climate change financing since 2009, it seems highly likely that aid financing for GPGs will have continued to grow strongly in absolute terms between 2001 and 2011, and probably also as a proportion of aid.

An analysis of CRS data for the decade from 2002 to 2011 confirms that the use of aid for GPGs has increased substantially. (It appears that nobody has undertaken such an analysis since around 2004.) In constant 2011 US dollar terms, DAC donor funding for GPGs grew from about $4 billion annually during 2002–03 to about $12 billion for 2010–11. Multilateral spending on GPGs grew from about $1 billion to about $3 billion. DAC donors' complementary spending grew from about $12 billion to $22 billion, and multilateral complementary spending from about $4 billion to about $7 billion. As a share of official development assistance (ODA) from DAC donors, spending on GPGs went from under 4 percent to more than 8 percent. As a share of multilateral spending, it went from 5 percent to 15 percent.

Figures 5.5 and 5.6 illustrate trends in the level and share of aid for GPGs over the decade up to and including 2011, distinguishing between bilateral and multilateral outflows.

While increasing allocations for global health and environment programs account for the bulk of the recent growth in aid for GPGs, strong growth in aid budgets up to 2010 or so for most donors coincided with an increased level of interest in the use of aid for other GPG-related purposes. These uses include costs associated with international peacekeeping, the presence of refugees and asylum-seekers within donor countries, the negotiation of trade liberalization agreements, and the promotion of private investment in developing countries through bilateral development financing institutions or various public-private partnerships for development. The general trend is toward much greater use of aid for both mutual interest and global interest purposes, though some of the uses listed have aroused considerable controversy.

Figure 5.5 Trends in Aid for Global Public Goods

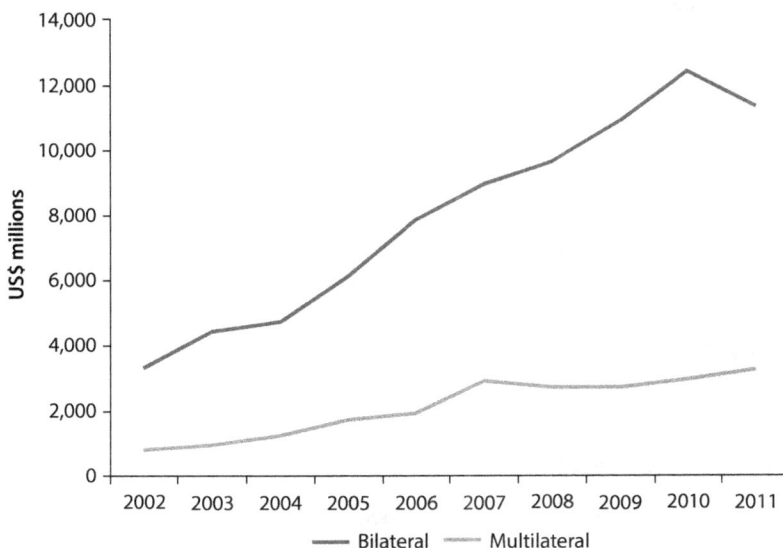

Source: Calculations based on OECD Creditor Reporting System data.

Figure 5.6 Trends in Share of Aid Used for GPGs

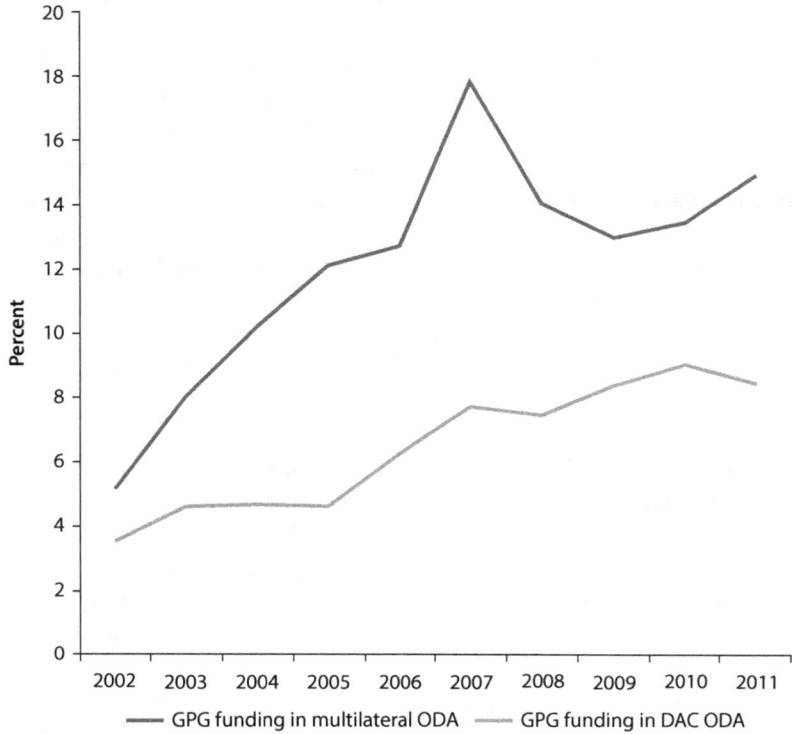

Source: Calculations based on OECD Creditor Reporting System data.

Overall, the sharp increase in global aid, commencing around the turn of this century and falling off only recently, permitted a similarly sharp increase in funding for GPGs without any very noticeable impact on allocations to country-specific purposes. Thus a sort of additionality was achieved—the sort of additionality that many donors clearly had in mind when they agreed, in negotiations on the Copenhagen Accord (UNFCCC 2009), that their climate change financing commitments would be "new and additional." This might help to explain the seeming paradox that aid for GPGs experienced a major acceleration at exactly the time when international interest in GPGs as an object of international public financing appeared to evaporate. It is possible that the onset of the global financial crisis, and the resultant preoccupation with its national-level impacts and related response measures, might also have played a role in drawing discussion on this topic to a close.

The Changing Context for Aid

At the same time as aid for GPGs has been growing strongly, some quite dramatic shifts have taken place in the level, composition, and origins of international financial flows to poor countries, as well as in the distribution of growth and poverty across the world. As these have been well-discussed elsewhere, the four main such shifts are discussed only briefly below.

First, aid from traditional sources is currently declining in overall volume. Over the last 40 years, global aid from official donors—ODA, as defined by the OECD Development Assistance Committee—has mostly followed a quite steep upward trajectory. In fact, it has trebled in real terms since 1970. In constant 2011 dollars, ODA more than doubled, from $43 billion to $93 billion, between 1970 and 1992, declined somewhat over the five years to 1997 to $73 billion, then climbed steeply from 1998 to 2010. It hit an all-time peak of $137 billion in 2010. In 2011, however, it fell by 2 percent, and in 2012 by a further 4 percent. It is expected to remain stagnant, at best, over the several years ahead.

Second, even without the recent volume declines, aid was becoming much less important than it was compared with other sources of finance. Foreign direct investment and migrants' remittances, in particular, were both about half the size of global ODA in 1990, but now, taken together, are some eight times larger. The level of private flows with an explicit development objective is growing rapidly too. By some estimates, private philanthropic flows have grown from a very low base in 1990 to more than $50 billion per year now. Domestic sources are also assuming much greater importance. Tax receipts in Africa are now thought to be equivalent to about 10 times the level of ODA.

Third, aid from traditional sources is now competing with aid or aid-like flows from emerging economies. While not well understood, these flows are thought to be anywhere between $10 billion and $50 billion per year (Walz and Ramachandran 2011). These donors, or "South-South cooperation partners," have so far shown little interest in financing GPGs. Their emphasis is on mutual interests within bilateral relationships rather than on global interests. Their priorities tend to be those neglected in the Millennium Development Goals (MDGs) and in the programs of traditional donors over the last two decades: economic infrastructure and production. In some cases, of course, this emphasis on mutual interest and infrastructure will in fact lead them to support the provision of important regional public goods (RPGs), such as international road, rail, and seaport networks.

Fourth, there are fewer poor countries and, as a result, more poor people in middle-income countries (MICs). The Center for Global Development argues that by 2025, the client base of the World Bank's concessional financing arm, the International Development Association (IDA), could shrink by more than half in terms of the number of eligible countries (37 of 68 could graduate) or by two-thirds in terms of the population of eligible countries (from 3 billion to 1 billion people) (Moss and Leo 2011). The number of low-income countries fell from 63 in 2000 to 35 in 2010 and might be as few as 16 by 2030 based on IMF (2012) World Economic Outlook projections (Sumner 2012). At the same time, MICs now account for around 70 percent of the world's poor, compared with less than 10 percent two decades ago. In addition, almost 90 percent of the world's poor are concentrated in just 10 low-income countries and 10 MICs. Persistent inequality in these countries could in some cases have negative regional or global spillover effects.

GPGs versus the standard aid policy narrative

We have seen that dramatic shifts have taken place in the level, composition, and origins of international financial flows to poor countries, as well as in the distribution of growth and poverty across the world. These developments pose major questions for traditional development agencies, whose institutional mandates and resource allocation processes are carrying them toward a narrow focus on the poorest and most fragile states with the most intractable development problems, mainly in Africa. As a result, the traditional donor community is undergoing much self-examination with respect to aid volume, resource allocation priorities, financing instruments and delivery channels.

To some extent, this self-examination is taking place in the context of ongoing discussions about the post-2015 international development framework. The priorities of traditional donors, as expressed in the MDGs, have often been seen as biased toward the charitable concerns of their own citizens and somewhat ill-matched with the primary concerns of people in poor countries, namely, jobs and growth, social security, peace and freedom, and, increasingly, climate change. These "missing" elements of the MDGs are likely to assume greater prominence in the post-2015 framework. However, fundamental and interrelated questions about the use of aid for climate change and other GPGs, the allocation of aid to MICs, and the overall level of financing for international development have not yet begun to be considered and could make agreement on the post-2015 development agenda much more difficult than is presently expected.

The self-examination referred to above is also taking place in the context of individual donor countries' policy-making and budget processes. At the level of policy, there is an increasingly evident inclination to use, or revive, mutual-interest rationales for aid in traditional donor countries. Such rationales typically emphasize generalized benefits, as in the case of the United Kingdom's aid narrative, quoted in box 5.1 below. In some cases, though, they emphasize narrower,

---

Box 5.1 The U.K. Aid Policy Narrative

Combating poverty, disaster, and conflict is in the best traditions of our country. Whether it was the campaign to abolish slavery in the 19th century, the fight against fascism in the 20th century, or campaigns like Live 8 and Make Poverty History in the 21st, the UK has a proud history of showing compassion to those who are suffering beyond our borders.

And this aid commitment is not just morally right—it is also firmly in our national interest. We live in an increasingly interconnected world, where problems in faraway places can reverberate back home. Aid is vitally important to tackling the root causes of those global problems—disease, drugs, terrorism, and climate change—that threaten our own future.

—*Statement of David Cameron MP, Prime Minister, and Nick Clegg MP, Deputy Prime Minister, United Kingdom*

Source: DfID 2011.

---

usually commercial, benefits for the donor country. At the time of writing, at least two DAC donors—Canada and Australia—were describing their aid programs as instruments of "economic diplomacy." There are in fact two divergent tendencies here: one toward a new, GPG-based rationale for aid, the other toward a "bilateral-benefits" rationale of the kind used by emerging donors. Traditional donors might be coming to perceive that there is a choice to be made between, on the one hand, competing with emerging donors on their terms in bilateral arenas and, on the other hand, ceding some ground to those donors and pursuing complementary investments in RPGs and GPGs. These options are not mutually exclusive in practice, but they represent such different conceptions of the role of aid that it is hard to imagine a donor juggling them.

One might hope that with all the contextual changes outlined above, the use of aid for GPGs by traditional donors would naturally further increase in order to complement, progressively, the bilaterally oriented investments of emerging donors—in other words, that for these donors the "global-benefits" tendency would prevail over the "bilateral-benefits" tendency. This is certainly not a foregone conclusion. It is entirely possible that aid for GPGs will actually diminish if a significant number of traditional donors elect to compete with emerging donors at the bilateral level. However, it is clear that such competition would be inefficient and retrograde from an aid effectiveness perspective. For present purposes, then, assume that traditional donors do see reason to further increase aid for GPGs. The question then arises as to how easy it would be actually to achieve such an increase.

Even if there were strong interest among traditional donors in increasing the share of aid allocated to GPGs, this enterprise faces a significant barrier in the form of the standard aid policy narrative. Most DAC donors' aid policy narratives, read strictly, are largely inconsistent with the use of aid for purposes other than poverty reduction and humanitarian action within the poorer developing countries. They present aid as a resource for national and local poverty reduction and social development efforts, in line with partner governments' national development strategies. They place little or no emphasis on the importance for poor countries themselves of actions to supply GPGs. Three factors, not entirely independent of one another, explain the nature of the dominant aid policy narrative, as follows.

First, the notion that aid is focused on poor or at least fragile countries is generally considered to be important in building and maintaining public support for aid. The MDGs, which crystallized over the period 2000–01, increasingly became a rallying point for aid advocates as the decade progressed. By the time of the G8's Gleneagles Summit in 2005, many bilateral donors had given the MDGs pride of place in their aid policy frameworks. It should be noted that the MDGs are not in themselves antithetical to the use of aid for GPGs. In fact, it is often argued that the emergence of several "vertical" funds, including the health-related funds that account for a large part of the recent growth in aid funding for GPGs, was linked to the centrality of the MDGs in donors' aid policies and sector strategies. However, the MDGs, despite being established as global goals, were quickly translated to the country level, to the dismay of at least one of their architects (Vandemoortele 2012). In effect, the MDGs have been localized in order to make them more vivid and consistent with the message that aid is for poor countries. As a result, the measures necessary for the achievement of the MDGs are generally conceived as national measures, and vertical funds have faced strong pressure to become more responsive to national priorities.

Second, a body of aid effectiveness doctrine was developed over the course of the last decade that essentially elaborated on the 1990s donor dictum that for aid to work, developing country governments needed to be "in the driver's seat." The Paris Declaration on aid effectiveness and the subsequent Accra Agenda for Action (OECD 2005/08) called for aid to be provided in ways that maximize ownership by beneficiary governments and alignment with their development strategies. At the same time, there was a strong emphasis on managing aid for results (which also found expression in the MDGs) and on harmonizing donor processes (IEG 2008). While the results orientation of global funds and programs was applauded, the need for such mechanisms to be integrated into country-level assistance efforts was, as noted above, strongly emphasized. The need to integrate assistance related to HIV/AIDS into national development strategies, for example, was explicitly mentioned in the Paris Declaration. This heavy emphasis on the national development strategies and priorities of developing country governments also helps to explain the localization of the MDGs, which appealed to many donors and some developing country governments as templates for such strategies where they did not already exist.

It is worth mentioning here that the concept of "policy coherence for development" is an important part of the above aid effectiveness doctrine, though a somewhat neglected one in the view of the OECD, which regularly criticizes donors for inconsistencies between their aid and non-aid external policies. This concept recognizes that action outside the borders of developing countries is important for their development. It is, however, usually concerned only with policy consistency, primarily within individual donor countries and specifically between externally oriented ministries. A commitment to policy coherence does not in any strong way entail a commitment to collective action for the purpose of supplying GPGs, even if it might be expected to. Certainly some donors will present their commitment to an open, rule-based, non-discriminatory trading system—a GPG—as an instance of policy coherence. However, this particular GPG is prized primarily for its benefits to the economies of the donors in question.

Third, the notion that aid is used in support of developing countries' priorities is important in maintaining those countries' support for aid and therefore in maintaining aid's diplomatic impact. Bilateral aid is inevitably embedded within diplomatic and trade strategies, even where it is not actually subservient to such strategies. For this reason, quite apart from any attachment to the above aid effectiveness doctrine, a donor country will wish to convey to its bilateral aid partners that its aid is above all responsive to their needs and priorities. In fact, donor countries' attachment to the aid effectiveness doctrine is likely, in part, to be a reflection of their diplomatic and trade objectives.

The several factors just described help to explain the nature of the aid policy narrative that is now dominant, and therefore donors' heavy reliance on country-based aid allocation processes, as well as the related incentive structures within development agencies. Clearly these factors should tend to limit the quantity of aid allocated to GPGs, particularly in a straitened fiscal environment. However, it is less clear exactly where that limit might start to assert itself. As demonstrated above, aid for GPGs has so far been able to grow very substantially, somewhat faster than global aid has grown, without evident impact on the dominant aid policy narrative. At some stage, however, funding for GPGs could become so significant and prominent that the narrative ceases to be relevant, perhaps with something of a lag. At that stage, it might be assumed, the obvious course of action is simply to qualify the narrative in some way, such that it articulates a secondary purpose for aid in supporting the provision of GPGs important for development. But now further barriers arise.

One barrier is that—for full-blown GPGs, as distinct from international public goods benefiting only developing countries—moral objections tend to inhibit reliance on aid. If the weight of benefits is too strongly in favor of wealthier countries, this could lead to reductions not only in public support for aid in developed countries, but also in cooperation from the governments of developing countries.

A second barrier, which arises even where the weight of benefits strongly favors developing countries, is that much of the action necessary to supply certain GPGs—namely those described above as "cumulative" GPGs—must happen, not extraterritorially, but within the borders of fast-growing MICs. These countries are generally characterized by growing inequality, weak social protection systems, and inadequate infrastructure. They are unlikely to pursue policies and programs that yield global benefits without some level of subsidy for the incremental costs of doing so. However, if aid is used to fund such subsidies, this creates the perception that aid is being allocated to richer countries at the expense of poorer ones. It would be a very challenging public relations task to dislodge this perception. Indeed, public relations imperatives are tending in the opposite direction: the United Kingdom and some other donors have announced the cessation of all aid to China, India, and South Africa. Norway is an interesting exception to the general trend: its largest aid recipient in 2012 was Brazil, a principal site of Norwegian-funded action to reduce carbon emissions from deforestation and forest degradation.

A third barrier is one of principle. As just noted, even emerging economies will often require an external subsidy in order to adopt this or that specific policy or measure that yields global benefits. However, a traditional donor country might accept that reality without conceding that the emerging economy in question should make no contribution at all to the cost of providing GPGs. The argument will be that as an economy grows, it should accept an increasing level of overall responsibility for sharing the burden with respect to GPGs. This might mean, for example, that the emerging economy in question is expected to make contributions to certain global mechanisms commensurate with its growing financial capacity, while remaining eligible for international subsidies for certain purposes. Unless the burden-sharing obligation is accepted, the subsidies are withheld. This was the model proposed by Mexico in 2008 for a World Climate Change Fund, known generally as the Green Fund (Quesada 2009). However, gaining the cooperation of major players in such an arrangement, and negotiating precise burden shares, would be very difficult indeed.

This latter set of essentially moral factors—relating to reflexive benefits, the special entitlement of poor countries to aid, and global burden sharing—strongly tends to limit the extent to which the dominant aid policy narrative can be modified or qualified in order to make space for GPGs. Perhaps space can more easily be made for actions in support of GPGs that strongly benefit poor countries where those actions are taken at the global level. The paradigm of such action is support for the development of vaccines and drugs for neglected diseases. The anti-paradigm, however, is the provision of concessional financing to large emerging economies as an inducement to switch from high-emission to low-emission energy generation.

This set of moral factors accounts for various calls for GPG financing to be made separate from and, more important, additional to aid. This call for additionality is a common refrain in the Zedillo report prepared for the Monterrey conference on financing for development (UN 2001), in the 2006 report of the International Task Force on Global Public Goods (ITFGPG 2006), in the 2009 Copenhagen Accord (UNFCCC 2009) with respect to climate change financing, and in several pieces of work led by Inge Kaul, the primary author of the 1999 United Nations Development Programme report that sparked international interest in the topic of GPGs for development (Kaul, Grunberg, and Stern 1999).

The additionality here called for is not merely additionality with respect to baseline levels of aid, but additionality in one of several much stronger senses, according to which the resources in question must not come from the same sources as aid, or disturb the existing pattern of aid allocation to countries and sectors, or be counted as aid in the context of assessing progress toward ODA/GNI targets, most notably the United Nations' 0.7 percent target. For example, the resources might be extracted from the budgets of relevant domestic sectoral ministries, with no offsetting savings harvested from aid programs. Or they might be raised by means of new taxes or levies on certain types of international transactions that are currently untaxed or generate global public bads.

However, such proposals have made no appreciable progress thus far. In part this reflects their complexity and the fact that governments generally prefer to maintain a clear separation between revenue and spending policies. (It must also be assumed that if any new international tax or levy proved particularly lucrative, it would tend to depress aid budgets or else lead to the diversion of some share of the proceeds to domestic purposes.) In part, however, the poor uptake of these proposals likely also reflects a view that the existence of reflexive benefits and displacement effects does not constitute a compelling argument for creating a separate category of international public finance.

Not everybody argues that GPG financing should be additional to aid. Severino and Ray (2009) have called for abandonment of the traditional concept of aid in favor of a broader concept of international public finance (presumed to be concessional in character). This would encompass GPG financing and financing for poverty reduction at the national level. It would essentially be a category of financing for the resolution of a variety of global problems, some of which would concern developing countries only and some of which would concern the world as a whole. However, this call has attracted little support, probably because it is unclear what allocation and burden-sharing principles would apply and how public support, which is strongly linked to the dominant aid policy narrative, would be preserved.

Where the Zedillo strategy would situate GPG financing in a parallel space, not impinging on that occupied by traditional aid, the Severino and Ray strategy would eliminate the distinction entirely. In both cases, any amount of growth in GPG financing would in principle be possible. However, in the real world, GPG financing simply is aid, and its growth is strongly constrained by both the standard aid narrative and the quantity of aid. At some point, the use of aid for GPGs is likely to start grinding against these constraints, and it will not be possible to relieve the resultant pain simply by adding a GPG "wrinkle" to the existing aid policy narrative.

Conclusion

International aid donors are in a fundamentally unstable situation. On one side is a level of investment from traditional donors in GPGs that is increasingly out of balance with their own dominant rationale for aid, and probably with the allocation preferences of their partner countries. On the other side is an increasingly concentrated and assertive group of developing countries whose priorities cannot be read off from the MDGs and who have access to new and flexible sources of finance. They are more often finding themselves in a position to refuse aid that might once have been accepted for its national benefits, even if the motivation for its provision related more to its global benefits. Surely, sooner or later, something has got to give. Unless global aid resumes its rapid growth, either the standard aid rationale will have to be decisively revised, or the growth of aid for GPGs will have to end.

In the latter outcome, traditional donors would flatline or reduce aid for GPGs, restore faith with their own policy narratives, and compete in bilateral arenas with newer donors. In the alternative outcome, they would further increase aid for GPGs, substantially revise their narratives and try to work in a complementary fashion with newer donors. In other words, aid for GPGs would either subside or move to the foreground in the narratives and portfolios of traditional donors. Subsidence looks unlikely, given the trends of the last two decades and the nature of the challenges ahead. So a sensible modification of the dominant aid policy narrative should be contemplated. How such a modification might be undertaken is the subject of chapter 6.

Box 5.2 What Young Development Professionals Think About Financing Global Public Goods

Nasser Brahim, Climate Investment Funds

Of the four global public good (GPG) topic areas introduced in the beginning of this chapter, the climate-related narrative and evidence that follows focus primarily on the financing of climate mitigation activities. The frictions described in the chapter between the dominant aid policy narrative and the evidenced practice of increasing financing for GPGs are very real in the context of climate mitigation given the moral, public relations, and delivery challenges noted. However, another topic area mentioned deserves arguably greater attention in the context of climate change and the role of development finance institutions like the World Bank Group in 2025, namely, sustainable [management and] consumption of internationally-important resources.

Increasing financing for sustainable management of forest, fresh water, coastal, and marine ecosystems and consumption of their goods and services should result in both reduced emissions and increased resilience of the poorest and most vulnerable people to the effects of climate variability and change. This "sustainable management" subsector of adaptation merits and could sustain large growth in public financing flows by 2025 and beyond, building substantially on existing trends. After all, there is no evidence to suggest that the current pace of incremental mitigation action will solve the climate crisis completely, leaving all countries, including poor and vulnerable populations now concentrated in middle-income countries (MICs), to cope with the unavoidable and residual consequences.

Unlike on the mitigation side of the equation, financing for climate adaptation fits nicely into the dominant aid policy narrative described in this chapter. The benefits are national or local; the purpose is to reduce poverty or increase welfare; and the provision of such finance can be integrated in donor countries' trade and diplomatic strategies as well as the mainstream operations of development finance institutions, such as the World Bank Group. Through their actions and commitments, donor countries have shown that while they may not formally acknowledge "historical responsibility" for climate change, they are able to justify and deliver large levels of "new" financing for adaptation, including through multilateral institutions like the Bank. But current levels of financing are in no way adequate "compensation" for the historical failures of rich countries to provide their fare share of GPGs.

I was in the Bella Centre assisting the chair of the Small Island Developing States negotiating block when the resolution recognizing the Copenhagen Accord was passed. A major sticking point for the support of island leaders from Grenada and the Maldives was donors' agreement to provide "balanced allocation [of support] between adaptation and mitigation." Why then, do recent analyzes show that climate finance flows for mitigation have vastly outstripped those for adaptation, including in the public finance category? The multiwindow Climate Investment Funds (CIF), a microcosm of the vast climate finance space, illustrates this point. The CIF's adaptation financing window—the Pilot Program for Climate Resilience (PPCR)—accounts for roughly 17 percent of the $7.6 billion in funds pledged to the CIF by donors to date, with the balance going to mitigation programs. Of the $1.1 billion that donors have pledged to the CIF after the initial start-up phase (establishing pledges totaled $6.5 billion), less than $200 million have been for the PPCR. Meanwhile, the PPCR supports a greater number of countries than any other CIF program.

Substantially increasing funds for the PPCR and for broader adaptation finance, with the goal of reaching at least parity with mitigation finance by 2025, should be the priority of donors and the MDBs. Also, sustain investments in current PPCR countries who have both paid substantial transaction costs to participate in the program and benefitted greatly from the new experience and capacity in climate resilient development planning and implementation. Open up the PPCR to the scores of countries knocking on the CIF's doors, and welcome the participation of MICs with large economies. A large proportion of the demand for adaptation finance in 2025 will come from them, and they still look to the Bank's technical and financial assistance to help them solve long-term and difficult challenges and to crowd in private finance.

Given the risks and long lead times associated with these types of investments, the World Bank will also need to build the foundations for them now by investing in human capacity within the World Bank and the International Finance Corporation (IFC) and increasing the prominence of climate risk and adaptation in dialogues with public and private sector clients. Climate risk and adaptation curriculum (an "Adaptation Academy"), similar to that now used to train environmental and social safeguards specialists, could be developed and mandated with different tracks for sector specialists, investment officers, and country directors and managers. Achievement of annual training targets should be developed and included in performance assessments of operational staff. This would ensure that World Bank Group representatives involved in policy and technical dialogues would be capable of offering the best advice to their client counterparts.

This strategy ultimately hinges on two preconditions: wealthy countries delivering on their political commitment and moral obligation to increase financing for adaptation, and the Bank and IFC showing top performance as a financial and technical mediator for adaptation financing programs like the PPCR. Only with "cash in hand," a good track record, and the above-noted capacities can Bank representatives be taken seriously by clients as they work to steer them toward a more climate-resilient development.

Notes

1. All funding amounts cited in this chapter are in U.S. dollars.
2. This is not quite the same as distinguishing them, based on Sandler (1998), according to their "aggregation technology"—best shot, summative, or weakest link. Sandler's approach, which has been widely taken up, is essentially quantitative. It is concerned with the manner in which the total quantity of the good supplied depends upon the quantities supplied by each of the relevant actors. The mode-of-production approach is qualitative. The main difference between the two approaches is that in the mode-of-production approach, structured public goods include weakest-link public goods, but much else besides. For example, regional water resources management regimes and regional transport corridors are structured public goods, but not

weakest-link public goods, because non-cooperation by one party may reduce but not necessarily eliminate their benefits to other parties.

3. Reisen, Soto, and Weithöner (2004) claim to find such an effect, though not large.

4. Raffer (1999) estimates 25.3 percent; Reisen, Soto, and Weithöner (2004), 30 percent; World Bank (2001), 12.5 percent; te Velde, Morrissey, and Hewitt (2002), 8.8 percent (though they allow that this might be a substantial underestimate); and Anand (2002), only 3.7 percent. These estimates include aid for regional public goods. Reisen, Soto, and Weithöner (2004) suggest that about half of aid for international public goods is for GPGs and half for RPGs.

5. Of the $7 billion total, the World Bank had operational responsibility for about $1 billion and acted as trustee for about $5 billion. The Climate Investment Funds were not included in IEG 2011b, but were included in IEG 2011a.

References

Anand, P. B. 2002. "Financing the Provision of Global Public Goods." Discussion Paper 2002/110, World Institute for Development Economics Research, United Nations University.

BMGF (Bill & Melinda Gates Foundation). 2011. *Building Better Lives Together*. 2011 Annual Report. Seattle, WA: BMGF.

DfID (U.K. Department for International Development). 2011. *UK Aid: Changing Lives, Delivering Results*. London: DfID.

IEG (Independent Evaluation Group). 2008. *Annual Review of Development Effectiveness 2008: Shared Global Challenges*. Washington, DC: IEG, World Bank.

———. 2011a. *Trust Fund Support for Development: An Evaluation of the World Bank's Trust Fund Portfolio*. Washington, DC: IEG, World Bank.

———. 2011b. *The World Bank's Involvement in Global and Regional Partnership Programs: An Independent Assessment*. Washington, DC: IEG, World Bank.

IMF (International Monetary Fund). 2012. *World Economic Outlook 2012: Growth Resuming, Dangers Remain*. Washington, DC: IMF.

ITFGPG (International Task Force on Global Public Goods). 2006. *Meeting Global Challenges: International Cooperation in the National Interest—Report of the International Task Force on Global Public Goods*. ITFGPG, Department for Development Policy, Ministry for Foreign Affairs, Stockholm, Sweden.

Kaul, Inge, Isabelle Grunberg, and Marc A. Stern, eds. 1999. *Global Public Goods: International Cooperation in the 21st Century*. United Nations Development Programme. Oxford, U.K.: Oxford University Press.

Kaul, Inge, Pedro Conceição, Katell Le Goulven, and Ronald U. Mendoza, eds. 2003. *Providing Global Public Goods: Managing Globalization*. Oxford, U.K.: Oxford University Press.

Moss, Todd, and Benjamin Leo. 2011. "IDA at 65: Heading toward Retirement or a Fragile Lease on Life?" Working Paper 246, Center for Global Development, Washington, DC.

OECD. 2005/08. "The Paris Declaration on Aid Effectiveness (2005) and the Accra Agenda for Action (2008)." Paris.

———. 2013. "OECD DAC Statistics on Climate-Related Aid." Paris.

Quesada, Juan Rafael Elvira. 2009. "Mexico's Proposal of a World Climate Change Fund (The Green Fund)." Mexico Ministry for the Environment and Natural Resources, PowerPoint presentation at 2009 United Nations Climate Change Conference, Copenhagen, December 2009.

Raffer, Kunibert. 1999. "ODA and Global Public Goods: A Trend Analysis of Past and Present Spending Patterns." Office of Development Studies, Bureau for Development Policy, United Nations Development Programme, New York.

Reisen, Helmut, Marcelo Soto, and Thomas Weithöner. 2004. "Financing Global and Regional Public Goods Through ODA: Analysis and Evidence from the OECD Creditor Reporting System." Working Paper 232, OECD Development Centre, Paris.

Sandler, Todd. 1998. "Global and Regional Public Goods: A Prognosis for Collective Action." *Fiscal Studies* 19 (3): 221–47.

Severino, Jean-Michel, and Olivier Ray. 2009. "The End of ODA: Death and Rebirth of a Global Public Policy." Working Paper 167, Center for Global Development, Washington, DC.

Sumner, Andy. 2012. "Where Do the World's Poor Live? A New Update." Working Paper 393, Institute of Development Studies, Brighton, U.K.

te Velde, Dirk Willem, Oliver Morrissey, and Adrian Hewitt. 2002. "Allocating Aid to International Public Goods." In *International Public Goods: Incentives, Measurement and Financing*, edited by Marco Ferroni and Ashoka Mody, 23–28. Netherlands: Kluwer.

UN. 2001. "Report of the High-level Panel on Financing for Development." Document A/55/1000, United Nations General Assembly, 55th session, United Nations, New York.

UNFCCC (United Nations Framework Convention on Climate Change). 2009. Copenhagen Accord. Draft decision –/CP.15. UNFCCC Conference of the Parties, 15th session. Copenhagen, December 7–18.

Vandemoortele, Jan. 2012. "Advancing the Global Development Agenda Post-2015: Some Thoughts, Ideas and Practical Suggestions." Background paper prepared for the UN System Task Team on the Post-2015 UN Development Agenda, United Nations New York.

Walz, Julie, and Vijaya Ramachandran. 2011. "Brave New World: A Literature Review of Emerging Donors and the Changing Nature of Foreign Assistance." Working Paper 273, Center for Global Development, Washington, DC.

World Bank. 2001. *Global Development Finance: Building Coalitions for Effective Development Finance*. Washington, DC: World Bank.

———. 2007. "Global Public Goods: a Framework for the Role of the World Bank." Paper DC2007-0020, World Bank Development Committee, World Bank, Washington, DC.

CHAPTER 6

Aiding Global Public Policy: Rethinking Rationales and Roles

Robin Davies

Traditional development agencies, emerging aid providers, and recipient countries are in strong agreement that the fundamental purpose of aid is to help achieve the development priorities of sovereign states in need. This agreement serves both aid effectiveness and national interest objectives. At the same time, a range of global problems is rendering development gains ever more precarious and making increasing calls on aid budgets. Such problems include instability in highly integrated global markets for food, fuel, and finance, natural resource depletion, the persistence or emergence of infectious diseases, and the increasing impacts of climate change. Moreover, after growing by some 60 percent over the previous decade, global aid peaked in 2010 and now looks set to decline or at best stagnate, as most donor countries pursue fiscal consolidation and public debt reduction strategies and as more and more countries graduate from low-income status.

So now there is a fixed "lid" on aid, growing pressures to apply it to global challenges, and a dominant aid narrative that says it should be applied to the national challenges of the poorest countries. As argued in the previous chapter, at least one of these three things has to give, sooner or later. Either the purpose of aid must be reconceived, or more aid must be provided, or financing for global public goods (GPGs) must be mobilized in some new way without prejudice to existing aid budgets.

It is reasonable to assume that aid volume will not continue to grow at anything like the rate witnessed in the decade up to 2010 and that there is no realistic prospect that international public financing additional to current levels of aid will be mobilized on any significant scale by means of "innovative" financing mechanisms. Therefore, it must be concluded that if aid for GPGs is to be maintained or increased, the purpose of aid must at some point be reconceived—a corollary of which is that the institutions and instruments used to deliver it are likely to require a degree of modification in order to maintain their fitness for purpose.

This chapter proposes a relatively conservative modification of the rationale for aid, which carries implications for resource allocation, delivery mechanisms,

To see Robin Davies discuss global public policy aid: http://youtu.be/HdSJS4AH2X0

the institutional and global governance of the relevant financial flows, and also to an extent for the measurement of those flows. It complements the previous chapter, but goes beyond posing a quandary to sketching the broad features of a possible way forward. The structure of this chapter is as follows. The first Section explores the formal definition of official development assistance (ODA) as it stands and finds that it can already accommodate a concept of aid that is somewhat broader, and more favourable to GPGs, than the concept currently in general use. The second section examines some obstacles that stand in the way of making greater use of the multilateral GPG delivery "system." The third section sets out in broad terms some proposals for overcoming these obstacles and for mobilizing and allocating financing for multilateral GPG-related efforts. The conclusion summarizes the foregoing discussion in the form of five general recommendations for action.

Revising the Rationale for Aid and Redefining ODA

There is at the time of writing a move afoot to "modernize" the concept of ODA. The 2012 High-Level Meeting of the Organisation for Economic Co-operation and Development's (OECD) Development Assistance Committee (DAC) determined that the DAC should "elaborate a proposal for a new measure of total official support for development" and "investigate whether any resulting new measures of external development finance … suggest the need to modernize the ODA concept" (OECD 2012: paragraph 17). This move appears to have been driven by a desire, not necessarily to alter fundamentally the concept of ODA, but rather to achieve better recognition of other expenditures relevant to development and explore ways of including as ODA some expenditures that are developmentally motivated but not currently captured by the ODA definition. An example is providing official support for inclusive business ventures in low-income countries by means of guarantees and equity investments—which do not figure as "flows" or as concessional expenditures under the current ODA definition (OECD 2008).[1] There is also an ongoing debate about the ODA status of some official loans to developing countries—loans that are developmentally motivated and meet a technical grant-element test[2] but are not actually concessional in character—in that the interest rate charged to recipients is above the donor's cost of borrowing, which is currently extremely low.

In short, the DAC's objective, or at least the objective of some of its members, is to tidy up the ODA concept by folding in some additional expenditures and pushing out others while at the same time investigating the use of a broader expenditure category that would incorporate ODA and capture total official support for development more fully, in some sense, than existing measures. Presumably, some donors calculate that if they fail to expand the ODA definition in the way that they might wish, they will still be able to incorporate the expenditures in question within the broader measure of total official support for development. It is conceivable that some DAC members would wish to exclude financing for GPGs, most notably climate change financing, from a revised ODA definition and include it instead under the broader concept of total official support for development. However, it is likely that an overwhelming majority of members would wish it to remain within the ODA category where, by default, it currently sits. The decision to revisit the ODA concept certainly does not appear to have been motivated by any broad-based desire to exclude GPG financing from ODA.

Just as there is no push to exclude financing for GPGs from ODA, there is no evident push to give it explicit recognition as a claim on ODA budgets. At present most such financing gets counted as ODA simply because it is generally provided in the form of grants to international organizations that are recognized as development organizations and generally ends up flowing on concessional terms to one or another country on the DAC's list of ODA-eligible countries, which excludes only high-income countries.[3]

Even grants to the Global Environment Facility (GEF), established with the explicitly limited aim of financing national and regional project costs only insofar as they yield global benefits, are 100 percent reportable as ODA.[4] Some core funding for international organizations that have a substantial normative function—such as the World Health Organization, the UN Food and Agriculture Organization and the International Labour Organization—is excluded from ODA and is generally drawn from the budgets of the relevant domestic ministries in contributing countries, but the amount of money concerned is not large. The vast bulk of international public financing for GPGs comes from ODA.

The formal concept of ODA has several elements.[5] First, ODA involves a flow of resources from the official sector, either from a developed to a recognized developing country or from a developed country to a recognized international development organization.[6] Second, the flow must have the "main objective" of promoting the economic development and welfare of developing countries. Third, it must be concessional in character, meaning that it must incorporate a subsidy. If the flow takes the form of a loan, the loan must be equivalent to a grant worth no less than 25 percent of its face value, and principal repayments figure as negative ODA in the year in which they are made.[7] ODA is fundamentally aid as given by donors. Measuring ODA measures donors' fiscal effort. It does not measure aid as experienced by recipients,[8] both because much ODA does not actually cross borders and because some ODA is not passed on to developing countries in concessional form by some international organizations.[9]

The ODA definition looks to be quite narrow in two respects. First, it would appear at first glance to exclude expenditures that benefit developing countries but do not involve cross-border flows, such as expenditures on aid administration and on universities that might in some cases educate students from developing countries at less than full cost. Second, it also appears at first glance to exclude expenditures related to GPGs that are primarily of benefit to people in or from developing countries, such as research undertaken by developed countries' national research institutes into neglected tropical diseases or smallholder agricultural productivity, and, controversially, costs associated with the presence in developed countries of refugees and asylum-seekers from developing countries.

However, in practice the DAC has taken a series of ad hoc decisions that have incorporated these and other expenditures within the category of ODA by fiat. The core of the ODA concept has not, in that process, been revisited. As already noted, recent moves to "modernize" the concept seem unlikely to involve fundamental reconsideration of the ODA definition.

What notion of aid, then, would be more conducive to the allocation of an adequate amount of aid for GPGs? (Rather than seeking to quantify "adequate," we simply assume that an adequate amount would be equal to or greater than the present amount.) Broadly speaking, such a notion might have several features. First, it would still be a notion of aid, not of something much broader, such as "official global public finance."[10] That is, it would relate to public expenditures that are primarily for the benefit of developing countries, including expenditures on GPGs important for development. Second, it would recognize the fact that international organizations are in themselves GPGs, as well as mediums for the provision of GPGs through action in developing countries, and would give effect to this recognition by counting as aid all contributions to a defined group of international development organizations, regardless of the specific utilization of those contributions. Third, it would incorporate a concessionality requirement, but allow that contributions to some international development organizations might be used by those organizations to fund non-concessional expenditures with a developmental objective.

Would this be a very substantial departure from the concept of aid embodied in ODA? In fact, it would be no departure at all. It is quite possible within the existing formal definition of ODA to give substantially greater prominence to financing for GPGs through international organizations. It is common but not entirely correct to regard ODA as a flow to developing countries, with multilateral organizations functioning as one channel for ODA flows. On more careful examination, the ODA concept gives multilateral organizations a more privileged role than that. ODA is defined as "those flows to countries and territories on the DAC List of ODA Recipients *and to multilateral institutions* which are provided by official agencies ... and each transaction of which is administered with the promotion of the economic development and welfare of developing countries as its main objective; and is concessional in character" (OECD 2008). The institutions mentioned are, like developing country aid recipients, identified in a separate list that is regularly revised. So, putting the point very roughly, to fund multilateral organizations to do whatever they do is to provide ODA, by definition. Some of their outflows do not meet the ODA definition, but that has no bearing on the ODA status of contributions to them.

It would perhaps be less confusing if concessional outflows from international organizations were not labeled as ODA in statistical reporting, such that the term "ODA" were applied only to outflows from original sources, and a term like "official development finance" (ODF), or country programmable aid (CPA), or something else that measures aid received, were applied to inflows to developing countries. However, the key point is that the existing concept of aid in fact is not unfriendly toward aid financing for GPGs. There is certainly no need to turn the tables by replacing the concept of ODA with that of official global public finance (as above) or some similar construct.

The central idea at work here, requiring no change in the formal concept of ODA, is to change the way we think about international development organizations, which play an indispensable role in supporting the provision of GPGs through their global-, regional- and country-level work. Rather than thinking of such organizations primarily as channels for aid to developing countries, we may think of them primarily as objects of aid in their own right. Essentially, funding to them is aid if their mandate is developmental.

The notion of aid outlined above involves not a change in the formal concept of aid, but rather a change in the rationale for, or the narrative about, aid. This change would involve moving to a two-part, public good rationale for aid. According to this rationale, aid supports the provision of national public goods[11] for growth and poverty reduction[12] and the provision of regional and GPGs to meet transnational challenges of particular importance for developing countries. Funding for international development organizations would be considered to inhabit the latter category, even where their country-specific operations are concerned. Thus, roughly speaking, bilateral aid (aid to countries) would be about national public goods; multilateral aid (aid to international development organizations) would be about GPGs.

If strictly accepted, this approach would have substantial implications for the way one would think about, and in fact manage, the operations of both bilateral and multilateral agencies. One implication is that it becomes unimportant and indeed unhelpful to distinguish so sharply between the hard and the soft arms of the multilateral development banks (MDBs). Currently it is the case that all capital and grant contributions to the World Bank Group are considered aid and that outflows from the International Development Association (IDA), but not from the International Bank for Reconstruction and Development (IBRD),[13] are considered aid. IDA, under the approach proposed above, would no longer be described, as it is now, as the "aid agency" of the World Bank Group, because its outflows would be treated in the same way as IBRD outflows for accounting purposes—in the "development financing received" category.

A second implication is that given an explicit license or even a mandate to concentrate more of its resources on the provision of GPGs, consistent with the above notion of aid, the World Bank would be better able to offer incentives to clients in the form of flexible financing packages, blending funds borrowed against its capital and funds received from donors in grant or at least concessional form. At present, such blending is practiced mainly in order to achieve financing terms of intermediate hardness for countries graduating from IDA to IBRD financing—though it has also been practiced to some extent in connection with global environmental public goods, through the blending of GEF resources or resources from the Climate Investment Funds (CIFs) with resources from the nonconcessional arms of the MDBs. The same approach would be open to other MDBs.

A third implication is that the job descriptions of both bilateral and multilateral development agencies would be sharpened considerably. Bilateral agencies—in line with the two-part, public good rationale outlined above—would be less likely to attempt direct support for the provision of GPGs and more likely to provide such support through the multilateral system. Multilateral agencies, and particularly the MDBs, might well continue to be strongly oriented toward support for the priorities of sovereign states but, with an explicit GPG mandate and more flexible financing instruments, would seek to select and manage their investments in a way that is consistent with the objectives of an overarching GPG strategy.

The two-part rationale offered here, like any rationale for aid, faces an important test: Would it weaken public and political support for aid? It seems unlikely that it would do so. For one thing, it is still recognizably a concept of aid, unlike the alternative concept of official global public finance. If anything, it sharpens the focus of bilateral aid on poverty reduction. Further, it gives a clearer account of the role of international organizations, which at present are often perceived either as servants or competitors of bilateral development agencies. Finally, it does not take multilateral organizations away from country-based work, on which their influence and credibility partly depends, but it does add a higher, global purpose to that work. This last point is important from a substantive perspective too: It is a mistake to think that all GPGs can be provided in a sort of global ether. Many such goods, as noted in the previous chapter, are provided in a cumulative fashion—through coordinated or replicated action across multiple countries, supported where necessary by advice and incentives.

The Multilateral GPG Delivery System

Is the multilateral GPG delivery "system" actually up to the task proposed for it above? Even if more public finance were supplied for GPGs, and even if this use of public finance met with no resistance from any quarter, there remains the question of whether the multilateral system is well adapted to support the production and adoption of GPGs important for development. There are several reasons to believe that it is not. These relate broadly to an absence of overarching strategy, a failure to integrate efforts in various ways, a bias toward some types of GPG at the expense of others, and an unsystematic approach to evaluation and learning.

The Strategic Deficit

With one exception, there has never been an attempt to organize the work of international organizations, let alone development agencies in general, in support of GPGs. Priorities and mechanisms have for the most part emerged piecemeal. This is reflected in the composition of the World Bank's portfolio of global and regional partnership programs, which number some 120. It is reflected also in the array of mechanisms that contribute to the achievement of global health objectives, as well as the growing stable of mechanisms that seek to achieve climate change mitigation or "green growth" objectives. The exception just noted is the Consultative Group on International Agricultural Research (CGIAR), which is trying to implement a strategic approach to the definition of research priorities for, and the allocation of resources to, its 15 affiliated research centers. Even here, though, there is considerable uncertainty about the extent to which individual donors and individual centers will cooperate in a sustained manner.

Outcome-oriented financiers, particularly private foundations, will often perceive cross-institutional strategies as straitjackets or disdain the bureaucracy associated with centralized resource allocation. One reason for this is the view that centralization and bureaucracy are antithetical to innovation—that modular, nimble, and competing approaches are better able to achieve results where innovation is needed. To make matters worse, individual bilateral donors for the most do not themselves have GPG financing strategies. In allocating resources to global programs, they tend to finance the priorities of today, often at the expense of the priorities of yesterday. The World Bank, which plays a central role as trustee for the majority of the donor funds allocated to global mechanisms, also has no explicit policy basis for determining which GPG-related priorities should be primary, taking into account likely development impacts, the scale of resourcing likely to be available, and its own institutional capabilities. Its 2007 GPG policy framework does not serve this purpose and cannot have been intended to do so.

Often the strategic deficit described above is evident even within single sectors, most notably that of global health. It is not possible, for example, to discern any logic underlying the distribution of resources between mechanisms such as the Global Fund to Fight AIDS, Tuberculosis and Malaria (GFATM), the GAVI Alliance (formerly the Global Alliance for Vaccines and Immunisation), the 2006 pilot Advance Market Commitment for pneumococcal vaccines, and the many product development partnerships working on vaccines, drugs, and diagnostics.[14] The 2001 Commission on Macroeconomics and Health (WHO 2001), it should be acknowledged, did provide reasoned recommendations relating to the allocation of resources for public health, including resources for GPGs. The commission argued for the allocation of $7 billion in ODA per annum to GPGs in the health sector, within total health sector spending of $38 billion by 2015. It also provided a breakdown of how these resources might be used. However, there is no evidence that its GPG-related recommendations achieved any impact beyond the creation of the GFATM.

Fragmentation of Effort

GPG financing mechanisms are extremely numerous and for the most part small and issue specific. The mean fund size for the global and regional partnership funds in which the World Bank is involved is $58 million, given a total of $7 billion across 117 funds (IEG 2011b: table 2.1). The median size is not known but would be much lower, as most funds are quite small—86 percent of the money is in one-quarter of the funds. Only a handful of GPG mechanisms are substantially larger, most notably the "big five": the GEF, GFATM, GAVI Alliance, CGIAR, and the CIFs.

The GPG financing mechanisms with which the World Bank is associated have tended to emerge incrementally;[15] for every problem, or set of closely related problems, a fund is formed with associated governance arrangements, resource (usually grant) allocation processes, and administrative support structures. They are incremental in other senses too. First, they are generally separate from and supplemental to the country operations of the Bank and other development agencies. And second, in some cases they provide resources to countries only for the incremental costs of delivering global benefits. While the concept of incremental cost is clear enough, actually calculating the level of such costs for resource allocation purposes has proven to be difficult. In fact, it has been judged ultimately unproductive by the GEF, which in 2007 retreated to the much looser requirement that investments be based on "incremental cost reasoning" rather than incremental cost assessment.

The fragmentation and the related incrementalism described above inflicts quite high transaction costs on the countries that might benefit from GPG financing mechanisms, as well as the organizations that host them. Those costs include, most importantly, a diversion of attention away from the main strategic priorities and decision-making processes of the relevant government or organization.

It might be argued that economies of scope are important in the production of GPGs, such that numerous mechanisms should be tolerated rather than seeking to overconsolidate. The point made earlier about the importance of diversity and competition in spurring innovation is also relevant here. However, it seems beyond doubt that in many cases GPG financing mechanisms, without good reason, have taken on lives of their own, becoming in effect new micro-development agencies that compete for the attention of donors and partner governments.

For the most part, then, GPG financing mechanisms do not occupy a central place in either the mainstream operations of country-oriented international development organizations or in the national development strategies of partner governments. Real complementarity—that is, coordination and mutual reinforcement—between these mechanisms and those that finance national public goods is absent. However, partial exceptions to this observation exist in the case of larger mechanisms. The GFATM, for example, wields enough market power to influence the allocation of complementary resources by donors. In addition, both the GFATM and the GAVI Alliance have broadened the scope of their investments over time in response to criticisms that they did not sufficiently recognize the importance of health system strengthening at the national level. And the GEF by design employs cofinancing, blending its resources with those from mainstream sources. These instances of complementarity are described as partial, however, because from the developing country perspective there are still many actors and products in play, with correspondingly high transaction costs.

The case of the CIFs, in particular the Clean Technology Fund (CTF), bears closer examination. By contrast with the situation in the GEF, in the CTF cofinancing is more an operating principle than a requirement. For reasons of speed and efficiency, the CTF has allocated resources as far as possible in conjunction with mainstream IBRD and IDA operations, or the equivalent operations of other MDBs, using those resources to generate incentives for low-emission investments. CTF funds are used to soften the terms of, or grant-finance discrete components of, larger financing packages—which is attractive both to geographic departments of the MDBs and to their customers.

While the GEF's 2007 shift to incremental cost "reasoning" effectively made its investments complementary in the same sense as the CTF's, there is an important difference. Although technically part of the Bank, the GEF is its own institution, whose involvement in a transaction adds greatly to processing times and transaction costs for all parties. It is not merely a pool of resources that can be blended with others. The CTF, admittedly, is not exactly the latter either, as it has its own governance arrangements. Nevertheless, the way it is managed does provide a higher degree of complementarity with mainstream MDB operations than is typical of other GPG financing mechanisms. This strength of the CTF model is, at the same time, also a source of weakness. The CTF's light management arrangements mean that it is at the mercy of the vagaries of demand from geographic areas of the participating MDBs. It has limited capacity to generate such demand or to establish and enforce internal accountability arrangements within the banks for activities already approved.

The underlying problem with existing GPG financing mechanisms is that they exist at the margins of their host institutions, such that they are either good at complementarity but organizationally weak or less good at complementarity but organizationally stronger. Ideally, their priorities would be central priorities of their host organizations. Were that the case, aggregating resources in GPG financing mechanisms might not always be necessary. In principle, at least for cumulative GPGs, it might be sufficient simply to use existing country-oriented financing mechanisms and instruments, but with a modified approach to program selection that favors programs with greater global benefits over those with lesser benefits and seeks to support coordinated or parallel interventions in multiple countries.

Bias Toward Some Global Public Goods

The existing array of GPG financing mechanisms tends to favor certain types of GPG, namely, those described in the previous chapter as "singular" and "structured" GPGs. There is considerable, if still inadequate, resourcing for agricultural and health research for the production of singular GPGs. There is much support for global and regional institutions that mediate international cooperation on a regional or topical basis to produce structured GPGs. But there is much less in the way of support for the provision of cumulative GPGs, which depend on serial or parallel action in all countries that are particularly important for the solution of a problem. The Multilateral Fund of the Montreal Protocol, which supports developing countries in eliminating ozone-depleting substances, is one example of a GPG financing mechanism for a cumulative GPG. World Bank–managed mechanisms, such as the Forest Carbon Partnership Facility, the Forest Investment Fund, and the CTF, are other examples, though they are only conceived as pilots and do not claim to be able to take in a large number of the important countries, whether considered as such for their impact on emissions from deforestation or from energy generation.

The imbalance noted here is not an arbitrary one. Singular and structured GPGs are suitable for stand-alone funding, which can be provided directly to the singular producer or to the structuring institution. Cumulative GPGs can only be provided through mainstream operations, drawing as necessary on concessional resources for incentive purposes. Thus priorities and mechanisms that are perceived and often conceived as marginal to those operations are of little relevance to the provision of cumulative GPGs.

Evaluation and Learning

GPG financing mechanisms are often individually well evaluated. The GEF, for example, has a strong evaluation office and is also evaluated indirectly by the World Bank's Independent Evaluation Group (IEG), which regularly examines the quality and impact of the Bank's partnerships with global funds. The major global health mechanisms are also closely scrutinized and again also indirectly by the IEG. The CIFs are at the time of writing the subject of a major evaluation, which will make findings on impacts achieved and lessons learned since the establishment of the CIFs in 2008. The CGIAR system was fully evaluated by the IEG in 2004, and the findings of that evaluation were important in shaping the systemic reforms subsequently put in place.

However, there is a deficiency at the level of strategic and comparative evaluation. This can be seen, for example, in the way that World Bank–related GPG mechanisms were, in a sense, evaluated twice over—through the IEG's twin, overlapping 2011 evaluations of the Bank's involvement in global and regional partnership programs (IEG 2011b) and of its trust fund portfolio (IEG 2011a)—yet not evaluated in a way that specifically considers the impact and coherence of the Bank's involvement in GPG financing mechanisms.

There has been only one dedicated effort to assess the World Bank's work in support of GPGs—the IEG's 2008 Annual Review of Development Effectiveness, which took as its special theme "shared global challenges" (IEG 2008). However, this review reached quite broad and predictable conclusions about the disconnect between country priorities and global priorities. It did not make actionable recommendations as to how the Bank might better marshal its resources—IBRD, IDA, International Finance Corporation (IFC), and trust fund resources—in support of GPGs. Its recommendations set out no operationally specific policy framework for such investments and, therefore, represented no advance on the Bank's own 2007 framework. No other MDB has even attempted something comparable to the IEG's 2008 exercise.

Individual bilateral donors likewise do not conduct comparative evaluations of the GPG financing mechanisms they support. Their mechanism-specific evaluations tend to be directed toward those mechanisms in which, for often purely accidental reasons, they already have a significant financing stake. This multilateral and bilateral evaluation deficit mirrors the strategy deficit already discussed.

A Way Forward

What follows takes a more constructive turn. It is suggested that a number of measures would need to be taken in order to make the World Bank, other MDBs, and other multilateral organizations fit as GPG delivery mechanisms. Those measures, set out in general terms below, include rethinking financing instruments and programming strategies; reforming policy and governance frameworks; aligning country and global priorities; streamlining the mobilization and allocation of concessional financing for GPGs; and managing for impact.

Rethinking Instruments and Strategies

Suppose that the World Bank has at its disposal a substantial, IDA-like pool of concessional resources to supplement the resources it can raise on its own account. Suppose also that this pool of resources, unlike IDA, is available for use in any developing country. The question then is how might all the Bank's financial resources be deployed so as to achieve a meaningful impact on key global challenges? The answer suggested below involves three strategies: blending, replication, and leveraging.

Consider first the concept of blending—that is, the blending of concessional and nonconcessional resources within financing packages. At present, as noted earlier, blending is used primarily to wean countries off concessional financing, though it has been used to some extent to create incentives for action on global environmental public goods in the past and also to promote food security in the aftermath of the food price crisis of 2007–08, via the Global Agriculture and Food Security Program.

The latter type of blending is not much remarked upon, perhaps in part because it tends to involve the spending of concessional resources in middle-income countries rather than low-income countries. (Countries in the latter category will generally not accept financing on nonconcessional terms, even with blended packages.) However, there is clearly considerable scope to induce action on GPGs through the provision of financing on sufficiently favorable terms, as has been demonstrated by the experience of the CIFs.

Here "sufficiently favorable" means simply favorable enough to persuade a government to opt for a better alternative over a worse one, in circumstances where the better alternative helps to supply a GPG and the worse one would have been acceptable to the government in question when considered in purely national interest terms. This is quite different from an approach where financing terms are determined by the characteristics of the borrower or of the investment itself, and also from an approach that seeks to limit the use of the concessional component of the package to support for the "incremental" costs of supplying a global benefit. What is here proposed is rather that the concessional financing be used, as sparingly as possible, to create incentives for action.

Now consider the concept of replication—that is, the replication of programs across countries to achieve a sort of domino effect, spreading impact but also creating shared and linked strategies that are mutually reinforcing. This happens now on an ad hoc basis—for example, in the case of support for smart energy grids or rapid urban transit systems—but there is at present no strategic approach to replicating programs, within or across major multilateral organizations, for the purpose of increasing the supply of GPGs.

There are few incentives to do this. MDB staff would generally prefer to be known for creating blueprints than for applying others' blueprints, and their clients are on the whole resistant to investment proposals that appear to be driven by the financier or cut-and-pasted from other and quite different country contexts. However, deliberate and strategic replication would seem to be essential if cumulative GPGs are to be supplied in sufficient quantities. Programs with similar objectives need to be supported in multiple countries, and those programs should as far as possible have similar characteristics for reasons both of efficiency and mutual reinforcement.

And now consider the concept of leveraging—which is here intended to refer not merely to cofinancing but rather to the use of concessional resources to mobilize private investment for large and decisive impacts. ODA accounts for only about 7 percent of the total flow of resources from developed to developing countries (DI 2013), and cannot by itself achieve such impacts. It must wherever possible be combined with, and influence the allocation of, non-ODA flows. At present ODA is used to create incentives for private investment in at least five distinct ways:

- It funds risk reduction (by providing equity, quasi-equity and guarantees).
- It backs the issuance of bonds to finance large-scale, high-impact development interventions that promise to deliver long-run savings net of repayments to bondholders (the International Finance Facility for Immunisation, or IFFIm, being the only significant example of this approach to date).
- It provides, through "pull mechanisms," price incentives for investment in the discovery, development, and dissemination of products important for development (examples of which include the Pneumococcal AMC vaccines and the AgResults initiative).
- It helps developing countries participate in international permit trading mechanisms associated with the pricing of externalities (for example, the Clean Development Mechanism [CDM] or arrangements aimed at reducing emissions from deforestation and forest degradation and enhancing forest carbon stocks [REDD+]).
- It funds the public side of public-private product development partnerships (such as the Medicines for Malaria Venture [MMV] and other Geneva-based health sector partnerships).

A further possibility, which combines elements of the second and third approaches above, is the use of aid to back the issuance of "impact bonds," where returns to investors, and therefore costs to donors, vary with the results achieved.[16]

In addition to its support for risk reduction through the World Bank Group's IFC, which for the most part is not provided in the service of GPGs, the World Bank has been involved in a number of GPG-related efforts that fall into categories above, namely, the carbon funds, the Pneumococcal AMC vaccines and the G20-endorsed AgResults initiative (a pull mechanism that seeks to stimulate private sector innovation in smallholder agriculture), all of which seek to create the conditions for market-based investment in, or for the benefit of, developing countries—either by helping to establish new markets (carbon) or correcting market failures (vaccines and agricultural products). The Bank has acted as trustee for IFFIm, a front-loading initiative that raises funds for immunization through the issuance of bonds backed by long-term ODA pledges. In addition, the Bank has been involved in some push-financed product development partnerships, though it is less clear what it has to offer in this effort.[17]

Overall, the Bank's main attempts to engage the private sector in the provision of GPGs are of two broad types—those aimed at creating markets for products that help to yield GPGs and those aimed at securitizing anticipated aid flows in order to achieve immediate and decisive impacts. And corresponding to the two broad forms of leveraging just identified are two facts. First, action on global challenges that is taken in developing countries will yield greater benefits per unit of investment, given their cost advantage, than action taken in developed countries—which creates opportunities for trading where regulatory regimes permit. Second, action taken now will yield greater benefits, given its prevention potential, than action taken later.

These facts are rather straightforward and compelling, yet the various initiatives described are essentially all pilots, and none is large scale relative to the problem that it seeks to address. They have mostly been perceived as experiments in innovative financing, rather than as major efforts to make inroads into global problems or problems affecting developing countries in general. ODA for GPGs is heavily concentrated on public investment, with relatively short-term investment horizons. There might therefore be a good case for establishing a target for the share of any given ODA pool that should be devoted to the mobilization of private investment in GPGs. A target for the level of such investment itself would be very difficult to select and measure.

So, given a pool of concessional resources that can be allocated without restriction as to geography, country income (below the high-income threshold), or sector, the best way to achieve impacts on global problems is likely to be as follows. First, use concessional resources as incentives to influence investment decisions, by blending them with nonconcessional resources to deliver sufficiently attractive financing terms. Second, seek to replicate investment programs and associated financing arrangements across countries so as to achieve cumulative impacts with maximum efficiency and connectedness. Third, use concessional or blended financing in a much more determined fashion to facilitate private investment that contributes to the provision of GPGs, perhaps based on a target for the share of the ODA pool that should be used to facilitate such investment.

Strengthening Strategy and Governance

There are no effective global or institution-specific frameworks for action on GPGs. The World Bank's 2007 framework (World Bank 2007) does little more than indicate broad priority areas, of which there are five: preserving the environment; controlling communicable diseases; strengthening the international financial architecture; enhancing developing countries' participation in the global trading system; and creating and sharing knowledge relevant for development. The choice of areas may be questioned but, more importantly, the framework gives no indication of how or to what extent the Bank will seek to contribute in each of the areas identified. It is essentially a general policy statement, not an operational framework. Other institutions offer the same or less, so it is not surprising that there is nothing at all at the supra-institutional level. The existing supra-institutional development framework is by default that articulated in the Millennium Declaration (UN 2000) and subsequently elaborated in the Millennium Development Goals, but that framework gives muted treatment to GPGs and does little to create incentives for the allocation of ODA in support of them.

With the elevation of the G20 to become a leaders-level forum in the aftermath of the global financial crisis, and the adoption by the G20 in 2010 of a development "agenda" (G20 2010), one might in principle expect the G20 to play a role in establishing a supra-institutional framework for the provision of GPGs. However, that seems a distant prospect at present, given the way in which the G20's development agenda has unfolded to date. In the absence of any supra-institutional process, it would be desirable for the World Bank's Board of Directors to request that the Bank's 2007 framework be revisited, seven years on, and made much more operational as well as more relevant to today's challenges. As part of this process, two distinct but related needs should be met, as follows.

First, the current array of global and regional partnership programs, which are perceived as the Bank's primary way of contributing to the supply of GPGs, needs to be placed on a clearer strategic footing. This would facilitate some consolidation of these programs, something that is obviously needed but difficult to achieve in the face of donors' special interests and requirements. It needs to be recognized explicitly that partnerships are not the only vehicles for contributing to GPGs. Several large financial intermediary funds have the same objective, but are not considered to be part of the above constellation, falling instead into the general category of trust funds. A strategic framework is needed for all trust funds that contribute to the supply of GPGs.

Second, and more importantly, the manner in which country operations are expected to contribute to the Bank's objectives in this area requires clear and forceful articulation. At present, any such contribution is either largely a by-product of investment decisions made for national or mutual interest reasons or is dependent on the will of individual staff to make use of the limited concessional resources available to support investments in GPGs through country programs. There is nothing that resembles a set of targets for such investment. There are no positive incentives for individual staff to steer their clients in this direction, and there are no procedural requirements to seek to replicate and network successful investments across countries. The overall absence of incentives and accountability mechanisms that might ensure any particular level of investment in GPGs is perhaps understandable when the Bank has only quite rigid financing instruments at its disposal, but the situation could be quite different if the Bank were able to offer more flexible financing packages.

The likely emergence of a BRICS (Brazil, Russia, India, China, and South Africa) bank—combined with calls for the creation of a new global "infrastructure bank"[18]—might be seen to pull the World Bank even more strongly toward responsiveness to national priorities. However, the opposite conclusion can as easily be drawn—that any new institutions of the kind proposed (which are at the present time very far from becoming realities) would relieve pressure on the Bank's resources and allow it to reposition itself as an institution seeking to find and work at the intersection of national and GPGs.

Aligning Country and Global Priorities and Programs

As has been noted above, the Bank's primary contribution to the supply of GPGs is likely to be through its country operations. So, in addition to having a strategic framework that ensures consistency between country and global priorities, it would be important to ensure that global programs are connected to and directly support country operations and that country operations are mandated to make use of the concessional resources available in global funds. Of course, the extent to which this might be achieved depends in large part on the flexibility of donors, who will not always welcome the loss of identity involved in blending their trust fund resources into country-level investment packages.

Mobilizing and Allocating Concessional Financing for Global Public Goods

The discussion above has assumed, for the sake of argument, the availability of a pool of concessional resources that might be allocated to developing countries, without restriction as to geography or income level, for the purpose of contributing to the supply of GPGs. Even if this unrestricted approach is seen as unrealistic or insufficiently targeted, a clearly identifiable and bounded pool of resources would be a prerequisite for effective action to supply GPGs for development. Unless a specified quantity of resources is reserved for allocation to such GPGs, other uses will predominate, as this is in the nature of GPGs. The question is how such a pool might be created and managed.

One option is obvious, though not without problems. That option is to use the IDA. IDA is, as noted earlier, losing clients at a significant rate. This fact presents IDA's donors with three choices. They can cut IDA back, increase allocations to the remaining IDA-eligible countries, or keep the graduation dividend within IDA but use it for something other than operations in low-income countries—namely GPGs. GPGs, like poor countries, need grant financing.

This option, however, has two substantial problems. One is that IDA is strongly identified as the World Bank's fund for the poorest countries, and the loss of this clear identity could have a negative impact on perceptions of the Bank generally, even if the GPG component of IDA is quarantined. Another is that IDA is subject to the Bank's normal governance processes, which are unlikely to deliver more than marginal adjustments to IDA's country-based operating model.

There are two equally obvious alternatives to the IDA option. One is to create a parallel GPG fund within the World Bank Group on the model of IDA and to seek, at a minimum, to divert the IDA graduation dividend into this fund. The other is to create such a fund outside the Bank (which would not preclude the Bank's acting as trustee) but with a strong connection to the investment pipeline of the Bank and other MDBs, as well as to the project pipelines of certain other grant-based international development organizations. The former option is subject to the same reservation as the IDA option with respect to institutional governance: it is simply unlikely to happen. The latter option has much merit but faces a much greater challenge in capturing the IDA graduation dividend.

Leaving aside the latter challenge, the principal merit of creating an external mechanism is that it could be set up with governance arrangements that are both fit for purpose and reflective of the stakes that major countries, and perhaps other actors, have in the problems to be addressed—rather than of the amount of funding they might have contributed to the fund. It need not constitute a new international organization: it could be a fund on the model of the CIFs, whose board determines strategy, approves major investments, and monitors progress and impact, but whose administrative support structure, including the treasury function, might be provided by the World Bank.

In addition, an external mechanism need not establish direct funding relationships with governments or private sector actors. In an already crowded field, it would preferably channel its resources through existing institutions, supporting them to develop and executive GPG strategies. A further benefit of externality is that the fund could have associated with it an independent policy hub, which might assist in the development of both institutional and cross-institutional strategies for the supply of GPGs. Its leadership could also take on certain functions that presently reside within the Bank by default, such as coordination of the CGIAR system. It might be argued that the Green Climate Fund (GCF) should have developed according to this kind of model, rather than aspiring to become a self-contained institution, and in fact, it is currently quite uncertain that it will succeed in becoming the latter.

While resource mobilization for such a fund could proceed on the IDA model, which involves regular injections of concessional resources through negotiated replenishments, consideration could be given to folding into it many existing trust funds and also raising resources on the IFFIm model through the issuance of aid-backed bonds. For any new resources, burden-sharing arrangements would be challenging to negotiate, and traditional donors might need to tolerate a mismatch between voting power and cash contributions. To reduce this mismatch somewhat, developing countries might be allowed to count toward their shares the cost of domestically financed measures that contribute, either wholly or in part, to the supply of GPGs.

Managing for Impact

It is a particular, if not unique, feature of GPG financing mechanisms that funds and partnerships are established with considerable fanfare in connection with a recognized problem, but without any clear targets or theories of change. Certainly it is difficult to "size" such funds and partnerships a priori or devise plausible, realistic theories of change when action involves multiple actors and complex problems. But for these reasons, it is all the more important that a strong impact-monitoring regime be put in place. Strong impact monitoring is the flip side of a strong institutional GPG strategy: the two things are interdependent.

A robust independent evaluation function established in association with the financing mechanism sketched above, and reporting to its governing body, could examine the performance of all institutions receiving funds, individually and collectively. It should specifically examine their performance in supplying GPGs, not merely in managing partnership programs or trust funds. It might subsume, but need not do so, the capable, independent Evaluation Office of the GEF.

Conclusions

By way of summarizing this discussion, what follows is a set of broad conclusions regarding the role of international public financing in supporting the provision of GPGs—or, more concisely, financing global public policy.

Essentially, the argument made here has been that there is no need to redefine what constitutes aid in any technical sense—or make any dramatic changes in the way in which it is measured—in order to facilitate its use for financing global public policy. Aid is not bound to be provided as a flow of resources to countries. What is more likely to be needed, sooner or later, is a new rationale for aid that assigns it a dual role: financing national public policy and financing global public policy. An important element of this rationale is that global public policy is the domain of global institutions, so that this second purpose of aid entails a strengthened role for such institutions, and also very material changes in the way in which they conduct and present their operations.

By way of summarizing the main points made in this chapter, five concluding recommendations are set out below, then briefly elaborated upon.

- adopt a new, bifurcated rationale for ODA;
- develop strategic institutional frameworks for financing global public policy;
- pursue global goals through country operations, as well as global programs;

- shift to the use of more flexible financing packages to create incentives for deviations from business as usual; and
- establish a global financing facility to finance global public policy through existing institutions.

A New, Bifurcated Rationale for ODA

The international development community should change the rationale for ODA, not the definition of it. The existing ODA definition is interpreted too broadly in some ways, but too narrowly in others—certainly too narrowly with respect to GPGs. It is in fact capacious enough to support, without change, a new, bifurcated rationale for aid that gives much greater prominence to the role of international development organizations as agents for the supply of GPGs, rather than merely as agents for the delivery of bilateral resources. According to this rationale, the purpose of aid is to support both national and GPGs, where support for GPGs is provided through the multilateral system.

Outflows from international development organizations are best not conceived as aid in the above sense, though many of them will meet the concessionality requirement. They are already captured in the concept of official development finance, a measure of financing received by developing countries rather than a measure of aid given by donors, and are best considered in that category. The ODA concept's principal value is as a basis for assessing and motivating fiscal effort on the part of sovereign states.

Frameworks for Financing Global Public Policy

International development organizations should adopt institutional strategies for contributing to the supply of GPGs through both country and global programs. These should as far as possible be linked across key institutions and certainly across the MDBs. They should be more than policy statements: they should be operational strategies that set goals, drive resource allocation, articulate implementation arrangements, and provide a basis for monitoring and evaluation.

Such strategies should lead to a consolidation and rationalization of the existing patchwork of arbitrarily sized and unreliably funded global and regional funding mechanisms operated by the World Bank and, to a lesser extent, other MDBs. The impact of approaches and instruments tried to date needs to be more systematically assessed so as to support decisions about which to replicate and scale up and which to discontinue.

The G20 has a unique capacity to ensure that linked institutional strategies are developed, resourced, and implemented. It also has an obvious role in monitoring the supply of GPGs important for global stability and prosperity. This could become an important theme of its development agenda as that agenda further evolves.

Global Goals through Country Operations

From a sustainability perspective, the most important GPGs are not those that can be supplied by means of relatively small funds and tight-knit coalitions of like-minded organizations. Tiger preservation might be supplied in that way; climate change mitigation clearly will not be. The most important GPGs will be supplied by governments and private actors through cumulative action across multiple countries.

It is of paramount importance to create incentives for the pursuit of GPGs through mainstream country operations, rather than merely through global programs. Incentives are needed for clients and for World Bank staff, particularly in middle-income countries, which now have a much wider range of financing options than previously.

More generally, the way in which the Bank conceives its mission needs fundamental reconsideration. Its goal should increasingly be to find and work at the intersection between national and global public policy priorities.

Flexible Financing Packages

MDBs should be enabled and mandated to offer flexible financing packages to clients, packages that provide sufficient incentives to undertake or modify investment intentions in favor of GPGs. These might blend concessional and non-concessional resources in various degrees, with the blend determined not by the characteristics of the borrower or the operation, but by the level of incentive required to reach agreement in a particular case.

Allowing calibration of incentives would increase the MDBs' capacity to pursue global goals through country operations. Even where blending results in the provision of a "soft" financing package, the package should not be characterized as aid. It should be considered as ODF of a piece with non-concessional lending.

A Global Financing Facility

A dedicated GPG financing facility—a Global Financing Facility—should be established at arm's length from any existing institution, but using existing administrative structures and financing channels.

In addition to its financing function, the facility should be equipped with strong policy advisory and evaluation functions. It should be financed by folding in resources from a range of existing funds, possibly including the GCF, if that fund proves unable to get off the ground, as well as by raising cash contributions from donors and by raising funds in the capital markets through the issuance of bonds backed by long-term ODA pledges.[19]

The Global Financing Facility should be required to allocate a defined proportion of its resources to the mobilization of market-based investments in GPGs. Its governance arrangements might include government and nongovernment representatives and would reflect their stakes in global challenges, not their cash contributions to the facility.

Box 6.1 What Young Development Professionals Think About Financing Development

Benedikt Signer, Global Facility for Disaster Reduction and Recovery

To support the achievement of vital global public goods (GPGs), as outlined in this book and for development as a whole (in any case often overlapping agendas), the World Bank cannot maintain an edge through financing volumes alone. Instead, it is about *targeting* available funds more effectively.

The comparative advantage of the World Bank cannot come solely from the financing it has available, nor from the knowledge and experience it has accumulated. While both are necessary, neither by itself is sufficient. Change has to be the defining feature as the Bank looks toward 2025—not for the sake of self-perpetuation, but to fill an important void in the 21st century. Faced with global challenges, it should support the necessary knowledge, capacity, and incentives for governments to put the long term at the heart of decision making, invest in public goods, and enable global collective action.

Investing in GPGs means investing for the long term. Spending resources now for future benefits requires trade-offs, and policy makers—in developed and developing countries alike—are faced with difficult political choices. In the face of pressing immediate needs and opportunity costs, competing priorities, and high discount rates, every decision to invest in the long term is inherently political. The Bank's work should support this process, by giving decision makers the tools to ask the right questions, to evaluate different strategies, and to make better-informed decisions.

Additionally, the Bank can support developing countries escape the false dichotomy between investing for today or for the future. Financing short-term development interventions linked to policies with long-term benefits can help overcome trade-offs. It can compensate countries that are willing to turn to more expensive alternatives that contribute to the achievement of GPGs for the difference in cost so as not to compromise their development.

Many of the challenges the world faces in the 21st century are increasing in severity. Actions will get more costly over time, and in many cases we risk passing irreversible thresholds. Considering the impact of our actions today on future generations has to be a guiding principle as we look to achieve the highest impact with limited resources. Through funds well targeted, the World Bank can support national governments to make difficult choices now and leverage development processes over the long term.

Role of Global Partnership Programs

The Global Facility for Disaster Reduction and Recovery GFDRR, for instance, provides an example of how the World Bank can support vulnerable countries to consider the long-term effects in their decisions today. Rising disaster losses are mainly driven by increasing exposure of assets and people to natural hazards. A changing climate will exacerbate this further. GFDRR financing supports governments with the knowledge, tools, and supporting institutions to integrate risk considerations in long-term planning and investments across all sectors. Targeting limited finances strategically helps countries plan for the long term, to reduce existing risk, and prevent the creation of new risk.

The joint GFDRR–World Bank Disaster Risk Financing and Insurance (DRFI) Program is a good example how small, well-targeted Bank investments can catalyze larger reforms. In the context of increasing exposure to disaster risks and climate variability, there is an urgent need for governments to better understand, manage, and reduce the financial and fiscal impacts natural disasters inflict. Through the DRFI Program, GFDRR partners with countries to help increase their financial resilience, be better prepared for future uncertainty, and become less dependent on donor support.

Having access to cost-effective and rapid liquidity immediately after a disaster and the budgetary mechanisms to execute disbursements wisely can speed recovery, safeguard assets, minimize budget disruption, and reduce the total economic and human cost of the event. In addition, implementing a disaster-risk financing and insurance strategy also introduces discipline, transparency, and a long-term perspective in financial planning and supports comprehensive approaches to risk management through putting a price on risk.

Targeting limited funds to support governments prepare for the future is a win-win investment. It allows the World Bank to invest today in support of its core mission of poverty reduction, while supporting long-term thinking to ensure we are better prepared for future challenges than current behavior suggests.

Notes

1. Some relevant expenditures are already captured in the OECD's category of official development finance (ODF), which takes a receiver's perspective and includes the following receipts except where not provided for developmental purposes: bilateral ODA, concessional and non-concessional financing from multilateral financial institutions, and other official flows whose grant element is too low for them to qualify as ODA. ODF does not include non-ODA expenditures by bilateral development financing institutions, which appears to be the reason for the call for a new measure of total official support for development.

2. Namely, that the loan in question must convey a grant element of at least 25 percent based on a discount rate of 10 percent. The discount rate is much higher than prevailing interest rates and was set long ago on the basis of the presumed opportunity cost to the donor of providing the loan.

3. In 2012 a country was considered high-income if its per capita income exceeded $12,615.

4. This was not always the case. For many years, the DAC counted only 77 percent of contributions to the GEF as ODA. However, this reflected the fact that some of its recipients were economies in transition, not the fact that some of the benefits of its investments were global benefits.

5. For a fuller but still non-technical account, see "Is it ODA?" (OECD 2008).

6. The DAC maintains and regularly revises lists of developing countries and international development organizations.

7. Interest is not included as negative ODA on the basis that in constant price terms, its inclusion would cause total reflows to exceed the size of the loan originally recorded

as ODA, thus creating a net loss for the donor. However, Tew (2013) has noted that when one looks at the situation from the receivers' perspective, the exclusion of interest causes ODA receipts to be overstated quite substantially.

8. The DAC in fact has devised two such concepts: ODF, already mentioned, and country programmable aid (CPA), which is used to measure a subset of aid inflows from bilateral and multilateral sources to developing countries. CPA is a quite restricted concept, limited to actual flows available for long-term development financing, and accounts for around half of all ODA.

9. There can be a substantial time lag between the provision of contributions to multilateral organizations and the consequent flow of resources from those organizations to developing countries.

10. This is a term suggested in Severino and Ray (2009).

11. Such public goods need not be the exclusive domain of national governments, though in general they will be the primary providers.

12. Some aid is used as direct support for business ventures in developing countries, but it is almost insignificant in quantity. The jury is out as to whether such support is worthwhile, with many people arguing that aid for private sector development should be confined to the provision of relevant public goods.

13. This leaves outflows from special-purpose trust funds aside.

14. Grace (2006) is a partial counter example. The U.K. Department for International Development commissioned Grace to advise on the relative merits of "push" vs. "pull" mechanisms in health in order to inform resource allocation decisions.

15. Some of these are funds to which the World Bank has contributed through the Development Grant Facility, rather than funds that the Bank itself manages.

16. "Social impact bonds" are being piloted in a number of developed countries, including Australia, the United Kingdom, and the United States. The Center for Global Development has explored the idea of extending the model for international development purposes (CGD 2013). The term "bond" is something of a misnomer, as returns to investors are not fixed.

17. For example, an Independent Evaluation Group evaluation of the Medicines for Malaria Venture, to which the Bank contributes, found MMV to be successful but was less positive about the value of the Bank's engagement with it.

18. A global Development Bank for Infrastructure and Sustainable Development was proposed in 2012 by Bhattacharya, Romani, and Stern (2012).

19. These bonds might be identified with the various specific problems to be tackled with support from the facility on the model of vaccine bonds (issued by IFFIm) or green bonds (issued by the IBRD).

References

Bhattacharya, Amar, Mattia Romani, and Nicholas Stern. 2012. "Infrastructure for Development: Meeting the Challenge." Policy Paper, Centre for Climate Change Economics and Policy and the Grantham Research Institute on Climate Change and the Environment, in collaboration with the Intergovernmental Group of Twenty-Four, London.

CGD (Center for Global Development). 2013. "Investing in Social Outcomes: Development Impact Bonds." Report of the Development Impact Bond Working Group. Published jointly with Social Finance, CGD, Washington, DC.

DI (Development Initiatives). 2013. *Guide to Official Development Assistance*. Development Initiatives, Bristol, U.K.

Grace, Cheri. 2006. *Developing New Technologies to Address Neglected Diseases: The Role of Product Development Partnerships and Advanced Market Commitments*. DFID Health Resource Centre, U.K. Department for International Development, London.

G20. 2010. "Seoul Development Consensus for Shared Growth." Annex I to leaders' communique, G20 Seoul summit, November 11–12.

———. 2008. *Annual Review of Development Effectiveness 2008: Shared Global Challenges*. IEG, Washington, DC: World Bank.

———. 2011a. *Trust Fund Support for Development: An Evaluation of the World Bank's Trust Fund Portfolio*. Washington, DC: World Bank.

———. 2011b. *The World Bank's Involvement in Global and Regional Partnership Programs: An Independent Assessment*. Washington, DC: World Bank.

OECD (Organisation for Economic Co-operation and Development). 2008. "Is it ODA?" Supplement to OECD Development Assistance Committee (DAC) Statistical Reporting Directives. OECD, Paris.

———. 2012. "Communique of the 2012 High-Level Meeting of the OECD Development Assistance Committee." OECD, Paris.

Severino, Jean-Michel, and Olivier Ray. 2009. "The End of ODA: Death and Rebirth of a Global Public Policy." Working Paper 167, Center for Global Development, Washington, DC.

Tew, Rob. 2013. "ODA Loans: Investments to End Poverty Discussion Paper." Development Initiatives, Bristol, U.K.

UN (United Nations). 2000. "Millennium Declaration." Resolution A/RES/55/2 adopted by the General Assembly at its 55th Session, September 2000.

World Bank. 2007. "Global Public Goods: A Framework for the Role of the World Bank." Paper prepared by staff of the World Bank for the Development Committee, October. World Bank, Washington, DC.

World Health Organization. 2001. "Macroeconomics and Health: Investing in Health for Economic Development." Report of the Commission on Macroeconomics and Health. Geneva.

CHAPTER 7

Financing Global Public Goods at Scale

Kenneth Lay

The Problem: Public Credit Alone Cannot Meet the Biggest Challenges

The two major tools that need to be brought to bear in tackling any of the major issues facing the international community (that is, to deliver global public goods GPGs) are (1) the technical capacity to design solutions and (2) the money to pay for them.

The principal constraint on the financial side, of course, is that political reality (and sometimes fiscal and macroeconomic reality) makes it impossible for direct, unlevered government money sourced from taxes and government borrowing official development assistance (ODA) aid to provide resources at the scale required. This problem has become more evident over the past several decades as the international community has come to appreciate the full magnitude of issues such as climate change and as government resources have been stretched in response to developments such as aging populations or the need for basic infrastructure to support improving standards of living in emerging market countries.

Moreover, as discussed elsewhere in this report, it has been challenging for the international community to develop the consensus needed to "repurpose" the World Bank Group and similar institutions and broaden their respective franchises to address issues beyond economic development and poverty alleviation in developing countries. This is not to say that the World Bank and others haven't tried: The green bonds that the International Bank for Reconstruction and Development (IBRD) pioneered late in the last decade are a good example of creativity in directing finance into a specific set of global priorities. It is important to keep in mind, however, that even if such an institutional transformation were to occur, the public sector capital investment required to fully address the broader set of global priorities would be infeasible even in the most financially efficient of these institutions.

Global Savings: The Resource, Its Potential, and Its Constraints

The challenge under these circumstances is to develop ways to access at scale the much larger, and extensively institutionalized, pools of public and private sector savings that have accumulated in many countries in the years since World War II.

To see Kenneth Lay discuss institutionalised savings for long-term financing: http://youtu.be/kmaYKlci1Eo

(Box 7.1 describes how IBRD has leveraged donor country commitments for credit) To get at this issue, it is useful to review, for readers who may not be familiar with the landscape in institutional investment, the sources and scale of these resources and the way in which the managers of these pools of savings make investments. Obviously, any successful effort to see this money directed to the challenges that are the focus of this volume will require structuring their financing to meet the needs of the institutions managing these savings.

Institutional investors (pension funds, insurance companies, mutual funds, endowments/foundations, and sovereign wealth funds) now hold roughly $75 trillion in assets that they manage for the various beneficiaries that are the ultimate owners of these pools of resources.[1]

A surprising amount of this money is managed pursuant to relatively consistent fiduciary standards and a more or less common investment philosophy. These are grounded in institutional investors' obligation to serve the financial objectives of the beneficiaries for which they invest, and they are broadly

---

Box 7.1 IBRD: Efficient Leverage of Global Public Credit

From its establishment early in the process of the institutionalization of savings in the developed countries, the International Bank for Reconstruction and Development's (IBRD) capital structure and business model have been brilliant solutions to the challenging of leveraging global public credit to mobilize savings to fund public purposes. The IBRD capital structure, coupled with conservative financial management, has enabled it to offer a triple-A, fixed-income investment opportunity even though (1) only a handful of its members carry that rating themselves, (2) its loan assets are obligations of unrated or much less highly rated emerging market countries, and (3) IBRD leverages more than three times its paid-in capital and retained earnings. The contingent obligation on the books of IBRD's owners—its "callable capital"—has never been drawn, even through successive emerging market and global financial crises.

A key point for the present discussion is that IBRD's triple-A-rated bonds go into the high-grade, liquid part of institutional investors' portfolios—the asset class for which investors expect the lowest return, given the high credit rating, relatively low price volatility and good liquidity of the instruments comprising it.

While offering concessional financing terms to its developing country members, moreover, IBRD's low financing costs have enabled it—over most of its history—to lend to members at rates far below market. Even so, the interest margin it has maintained on its loans, together with returns on its reserves, have been sufficient to fund (1) the world's preeminent development resource management capacity (country teams and the teams orchestrating solutions to GPGs—the signature business of the institution) and (2) an extensive consultancy across every major development-related discipline that it offers essentially for free to members. Even after funding its share of World Bank Group knowledge and development resource management work, IBRD generates a profit that, even after additions to reserves, enables its owners to direct a dividend to the aid agency—the International Development Association (IDA)—they asked IBRD to administer from about 1960.

Note: To see Kenneth Lay discuss the scale of financing needed for global public goods: http://youtu.be/KojADe9nXXk

---

informed by the tenets of modern portfolio theory, pursuant to which practitioners diversify portfolio holdings across assets to optimize return for a given level of portfolio volatility. Modern portfolio theory and its variants, despite numerous and varied criticisms, nevertheless remains core to the investment process for most institutions managing their share of the pool of global savings.

Reduced to essentials, and acknowledging substantial variation in the detail, investors typically manage their investments on a portfolio basis in order to achieve long-term savings objectives or fund long-term liabilities (as in the case of pension funds and insurance companies). Within the portfolio, most continue to make allocations to asset classes, each with a more-or-less characteristic risk and return profile. Historically, these have been variations (e.g., public and private equity, investment-grade and non-investment-grade debt) on equity and debt. In many cases, investors seek exposure to the average performance of the asset class as a whole. Other investors attempt to select the best-performing individual investments with the asset class or engage third-party specialists to make the investment selection for them.[2]

Given their fiduciary obligations to the sponsors and beneficiaries of the assets they manage, moreover, institutional investors make these asset allocation and investment selection decisions with a view to achieving the best possible financial return, taking into account the appropriate time horizon and degree of tolerance for price volatility and principal loss given the objectives of the investment.

Against this background, decisions on the part of these funds to invest to help achieve "public goods" may be inappropriate and are likely to be controversial (and perhaps illegal), unless there is a persuasive case that the proposed investment is competitive in terms of risk-adjusted returns with the other opportunities available.[3, 4]

Table 7.1 is a summary of total-portfolio asset allocations, variations of which are typical in the portfolios of institutionally managed savings pools. It is intended to be broadly illustrative, not precise or exhaustive. There are categories of

Table 7.1 Institutional Investors' Allocations and Return Expectations

Investor category	Asset classes, typical expected real returns (% annualized) and typical allocations (% of total portfolio)				
Asset class (expected real return) Type of institution	Public equity (5 to 6%)	Liquid fixed income[a] (1.5 to 2%)	Private equity (8 to 10%)	Other illiquid (5%)	Cash (−1 to 2%)
Pension funds	50	25	10	10	5
Insurance companies	10	70	5	10	5
Endowments/foundations	45	15	10	25	5
Sovereign wealth funds[b]	45	40	10	10	5
Mutual funds (U.S.)	45	25	Not material	Not material	20

a. 10-year maturities.
b. Asset allocations among sovereign wealth funds vary widely depending on their respective purposes and on the authorizing environment in which they operate. Stabilization funds invest much more heavily in fixed income, while long-term national savings funds invest in fully diversified portfolios similar to pension funds or endowments.

Too Global to Fail • http://dx.doi.org/10.1596/978-1-4648-0307-9

savings not included, and within each there are many individual institutions whose allocations and return expectations will diverge—often substantially—from those shown here. It is based on the author's experience and observation, validated with reference to many sources.

The good news is that the asset class (other than cash) with the lowest expected return (and therefore, producing the lowest cost of capital for borrowers)—liquid fixed income—also is one of the largest. Worldwide, the bond market totals roughly $80 trillion in outstanding securities, with new-issue long-term debt volumes in the neighborhood of $5 trillion per annum (this rough estimate is based on a review of data published in 2012 by Reuters).

The bad news is that a relatively small proportion of the financing for GPGs has been drawn from investors' high-grade fixed-income (HGFI) allocations, and much of that has come from bond issues by international institutions such as IBRD and the regional development banks that themselves have allocated only a modest proportion of their own long-term lending to fund these major international priorities.

Most of the activity to-date financing, for example, renewable energy, energy efficiency, sustainable forestry and agriculture, and other sectors that have a nexus with some of the major issues of concern to the international public sector, has produced assets drawing investment from the illiquid private equity or "real assets" parts of investors' portfolios. As evident in table 7.1, these are relatively small parts of institutional portfolios, and investors' return expectations, given the illiquidity and other characteristics of the risk profile, are relatively high. The bottom line: There remains a great deal of work to be done to attract large-scale, low-cost, long-term financing into these sectors.

Tapping the High-Grade Fixed-Income Resource: Quality and Liquidity Needed

What will enable assets originated in these sectors to work in investors' HGFI portfolios? Instruments with three characteristics: credit quality, liquidity, and competitive return.[5]

Credit Quality

The source for each periodic payment and for redemption at maturity must meet minimum standards of reliability to achieve an investment-grade (Moody's Baa3/S&P and Fitch BBB-, or better) credit rating from major rating agencies. There are two essential foundations to credit quality:

- **Economics of the business.** The business or activity itself has to generate a cash flow, covering both interest and principal, predictable enough to warrant investment-grade rating.
- **Enforceability of the obligation.** The legal arrangements surrounding the activity and the financing, and the legal system and political economy in which they are grounded, must provide a reliably enforceable obligation in favor of investors.

Where these may be in doubt, credit enhancement will have to be applied from a public or private source.

Liquidity

Investors have to anticipate that there are likely to be reliable offers for their holdings at a narrow spread to the price at which the same position then could be bought—in short, on a tight bid-offer spread. Given the scale of institutional investors' holdings, moreover, this bid-offer spread has to work for trades of, say, $5 million or more.[6] This level of liquidity or better is routinely achieved in conventional bond issues by governments and their agencies, IBRD and other MDBs, and major corporate borrowers. It is provided by entities with capital committed to market making in these instruments—typically, the investment banks that underwrite and distribute securities in the HGFI market.

Competitive Return

Most institutions, given their fiduciary obligations, will want to see a financial return for an investment with a given credit risk and liquidity that is as good or better than others available.

Virtually without exception, instruments that meet these three criteria are offered or guaranteed by entities (developed country governments, supranational institutions, and major corporations) that themselves carry investment-grade credit ratings. Typically they are issued in large transactions (say, $300 million or more) originating in established global financial centers.

Quality and Liquidity in GPG Finance: Pooling and Securitization

The challenge, or course, is that much of the most important work being done to provide GPGs is local, relatively small scale, and idiosyncratic. This is probably unavoidable, so the question becomes how to assure a minimum degree of consistency to enable the resulting assets to be aggregated (pooled) and securitized, with any required application of public credit enhancement occurring in the most efficient manner to reach investment grade.

The basic mechanism for delivering these solutions—pooling and securitization—is certainly not novel, and in certain sectors supports a major financial industry.[7] But despite extensive discussion, there has yet to emerge in key areas of global import—sustainable energy and infrastructure development, energy efficiency, and the like—the credible sponsorship and consistency of approach across projects, sectors, and countries that could permit pooling projects into the kind of large-scale, high-grade, liquid financial instruments commanding the highest prices from investors and achieving the lowest cost of capital for these crucial undertakings.[8] And these characteristics have to be met while providing certainty for project developers that this form of long-term "take-out" financing will be available to justify the risk they take and the cost they incur in the development stage.

Achieving this goal is simply not possible for all of the myriad activities supporting delivery of GPGs. But certainly it can be achieved in important areas if the international community is willing to coalesce around a few of the most promising, scalable approaches to tackling key challenges like climate change and sustainable infrastructure. If these can be agreed upon, and if simple, standardized implementation and legal arrangements are adopted, then pooling and securitization could be accomplished with the creditworthiness, size, and liquidity necessary to dramatically reduce the cost of capital for these activities.

For the foregoing to occur, the following conditions and tasks to meet them would be needed:

1. **Agreement on HPAs:** Broad international agreement on a limited number of high-priority activities (HPAs) that would benefit from pooling and securitization. The criteria for inclusion on this list are straightforward: An HPA must (a) have the potential for major positive impact in a high-priority area; (b) generate cash flow to service debt or enable cost avoidance that then can enable the funds thus freed up to be directed to service debt; and (c) be susceptible to a standardized approach across jurisdictions. Some examples are urban conversion to LED street lighting, distributed generation of renewable energy, bio-shield restoration, and multi-peril/multi-jurisdiction catastrophe risk insurance.

2. **Defined project criteria:** For each HPA, there will need to be developed and agreed upon a set of minimum criteria to create a "conforming" project that can be pooled with others and securitized. Part of the objective in limiting the HPA universe to high-impact activities susceptible to standardization is to minimize the impact of idiosyncratic local approaches to essentially similar challenges. This ex ante classification of activities should make it possible to develop in each activity category a small number of essential criteria for pooling, while allowing significant variation across jurisdictions in all other aspects of projects.

3. **Minimum legal standards:** Similarly, for each participating jurisdiction there will need to be a set of minimum legal standards to ensure enforceability of each project's obligations to investors in the pool. Meeting these standards ex ante would qualify a national or subnational jurisdiction to originate HPA projects for pooling and securitization.

4. **Established issuing vehicle:** For each HPA, there will need to be established a vehicle to act as issuer of the fixed-income instruments created from the aggregated and securitized projects meeting the requirements of items 2 and 3 above. An example of a vehicle of this kind is the International Finance Facility for Immunisation (IFFIm), which pools and securitizes future aid commitments of up to 20 years from several countries to support issuance of high-grade bonds in the international capital markets. As with IFFIm, each HPA

vehicle could outsource project and jurisdiction validation functions (tasks 2 and 3) as well as the execution of financing and other aspects of financial management.[9] In addition, and again as illustrated in the IFFIm experience, each HPA vehicle could provide modest intermediation services, maintaining sufficient liquidity derived from borrowings to accommodate timing differences between receipt of HPA project revenues and interest and principal payments on HPA vehicle bonds. To the extent that project-related cash flows may not be sufficiently reliable to warrant investment-grade credit rating, an HPA vehicle could be an appropriate and efficient recipient of bilateral or multilateral public credit, for example, in the form of guarantees, participation in financings, hedging facilities, or capital contributions.

Obviously, the devil is in the details in this approach, and the details are highly dependent on the specifics of the activities being financed, the characteristics of the institutions undertaking them, forms of available credit enhancement (to the extent necessary), and the complexity of the governance arrangements which, if not handled well, can vastly and unnecessarily increase administrative costs. Again, simplicity is the watchword in any effort of this kind—indeed, experience in the international community so far has been that expansive institutional mandates have led to complex negotiation over governance and "voice" issues, seriously impeding progress toward delivery of GPGs in areas such as climate change mitigation and adaptation.[10]

Box 7.2 What Young Development Professionals Think About the Private Sector

Jun Rentschler, Office of the Chief Economist of the Climate Change Group, World Bank

As international development banks turn to the private sector in search of new financing sources, they need to discover more takeaways than just funding.

The funds of international development banks and agencies have traditionally relied heavily on contributions from individual governments. However, facing tight budgets and stagnating growth, developed donor countries are increasingly concerned with their own, rather than foreign, development. In addition, many of the low-hanging fruits of development and poverty reduction have been picked, and future challenges are thus likely to be more complex—not least considering the challenges around climate change and development in conflict-affected states. Development operations thus follow a trend of becoming increasingly costly and risky. In the search for financing to fill the resulting gaps, development agencies are turning to flirting with the private sector.

However, when private funds are to be won for the development agenda, conventional development agencies will find themselves subject to a different measure of scrutiny. The standard expectations and benchmarks of private sector investors and asset holders are likely to differ from those of bureaucratic donor governments. Thus, the development industry must go beyond finding new sources for funding old ways.

In fact, the very discovery of the private sector as a source of potential funding could be a tremendous opportunity for players in the development industry to reform and restructure their operations. In line with the tradition of many public institutions, development agencies have evolved into complex bureaucracies (or at least have a reputation to have done so), gaining in inertia at the expense of efficiency and competitiveness. Thus, in addition to tapping into new funding sources, it will be crucial for them to adopt more cost-effective and results-oriented approaches adequate for attracting competitive financing, as well as for the future challenges of development.

In this context, many private companies have set business standards that may offer crucial lessons. For instance, it will be useful (or in some cases even urgently needed) for development institutions to strengthen operational efficiency by drawing on practices such as leaner management, flatter hierarchies, risk management, culture of innovation, and results-oriented organizational architecture. Furthermore, transparent, open, and competitive hiring systems, merit-based progression opportunities, and skill-development programs will be absolutely essential to attract (young) talent and maintain long-term institutional capability. In turn, without such qualities in place, development agencies may not only find that their interest in private institutions is not reciprocated, but in the long run they may see their ability to tackle development challenges fade, and thus maneuver themselves into irrelevance.

On a more positive note, development agencies may find that private organizations can be not just financiers and models of good business practice, but also important partners—with tremendous technical expertise, regional experience, and effective networks and infrastructure. In addition to these assets, some private institutions and industries have enormous economic significance and political influence (e.g., the oil and mining sectors), which may be an even more valuable contribution than private sector funding per se. Thus, winning the private sector as partners for the development agenda could bring game-changing progress in areas such as climate change mitigation and environmental and social sustainability standards. Indeed, as development institutions turn to the private sector, they may discover that shaking hands rather than pointing fingers will result in more constructive cooperation. This could lead to opportunities that go well beyond funding and could significantly leverage efforts toward sustainable development.

Notes

1. Traditional commercial bank lending has never been a great source for low-cost, long-term financing needed to finance GPGs. Although total assets in the global banking system are immense—roughly $100 trillion in the top 1,000 banks—most of that is sourced from deposits and other short-term liabilities, and the term transformation that banks provide necessarily comes at a significant cost. That said, commercial banks play an important role in the early stages of project financing and, of course, in the underwriting and distribution process that facilitates access to the long-term investment discussed in the text.

Too Global to Fail • http://dx.doi.org/10.1596/978-1-4648-0307-9

2. In the interest of completeness, it is worth noting that the highly correlated behavior of traditional asset classes during the recent financial crisis and its aftermath is leading some investors to seek to better diversify their portfolios by allocating to "factors"— e.g., macroeconomic performance and its constituents, real interest rates, currency exchange rates, credit, commodity prices, etc. It remains to be seen to what extent this approach gains traction.

3. Not surprisingly, an industry of sorts has grown up around the issue described in the text, with nongovernmental organizations (NGOs), academics, consultancies, and "sustainable" asset managers striving to demonstrate that some sacrifice of conventional risk-adjusted return is warranted in return for achieving broader public goods. These public goods—so the arguments often go—serve to reduce risks to institutional investors' beneficiaries in other ways, a risk reduction that should be valued ("priced") and taken into account in asset allocation and investment selection.

4. In this context it is worth recalling the difficult experience of some institutional investors, for example, when authorities in jurisdictions sponsoring investment funds have sought to pursue local economic development objectives by directing fund investments into favored businesses or other activities. Well-intentioned special pleading of this kind can give way to wholesale departure from sound investment practice as authorities find it difficult to say "yes" to one or several ostensibly salutary purposes while saying "no" to others.

5. To see Kenneth Lay discuss new financial products for sustainability: http://youtu. be/omjqnEuF-WY.

6. Bid-offer spreads in the institutional-scale market, for example, a plain-vanilla 5-year bond, can be in the neighborhood of 5 basis points (.05%) for a $5 million ticket in high-grade corporate debt to well under 1 basis point (that is, less than .01%) for tickets in the tens of millions in "on-the-run" U.S. Treasuries. It is important to note, of course, that compared with government-bonds, liquidity in other sectors of the fixed-income market can vary widely; it is especially name-specific and tiered by credit rating, and it can improve or deteriorate with much greater sensitivity to overall market conditions. It also is significantly more exposed to the impact of declining balance sheet commitments by traditional market makers in the current climate of uncertainty around the structure and regulatory capital requirements in the banking sector.

7. Variations on the pooling/securitization theme include mortgage-backed securities, asset-backed securities, and their collateralized debt obligation variants, as well as covered bonds (issued as plain-vanilla debt, carrying the credit of an issuing institution, but with backing as well from a specified pool of assets held by the institution).

8. Pooling and securitizing assets has been employed widely and often without creating the "plain-vanilla" investment grade instruments that enable financing at the lowest cost. In the United States, for example, conventional mortgage-backed securities, carrying federal agency guarantees, nevertheless require market participants to undertake complex modeling to allow for prepayment risk and disparate cash-flow patterns among the mortgages in a pool.

9. IFFIm, which is organized as a U.K. charitable corporation, outsources to the GAVI Alliance (formerly the Global Alliance for Vaccines and Immunisation) the delivery of vaccination services and outsources to IBRD implementation of its bond issue program, liquidity management, accounting, and other financial services.

10. An alternative approach to pooling and securitizing GPG-related financing is to establish a separate "special-purpose vehicle" for each transaction. This has been the approach in, for example, "multi-cat" parametric catastrophe risk bond issue arranged by the World Bank Treasury.

PART 3

Strategic Directions for the Provision of Global Public Goods

CHAPTER 8

Emerging Economies, Emerging Development Partners

J. Warren Evans, Laura Tlaiye, Tae Yong Jung, and Esther Choi

Much has been written about the likely changes in the International Development Association's (IDA) clientele and operations over the coming years. This of course will have profound effects on the broader workings of the World Bank Group. But less has been said about the future relationships that the World Bank Group, particularly the International Bank for Reconstruction and Development (IBRD), might have with emerging economies. The IBRD's biggest clients in terms of lending volume over the last five years have been China, Brazil, Mexico, and Turkey—these four countries together have averaged more than 36 percent of total IBRD lending in recent years. Will they still be borrowing billions of dollars from IBRD in 10 years? It seems safe to assume that they will start to transition to a different role much as the Republic of Korea (hereafter, Korea) has done since the late 1980s—moving toward a recipient/donor role and eventually a donor role.

How might the relationship of these and other rapidly growing economies with the multilateral development finance community evolve? Is there potential to work together over the coming years to jointly shape partnerships whereby World Bank and other similar organizations with decades of development assistance experience can facilitate effective and efficient South-South and South-North programs that are designed to address regional and global public goods (GPG) challenges? In order to further explore these questions, country case studies were prepared for Brazil and Korea. These two countries were selected because they each are already engaged in providing bilateral development assistance to developing countries, while at the same time contributing to multilateral assistance programs, such as the IDA and the Global Environment Facility (GEF).

These two countries also bring very different types of expertise and experience to the GPG and environmental sustainability agenda—Korea has pioneered green growth in terms of urban, infrastructure, and industrial development, while Brazil is a global leader in agricultural innovation and natural resource management.

Brazil's recent economic performance and progress in reducing poverty and inequality, combined with its share of the world population, natural assets, and output, have earned it a visible position in world affairs. Its size and standing give its voice strength in shaping the debate on GPG in an emerging economy context. How much muscle Brazil will show in the GPG arena in 10 years is hard to predict, but it clearly will depend on how much its economy and population eventually benefit from the global marketplace and greater involvement in global issues.

Brazil is a large country with great regional disparities and contradictions—a technological powerhouse in selected sectors (for example, aviation and agrotechnology), with Africa-like poverty levels in some parts of the north and northeast. The recent riots across the country offer a glimpse of popular dissatisfaction with the poor quality and high costs of public services and weak governance of the political system. Furthermore, while externally Brazil is seen as an engine of regional development, some analysts worry about its medium- to long-term growth prospects because of structural impediments and risks (for example, low labor productivity, poor education quality, infrastructure gaps, and regulatory inefficiency). Yet, the country is endowed with vast natural resources, cultural and biological diversity, and unique capabilities for sustainable production of food, biofuels, and certain manufactured goods.

This case study explores how Brazil's growing share of and connectedness to the world economy might translate into a growing presence and influence among other developing countries, notably in Latin America and Africa, and how it might participate in the GPG debate. Less guided by an explicit strategy or policy, recent presidential initiatives and commercial interests have expanded Brazilian overseas private and public investment and development cooperation and assistance. Examples of recent South-South cooperation arrangements are presented, showing how Brazil helps abroad and also serves its own interests.

What does the emergence of Brazil as a regional and global leader mean for its relationship with the World Bank over the next 10 years? It is likely that the remaining domestic challenges will sustain the stable but evolving relationship developed in recent years. Based on informed opinions, Brazil is likely to continue to value investment lending support for state- and municipal-level development programs and the provision of infrastructure and other services via public-private partnerships. At the federal level, Brazil is likely to seek advice in specific, complex policy areas, while also partnering with the Bank in bringing its expertise to other regions of the developing world. Hence, under a sustained relationship, the World Bank can explore and debate issues of global relevance with Brazil for the foreseeable future.

This case study concludes that Brazil's engagement in development assistance is increasing and more visible in Africa and Latin America. From the interviews conducted and literature consulted, no clear national consensus has emerged about how prepared the country should be in shaping the discussion and in participating in the provision of GPGs. However, as seen with issues such as HIV/AIDS and climate change, Brazil has taken leadership toward positions that benefit itself and other developing countries while contributing to negotiated solutions. This study ends with a series of open questions that might be useful in observing the evolution of Brazil's position through 2025.

A Growing Presence in Regional and Global Affairs

Brazil's economic growth, improved income distribution, and strengthened democracy in recent years have given the nation a more prominent presence in the international arena. Its domestic achievements and less timid foreign policy have strengthened its external visibility, earning it recognition as a key player in diplomacy and world politics.

Brazil is the world's fifth-most populous country (196 million in 2011) and seventh-largest economy (gross domestic product [GDP] in 2011 was $2,477 billion) (EIU 2013), and it lifted 22 million people out of poverty from 2003 to 2009 (World Bank 2011). Brazil weathered the global financial downturn with relatively minor impacts. The country was one of the last to fall into recession in 2008 and among the first to resume growth in 2009. Brazil's GDP grew 7.5 percent in 2010, 2.7 percent in 2011, and only 1 percent in 2012 because of the global slowdown. Still, the country's strong domestic market is less vulnerable to external crisis, and Brazilians are benefiting from stable economic growth, historically low unemployment at around 5 percent, relatively low inflation rates, and improvements in social well-being (World Bank 2013).

A growing middle class in Latin America's largest market is likely to remain an attractive destination for foreign investment, Brazil being second only to China in foreign direct investment. Brazil's national development bank, Banco Nacional de Desenvolvimento Econômico e Social (BNDES), is a major player in domestic finance and increasingly so in international infrastructure projects, disbursing an average of approximately R$150 billion per year—about $75 billion in today's exchange rate (BNDES 2013). The football World Cup in 2014 and the Olympics in 2016 have spurred upgrades and development of new infrastructure and will further showcase Brazil as a multicultural and open society to international audiences.

From a Cautious Foreign Policy to 'Punching at its Weight'

Brazil's economic and social transformation has permeated its foreign policy. From the first administration of President Luiz Inácio Lula da Silva onward, foreign policy has been shifting from a cautious stance anchored on multilateralism and defense of self-determination and sovereignty and toward a more visible and bolder position in world affairs (Amorim 2011). The significance of extensive and diverse trade relations,[1] sustained interest in regional solidarity and peace, and greater public recognition of Brazil's connectedness with the rest of the world have contributed to making Brazil more courageous in foreign policy. A good example was Brazil's role during the 2003 World Trade Organization (WTO) Ministerial Conference in Cancun, Mexico, rallying other developing countries to negotiate an agreement against farm subsidies that would have disproportionately benefited the European Union and the United States.

In making its influence more visible, Brazil has been actively advancing a South-South agenda and a stronger voice for developing countries in multilateral institutions. For example, Brazil participated with Russia, India, and China (BRICS) in creating a forum, which since 2011 also includes South Africa. Since 2009 the BRICS group has held summits on the financial crisis, pursuing an agenda of economic coordination, and recently confirming the creation of a BRICS development bank. Brazil also participates in the IBSA forum, established with India and South Africa to strengthen economic partnerships among them, coordinate world trade negotiation efforts, and discuss the expansion of the UN Security Council. Likewise, Brazil has worked through the Group of 20 (G20) to advance its efforts for increased voting powers for emerging economies within the International Monetary Fund (IMF) and the World Bank and has increased its voting powers in various multilateral organizations.

While recognizing this recent shift toward working with different country groupings, it should be noted that the Brazilian foreign policy establishment prefers a "South orientation" in its geopolitical actions. That is, rather than seeking closeness to the Organisation for Economic Co-operation and Development (OECD) and other "North oriented" organizations, Brazil has a strong preference for the G-77 (Group of 77 UN countries) as a platform for exerting its international influence (Gratius 2008; Fonseca 2011).

South American Integration and Development Assistance

Consistent with this South orientation, nowhere else is Brazil's determination to demonstrate its leadership than in fostering integration and peace in South America. It shares borders with 10 of the 12 South American nations and, although language and relatively peaceful history sets it apart from its neighbors, Brazil emphasizes a common South American identity and a pursuit of peace and prosperity through growing trade and investment. Investments in gas, mining, underwater oil, construction, and other sectors, often supported by BNDES, have made Brazil a visible investor in other South American economies.

Brazil reinforces its efforts to promote economic integration by supporting MERCOSUR (a trade agreement between Argentina, Brazil, Uruguay, and Paraguay and to which the República Bolivariana de Venezuela later acceded) and by supporting a 12-member Union of South American Nations, UNASUR. It has played a leading diplomatic role by helping mediate internal conflict (in Ecuador and Bolivia) and tensions between countries (Colombia and the República Bolivariana de Venezuela), and in opposing takeovers by the military (Ecuador in 2000 and Honduras in 2009). Beyond South America, Brazil has a prominent presence in Haiti working with the UN on security and development, increasing its financial and personnel support after the 2010 earthquake.

In the area of development assistance, Brazil has a long history of collaboration with its neighbors and other developing countries. In terms of its financial contributions, it tends to prefer multilateral mechanisms over bilateral cooperation. According to data compiled by the Brazilian Cooperation Agency and the Institute for Applied Economic Research (ABC and IPEA, respectively, for their acronyms in Portuguese), Brazil contributed $1.6 billion over the period 2005–09 ($320 million per year on average) for international development assistance.[2] Of this total, 76 percent corresponds to contributions to multilateral institutions and funds, such as the World Bank's IDA,[3] the Inter-American Development Bank's Special Operations Fund, and thematic global funds administered by other UN agencies (for example, UNICEF), among others. The remaining 23 percent went to bilateral cooperation.

What explains this preference? From personal communications and media coverage, three factors seem relevant. First, Brazilian bilateral cooperation rules require partial cofinancing of expenses by collaborating entities, which may be difficult for some partners. Second, ABC's budget has remained relatively small, and it relies on other agencies to provide the staff with the relevant technical expertise. Finally, multilateral mechanisms offer Brazil a platform to work with many more developing countries, and evaluations point to less fragmented, more efficient, and focused development assistance (IPEA 2012).

Yet, the Lula government and Brazil's current president, Dilma Roussef stressed the importance of South-South relations, particularly more from a business rather than an "aid" perspective. In particular, relations with Africa flourished under **Lula** (president 2003–11). He traveled there a dozen times, and African leaders flocked to Brazil. President Rousseff is continuing those policies, though with more emphasis on how the relationship benefits Brazil (*The Economist* 2012). Leveraging Brazil's affinity with Africa—Brazil has the largest number of people of African descent outside of Africa—Brazilian public and private sector corporate giants (Vale, BNDES, Petrobras, Odebrecht, and so on) are participating in natural resource and infrastructure projects in Africa.

Trade with Africa has grown from $3 billion in 2001 to $26 billion in 2008 (CFR 2011). Brazil is supporting Africa in various biofuel and associated technology initiatives (Hochstetler 2012), with the private sector supporting the development of expertise in this renewable energy source. As discussed in the next section, Brazil is playing an important role in transferring knowledge and fostering innovation in the African agriculture sector.

South-South Exchanges of Globally Relevant Knowledge

Brazil is recognized as a powerhouse in agricultural research and technology due to its private agribusiness enterprises and its research and technology development agency, Empresa Brasileira de Pesquisa Agropecuaria (EMPBRAPA), both filling historical gaps in science and technology for tropical agriculture. A dynamic agricultural sector fueled by favorable demand and price outlook plays a key role both in Brazil's exports and in its rural economy. Its coffee, orange juice, sugar, beef, and poultry sectors thrive along with those for soybeans, rice, and wheat.

Once a food-importing nation focused on coffee exports, Brazil in 2008 exported more than 1,500 types of agricultural products to foreign markets. Around 79 percent of the nation's food is consumed domestically; the rest is shipped overseas. Food exports amounted to $76 billion in 2010.

EMBRAPA has approximately 9,800 employees and 41 development units dedicated to enhancing Brazil's agriculture and agribusiness, addressing traditional and non-traditional crops and animal husbandry. Its expertise ranges from improving small-scale agriculture practice to advanced biotechnology and nanotechnology, agro-forestry, and silviculture. The agency has a long history of international cooperation, with 78 active bilateral agreements with research laboratories and agencies in 56 countries, including joint research programs (EMBRAPA 2013). In terms of South-South cooperation, EMBRAPA has set up centers in Ghana, Panama, and the República Bolivariana de Venezuela. The Africa-Brazil Agricultural Innovation Marketplace is an example of an international cooperative program facilitated by the World Bank and other partners, which brings together EMBRAPA and African research bodies to work on joint projects (see box 8.1). For example, through EMBRAPA, Brazil has provided technical assistance to the cotton industry in Benin, Burkina Faso, Chad, and Mali.

Box 8.1 Brazil Partnerships with Africa in Agriculture Science and Technology

Brazil's success in reducing internal poverty and hunger is in part due to the expertise of Empresa Brasileira de Pesquisa Agropecuaria (EMBRAPA) in small-scale farming and traditional crops (beans, rice, cassava, maize, and vegetables). With Brazil and Africa having recognized the importance of agriculture in their economies and the similarities in climate, ecosystems, and agricultural practices, a natural association of knowledge sharing and technological cooperation has developed over the years between individual African governments and Brazil. EMBRAPA had an ongoing program of outreach to Africa that received increased support after former president Luiz Inácio Lula da Silva made support to Africa a priority.

The concept of an "innovation marketplace" emerged to foster increased collaboration with Africa on agricultural innovation and research. Linking EMBRAPA with the Forum for Agricultural Research in Africa (FARA), which coordinates and advocates agricultural research across the continent, enabled the Africa-Brazil Agricultural Innovation Marketplace to reach numerous research organizations in Africa and helped target the program's activities in three areas:

• Policy dialogue in the agricultural sector;
• A forum for presentation and discussion of research for development ideas, including proposal selection, and projects that would be competitively supported; and
• Support and implementation of joint agricultural research for development projects.

The agricultural research program was later extended to other Latin American countries. In a little more than two years, the marketplace mobilized almost 200 research and development institutions from more than 40 countries. More than 50 percent of the EMBRAPA research centers have participated in the initiative. A dozen international, national, and private organizations

box continues next page

Box 8.1 Brazil Partnerships with Africa in Agriculture Science and Technology *(continued)*

support and participate in the administration of the marketplace, such as, the World Bank's Development Grant Facility, the United Nation's International Fund for Agricultural Development (UNIFAD), and the United Kingdom's Department for International Development (DfID), and the Bill & Melinda Gates Foundation. In addition to the 10 projects from previous selections already running on the African continent, 35 projects were in operation in 2012 within the scope of the Marketplace, encompassing 30 African and 5 Latin American and Caribbean countries.

The World Bank has played a prominent role in the development of Brazil's agricultural research and innovation advances. First, EMBRAPA and FARA have long-standing relationships with the Bank through the Consultative Group on International Agricultural Research (CGIAR) and other programs. Second, although the relationship between EMBRAPA and FARA existed before the marketplace partnership, the World Bank helped them work together on a concrete program concept, thus building trust and expectations of the possibilities of a larger collaboration. Third, the World Bank helped mobilize the initial seed funding from trust funds, and later facilitated additional funding from other sources, including DfID, the Gates Foundation, and UNIFAD. The program's budget grew from US$1.5 million to US$7 million in liquid contributions in 2013, of which US$1.4 million was provided by EMBRAPA (not counting the significant in-kind contribution of EMBRAPA's staff time).

Source: http://wbi.worldbank.org/sske/story/africa-brazil-agricultural-innovation-marketplace-incubating-agricultural-innovations-african

Scientific knowledge exchange on topics relevant to other developing countries can be a public good when the costs and benefits of its development are shared as agreed by the participating partners. The question of how a country with the capabilities and characteristics of Brazil views public goods of global significance is addressed in the next section.

Recent Policies and Initiatives Shaping Brazil's Role in Global Public Goods

Brazil's opinion on GPGs matters a great deal, not just because its views are increasingly influential among developing and developed countries, but because its sheer size (the world's fifth largest land mass), vast natural endowment, technological capabilities, and demographics affect the condition of global systems, such as climate, biodiversity, and water resources. The knowledge Brazil has developed and is acquiring to steer development toward a sustainable future is also a valuable asset that can be shared globally.

Foreign Policy and Global Public Goods

Observers of Brazil's foreign policy stance on global environmental issues comment that traditional concerns over national security and interests, fair distribution of costs, and a preference for the United Nations as the eminent multilateral institution now share space with a new pragmatism toward GPGs. The architects of the new pragmatism, without abandoning the principle of shared but differentiated responsibilities, seem to be more willing to accept a greater role in addressing and in constructing negotiated solutions to global challenges. A more engaged Brazil in GPG issues is also partly the results of an active civil society that has benefited from more than two decades of democratic openness. An example of useful convergence between addressing national interests while also strengthening Brazil's international leadership and engagement is its globally recognized HIV/AIDS program (see box 8.2).

Tackling Sustainable Development: Energy Security

With the end of 20 years of military government in 1985 and the rise of democratization, Brazilian public opinion and civil society organizations, often connected to international nongovernmental organizations, have been critical of a development pattern that has degraded the environment and brought hardship to local populations. From the outrage about the effects of pollution in the industrial belt of São Paulo to the Amazon rubber tapper movement led by the later-assassinated Chico Mendes, a national consciousness gave rise to new institutions and laws to address environmental issues. The first democratically elected president, José Sarney, offered to host the first United National Conference on Environment and Development in Rio de Janeiro in 1992. Since then, sustainable development has become a centerpiece of government policy, and much of Brazilian society identifies with the objectives of environmental and social sustainability.

In finding a balance in order to meet Brazil's many development needs, nothing presents a greater challenge and more international relevance than the goal of addressing energy security while acting responsibly regarding climate change. Meeting the needs of Brazil's growing economy and its voluntary low-carbon commitments will be extremely challenging. As described below, existing renewable resources (mainly hydropower), even if tapped to the maximum scale, may not be sufficient to meet demand and are located in sensitive areas. Brazil may have to resort to increasing its fossil fuel–based generation capacity. However, addressing growing energy needs also offers the opportunity to capitalize on the country's competitive advantages over energy, land, water, and genetic resources while building greater climatic resilience.

Brazil has committed to a voluntary emissions reduction target of about 1,168 million tons carbon dioxide equivalent by 2020. This target represents a 20 percent reduction of a projected emissions trajectory using year 2005 emissions as the base year. Thanks to Brazil's current rather clean energy matrix of about 50 percent renewable sources, it may continue to sustain low-carbon energy development. However, meeting the growing demand from its cities, new industries, and expanding middle class will present challenges.

About 70 percent of Brazil's installed capacity and 80 percent of power generation come from hydropower, but more than 50 percent of the economically viable supply has already been tapped. The remaining large-scale projects are in sensitive locations, such as the Amazon, and distant from the main demand centers in the southeast. Opposition and inherent delays in such large projects are bringing on-stream smaller-scale hydropower projects (less than 50 megawatts) and gas-fired power.

Box 8.2 Brazil's Response to AIDS: A Case of Successful International Engagement

Considered among the most successful developing countries in tackling the HIV/AIDS epidemic, Brazil presents an interesting case of convergence between domestic interests helped by active international engagement. In the beginning of the 1990s, the HIV/AIDS epidemic appeared to be progressing in Brazil at rates comparable to some countries in Africa. Today Brazil has been able to contain the epidemic at 0.6 percent of adult population and has nearly halved the number of AIDS-related deaths. The strengthening of the entire health system combined with full access to free antiretroviral treatment for all qualifying patients (190,000) has resulted in increases in survival rates comparable to those of developed countries.

While initially the national government was slow to respond to AIDS, eventually national and international pressure increased, and Brazil's concern about its reputation motivated the government to respond. As public pressure and the civic movement advocating universal health care gained power (eventually enshrining free access to treatment in the constitution), AIDS officials sought strategic interaction with the international community. The government began by increasing its attendance and participation at conferences, while also inviting international organizations to Brazil. The goal was to convince the international community that the government was committed to responding and becoming a world pioneer in the fight against HIV/AIDS.

However, Brazil and other nations were confronting high drug prices among international drug companies. These suppliers were protected by the World Trade Organization's Agreement on Trade-Related Aspects of Intellectual Property Rights (TRIPS), enabling trade of AIDS drugs at free-market prices. Brazil led the fight against the TRIPS ruling on the principle that it made it impossible for developing nations to ensure universal access to medicines. Thus, Brazil played a key role in leading other nations to introduce the Doha Declaration of 2001, which further clarified and enforced the TRIPS ruling, stating that nations have the right to issue compulsory licenses for the production of antiretroviral medication in periods of health crisis, while giving governments more autonomy in defining such a crisis.

Brazil has consistently used the TRIPS agreement and the Doha Declaration as a bargaining chip when negotiating with pharmaceutical companies. By periodically threatening to produce generic versions of patented medication in its government-sponsored laboratories, the government has been able to acquire medicine at more affordable prices. To further strengthen the government's bargaining power, the Ministry of Health has also worked with the Ministry of External Relations to send medically trained diplomats to international health conferences to persuasively explain the drug-production process and the need for price reductions.

The experience of the HIV/AIDS program in Brazil has been extremely valuable to other developing nations and is the subject of numerous South-South exchanges. These include the Southern Ties Network Initiative, which brought eight Portuguese-speaking countries together, and the creation of the International Center for Technical Cooperation in Brazil, a partnership with UNAIDS and bilateral donors that works on capacity building in Latin American and Portuguese-speaking countries in the areas of clinical management of HIV infections, logistics, laboratory techniques, human rights, and civic society organizations.

Sources: Gomez 2011; World Bank 2010.

In the future, oil- and gas-fired power plants will greatly expand, particularly as the massive oil reserves discovered in 2006 off the coast of Rio in the deep pre-salt formation are commercially exploited. Increasing the share of biofuels in the fast-growing transportation fuels market is possible, but pricing and regulatory reforms may be necessary. Concerns over land pressure in the Amazon and the Cerrado may diminish if the biofuel industry significantly increases yields and productivity in other crops and regions, as has been the case for sugarcane in the southeast and soybeans in the Cerrado. Brazil is also encouraging expansion of other renewable sources, such as wind and biomass, and is enhancing its nuclear power capabilities: Brazil has the sixth-largest proven uranium resources in the world and is expanding its enrichment facilities. Overall, however, the shape of the energy matrix is likely to become much more carbon intense in the next 10–20 years.

Reducing Deforestation and Agriculture's Footprint

A similar challenge ahead is sustaining Brazil's achievement in reversing the trends in deforestation and land use change. Deforestation in the Amazon fell by about 11 percent, to 6,238 square kilometers between August 2010 and July 2011, and to 4,471 square kilometers between August 2011 and July 2012, reaching the lowest ever recorded for the fourth consecutive year. This constitutes only about one-third of the 21,000 square kilometers that were deforested in 1988, the year monitoring began. Importantly, this decline has occurred at the same time that Brazil has experienced impressive rates of economic growth, suggesting a decoupling of economic growth and deforestation. The gains are partially credited to improved monitoring and enhanced enforcement—led by the Brazilian Institute of Environment and Renewable Natural Resources (IBAMA) in cooperation with the Federal Police, the National Security Force, and the army—and high-level intersectoral cooperation.

In addition to strengthened control of illegal logging, a critical economic (dis)-incentive has been the law passed by the Central Bank that included conformity with environmental legislation as a key factor for concessioning agricultural credit. Another major economic factor has been on the demand side. Due to pressure from consumer groups and supermarket chains, as well as from producers of products such as beef and soybeans, products originating in the Amazon have been increasingly certified and monitored to ensure that they do not come from areas of illegal deforestation or other illegal practice. Thus, reducing deforestation has been possible through a combination of technological surveillance and enhanced speed and effectiveness of enforcement actions coupled with well-targeted economic incentives that have been increasingly pushing farmers toward conformity with social and environmental laws.

The National Climate Change Action Plan became law in 2009 and includes bold targets to decrease deforestation rates in the Amazon and Cerrado by 2020. And in setting a target of no net liquid loss of forest by 2015 with a reduction in deforestation rates in the Amazon, Brazil is voluntarily indicating its willingness to protect its significant natural wealth. This goal has high global significance as the Amazon is the largest remaining intact swath of natural forest and accounts for about 30 percent of the globe's remaining tropical forests and about half of the world's plant species.

Challenges remain as demand for new land persists. Given the strength of its agribusiness sector, Brazil will continue to expand its agricultural output and exports. While most of the increase in output in the last two decades has been a result of productivity gains, pressure will remain to expand the agricultural frontier—particularly in the Amazon and in the so-called MATOPIBA (the States of Mato Grosso, Tocantins, Piaui, and Bahia). About 80 percent of the increase in land use between 2018 and 2030 is expected to take place in the Amazon and the MATOPIBA, and it is possible that conflicts between conservation and the expansion agriculture and cattle ranching will also persist.

This pressure on resources may be countered in part by the continued productivity gains in agriculture and cattle ranching, as well as by the increasing recovery of degraded lands and significant increase in silvo-pastoral and agro-forestry practices. Hence, reducing agriculture's environmental footprint, currently accounting for 40 percent of total greenhouse gas (GHG) emissions, along with other environmental pressures (fertilizer runoff, pollution from meat processing, among others), represents an important concern for Brazil in the next decade.

Conclusions: Brazil's Potential Contribution to Sustainable Development Post-2025

Brazil's economic importance and rising influence in regional and global affairs makes it an influential participant in the discussion of GPGs. Its size, demographics, and natural endowments assign global significance to the domestic choices the country makes in the future, particularly in the areas of energy and land use.

Brazil is shifting from a traditionally conservative, nationally focused foreign policy toward more proactive engagement in world affairs and international development assistance. Though not abandoning the principles of respect for sovereign nations to define their own choices, Brazil—with a goal of equity in global solutions and a preference to work within the G77 platform—is now also actively working with new groupings of emerging economies on a number of global issues. In addition, since the first Lula administration, investment in and cooperation with Africa and a stronger integration with the rest of South America have taken center stage. Brazil is actively engaged in several South-South programs sharing its knowledge in a wide number of areas, from agricultural innovation and research to improving health and education systems. The World Bank has been a facilitator of some of these programs.

Energy security and land use change in the next 10–15 years will test Brazil's determination to seek the sustainable path enshrined in various laws and programs, including its climate change action plan. As large-scale hydropower opportunities have been almost exhausted, and other renewables are yet to reach their full potential, the availability of gas and the pre-salt oil likely to be commercially exploited in the future point toward a more carbon-intense energy matrix in the future. Brazil's ability to sustain the economic policies and enforcement actions needed to preserve the agricultural frontier from the Amazon and the Cerrado will also be tested in the coming decade.

In this challenging context, will Brazil choose to take an individual approach or prefer to partner with others in the search of solutions for the challenges affecting the planet? Will it continue to deploy its technical and diplomatic capabilities to help least-developed nations, even when returns to the country may only materialize in the long term? How will Brazil leverage the visibility of its cities during major sports events in the context of huge needs for environmental improvement and urban infrastructure in the development world?

The possible scenarios resulting from each of these questions will likely vary depending on whether Brazil has been able to satisfy domestic needs and concerns to a sufficient degree and when these converge with international pressures (such as in the case of HIV/AIDS reviewed earlier). Regardless, Brazil's voice will be increasingly influential in the decades to come.

The Republic of Korea's noteworthy economic success—per capita GDP increasing from $70 in the early 1950s to $17,000 some 50 years later—has been widely recognized and extensively studied by the international community. Despite its small land size and low endowment of natural resources, Korea has emerged as a highly industrialized, advanced economy, as well as an information technology (IT) powerhouse fueled by investment in human capital from the beginning of industrialization. Now, as the globe's 15th-largest economy, Korea is a world leader in several industries, including memory chips, LCD displays, mobile phones, and shipbuilding.

Korea is also emerging as a key member of the international donor community and partner of the multilateral development organizations, including as a contributor to the IDA and similar poverty-reduction funds. As a recently new member of the Organisation for Economic Co-operation and Development's (OECD) Development Assistance Committee (DAC), Korea took the bold step of pledging "green ODA" to reach 30 percent of its total official development assistance (ODA) by 2020. Its rise as a donor country places Korea in a unique position as a "bridge" between the developed and developing world.

This case study focuses on the process and mechanisms through which Korea addresses GPGs, especially climate change and related sustainability challenges, and Korea's contributions to the broader development agenda. It also highlights the demand for investment in climate-resilient urban development in Asia and examines various examples of successful and relevant Korean urban initiatives. The study concludes with remarks on the role that Korea can play in provisioning GPGs in the future and recommendations for the World Bank to strengthen its role as a knowledge-sharing institution that also serves as an intermediary to include one in which it leverages private sector resources in order to scale up investment for long-term, climate-resilient infrastructure development in emerging countries.

Korea's Role in Asia and the International Community

Korea has demonstrated one of the most successful economic transformations in the 20th century. In the aftermath of World War II, Korea was one of the world's poorest countries, and the subsequent Korean War, 1950–1953, worsened its economic and social conditions. The economy was on the verge of bankruptcy, as shown by the statistics on goods imported and exported. In 1960 the Korean government was importing 10 times more than it was exporting: $344 million in imports, mostly basic commodities for consumption by the population, while exports were only $33 million (O 2009).

Economic Success

The Korean government opted to exploit Korea's only resource—an abundant supply of labor—and use this cheap labor to produce and export goods. In 1964 the Korean government adjusted the dollar exchange rate to lower the average labor cost for its export-oriented growth strategies, making Korean labor more internationally competitive (O 2009). This cheap labor became the driving force in implementing the national economic strategy and reorganizing Korean industry to be export oriented. As industrialization progressed, however, the government decided it needed more skilled workers and prioritized the education of skilled workers and engineers as one of the most urgent national tasks. Special subsidies were given to technical high schools to encourage education, and government-operated enterprises, as well as large companies from the private sector, were strongly urged to establish technical schools (O 2009). Therefore, human capital was recognized as the integral part of the economy from the beginning of Korea's industrialization and continued throughout the process.

Thus government-led industrialization and export-oriented growth strategies, driven by investment in human capital, enabled Korea to overcome its small domestic market, low endowment of natural resources, and extremely high dependence on foreign fossil fuels. The highly successful results include increased exports from less than 5 percent of GDP in 1960 to more than 56 percent in 2011 (Jones 2012; OECD 2013). Accordingly, Korea's per capita GDP increased by more than 24-fold over the five decades since 1960 (see figure 8.1), and life expectancy increased from 53 to more than 80 years.

Despite its success, the Korean development model was called into question when the Asian financial crisis dealt a humiliating blow to Koreans through the "IMF crisis" in 1997, when Korea was embarrassed to have to receive a bailout from the IMF because of bank failures. The mechanisms of resource allocation by which the government wielded discretionary power over the market had been effective in the early, high-growth era, but the government

Figure 8.1 Comparison of GDP Per Capita of the Republic of Korea and Sub-Saharan Africa, 1960–2011

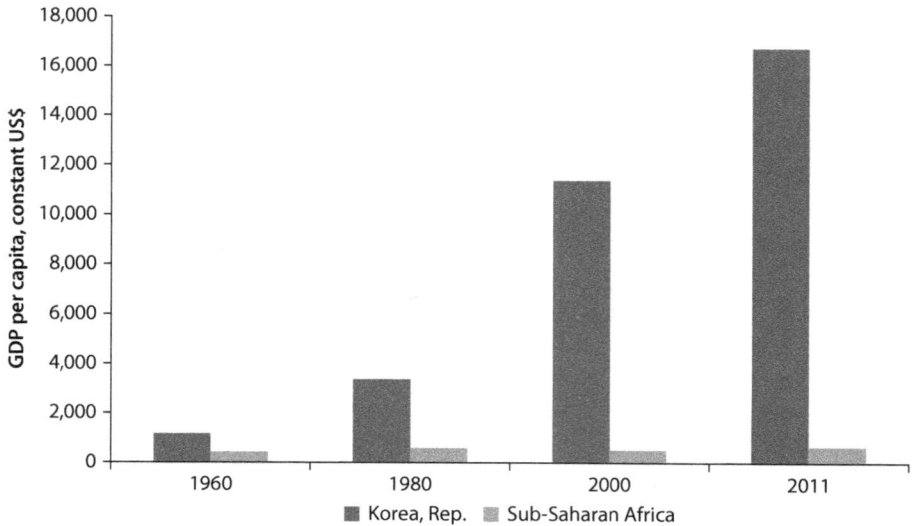

Source: World Bank Open Data (http://data.worldbank.org).

failed to restructure the policy framework and growth strategy to accommo-date the new, larger, and more complex economy (Suh and Chen 2007). Korea took a $60 billion bailout from the IMF and shut down excess production capacity, causing the collapse of 14 of the nation's industrial conglomerates, laying off legions of workers, and prompting a nationwide movement in which citizens donated their household gold to the national treasury. This collective trauma is remembered in Korea on the scale of the Great Depression in the United States (Fackler 2011). Recognizing the urgent need for widespread economic reform, the Korean government increased openness to imports and positioned itself as more market oriented, advancing Korea's further integration into the international community.

When the 2008 global financial crisis occurred, the economic restructuring and reform undertaken after the IMF crisis proved effective in dealing with external shocks. In fact, Korea was the first industrialized country to rebound; after seeing GDP growth fall to only 0.3 percent at the height of the crisis in 2009, it recovered to 6.3 percent in 2010 (Strangarone 2013). However, GDP growth fell to 3.6 percent in 2011 and to 2 percent in 2012, highlighting the need to reposition the government's national priorities and policy directions as a relatively mature economy.

Current and Future Economic Challenges

Korea's challenges today are different from those of the past few decades. Despite its significant GDP growth, Korea remains a manufacturing-led nation that is still catching up to the post industrial economy of countries like the United States (Fackler 2011). Its focus on manufacturing has resulted in a relatively under-developed service sector compared with other developed nations. Accounting for 57 percent of GDP, Korea's service sector is the second smallest in the OECD, with 2008 productivity only 53 percent of that of the manufacturing sector, far below the OECD average of 87 percent (OECD 2012). Increasing productivity and overseas expansion of the *chaebols* (family-controlled Korean conglomerates), whose industries account for nearly half the GDP, exacerbates conditions for Korea's service sector and its small and medium-sized manufacturing enterprises. The share of domestic employment by the chaebols has fallen by one-third, from 18 to 12 percent over the period 1995–2010, and job creation has fallen to sectors that do not have the capacity to absorb available labor force, especially the young and highly educated (Choi et al. 2013). One survey shows that the real number of unemployed young people in Korea stood at 1.1 million in 2010, which trans-lated into a striking 22 percent youth unemployment rate (HRI 2011).

Social and economic issues related to an aging society are also quickly emerging in Korea. While Korea has the third-youngest population in the OECD, its demographics are projected to shift to the second oldest by 2050, with the elderly making up 37 percent of the population due to a low fertility rate and rapid gains in longevity (OECD 2012; Rim 2013). In other words, every elderly citizen in 2013 is supported by eight young people; the same responsibility will be borne by only two younger in 2050 (Rim 2013). Given the current age profile of the population (figure 8.2), expenditure in pensions is also expected to increase rapidly, from 0.9 percent of GDP in 2010 to 5.5 percent in 2050 (Rim 2013).

The elderly also face the issue of unemployment. All age groups in Korea have suffered from increasing unemployment since the 1997 Asian financial crisis, but the elderly (in this analysis, group aged 60 and over) is the only age

Figure 8.2 Republic of Korea Demographic Profile, 1970–2050

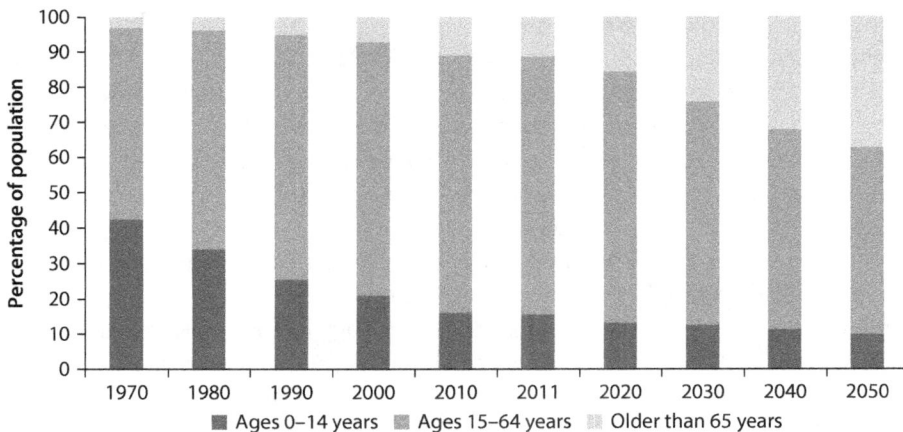

Source: Statistics Korea.

group that has shown a consistently rising unemployment rate. In fact, the elderly unemployment rate in 2012 was higher than at the pre-crisis level (Park 2013a). This phenomenon can be explained by two factors: first, most Koreans retire without sufficient means for a post-retirement living, both in terms of individual assets and social safety nets, and second, the tradition of children supporting parents is quickly disappearing with westernization (Park 2013a). The concomitant problems of a weak social safety net, limited job opportunities, and a large supply of elderly labor are contributing to increasing social instability.

Gender inequality is also a pressing social issue. A study places Korea 108th (ranked between the United Arab Emirates and Kuwait) in the world in gender equity, primarily due to women's lack of political and economic power (Hausmann, Tyson, and Zahidi 2012). Korean women without children earn about 13 percent less than men, but this pay gap nearly quadruples if they have children, at which point they earn 45 percent less than men (Fisher 2012). As a result, Korean women have only 55 percent labor force participation, compared with 76 percent for men (Fisher 2012). With the working-age population projected to start declining from 2017 (OECD 2012), the Korean government needs to incentivize the female and elderly workforce to sustain Korea's growth potential.

Export-oriented strategies have provided a solid ground for Korea's economic resilience during the past financial crises. However, Korea is now at the crossroads that Japan reached in the 1980s and that China is rapidly approaching—a point where a country that has tapped an investment-and-exports model to pull the population out of poverty must find a new growth path (Yoon 2012). The Korean development model has created a set of new economic and social challenges, including skewed industrial and commercial growth that favors conglomerates over small and medium enterprises, heavy dependence on the manufacturing sector, a weak service sector, a high unemployment rate, an aging population, growing inequality, and an inadequate social safety net.

Reducing domestic GHG emissions is another challenge for a country like Korea, whose GHG emissions almost doubled between 1990 and 2006—the highest rate among OECD countries (World Bank 2012a)—and that is still heavily dependent on manufacturing for its growth. Considering that nearly 85 percent of GDP growth in high-income countries over the past 25 years came from services (McKinsey & Company 2010), continued rapid economic growth in Korea is likely to become increasingly difficult if Korea continues to depend on an the export-led growth model.

Similar challenges will be facing today's developing and emerging countries in the next several years. Therefore, how Korea addresses and resolves these problems will serve as a case study for future emerging economies. Korea is seen by developing countries, particularly those in East Asia, as a source of knowledge and ideas on development drawn from actual experience (OECD DAC 2012). This particular comparative advantage gives Korea a good opportunity to maximize and share development knowledge as a GPG.

Korea's Standing with Regard to Global Public Goods

In the midst of the most recent global financial downturn, Korea chose "Low Carbon, Green Growth" as its new growth model, to improve both domestic economic performance and its international standing as a recent donor. As a national goal from 2008 to 2012, green growth represented an integrated strategy for Korea to achieve its vision of moving away from the traditional "brown economy," growth-at-any-cost model of the previous decades to a "green economy" model, where long-term prosperity and sustainability are the key objectives (UNEP 2010).[4]

A Green Growth Model Strategy

While it has characteristics of regional public goods and GPGs, much of the green growth agenda as a development strategy is intended to generate local public goods. Nonetheless, the knowledge generated through green growth initiatives in Korea and around the world is clearly a GPG of high added value. Korea's green initiative was largely embraced by the international community, its collective impact spreading at a global scale. All 30 member countries of the OECD, along with Chile, Estonia, Israel and Slovenia, signed a Green Growth Declaration in 2009 and approved a mandate to develop a Green Growth Strategy to include economic, environmental, technological, and developmental aspects within comprehensive policy measures. The World Bank adopted inclusive green growth as the pathway to achieve sustainable development (World Bank 2012b). Green growth has also been widely advocated by various other international entities—the United Nations Environment Programme (UNEP) and International Energy Agency (IEA) as well as at G8 and G20 meetings—and has spread to developing and emerging countries that hope to emulate Korea's economic success. For example, Korea's partner countries of Cambodia and Vietnam have started benchmarking Korea's model of green growth to apply in their national contexts.

The expanding network of green growth–focused institutions is facilitating the sharing of experience and knowledge as a public good, to be tailored and applied locally. The establishment of the Global Green Growth Institute (GGGI) as a vehicle to share knowledge of good practice on green growth was an important political decision by the Korean government. GGGI's conversion into an international organization to become a "global asset" was joined by 17 other developed and developing countries that recognized the importance of an international network dedicated to green growth.

Korea's Development Assistance Strategies in the Global Public Goods Context

As a beneficiary of development assistance and one of the clear aid success stories, Korea effectively utilized $12.7 billion of ODA received in the postwar period to spur economic development and decrease poverty. In turn, Korea began its aid activities in the late 1970s and 1980s with the provision of technical training, and in the late 1980s and early 1990s it made a more concerted effort to broaden and increase its ODA (OECD DAC 2008).

The Korean government established the EDCF (Economic Development Cooperation Fund) in 1987 under the Ministry of Strategy and Finance, and the KOICA (Korea International Cooperation Agency) in 1992 under the Ministry of Foreign Affairs to provide concessional loans and grants, respectively, to developing countries. Most of Korea's ODA is concentrated in these two ministries, which were responsible for 88 percent of the total fund allocation in 2011 (OECD DAC 2012). Korea was classified by the UNDP as a donor country in the technical cooperation field in 1992 and was removed from the list of recipient countries by the World Bank in 1996 (Kang 2011). In 1996 Korea became an OECD member and 13 years later, in 2009, an OECD DAC member.[5] By joining the DAC, Korea became one of only a few countries to transition from an aid recipient to a DAC member.

ODA Growth

Korea's ODA volume saw steady growth, reaching $1.325 billion in 2011, equivalent to 0.12 percent of its gross national income (GNI)—from $455 million and 0.05 percent of its GNI in 2006 (OECD DAC 2012, figure 8.3). Recognizing that its ODA volume and ODA/GNI ratio are still very low compared with other DAC members, Korea has committed to scale up its aid to achieve an ODA/GNI ratio of 0.25 percent by 2015. The ratio of Korea's bilateral to multilateral disbursements has shifted from 83:17 in 2006 to 75:25 in 2011 (OECD DAC 2012). Korea plans to strengthen its support for the multilateral system in the future, with its target ratio of bilateral to multilateral funding at the DAC average ratio of 70:30 by 2015 (OECD 2011).

For its bilateral assistance, Korea is concentrating on 26 priority partner countries based on their development needs, their capacity to use aid effectively, and their alignment with Korean foreign policy priorities, as shown in table 8.1

Figure 8.3 Republic of Korea's Official Development Assistance, 2006–15

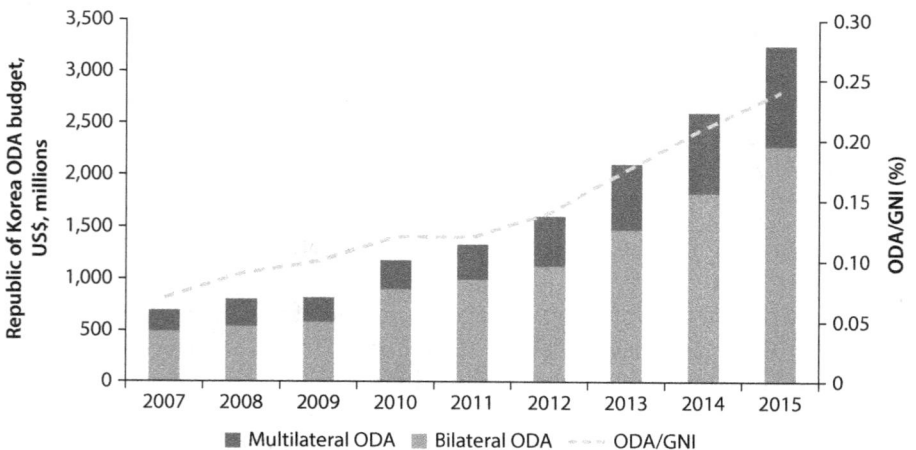

Sources: OECD DAC 2012; ODA Korea (http://www.odakorea.go.kr/index.jsp).

Too Global to Fail • http://dx.doi.org/10.1596/978-1-4648-0307-9

Table 8.1 Korea's Priority Partner Countries

Asia, Oceania, and Commonwealth of Independent States (14)	Africa (8)	Latin America (4)
Azerbaijan	Cameroon	Bolivia
Bangladesh	Congo, Dem. Rep.	Colombia
Cambodia	Ethiopia	Paraguay
Indonesia	Ghana	Peru
Lao PDR	Mozambique	
Mongolia	Nigeria	
Nepal	Rwanda	
Pakistan	Uganda	
Philippines		
Solomon Islands		
Sri Lanka		
Timor-Leste		
Uzbekistan		
Vietnam		

Source: OECD DAC 2012.

(OECD DAC 2012). Most of Korea's bilateral aid is delivered by grant or loan-funded projects and technical assistance.

One feature of Korean development assistance is its significant use of concessional loans. In 2006, loans constituted 31 percent of ODA, a high figure compared with most other DAC donors, and the portion actually increased to 42 percent in 2011.[6] Nearly all DAC donors' aid portfolios consist almost entirely of grants, with only three DAC donors using loans to any real extent (OECD DAC 2012). Korea's inclination for loans can be explained by its own positive experience as a recipient of loans during its development process and the profoundly held belief that this instrument imposes essential fiscal discipline on the recipient country.

Another characteristic of Korean aid is that it is extremely tied. An estimated 98 percent of Korean bilateral aid is either tied or partially tied (OECD DAC 2012), which is in striking contrast to other DAC members, who have either fully untied their aid or almost completely untied it. The Korean government is well aware of the need to untie its bilateral aid and foresees a gradual improvement in untying to meet the 2001 DAC Recommendation on Untying Official Development Assistance to the least developed countries by 2015.

Korea views the multilateral system as an important complement to its bilateral efforts, particularly in tackling transnational issues such as climate change, food security, and humanitarian issues. Korea's use of multilateral aid channels is expected to increase substantially, given its target to ensure that 30 percent of its ODA is multilateral and its intention to increase the overall ODA rapidly over the next few years to meet its ODA/GNI target. Korea intends to develop a comprehensive strategy for effective allocation to the multilateral development banks, the United Nations, and other multilateral organizations (OECD DAC 2012).

Korea's Partners

Based on its own experience, Korea is well aware that developing countries are interested in learning and applying successful development experience from other countries. The government is trying to make more use of its comparative advantage as a "bridging" country through various knowledge-sharing activities. The Knowledge Sharing Program (KSP), Korea's consultation program which the Ministry of Strategy and Finance launched in 2004 with the Korea Development Institute as the implementing body, serves as a representative example of Korea's such effort. The KSP draws from Korea's policy-making and development experiences to provide policy research findings, recommendations, and training activities on specific issues relevant to the partner country, with the goal of enhancing their national development capacities and institutional restructuring efforts.[7] Since 2011 the KSP has provided joint consultations with international organizations, including the World Bank, Asian Development Bank, and Inter-American Development Bank. By the end of 2012, the KSP had provided policy consultations to 107 countries on more than 440 topics (Kim and Tcha 2012). KOICA's recently launched Development Experience Exchange Program (DEEP) is another initiative to provide consulting service based on Korea's development experience, covering various thematic issues of social development as well as Korea's own experience of implementing ODA-funded activities.

More recently, Korea's development assistance shows a shift in focus to activities related to environment and climate change. For example, Korea's contribution in biodiversity, desertification, and climate change mitigation and adaptation shows a significant increase, from 1.7 percent of its bilateral ODA in 2007 to 14.1 percent in 2010 (OECD DAC 2012). Korea committed almost $250 million of its ODA to climate change action, including $27.5 million to the GEF for the period 2010–14, and $20 million to the Asian Development Bank's Future Carbon Fund for the period 2010–13 (OECD DAC 2012). In 2012 Korea committed to increase the proportion of environment-friendly green projects to 30 percent of its total ODA by 2020 (Yunhap 2012). This "green ODA" will help Korea's development assistance strategies evolve to meet the needs of developing countries that are generally not yet fully equipped to introduce and implement greener policies and tap into the benefits of environmentally sustainable future.

The East Asia Climate Partnership (EACP), KOICA's flagship program, highlights Korea's recent shift in development assistance towards green, climate change–related activities in the geographic area where Korea has a comparative advantage. With Korea's $200 million commitment for 2008–12, the goal of the EACP is to facilitate green growth and climate change mitigation in developing countries in Asia. KOICA has provided grant support for 20 projects in 10 countries, within five focal areas: water resources management, waste treatment, low-carbon energy, low-carbon city, and forestry. In addition, it is funding nine cooperation projects with seven international organizations, including the Asia Development Bank, UNESCAP, UNEP, and IFC; nine invitational training projects; and 19 research projects as part of the EACP program.[8] The EACP raised Korea's green ODA volume to 13.5 percent of total ODA in 2010 from 8.6 percent in 2008 (Jeong 2012), and it is set to become the foundation for expanding Korea's future green ODA.

Korea's Experience in Urban Development and Implications for Developing Countries

Between the 1960s and 1980s, the Korean government, taking into account the country's limited financial resources, adopted a strategy of concentrating industries in regions with high growth potential (KDI 2010). These "growth centers" allowed efficient use of limited resources to support the country's rapid economic growth. The regions selected for development included the Seoul-Incheon area, because of its existing infrastructure and availability of urban services; Ulsan, with its advantageous location and port; and the Mt. Taebaek area for agriculture and resource development (KDI 2010).

Financing the necessary infrastructure and industries for development during this period came from the Korean government's strategic choice of mobilizing public and private resources at different stages through social overhead capital (SOC) projects. One of the main objectives of the government's economic policy in the 1960s was to provide financial incentives to create an investment-friendly environment for private investors and to extend large sums of credit to businesses under various loan programs (Chung 2007). Therefore, the reconstruction and expansion of SOC were financed not with savings in the public sector, but largely with resources from two other sources—private funds and foreign savings. It has been estimated that approximately three-quarters of the credits (5.1 percent of GDP) extended by the financial intermediaries and government were to business for private investment (Chung 2007).

The government's initial investment played a fundamental role in the field of SOC, which included electricity, transportation, and communication, as well as some important large-scale pioneering industries, such as cement, chemicals, metals, steels, and ships. The government's subsequent contribution to investment in the manufacturing sector, where modern, innovative, capital- and technology-intensive, and large-scale operations took place, was also highly significant (Chung 2007). The main beneficiaries within the SOC sector, which captured the major portion of public investment, were the public enterprises that operated the electrical power, transportation, and communications networks. They received the largest amounts of loans among all economic sectors relative to their assets and at lower interest rates than all the others (Chung 2007).

Korea's early urban development was driven by a government strategy through which specific regions were targeted as growth centers and by financed development through SOC projects. Gumi City, located in Gyeongsang province, demonstrates such a case. It was built in the early 1970s to house the Korean electronics industry. The leading agent for Gumi City's construction was the

Korea Export Industrial Corporation (KEIC). As an arm of the national government belonging to the Ministry of Trade and Industry, KEIC had its own special trust fund to finance land clearance and development. Over the years, KEIC's operations have been increasingly funded out of the proceeds of its land and energy activities, but its development policy was still overseen by the national government (Park and Markusen 1999). Government subsidies and incentives, including land clearance, site preparation, tax breaks, and education and training programs, have played a major role in inducing domestic and foreign companies in Gumi City, and as a result, Gumi City has grown significantly as an industrial complex.

Pohang City is another successful example of the government's strategy of developing specific regions for different purposes. Pohang was selected to become the hub of steel manufacturing industry due to its geographical advantage and access to resources. When the Pohang Iron and Steel Company (POSCO) was established in the late 1960s using compensation claims of about $100 million from Japan as seed money, Pohang was a small coastal city with a population of 50,000 (Lee and Lee 2009). The Steel Industry Promotion Act was enacted in 1970 to enable various forms of government support for POSCO, including provision of long-term, low-interest loans, tax breaks, and infrastructure subsidies. Due to this government support, POSCO could save on the cost of railway use by 40 percent, port use by 50 percent, water by 30 percent, and gas by 20 percent (Lee and Lee 2009). The successful introduction of heavy industry to this city transformed the local economy into an industrial city known for iron, steel, and shipbuilding, with a population of 500,000 residents.

Korean Climate Change Efforts as Model for Asian Cities

Today, more than half of the world's population lives in urban areas, and this share is projected to reach 60 percent by 2030 and 70 percent by 2050 (OECD 2010). With a concentration of more than 80 percent of global economic activity, cities are also hubs of prosperity (Mohieldin and Allaoua 2013). However, cities also present complex economic, social, and environmental challenges, especially in the context of climate change.

Even though global urbanization took place predominantly in Europe in the first half of the 20th century, today Asia is the continent with the highest urban population (OECD 2010). Asia is urbanizing at an unprecedented rate. In 1950 Asia was predominantly rural—with only 17 percent of its 1.4 billion people living in cities or towns; by 2020, 55 percent of Asians, or 2.7 billion people, will live in urban areas (ADB 2012). Given that virtually all Asia's population growth will be in urban areas after 2015, and recognizing the significant impacts cities impose on climate and natural resources, Asian cities are increasingly embracing green urban development models specifically to reduce energy consumption by buildings, industries, and transport systems (ADB 2012).

Rapid urbanization in developing and emerging countries translates into a huge increase in the demand for infrastructure for electricity, telecommunications, rail, highway, and water and modern sanitation. A study of East Asian infrastructure needs estimated that the region needed to spend more than $165 billion per year in the period 2006–10, or roughly 6.2 percent of GDP (Jha and Brecht 2012). Another study showed that while the current annual investment required for urban (mainly environmental) infrastructure is about $40 billion, the total amount required of governments is valued at an estimated $100 billion, despite Asia's private capital markets flush with funds (ADB 2012). The only viable strategy for bridging Asia's investment gap, and an effective means to promote climate resilient growth, would be by leveraging private-sector funding.

Private Sector Role

The role of the private sector in addressing climate change has received increasing attention due to its unique capabilities: capital mobilization, risk management, innovative nature, and efficiency in delivering outcomes. For a practical, effective, and efficient sustainable development agenda, the private sector must take a prominent role. In fact, the private sector is already contributing the majority of global climate finance. In 2011–12 the private sector was responsible for $217–243 billion, or 63 percent, of the $364 billion for global climate financing (Buchner et al. 2012). The public sector ('$16–23 billion) acted as a catalyst for private finance as well as providing bilateral aid to developing countries.

Against this backdrop, Korea is well positioned and highly equipped to provide examples of climate-resilient, low-carbon, green urban development for other emerging and developing economies. The share of Korea's urban population grew significantly over the last five decades, increasing from 28 percent in 1960 to more than 80 percent in 2010, and is projected to reach 90 percent in 2050 (figure 8.4) (Henderson 2002).

Figure 8.4 Urban Population of Republic of Korea, Percentage of Total, 1950–2050

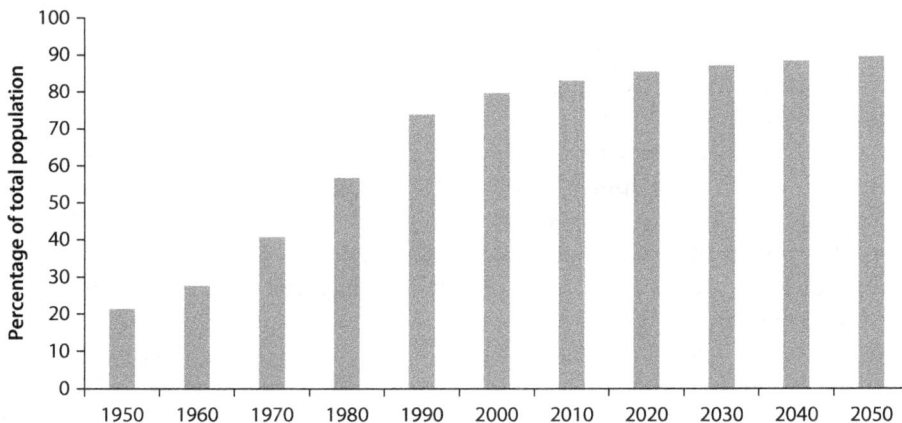

Source: UN 2011.

With about 70 percent of the country's land area comprising mountains and uplands, cities in Korea must have high urban density. In fact, the capital, Seoul, has the highest population density among large cities in OECD member countries, with 17,219 persons per square kilometer—roughly eight times the density of both New York City (2,050) and Sydney (2,100) (*Hankyoreh* 2009). Urban density facilitates the delivery of public services, including education, health care, and basic services. For example, it costs $0.70–0.80 per cubic meter to provide piped water in urban areas, compared with $2 in sparsely populated areas (Mohieldin and Allaoua 2013). Korean cities therefore benefit from high urban density. However, the other side of the coin is that other regional cities, such as Jeonju, are suffering from deteriorating urban centers due to development of suburbs and lack of sustained economic activities. Recently efforts have begun to address these issues (see next section).

Climate Change Vulnerability

Korea is highly vulnerable to climate change. According to the National Institute of Meteorological Research, the average temperature in Korea increased by approximately 1.7°C in the last 100 years, which is 2–3 times higher than the global mean temperature change. Rainfall intensity and frequency are increasing, as well as the number of extreme events, such as typhoon, heat wave, and heavy snow. For example, damage by typhoon increased 65 percent from 1999 to 2008 (Park 2013b). Given this immediate and increasing risk of vulnerability, and the fact that Korea's cities are both a major source of GHG emissions and a potential opportunity for mitigation, Korean decision makers have the opportunity to lead the region with low-carbon, climate-resilient urban growth.

Korea's Urban History

From Songdo (see box 8.3), a cutting-edge eco-city built from scratch on reclaimed land, to Gwangju, a historic city established in 57 BCE, with innovative new green initiatives now being implemented (see box 8.4), to Jeonju, where various urban regeneration projects are taking place (see box 8.5), Korea presents not only cities of various scales and characters that are relevant to cities in other developing and emerging countries, but also different measures and initiatives to restructure or establish cities so that they are more sustainable and climate-resilient.

With the right investment and planning, it would be relatively easy to implement new urban development projects that incorporate policies and relevant technology to maximize cities' capacity to address and mitigate climate change, as the developers of Songdo did. However, emerging countries already have cities of various scales, and will not necessarily be building new ones. Modifications to the built environment both to limit emissions and to adapt to climate change are costly and require long lead times. Given that new urban growth in the next few decades will primarily take place in small- and medium-scale cities and in peri-urban areas along existing and new growth corridors (ADB 2012), planning and mechanisms for urban renewal and regeneration need to be analyzed and

Box 8.3 Songdo International Business District: New Standard for Green Design for Large-Scale Development Projects

The Songdo International Business District (IBD) exemplifies a large-scale, top-down green urban development project with cutting-edge technologies. Located on 1,500 acres of the Incheon Free Economic Zone near Seoul, Songdo IBD is a US$35 billion private real estate project whose purpose is to set a new standard in sustainability through building design, systems engineering, urban infrastructure, and community planning. It is a development of Gale International and POSCO E&C, with the IFEZ Authority as the managing entity. Songdo IBD has been designated a LEED-ND (Neighborhood Development) pilot program—the largest outside North America—by the U.S. Green Building Council.

Songdo IBD's commitment to sustainability is driven by six core design goals:

1. **Open space:** Designation of 40 percent open space (600 acres) to maximize the connection to nature.
2. **Transportation:** Establishment of a new subway line, 25-kilometer network of bicycle lanes, infrastructure for electric vehicles, parking capacity allocated for fuel-efficient and low-emitting vehicles and carpool vehicles, and underground parking to minimize heat island effect.
3. **Water:** Establishment of water-saving irrigation systems and usage of reclaimed storm water and treated gray water from a city wide central system and green roofs to reduce storm water runoff, mitigate urban heat island effect, and promote biodiversity.
4. **Energy use:** Establishment of a central, citywide co-generation facility fueled by natural gas, energy-efficient LED traffic lights, and a centralized pneumatic waste collection system.
5. **Recycling:** Recycling 75 percent of construction waste, utilization of recycled/locally produced materials to the maximum extent possible, and incorporation of low volatile organic compound materials into all buildings.
6. **Operations:** Integration of sustainable procurement goals and recycling guidelines into the operational structure of the city through digital interfacing and mandating environmentally friendly (low/zero volatile organic compounds - VOC) facility management and maintenance.

Source: Songdo IBD website (http://www.songdo.com).

developed further. Innovative policy tools and initiatives in cities like Gwangju, some of which are already spreading nationwide, can serve as a benchmark to other cities in emerging economies.

Making existing cities more energy efficient, environmentally responsible, and livable is a constant task of urban renewal and regeneration. From here on, reuse and adaptation will be the predominant approach to environmentally sustainable regeneration and will help maintain the identities of existing cities (Steinberg 2008). Accordingly, initiatives with more specific focus on "regenerating" urban areas with consideration for climate change mitigation are taking place in Korea. The scale and intensity of urban issues—such as unbalanced economic

---

Box 8.4 Gwangju Metropolitan City: Successful Hybrid of National and Local Initiatives for Climate Change

Gwangju Metropolitan City demonstrates a hybrid of national and local green initiatives. Korea's national drive for green growth led Gwangju to establish its own Five-Year Plan for Green Growth, and the city also launched a local initiative, Creative Green City Gwangju, in 2011. Gwangju fosters green lifestyles in order to tackle greenhouse gas (GHG) emissions from the household and commercial sectors and to advance citizen-led programs with strong governance structures and has thus far produced successful outcomes. The Carbon Bank System and Low-Carbon Green Apartments programs are recognized as innovative and successful and have been benchmarked by other cities and national-level policies. These are described as follows.

- **The Carbon Bank System** was created by Gwangju City and the Gwangju Bank in 2008 to reduce GHG emission in the residential sector. It provides financial incentives in the form of carbon point or carbon money, which accrue as individual citizens reduce energy and water use and hence GHG emissions. This system also emphasizes the value of the local economy by engaging local actors, such as the Gwangju Bank, and by encouraging local stores to accept the carbon money as payment. More than 280,000 households in the city (51 percent of total households) have subscribed to the program since its launch, resulting in a 25,550 ton CO_2 reduction. For a city like Gwangju, where 47 percent of all GHG emissions result from residential and commercial sectors, the Carbon Bank System can be an effective instrument.
- **Green Card System.** In 2009 and 2011, the Ministry of Environment launched a similar program at the national level called the Green Card System. By May 2012, 2.6 million people (more than 10 percent of the economically active population) had joined the program.
- **Low-Carbon Green Apartment** is a program targeted to residents in apartment complexes with at least 150 units by engaging buildings and complexes to compete with one another in achieving GHG reduction. The evaluation criteria include the residents' participation rate in the Carbon Bank System and the GHG mitigation education program called Green Home Designer, in which consultants visit homes to diagnose the household's behavior and advise mitigation action. The prize money can be up to US$5,454 per apartment. The winning group often decides to invest the prize in green activities, such as installing LED lighting and planting trees. As of 2011, 24 apartments with 733 households were participating.
- **The Green Way** project is one of the most famous cases of environmental governance in Gwangju, where the local government, citizens, private companies, and NGOs collaborated to create an eco-park from 7.9 kilometers of abandoned metropolitan railway tracks in the middle of the city. It was a successful infrastructure project that engaged citizens and various stakeholders for green urban initiative.

Sources: Chung et al. 2012; KEPB 2012.

Box 8.5 City of Jeonju: Green Regeneration of a Traditional Marketplace

Business at the Central Market of Jeonju had been declining over the last three decades due to old infrastructure and insufficient capacity to deal with food waste. A regeneration project aims to refurbish and upgrade old food waste and sewer treatment systems and other infrastructure by using green reuse/recycling technologies; establish an education center to foster understanding of environmentally responsible activities; attract more people, particularly young generations; and establish community-driven businesses. Also, rainwater discharge and management and energy efficiency are to be improved through the installation of a rainwater reuse system and solar panels. Greenbox, a locally developed odor-controlling technology, is being used to treat organic waste to produce biogas, electricity, renewable fertilizer, and hot water. Establishment of a self-sufficient urban farm and green education program are also features of this project.

Source: Park 2013b.

development, outdated and inefficient infrastructure, and aging populations—in small and medium cities (SMCs) in Korea are increasing, highlighting the importance of social and economic regeneration as well as physical regeneration for climate-change resilient growth (Park 2013b).

The Korean Urban Regeneration Projects were initiated in 2007 with a research and development fund of $120 million million from the Ministry of Land, Transport, and Maritime Affairs to establish legal, institutional, technological, and social capacities to promote green urban regeneration of SMCs, especially for their climate change resilient growth. A unique feature of these projects is that active and voluntary participation and activities driven by communities are at the core in order to induce self-regeneration of urban areas and enhance social capital. Enhancing the local ownership of large projects can improve the quality and efficiency of public spending.

In sum, successful coordination for GHG emissions reduction and climate change adaptation can be driven from the top by national or regional authorities, can be grown from the bottom up by local policy innovations that can also provide models for regional or national action, or can feature a hybrid of both approaches.

Implications for Developing Countries in Future Urban Development

Efficient and strategic use of land has been crucial for Korea's economic development because of its limited land area. Korea's early urban development in the 1960s and 1970s was based on the national government's strategic planning and financing for the SOC sector. However, climate change was not taken into account in urban planning and development, and major cities today in Korea are becoming increasingly inefficient in their energy use and reduction of GHG emissions.

Korea's recent focus on green growth includes an upgrade of the urban development model in support of low-carbon development. The Songdo International Business District was established using a top-down planning approach and state-of-art technology, while old cities like Jeonju underwent regeneration programs using relevant green technologies. Gwangju demonstrated that cities do not have to focus only on infrastructure to improve their energy efficiency and change consumer behavior but rather that such improvements can be achieved through implementation of innovative policies and programs.

Korea's experience and knowledge will become a GPG only if developing countries "leapfrog" Korea's long early urban development stage of the 1960s and 1970s by tailoring various approaches employed in Korea in the 21th century to fit their local context. For example, nationally led top-down approaches, such as the Songdo development project, do best when they leave wide latitude for local authorities to shape policies on climate change to fit local contexts. Bottom-up frameworks allow for experimentation on models for urban climate action that regional or national governments can subsequently adopt or promote, as demonstrated by the Gwangju case.

On the basis of Korea's various green urban initiatives and SOC experience, such practices would greatly facilitate urban development in developing and emerging countries to meet their short-term economic and development needs and long-term sustainable development agenda. Korea's experience in climate-resilient urban development can be further developed and shared with the international community by exporting the model applicable to local contexts.

Conclusion: Korea's Contribution to Sustainable Development Post-2025 and the Role of the World Bank

Korea continues to be one of the most dynamic economies in the most economically dynamic region of the world. As one of only a few countries that has risen from aid recipient to OECD DAC member, Korea has thrust itself onto the international stage as a would-be leader on global development, especially in the context of green growth, achieving much in terms of international recognition. Its unique position between developed and developing countries, expertise in industrial and urban development, and commitment to increase green ODA allow Korea to contribute by its own means to provisioning GPGs and devising collective solutions for developed and developing countries.

Korea's experience in dramatic economic growth enables it to relate to developing countries of various economic stages, and this strengthens the ties between Korea and the international community, especially with developing and emerging countries. And Korea has a lot to offer. How it addresses today's economic, social, and environmental issues—skewed economic growth, unemployment, aging population, weak social safety net, urbanization, and GHG emissions—matters greatly to today's developing countries, because these issues will soon be relevant to them. The various urban case studies, ranging from large-scale urban development equipped with cutting-edge technology to deteriorating old cities, not only demonstrate Korea's strengths and experience in urban development, but also provide a specific platform for various stakeholders to collaborate and exchange their expertise in devising effective and tailored strategies for their urban areas. As the host country of international organizations and agencies such as GGGI, the Green Climate Fund, and the World Bank regional office focusing on advancing strategies for sustainable development, Korea has significant potential to become a regional and global hub for addressing GPGs.

Demand for policies and infrastructure for green urban development will be high, especially in Asia and Africa. The success of Korea's SOC sector demonstrates how effective the synergy between the public and private sector can be in leveraging the private resources. The interactions between the public and private sectors in Korea in the SOC sector highlight the role of public financing institutions like the World Bank in fostering such investment environment. Donors like the World Bank provide such support by strengthening the public sector of developing countries through capacity building and policy recommendations, which in turn attracts the participation of the private sector in infrastructure and urban development sectors in developing countries. Korea has the capacity, knowledge, and experience—through its diverse urban initiatives and knowledge-sharing programs—to cooperate with the World Bank to achieve its aim to be one of the leading global institutions helping countries meet short-term and long-term economic, social, and environmental needs.

The opportunities for the World Bank and other donors to partner with Korea to help shape and optimize benefits to developing countries from the growing international assistance are many and significant. Such partnerships could help several countries leapfrog technologies in industry and urban environs. Perhaps more important is the opportunity for the World Bank to work with Korea to assemble Korean lessons learned in devising low-carbon and climate-resilient urban growth at scale and to assist Korea in extending lessons and development finance to other countries.

In late 2011, Walz and Ramachandran (2011) reported estimates of $11–41.7 billion in aid flows from emerging (non-DAC) donors, many of which are currently IBRD recipients. This is equivalent to 8–31 percent of ODA (Walz and Ramachandran 2011). The discussion relevant to the impact this is having on overall aid architecture is presented in chapter 5, but it is also highly relevant to the current discussion on the relationship of the World Bank and emerging economies such as Brazil, as well as countries like Korea, that have transitioned from developing to developed.

These emerging economies are diverse, and they are certainly not consistent in how they support the development of other countries. However, they all have one thing in common: each has experience both as recipients and as aid donors and therefore possess a unique understanding of the challenges faced by those countries they are supporting with bilateral assistance. Countries like China, Brazil, and India are not emerging or new donors. They have each been supporting other developing countries for many years, and, as described in the Brazil case study, these assistance programs are diverse and substantial.

Technical and financial assistance from emerging economies to other developing countries does not generally follow the OECD DAC model. In a recent conference on the future of aid at the Australia National University, representatives of Brazil, China, India, Korea, and South Africa, agreed on one major point—their bilateral assistance is not purely altruistic, but rather designed for mutual economic and social benefit. Economic and foreign policy objectives are cited as key drivers for their bilateral assistance (Mulakala 2011). For example India's bilateral assistance is mainly in the form of credit lines that enable partner countries to export to India or via India to other parts of the world (AusAID 2012).

Recognizing the changing development assistance landscape—including the changing relationship between how "old" and "new" donors might collaborate—has spurred the OECD DAC to establish the Global Partnership for Effective Cooperation. Established in 2012, jointly managed by OECD and UNDP, it is too early to tell what might come from the partnership or how it might impact on the role of multilateral development finance institutions.

The World Bank is already deeply engaged with the new donors as shown in both the Korea and Brazil case studies. The World Bank Institute established the South-South Experience Exchange Facility in 2008 and has worked with a number of middle-income countries and lower-income countries to facilitate knowledge and technology transfer. Several country assistance strategies and partnership agreements have positioned the Bank as a broker to facilitate such exchanges.

There is a remarkable opportunity now to work with these new donor countries to the mutual benefit of the recipient and donor countries and the World Bank in terms of delivering on its commitments for sustainable development. The natural resource depletion and climate change challenges are a relatively new (at least from a priority issue point of view) and extremely complex global agenda that requires different approaches, and the World Bank has the capacity and resources to devise and implement these solutions.

For collective solutions for developing, emerging, and developing countries in the future, the World Bank needs to devise strategic approaches to tap into the resources and capacities of the new donors—not just their governments but also their private sectors, civil societies, and think-tanks. The World Bank is also well positioned to capture the lessons from their development experiences and development assistance experiences to draw common lessons to share as a public good. This would be a cost-effective way to spread the development knowledge, and the World Bank is well positioned to play the role of bridging countries of all development stages.

Box 8.6 What Young Development Professionals Think About Urbanization

Mark Hirschboeck, World Bank Institute

First, some good news. In an era of rapid urbanization, the World Bank's urban portfolio is expanding significantly. Average annual commitments by the International Development Association and International Bank for Reconstruction and Development (IBRD) classified under the "Urban Development" theme increased from US$1.87 billion during 2003–07 to US$4.14 billion during 2008–12.[9]

The bad news. These figures are a drop in the proverbial bucket. Global requirements for urban public infrastructure investment alone are roughly estimated at US$120 billion annually (Kharas and Linn 2013). Only a fraction of these needs (about 50 percent, according to ADB [2006]) is currently being met. Addressing the full range of issues raised in this chapter will require vastly more resources.

Given these realities, it's imperative that the Bank wring the maximum impact out of every urban dollar. This requires moving beyond a project-by-project or sector-by-sector approach and focusing instead on programmatic, long-term interventions that crowd-in and empower a full set of actors (including individuals and communities, local, regional, and national governments, nongovernmental organizations other donors and development agencies, and the private sector).

In a sense, the ultimate goal should be to transform municipalities into micro-World Banks, that is, agents that have the technical expertise and financial resources to plan and implement projects themselves. In the short and medium term, the Bank could undertake the following measures:

- Promote wide-reaching wholesale mechanisms. Bank lending originates out of national development strategies, which, even when emphasizing urban development, often prioritize large flagship cities over secondary cities and towns. Compounding the problem, cities with high degrees of technical capacity are often the most attractive and willing Bank clients. In the interest of inclusiveness, the Bank could support urban development in the broadest possible sense through mechanisms like credit pooling and municipal development funds (MDFs) and couple them with appropriate policy and technical assistance (e.g. on urban planning, procurement, franchise and concession granting, financial structuring, and own-revenue raising).
- Develop sources of municipal data. The lack of data on fiscal performance of municipal governments hinders effective policy making and impact evaluation. The Bank could help build capacity in local and national statistical and planning departments. This could involve replicating projects like HABISP, a Bank-supported housing information and mapping system in São Paolo, which allow municipal staff to better plan and monitor interventions (Cities Alliance 2012).
- Combine physical investments with broader policy and capacity-building efforts, capitalizing on demonstration effects. Financing a slum-upgrading project or BRT system is not enough. To be meaningful, interventions need to respond to community

needs, be sustainable in the long-term through appropriate financial and policy support (e.g., targeted/equitable user fees and subsidies), and catalyze further investment and wider reform.

- Increase staff incentives for engaging in long-term, innovative, and multisectoral urban projects. Evaluations have found that Bank staff are wary of engaging in potentially transformative urban initiatives, particularly infrastructure projects, due to the risks presented by complex regulatory environments, resettlement/safeguard issues, and working with multiple stakeholders (World Bank 2007). Given the resource constraints, it's important that staff are encouraged to be as ambitious and as innovative as possible with the finance that is available.

One could object that these proposals are a bit repetitive and not particularly original. I would largely agree, but underscore that they and other similar proposals have cropped up repeatedly in various sector strategies and reviews over the past ten to fifteen years.[10] The key challenge remains implementation. For understandable reasons, programmatic, capacity-building approaches haven't been mainstreamed into operations. The Bank, a risk-averse institution, has a proven record in financing discrete projects and a largely unproven one in effectively delivering advisory services and technical assistance. A movement away from project-related lending also raises questions about the long-term financial viability of the IBRD. For their part, clients are generally more interested in concrete projects rather than development policy loans and analytic and advisory activities (DPLs and AAAs). But if the Bank wants to help its clients solve the complex, long-term challenges of urbanization, a distinct shift in emphasis is needed. Unfortunately, we don't have much time to get things right. Decisions made (or postponed) today will influence urban development for decades.

Notes

1. In 2011 Brazil's top trading partners were China (17.3 percent), the United States (10.2 percent), and Argentina (8.9 percent) (EIU 2013).

2. The Brazilian Cooperation Agency study (ABC 2010) took stock of flows administered by ABC directly and those reported by federal agencies responding to a survey. Figures were normalized to constant 2009 reais.

3. Brazil's contribution to the 2010 replenishment (IDA 16) made it the 20th largest donor (0.3 percent of total contributions) of 52 contributing countries, and among the G20 developing countries contributing to IDA, it contributed more than Argentina, Mexico, South Africa, and Turkey (IDA 2011).

4. The National Strategy for Green Growth (2009–50) and the Five-Year Plan (2009–13) provide a comprehensive policy framework for both short- and long-term green growth in Korea.

5. The OECD DAC is the leading source of best practices and review of priority development cooperation issues. It mobilizes the majority of the world's ODA, especially for poverty reduction.

6. Data from http://www.koica.go.kr/.

7. For more details, visit http://www.ksp.go.kr/.

8. For more information, visit: http://eacp.koica.go.kr/.

9. http://www.worldbank.org/en/results/2013/04/14/urban-development-results-profile.

10. To choose one example, "Cities on the Move: An World Bank Urban Transport Strategy Review" (2000) speaks approvingly of a corporate-led shift "from infrastructure project finance toward knowledge building, advisory services, and capacity building" and "from stand-alone project finance toward more-programmatic lending."

References

Brazil

ABC (Brazilian Cooperation Agency). 2010. "Cooperação Brasileira para o Desenvolvimento Internacional: 2005–2009." Agência Brasileira de Cooperação, Instituto de Pesquisa Econômica Aplicada, Brasília.

Amorim, C. 2011. "Reflections on Brazil Global Rise." *Americas Quarterly* 5 (2): 50–55. Special issue: The New Brazil and the Changing Hemisphere. Americas Society and Council of the Americas.

BNDES (National Bank for Economic and Social Development). 2013. "The BNDES in Numbers." BNDES, Brasília. http://www.bndes.gov.br/SiteBNDES/bndes/bndes_en/Institucional/The_BNDES_in_Numbers/.

CFR (Council on Foreign Relations). 2011. "Global Brazil and U.S.-Brazil Relations." Report of Independent Task Force 66. Washington, DC: CFR.

Economist, The. 2012. "Brazil in Africa: A New Atlantic Alliance." November 12.

EIU (Economist Intelligence Unit). 2013. "Country Forecast—Brazil." February.

EMBRAPA. 2013. (Brazilian Enterprise for Agricultural Research). "Mission and Activities" (in Portuguese) EMBRAPA. http://www.embrapa.br/a_embrapa/missao_e_atuacao.

Fonseca, G., Jr. 2011. "Notes on the Evolution of Brazilian Multilateral Diplomacy." *Global Governance* 17: 375–97.

Gomez, E. 2011. "How Brazil Outpaced the United States When It Came to AIDS: The Politics of Civic Infiltration, Reputation, and Strategic Internationalization." *Journal of Health Politics, Policy and Law* 36 (2): 317–52.

Gratius, S. 2008. "Brazil Emerges as a Regional and Global Power." *Quorum* 22: 135–46.

Hochstetler, K. 2012. "Brazil as an Emerging Environmental Donor." Policy Brief 21, Centre for International Governance Innovation, Ontario, Canada.

IDA (International Development Agency). 2011. "Donor Contributions Table 1: Contributions to the 16th Replenishment." IDA, World Bank, Washington, DC. http://www.worldbank.org/ida/papers/IDA16_Donor_Contributions_Table_1.pdf.

IPEA (Institute for Applied Economics Research). 2012. "Cooperação Brasileira para o Desenvolvimento Internacional (COBRADI): O Brasil e os Fundos Multilaterias de Desenvolvimento." Comunicados do IPEA No. 136, Instituto de Pesquisa Econômica Aplicada, Brasilia, Brazil.

World Bank. 2010. "Brazil: National AIDS Program—National Health Service: Project Appraisal Report." *World Bank*, Washington, DC.

———. 2011. "International Bank for Reconstruction and Development and International Finance Corporation Country Partnership Strategy for the Federative Republic of Brazil for the Period 2012–2015." September 21, World Bank, Washington, DC.

———. 2013. "World Bank Brazil Overview." World Bank, Washington, DC. http://www.worldbank.org/en/country/brazil/overview.

Korea

ADB (Asian Development Bank). 2006. "Special Evaluation Study on Urban Sector Strategy and Operations." ADB, Manila.

———. 2012. *Urban Development Series: Green Cities*. Manila: ADB.

AusAID (Australian Agency for International Development). 2012. "ODE Talks Podcast: Asian Approaches to Development Cooperation." Office of Development Effectiveness, AusAID, Canberra. http://www.ode.ausaid.gov.au/publications /documents/transcript-ed-emerging-donors.pdf.

Buchner, B., A. Falconer, M. Herve-Mignucci, and C. Trabacchi. 2012. *The Landscape of Climate Finance 2012*. A CPI Report, Climate Policy Initiative, London. http:// climatepolicyinitiative.org/wp-content/uploads/2012/12/The-Landscape-of-Climate -Finance-2012.pdf.

Choi, W., R. Dobbs, D. Suh, J. Mischke, E. Chon, H. Cho, B. Kim, and H. Kim. 2013. *Beyond Korean Style: Shaping a New Growth Formula*. McKinsey Global Institute.

Chung, W. H., J. E. Kang, T. G. Kang, and H. Yoon. 2012. "Cities and Green Economy: Comparative Study of Korea, China and Japan." Policy Study 2012-01, Korea Environment Institute, Seoul, Korea.

Chung, Y.-L. 2007. *South Korea in the Fast Lane: Economic Development and Capital Formation*. New York: Oxford University Press.

Cities Alliance. 2012. "Technology That Transformed Urban Planning in São Paulo: HABISP." http://www-wds.worldbank.org/external/default/WDSContentServer/ WDSP/IB/2012/11/02/000333038_20121102033848/Rendered/PDF/734590BRI0 P09800in0S0o0Paulo0HABISP.pdf.

Fackler, M. 2011. "Lessons Learned, South Korea Makes Quick Economic Recovery: Memo from Seoul." *New York Times*, January 6. http://www.nytimes.com/2011/01/07/ world/asia/07seoul.html?_r=0.

Fisher, M. 2012. "Can South Korea's First Female President Fix the Developed World's Worst Gender Gap?" *Washington Post*, December 19. http://www.washingtonpost. com/blogs/worldviews/wp/2012/12/19/can-south-koreas-first-female -president-fix-the-developed-worlds-worst-gender-gap/.

Hankyoreh. 2009. "Seoul Ranks Highest in Population Density among OECD Countries." http://www.hani.co.kr/arti/english_edition/e_international/393438.html.

Hausmann, R., L. Tyson, and S. Zahidi. 2012. *The Global Gender Gap Report*. World Economic Forum, Geneva.

Henderson, V. 2002. "Urbanization in Developing Countries." *World Bank Research Observer* 17 (1): 89–112.

HRI (Hyundai Research Institute). 2011. "Characteristics and Implications of the 20 Percent de Facto Youth Unemployment Rate Era." *HRI Weekly Economic Review*, December 9 [in Korean].

Jeong, H. J. 2012. "Sharing Outcomes of the East Asia Climate Partnership." Unpublished Powerpoint presentation. https://portals.iucn.org/2012forum/sites/2012forum/files /workshop-mr.hoejin-jeong-koica.pdf.

Jha, A., and H. Brecht. 2012. "An Eye on East Asia and Pacific: East Asia and Pacific Economic Management and Poverty Reduction." In *Building Urban Resilience in East Asia*. Washington, DC: World Bank.

Jones, R. 2012. "Developing a New Growth Model for Korea: Korea's Economy 2012." *Korea Economic Institute and the Korea Institute for International Economic Policy* 28: 13–19.

Kang, S. J. 2011. "Green Growth ODA: Green Growth: Global Cooperation." *Green Forum* 2: 35–55.

KDI (Korea Development Institute). 2010. "The Korean Economy: Six Decades of Growth and Development." Committee for the Sixty-Year History of the Korean Economy, Korea Development Institute, Seoul.

KEPB (Korea Environmental Policy Bulletin). 2012. "Green Card System." *Korea Environmental Policy Bulletin* 1 (10), Ministry of Environment/Korea Environment Institute, Seoul.

Kharas, H., and J. F. Linn. 2013. "External Assistance for Urban Finance Development." In *Financing Metropolitan Government in Developing Countries*, 395. Brookings Institution.

Kim, Y., and M. Tcha. 2012. "Introduction to the Knowledge Sharing Program (KSP) of Korea." In *Korea Compass: Tracing the Impacts of Korea's Engagements Around the World. Seoul*: Korea Economic Institute.

Lee, S. J., and E. H. Lee. 2009. "Case of POSCO: Analysis of Its Growth Strategy and Key Success Factors." KDI School Working Paper Series 09-13, Korea Development Institute, Seoul.

McKinsey & Company. 2010. "South Korea: Finding Its Place on the World Stage." *McKinsey Quarterly*, April.

Mohieldin, M., and Z. Allaoua. 2013. "Getting Cities Right." Project Syndicate. http://www.project-syndicate.org/commentary/managing-urbanization-in-developing-countries-by-mahmoud-mohieldin-and-zoubida-allaoua.

Mulakala, A. 2011. "Is There an Asian Approach to Development Cooperation?" In *Asia: Weekly Insight and Analysis from the Asia Foundation*. Asia Foundation, San Francisco, CA. http://asiafoundation.org/in-asia/2011/04/06/is-there-an-asian-approach-to-development-cooperation.

O, W.-C. 2009. *The Korea Story: President Jung-Hee's Leadership and the Korean Industrial Revolution*. Seoul: Wisdom Tree.

OECD (Organisation for Economic Co-operation and Development). 2010. *Cities and Climate Change*. Paris: OECD Publishing.

———. 2011. *2011 DAC Report on Multilateral Aid*. Paris: OECD Publishing.

———. 2012. *OECD Economic Surveys: Korea 2012*. Paris: OECD Publishing.

———. 2013. "Country Statistical Profile: Korea." Country Statistical Profiles: Key Tables from OECD. OECD, Paris. doi: 10.1787/csp-kor-table-2013-1-en.

OECD DAC (OECD Development Assistance Committee). 2008. *Development Co-Operation of the Republic of Korea*. DAC Special Review. Paris: OECD.

———. 2012. "Korea." In *Peer Review*. Paris: OECD.

Park, H. K. 2013b. "Community-Driven Urban Infrastructure Regeneration for Climate–Change-Resilient Growth: A Case Study." Presentation at the World Bank Workshop, KDI School of Public Policy and Management, Seoul, March 7.

Park, J. 2013a. "The Unemployment Issue of the Elderly in Korea and Its Policy Implications." *KIF Weekly Financial Brief*. Korea Institute of Finance, Seoul. http://www.kif.re.kr/KMFileDir/130046048600680000_WFB13-05(Policypercent20Issue).pdf.

Park, H. K. 2013b. "Community-Driven Urban Infrastructure Regeneration for Climate–Change-Resilient Growth: A Case Study." Presentation at the World Bank Workshop, KDI School of Public Policy and Management, Seoul, March 7.

Park, S. O., and A. R. Markusen. 1999. "Kumi and Ansan: Dissimilar Korean Satellite Platforms." In *Second Tier Cities: Rapid Growth beyond the Metropolis.* Minneapolis: University of Minnesota Press.

Rim, C. 2013. "Korea's Age Boom: How South Korea Is Addressing the Reality of Low Fertility and a Rapidly Aging Society." *AARP International Journal*, http://journal.aarpinternational.org/a/b/2013/02/Koreas-Age-Boom-How-South-Korea-is-Addressing-the-Reality-of--Low-Fertility-and-a-Rapidly-Aging-Society.

Steinberg, F. 2008. "Revitalization of Historic Inner-City Areas in Asia: Urban Renewal Potentials in Jakarta, Ha Noi and Manila." Urban Development Series, Asian Development Bank, Manila.

Strangarone, T. 2013. "Why the Economy and Not North Korea Will Be Park Geun-Hye's Biggest Challenge." *Georgetown Journal of International Affairs.* http://journal.georgetown.edu/2013/03/27/why-the-economy-and-not-north-korea-will-be-park-geun-hyes-biggest-challenge-by-troy-stangarone/.

Suh, J., and D. H. C. Chen. 2007. "Korea as a Knowledge Economy: Evolutionary Process and Lessons Learned." Korea Development Institute and World Bank Institute, World Bank, Washington, DC.

UN (United Nations). 2011. "World Urbanization Prospects: The 2011 Revision." CD-ROM edition, Department of Economic and Social Affairs, Population Division, United Nations, New York.

UNEP (United Nations Environment Programme). 2010. "Overview of the Republic of Korea's National Strategy for Green Growth." Prepared by UNEP as part of its Green Economy Initiative, Nairobi. http://www.unep.org/PDF/PressReleases/201004_unep_national_strategy.pdf.

Urban Climate Change Research Network. 2011. *Climate Change and Cities: First Assessment Report of the Urban Climate Change Research Network.* Edited by C. Rosenzweig, W. D. Solecki, S. A. Hammer, and S. Mehrotra. Cambridge, UK: Cambridge University Press.

Walz, J., and V. Ramachandran. 2011. "Brave New World: A Literature Review of Emerging Donors and the Changing Nature of Foreign Assistance." Working Paper 273, Center for Global Development, Washington, DC.

World Bank. 2007. *A Decade of Action in Transport: An Evaluation of World Bank Assistance to the Transport Sector, 1995–2005.* Washington, DC: World Bank, xvii.

———. 2012a. "Korea's Global Commitment to Green Growth." Sustainable Development, World Bank, Washington, DC. http://go.worldbank.org/NR18WLLIV0.

———. 2012b. *Inclusive Green Growth: The Pathway to Sustainable Development.* Washington, DC: World Bank.

Yoon, S. 2012. "Koreans Fret World-Beating Chaebol Destroy Small Business." *Bloomberg*, November 13. http://www.bloomberg.com/news/2012-11-12/s-koreans-fret-world-beating-chaebol-destroys-small-busi.html.

Yunhap (Yunhap News Agency). 2012. "Lee: Green Growth Think Tank to Officially Launch as International Organization." Yunhap News Agency, May 10. http://english.yonhapnews.co.kr/national/2012/05/10/21/0301000000AEN20120510001700315F.HTML.

Shifting Priorities: Re-envisioning World Bank Partnerships for Transformational Impact

J. Warren Evans, Isabel Nicholson, Lelei TuiSamoa LeLaulu, and Alison Wescott

Introduction

The World Bank has taken a leadership role in a number of large-scale partnerships designed to improve the delivery of global public goods (GPGs) for developing countries. One of the earliest and longest lasting is the Consultative Group on International Agricultural Research (CGIAR), set up in 1971 by the World Bank through the direct intervention and foresight of its then president, Robert McNamara. The Bank has supported CGIAR financially and intellectually and with strong leadership for over 40 years. It led the reform effort reform in 2008/09 that changed the role of the World Bank as a CGIAR partner from overall Consultative Group manager to chairing its Fund Council and housing its Fund Office. The management of its operations was moved to a separate consortium Office. A newer partnership, the Cities Alliance, was similarly housed at and managed by the Bank until 2013, when it also moved offshore.

Until the late 1990s, the partnerships sponsored by the Bank tended to be with other development organizations. In the last 15 years, the Bank dramatically increased engagement with a broader range of stakeholders, in particular, with civil society organizations (CSOs). A more active global civil society, increasingly limited financial resources, recommendations from its own program evaluations, and new World Bank leadership are a few of the forces that have urged the Bank to ward more CSO engagement. In addition, the Millennium Development Goals catalyzed new types of collaboration by institutionalizing a sense of urgency and by bringing together different actors to accomplish ambitious goals. With a short timeline for accomplishing these goals, development actors—multilateral, bilateral, and CSOs alike—have found new ways to work together. In the course of this engagement, the Bank has accomplished some of its most innovative work yet, producing high-impact, once unattainable results. The CGIAR and the Partnership for River Blindness (discussed in chapter 2) are acknowledged success stories in this regard.

To see Vice President Rachel Kyte discuss new forms of development assistance: http://youtu .be/4ez5TbdOI2E

Yet new efforts inevitably bring new challenges. The World Bank was designed to work on an international scale to engage with sovereign nations, thus joint work with smaller, more dynamic entities, such as subsovereign entities and CSOs, has proven to be a challenge. Because the Bank's safeguard policies and procurement processes were designed for larger entities and greater funding, attempting to integrate CSOs into its systems has been a struggle for both parties. To address these challenges and to continue to adapt, the Bank can look to its existing partnerships for examples of applying innovative models for collaboration and developing best practices.

Current Partnerships: Examples of Strengths and Challenges

In the absence of an international governing body with the ability to manage and provide global and regional public goods directly, partnership programs with shared governance arrangements have become the principal instrument for providing this service, overseen at the World Bank by the Global and Regional Partnership Programs (GRPPs).

Examining the Bank's current partnerships shows which models have been successful and which have not. Evaluations by the Independent Evaluation Group (IEG)—the Bank's internal entity for program evaluation—provide explicit lessons in how to strengthen partnerships and move forward on tackling complex issues. GRPPs are characterized as follows:

- Partnerships exist in which the partners dedicate resources—financial, technical, staff, and reputational—toward achieving agreed objectives over time.
- The activities of the program are global, regional, or multicountry in scope.

Each GRPP is established as a new facility with shared governance and a management unit to deliver on its activities. The World Bank plays many roles in GRPPs, depending on the program, among them convener, financial contributor, trustee, member of the governing body, chair, host of the secretariat, administrative support, and implementing agency. Because GRPPs are a primary method by which the Bank manages and delivers GPGs, Bank leadership must maintain a dynamic and flexible position within the programs to ensure that the Bank is playing the role best suited for each partnership. The Bank's ability to engage at the country level and effectively support field offices and implementing partners is an area in which it must strive to ensure successful future collaboration. Still, the Bank faces significant challenges in these types of partnerships, often encountering the same pitfalls across different partnerships, especially in country-level implementation and coordination of similar programs.

The most successful of these partnerships have been those in which the Bank assumes *involvement* in the partnership, rather than *ownership*. A "lighter touch" within larger coalitions—rather than the Bank taking responsibility for program management—has allowed partnership managers to leverage the Bank's connections and create new linkages. This dynamic ultimately creates opportunities for actors to cooperate on a common agenda and pursue activities within their respective areas of strength. The Bank for its part does best in creating social, political, and economic linkages among actors.

Case Study: The Critical Ecosystems Partnership Fund

In the face of drastically declining ecosystem health, the Critical Ecosystems Partnership Fund (CEPF) was created to more effectively fund ground-level projects working to conserve biodiversity in the world's most biologically rich areas.[1] The CEPF supports CSOs through a grants program that connects field-level projects in biodiversity conservation to bilateral and multilateral funding. Conservation International and the World Bank together developed a model for a funder-based partnership, bringing together large donors to empower and support ground-level biodiversity conservation projects designed and implemented by CSOs.

The structure of the CEPF is unique: large funders—initially the World Bank, MacArthur Foundation, Conservation International, and Global Environment Facility—each pledged an initial sum of $25 million over a three-year period. Since then, Japan, France, and the European Union have joined as funding partners. These contributions provide the foundational funds the CEPF needs to consistently support CSOs, and it ensures ongoing involvement and interest from donors. Each funding organization is represented on the donor council and plays an important role in setting overarching strategic agendas.[2]

The type of grant that CEPF allocates to CSOs in a given country is determined by a regional team of scientific experts and leading actors in conservation. This regional implementation team (RIT) determines the most pressing threats to biodiversity in the area and the types of projects that have had and will have the most impact. This process enables those in-country to determine field-level needs, putting the power of setting country-level strategies in the hands of field practitioners, directly connecting project goals to biological threats and community resources. This allows projects to maintain the integrity of their field-work, with engagement from the CEPF secretariat ensuring regular incorporation of advisory board recommendations.[3]

To date, the CEPF has allocated funds to more than 1,800 civil society groups in more than 60 countries, with unparalleled biodiversity and conservation gains. Figure 9.1 provides an overview of CEPF's impact to date.

CEPF is an example of how the World Bank can be an innovative force creating new and extremely high-impact results, using partnerships to make enormous conservation strides. As a leading global development institution, the World Bank acts as a critical partner in many ways—at the global, regional, and country levels. As a donor, the Bank brings its credibility and the ability to bring in additional funders. Knowing that a CSO partner has fulfilled the Bank's extensive safeguards policy is appealing to funders and often makes the process of evaluating a prospective CSO partner shorter and easier. On regional and local levels, the World Bank's existing networks and in-country technical experts are an asset to creating RITs and building ecosystem profiles.[4]

Too Global to Fail • http://dx.doi.org/10.1596/978-1-4648-0307-9

Figure 9.1　Critical Ecosystems Partnership Fund Quick Facts

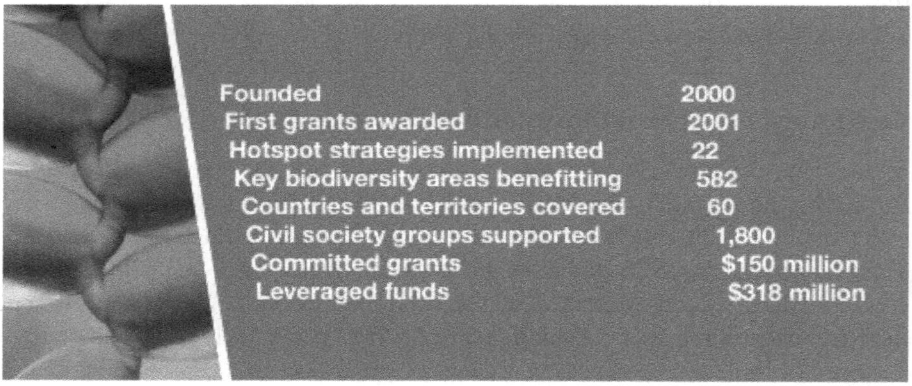

Founded	2000
First grants awarded	2001
Hotspot strategies implemented	22
Key biodiversity areas benefitting	582
Countries and territories covered	60
Civil society groups supported	1,800
Committed grants	$150 million
Leveraged funds	$318 million

Yet the CEPF model is relatively new, and the processes it uses to engage with the Bank have yet to be tailored to the unique nature of its work. The success of the CEPF model relies on it serving as a conduit for streamlined and open processes between CEPF and RITs and between CEPF and donors. Because World Bank safeguards and procurement processes were designed for larger clients, namely, countries, many of the demands on CSO partners are disproportionate to the scale of their work and the size of their funding, thus requiring more labor and resources than CEPF, or most other CSOs, have available.

In addition, given the global reach and scope of World Bank projects, partnerships like the CEPF will inevitably create conflicts of interest for the Bank and other large donors. As stated by the IEG,

> When a conflict of interest situation arises, one is not automatically in the wrong, just facing a problem. Given the pervasiveness of conflicts of interest in partnership programs, the key is to identify and manage them transparently. (IEG 2010: 41–42)

With CEPF, the Bank has been able to maintain a flexible role as partner. For example, when a program in China did not fit the Bank country strategy, rather than inhibit the implementation of the CEPF program, the Bank simply did not participate in it. This has not been the case with several other partnerships, such as the Forest Carbon Partnership Facility (FCPF), which was effectively blocked from implementation in countries where the FCPF was not included in the Bank's country strategy until additional implementing partners were brought on board to carryout FCPF activities in the countries (IEG 2011).

Case Study: The Global Tiger Initiative and Collective Impact: An Effective Conservation Model

Since 2008 the Global Tiger Initiative (GTI) has forged successful partnerships to engage the highest-level of government leaders in wild tiger conservation.[5] This has helped strengthen political will and significantly influenced public policy in support of biodiversity conservation as a GPG. Political leaders and champions in the tiger range countries are leading partnerships with governments, international organizations, civil society, the private sector, and committed individuals to help save the tigers.

GTI was formed in response to Asia's overwhelming crisis in biodiversity and against a status quo where "individual battles" may have been won, but "the war" was being lost. The organization has brought energy and urgency to tiger conservation and a paradigm shift in the way these ecosystems are valued and governed.

GTI has emerged as an innovative business model and changed the conversation about conservation. As a result, more funding has been injected into tiger conservation, with more than $200 million provided by tiger range governments (including increased funding by India and Nepal, for example) and multilateral and bilateral donors.

> GTI as a business model is not about saving a single species; rather it is about moving from isolated interventions to collective impact to address the common agenda articulated in the Global Tiger Recovery Program (GTRP).
>
> —John Seidensticker,
> Smithsonian Institution

However, GTRP is the first comprehensive strategic plan dedicated to the conservation of a single species. It was promulgated at the Global Tiger Forum in St. Petersburg, Russia, in 2010, co-hosted by Russian president Vladimir Putin and World Bank president Robert Zoellick. The event brought together delegations from all 13 tiger range countries, including heads of state, heads of leading international organizations, and top scientists, to sign the St. Petersburg Declaration. The parties to this declaration pledged to work together toward the goal of "T × 2"—to double the number of tigers across the range by 2022.

The common agenda is nested in the 13 National Tiger Recovery Priorities (World Bank 2012), developed by the participating governments to address their own goals for the recovery of wild tigers. At the Second Asian Ministerial Meetings in Thimphu, Bhutan, in 2012, the governments met again to renew their political commitment and further translate this vision into tangible goals and timely actions through the Thimphu Nine Point Affirmative Action Agenda (World Bank 2012).

GTI's core team realized that the challenges it faced were large and complex—habitat loss, fragmentation, rapid infrastructure expansion, poverty, and illegal trade and trafficking. A history of undervaluing and under-resourcing wildlife conservation prevailed. To save wild tigers, the partners focused efforts on the 13 tiger range countries, with broad cross-sector coordination, while working on several fronts at once. Today in addition to GTI's ongoing work in tiger conservation, the governments are discussing ways to mobilize global resources for conservation of the snow leopard and Arabian leopard. In addition, policy leaders from other regions, including Africa, have sought GTI's advice on replicating this business model to address their own challenges in the conservation of flagship species.

Figure 9.2 and table 9.1 illustrate how GTI has endeavored to achieve collective impact.

Figure 9.2 GTI Business Operations Model

Global Tiger Initiative as a
business model
is not about saving a
single species. It is
about moving from
isolated interventions to
collective impact to
address the common
agenda articulated in
the Global Tiger
Recovery Program.

—John Seidensticker,
Smithsonian Institution

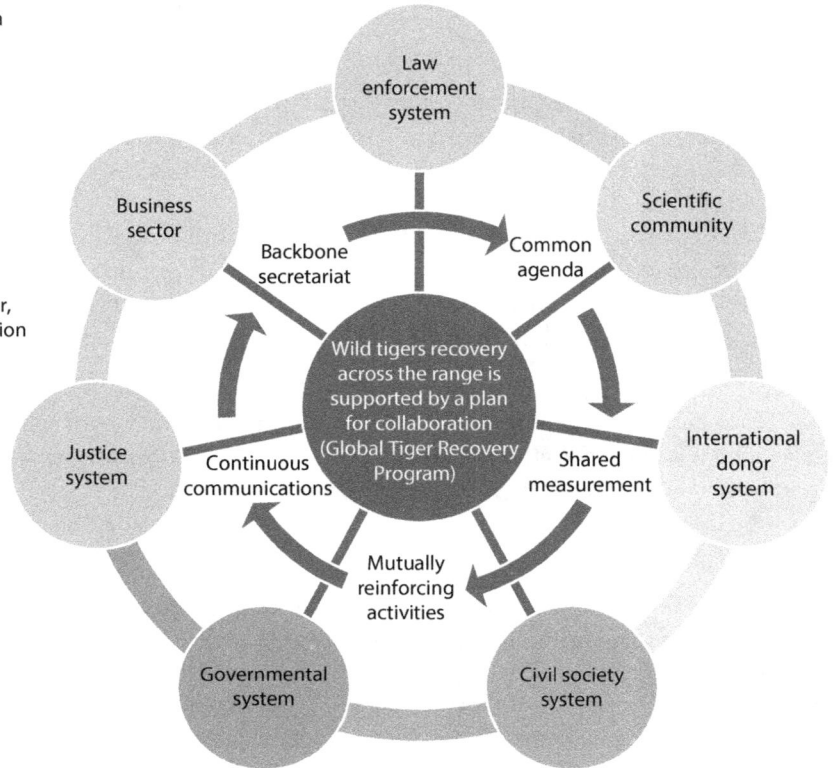

Sources: Quote in from correspondence from John Seidensticker, 2013; figure adapted from FSG.org, Collective Impact for Opportunity Youth, February 12, 2013; Kania and Kramer 2011.

Table 9.1 GTI Goals and Achievements for Collective Impact

Goals	Actions	Achievements
Common agenda	Partners agree on shared goals and vision	• T × 2 goal of St. Petersburg Declaration • Global Tiger Recovery Program–consensus, road map
Shared measurement	Partners keep track of the same data	• A common set of indicators • Common systems of monitoring and reporting
Mutually reinforced activity	Partners contribute key functions to the best of their capabilities (GTRP, mutual accountability frameworks)	• Impact not from numbers alone, but from the coordination of partners contributing the activities and functions that they do best toward shared goals and a common agenda
Continuous communication	Secretariat monitors and regularly shares results	• Regular results reports build trust and a common vocabulary • Regular meetings to learn and solve problems together
Backbone secretariat	Keeps goal in sight and keeps the process moving to report results and mobilize resources	• Separate dedicated staff to plan, manage, and support

Source: Adapted from Kania and Kramer 2011.

Case Study: The Global Partnership for Oceans

Despite global commitments—as well as the efforts of many organizations, governments, enterprises, and individuals—the oceans remain under severe threat from pollution, unsustainable harvesting of ocean resources, habitat destruction, ocean acidification, and climate change. By launching the Global Partnership for Oceans (GPO) in Singapore in 2012, then president of the World Bank Group, Robert B. Zoellick, initiated an ambitious attempt to deal with the dizzying array of multilayered problems the oceans, seas, and international waterways of the world are facing.[6] While numerous initiatives have been undertaken to address the "oceans challenge," they have been mostly piecemeal and inadequate to the enormous task of halting the relentless erosion of the health and productivity of the oceans.

The GPO is intended to reinforce and reinvigorate global efforts to ensure the sustainable use of the oceans and to further curb illegal, unregulated, and unreported fishing. As such, the GPO is vital to ensuring that a fair share of better-managed ocean resources is redistributed to benefit poorer countries. It aims to improve capacity and to close the recognized gap in action in implementing global, regional, and national commitments for healthy and productive oceans.[7]

Given the enormity and complexity of the challenge, President Zoellick decided it was time to bring together a coalition of governments, international organizations, civil society groups, philanthropic organizations, and private interests on a scale necessary to deal collectively with the well-known problems of overfishing, marine degradation, habitat loss, and other non-sustainable practices in the oceans and fragile coastal regions. Embodied in the GPO, this coalition represents active recognition of the inability of any one organization, country, or even clusters of countries to "go it alone" on ocean conservation. Rather, the GPO is a clarion call for global holistic approaches to a truly global issue, building on the commendable work already done to address the threats to oceans and to identify workable solutions.

All members of the GPO, including the World Bank Group, were already involved in activities to protect the world's oceans. The key next step is to mobilize around a set of agreed goals to reverse patterns of degradation and depletion and to scale up and coordinate the work of the various partners. It is hoped this focus will also help mobilize new financial, technical, and human support, working collectively across countries, civil society, and the private sector.

Ocean governance reform at all levels creates an enabling environment that in turn, can catalyze sizeable quantities of public and private sector finance to sustain ocean ecosystem services. The GPO provides a key opportunity to scale up proven approaches.

Among the GPO's goals are targets for significantly increasing global food fish production from aquaculture and sustainable fisheries; halving the current rate of natural habitat loss and increasing marine-managed and protected areas to at least 10 percent of coastal and marine areas; and reducing marine pollution, especially from marine litter, wastewater, and excess nutrients. The GPO is initially targeting three focus areas:

- sustainable seafood and livelihoods from capture fisheries and aquaculture;
- critical coastal and ocean habitats and biodiversity; and
- pollution reduction.

This case study chose two questions regarding the GPO as a way to better understand the magnitude of such global challenges. The first question is whether success has been adequately defined in terms of long-term objectives—in other words, what optimal, stretch targets might the GPO achieve by 2025 or 2030? The second question is will these stretch targets likely be met given the current norms for World Bank participation in such partnerships?[8]

What could the GPO accomplish by 2025 that would indicate that the partnership is facilitating the transformation needed to generate sustained optimal benefits from ocean ecosystems? In addition to the highly tangible objectives agreed by the GPO partners, some of the key accomplishments by 2025 might be as follows:

- In 2025 the GPO has evolved into a model of how the World Bank Group is able to support multipartner approaches to a global priority. Solutions unimaginable in 2012, when the GPO was launched, have emerged regularly as the partnership constantly and collectively adjusts its approaches to common problems. The GPO, with its commitment to forging collective impacts, is seen as a dynamic generator of emergent solutions.

- Eschewing the generally uncoordinated ocean aid efforts of the past, governments and other partners channel their ocean and coastal development assistance through the GPO.

- Accompanying the financial flows from donors is a steady stream of the top policy and technical talent seconded to the GPO secretariat, where they interact with counterparts from the recipient regions. Multiskilled, multinational teams systematically incorporate all collected data in any given area before analyzing and feeding it into the design and implementation process of the GPO membership.

- The cooperative, multistakeholder-driven conservation and sustainable development initiatives were double tracked by the GPO for global and for regional approaches. Once successful, the two were consolidated and their cooperative efforts resulted in healthier oceans that are productive and richer in biodiversity.

- To address the budgetary gap, WAVES, the Wealth Accounting and the Valuation of Ecosystem Services, of mainly terrestrial assets, was drawn offshore and adapted in "Blue WAVES" to include life forms that can be extracted from the oceans. With Blue WAVES serving as a GPO metric for programs, donor organizations have been more ready to justify contributions to GPO initiatives.

- Coastal and marine ecosystems and services are properly valued and accounted for. For example, the value of coral reef ecosystems, about $30 billion in 2012, has more than quadrupled since responsible reef-viewing tourism programs were scaled up and used to help fund GPO coral regeneration projects. In addition, reef valuation takes into account fisheries production, pharmaceutical potentials, and disaster reduction functions.

- Assigning a real economic value to the oceans results in budgets commensurate with its real contribution to the GDPs of countries.

- A more quantitative appreciation of the risks of climate change to ocean communities and resources helps stimulate a rapid reduction in greenhouse gas emissions so that the global target of limiting warming to 2°C is achievable.

What are some of the steps for achieving such major levels of success? Two actions are required in the immediate future: first, very high-level leadership needs to be reestablished, and second, that leadership needs to facilitate mobilization of sufficient funding commitments to meet the first five years of activities. Once these two actions are taken, it is suggested that the GPO establish a separate backbone organization, the GPO secretariat with staff and specific skill sets, to serve as the backbone for the entire partnership and to coordinate partner organizations. New studies on collective impact indicate that such a dedicated and somewhat independent group representing all of the partners is often of crucial importance for success. The CEPF experience is a good example of how this might work.

By 2015, the GPO should be recognized as the go-to organization as its carefully designed activities take root. Donors will better understand the potential returns on their investment in the GPO in terms of the development of productive oceans and coastal regions. The GPO approach has become a brand signifying a credible indication of the sustainability of proposed investment projects. At the same time, the GPO could quickly seek an expansion of partners, with the objective of including a significant percentage of Fortune 500 and most of the world's oceanic and coastal states.

Focusing on innovative financing will be an important step once the partnership is on a sound foundation. It could establish a GPO "Blue Exchange," say by 2016, matching financing with projects and programs of varying size and risk. The Blue Exchange would blend financing instruments to enable the private sector to record suitable returns on investment, while also offering multilateral development banks, bilateral development agencies, and venture capital a platform of offerings to participate in the financing of ocean-benefit activities. The tourism, fishery, extractive, and energy industries would be priority participants.

The Blue Exchange would also be tailored to support small island developing states (SIDS) by establishing subregional development funds (SDF). The GPO focuses on building the capacity of smaller island states to manage the SDF allocations to their needs. The SDFs, guided by sustainable development objectives and applying transparency and anti-corruption practices, are boosted by contributions from the regional private sector as well as from traditional donors. Recipient countries themselves are also investing in the SDFs to ensure a place at the governance table and to avoid the fiduciary distractions of domestic politics.

Blue carbon biofunds—promoting conservation and planting of coastal vegetation to reduce atmospheric carbon—are already under consideration by Abu Dhabi, which is working with the GPO. These programs should be well established by 2018, and by 2020 they should be funding at-scale replanting of mangroves, sea grasses, and other blue life forms at the global level.

Further to these broad 2025 measures of success already mentioned, by 2025 the work on valuation of ecosystems and resource and carbon pricing should set the stage for issuance of GPO Blue Bonds, an adaptation of the World Bank green bonds, fueling the sustained operations of the GPO. This effort would be enabled by the following:

- In the food sector, the GPO-branded (certified) capture of ocean protein has been accepted as an industry standard by the food production industry.
- It has become near impossible to secure funding for any coastal construction without the plans passing muster with the GPO sustainable construction guidelines.
- Tourism development proposals matching GPO criteria are fast-tracked for funding by the private sector.
- Governments, civil society, and the private sector save time and money by defaulting ocean-related funding and resources to the GPO and its many associated processes.
- Recognizing that energy generation and oil imports are the biggest budget drainers in small island and coastal states, as well as huge contributors to pollution, renewable energy has become a GPO priority. The SIDS Sustainable Energy Initiative (SIDS DOCK, http://sidsdock.org), the renewable energy driver of the GPO, with its formidable private sector backing, has converted the vast majority of SIDS and coastal developing countries to renewable energy. GPO-compliant tourism properties were able to quickly record heavily reduced electricity bills thereby rapidly repaying their loans from the SDFs. It wasn't long before the private capital community led the investment push in the tourism sector.
- A GPO Energy Fund, driven by the private sector and foundation contributions, funds efficiency and renewable energy development and production.
- Ocean-sourced energy systems, such as ocean thermal energy conversion and seawater air conditioning systems, are now the major forms of energy generation. Ocean thermal energy conversion systems have all but eliminated the import of fossil fuels to SIDs and coastal states, freeing up huge portions of

national budgets. Mixed ocean, wind, solar, and hydrogen systems, developed with GPO guidance, have enabled SIDS to be energy dependent.

A Model for the Future of World Bank Partnerships: Sustained Leadership for Collective Impact

The examples of the CEPF, GTI, and GPO and recommendations made by the IEG make clear the areas in which the World Bank can improve its partnership practice. GRPPs are innovative and multistakeholder partnerships that have incentivized an array of different groups to mobilize around common goals. The IEG reviews show the strength of the World Bank in these partnerships; it was most often effective at taking on a coordination role, and in other examples it provided valuable technical assistance. Correspondingly, the weaknesses in these partnerships also change, sometimes lacking uniform monitoring and evaluation systems and other times showing inconsistency between headquarters and country-level priorities. With a constantly changing international funding land-scape, urgent environmental and climate needs, and limited resources, World Bank must continually adapt to change and find new models of collaboration to accomplish its goals (IEG 2010).

Partnerships are increasingly complex, as they need to be able to tackle GPG challenges over the long term, and the Bank should continue to have a dynamic role as a partner, taking on responsibilities that are best suited to its strengths in a particular field and in conjunction with the resources of its partners. In the IEG reviews of the Bank's GRPPs, the Bank showed it can have enormous impact if it recognizes where it can add the most value to a larger partnership. As the Bank engages in partnerships that take on more complex, long-term GPG challenges, it is crucial to spell out the roles and responsibilities of partners at a project's inception and to put in place mechanisms that support the partners in meeting their obligations.[9]

An emerging practice, Collective Impact, appears to fit the emerging needs of mega-collaborative partnerships. Kania and Kramer (2011) outline the following five conditions that define collective impact initiatives and produce powerful results:

- **A common agenda.** All partners share a vision for change, including a common understanding of the problems and a joint approach to solving them through agreed actions.
- **Shared measurement.** Collecting data and measuring results consistently across all partners in a large and complex landscape or oceanscape ensures efforts remain aligned and partners hold each other accountable.
- **Mutually reinforcing activities.** Partners must be differentiated, but they have to coordinate through a mutually reinforcing plan of action.
- **Continuous communication.** Consistent and open communication lines are critical across a large and diverse partnership in order to build trust, assure realization of mutual objectives, and create common motivation.

- **Backbone support.** Creating and managing collective impact requires a separate organization with staff and specific skill sets to serve as the backbone for the entire partnership and to coordinate partner organizations.

For the World Bank to achieve significant impacts on global problems, it is not enough for it put in place a better overarching strategy, mobilize enough money, or receive that money in the right way. It must also become more agile and effective as a participant in broad coalitions. Consider the following glimpse of a possible future:

- By 2025, the number of IDA-eligible countries is halved and today's emerging economies, and largest IBRD borrowers, are partners in funding the development of other developing countries.
- ODA remains flat at around present levels or declines, and a large share of it is used in support of global public goods, including support for private sector–led green growth, with the balance allocated to a residual group of fragile and conflict-affected countries.
- ODA from traditional OECD sources is rivaled or even overtaken by contributions from emerging official donors, private foundations, or "direct giving" mechanisms.
- Action on global challenges is increasingly taken forward by coalitions of like-minded parties—incorporating sovereign states, cities, CSOs, businesses, institutional investors, regional and international organizations, and youth movements—with coalition governance geared toward achieving "collective impact" on large-scale challenges.
- The vehicles for dealing with such challenges are increasingly special-purpose, internationally coordinated, and long-term mega-programs designed to solve the problems, rather than put dents in them.

The scenario outlined here might appear far-fetched. But aspects of it are already coming to pass. Consider, for example, the emergence of the Global Fund to Fight AIDS, Tuberculosis and Malaria or the GAVI Alliance or more recently the GPO.[10]

The question now is whether the World Bank and similar organizations can adapt their ways of working to assure their long-term relevance as coalition partners. To do this, they will need to be ready to engage in both leadership and non-leadership roles in new forms of partnership that exhibit the vision, scale, resourcing, and durability required to match large and uncertain global challenges—including those of promoting healthy oceans and productive ecosystems, assuring sufficient freshwater supplies, and achieving a stable and hospitable climate.

It should be a given that the World Bank—with its strong technical and financial knowledge and operational capabilities—will ultimately play a fundamental role in most such large-scale, long-term partnerships. However, significant barriers to such partnerships exist at the institutional level. First among these is the

Bank's governance—the primary factor cited by the designers of the Green Climate Fund (GCF) when arguing for a limited role for the World Bank. The dominance of developed countries on the Bank's board was seen as a major problem, even though many recognized the Bank would have been the logical place to house the fund. A second barrier is the Bank's heavy reliance on external, special-purpose funding for regional and global initiatives. A third is the Bank's heavy and often risk-averse bureaucratic processes—geared more toward large, loan-financed operations than toward partnership-based and grant-financed programs—which tend to impede flexibility, innovation, and speed, and therefore limit impact. A final barrier, identified by some observers, is that the Bank tends to be a serious, engaged partner only when in the lead and in control.

The authors of this book believe the Bank does have the capacity to dismantle the above barriers and play a fundamental role in meeting global challenges within global coalitions. Indeed its place in the institutional architecture would be strengthened if it were to assume this role. But sustained leadership is also a key ingredient to sustainability and success. The CEPF and GPO are examples of partnerships that seek collaborative, transformational impact on complex, long-term GPG challenges. Both partnerships were established with challenging stretch goals. Both were established with strong leadership at the outset by two different World Bank presidents. The CEPF enjoyed that leadership over a long enough period to move the partnership beyond its initial phase by securing significant, relatively long term funding. The GPO has not had such sustained leadership since President Zoellick left the Bank shortly after launching it.

CEPF was set up from the outset with an independent secretariat housed in Conservation International, although achieving real independence was a challenging task and took about four years. GPO was set up with an informal secretariat inside the Bank. CEPF implementing partners and the CEPF secretariat have periodically struggled to meet Bank safeguard and procurement policies and procedures. It is too early to tell whether the GPO partners will experience similar difficulties.

The emerging model of collaborative impact partnerships has the Bank in a dynamic role as a partner, taking on responsibilities that are best suited to its strengths in a particular field in conjunction with the resources of its partners. Dynamic leadership is key to getting such initiatives under way. The Bank can often play that role by bringing top-level leaders together and keep their engagement active over time. Effective leadership will result in the partners tackling the challenges in a collaborative manner and avoiding their pushing a particular agenda.

GPG challenges like climate change, oceans, and water and food security require visionary, long-term strategies that can be broken into sequential activity programs with clear responsibilities and accountabilities for each partner. Financial resources must be adequate to carry out the immediate time slice and get the next one under way, thus funding for five or six years is required. When these conditions are met, the World Bank is in an ideal position to deliver collective, long-term impacts at a scale commensurate to the challenges.[11]

Box 9.1 What Young Development Professionals Think About Crowdfunding Sustainability

Anna Lerner, Energy Specialist, Latin America and Caribbean

In 1886 Joseph Pulitzer and his newspaper *The New York World* famously raised $100,000 in micro-donations from more than 160,000 people in five months for the completion of the Statue of Liberty's granite foundation. While crowd-funding to attract donations or investments from multiple individuals for a specific purpose is not a new concept, the advent of the internet and subsequent adoption of social media and other forms of technology have made it possible for almost anyone, anywhere, to invest any amount of money in any number of ideas imaginable. Crowdfunding has emerged as a viable, scalable alternative to traditional sources of public and private finance, capable of overcoming barriers to accessing finance and catalyzing innovation and entrepreneur-ship. While presently most prominent in developed countries, crowdfunding has the poten-tial to be a game changer for emerging markets and developing countries, allowing them to capitalize on their ability to leapfrog technology adaptation and innovation. Underpinned by universal connectivity, coupled with a favorable ecosystem that encourages risk taking and entrepreneurship, crowdfunding can offer a new frontier for innovation. The World Bank Group faces a unique opportunity to pioneer the creation of this enabling global system.

Through Kickstarter, one of the world's largest crowdfunding platforms, more than 12 million people from 177 countries have pledged in excess of US$300 million. They have contributed to around 18,000 successfully funded projects. In 2012 the crowdfunding indus-try grew 81 percent, reaching US$2.7 billion and funding more than 1 million campaigns. Industry experts project an exponential increase over the years ahead.

Small and medium enterprises (SME), social ventures, and entrepreneurs all cite financing as one of the primary barriers to growth. In developing countries, low avail-ability of traditional financing and high-risk financial markets exacerbate these hurdles. Many SMEs rely on friends and family for startup or growth capital due to lack of credit history, high transaction costs, and other barriers. Traditional capital markets have also limited large groups of non-accredited financial investors to capitalize high-growth entrepreneurs and local businesses. Crowdfunding offers a previously nonexistent opportunity for this market failure to solve itself, strengthening shared prosperity among community members. Funding Circle, for example, was launched in 2010 as a response to business "being starved of finance by the big banks, while people were getting a poor return on their money." Crowdfunding can become a unique vehicle matching foreign direct investment and remittances with high-growth entrepreneurs and profitable local investments, allowing for lucrative investments and social impacts.

The crowdfunding business models of choice depend on the type of capital needed by the venture, its industry affiliation, and what type of backers the project proponents are seeking. Early crowdfunding campaigns predominantly solicited donation crowdfunding and offered their backers a reward depending on how much they contributed to the campaign. Recent ventures have increasingly been seeking debt- or equity-based investments targeting high-growth entrepreneurs.

"Social cause" is the most active crowdfunding category, with more than 30 percent of market size, often using donation or interest-free, loan-based campaigns. Three other prominent categories in 2012 were entrepreneurship (17 percent), film and performing art (11 percent), and energy and environment (6 percent). Crowdfunding platforms exist in 27 countries, but North America and Europe presently account for 95 percent of the crowdfunding market.

While crowdfunding offers a real alternative to traditional financing, a democratization of impact investments of sorts, a number of risks are associated with the growth of the industry. Credible crowdfunding systems require the right mix of supportive ecosystem, enabling institutions, policies, technology, capital, and entrepreneurs as well as protection for investors. Multilateral finance institutions, like the Bank, could play an important role in mitigating these risks.

As a start, the Bank could act as an honest broker and support national regulatory frameworks that protect investors while facilitating capital formation, providing trust to the system. Forward-thinking regulators who understand the opportunity posed by crowdfunding will be key to transforming national markets. A strong pipeline of sustainable and profitable projects could also be supported by the Bank, particularly considering that projects directly relevant to the core business of the Bank (social cause, energy and environment) are dominating the existing crowdfunding market. Risk-averse investors often shy away from new emerging markets, where their investments could sometimes make the most impact. Social media market penetration and increased internet access are two of the most important drivers to recent expansion of crowdfunding. To allow new markets to leapfrog regulation and technology development and continue the expansion, the Bank should continue to support increased connectivity and widespread dissemination of information and communication technology in client countries.

Whereas the crowdfunding industry will innovate out of necessity, the transformational innovation argued here is related to connecting the financing mechanism to the global knowledge and the convening power of institutions like the Bank. With decades of experience operating in risky new markets, and with a global reach like few others, the Bank has a unique opportunity to leverage one of its core comparative advantages in order to fast-track the industry to scale and global reach. By engaging as a trusted convener, the Bank can address market failures for the provision of public goods while bringing renewed relevance to its operations and core mission. Crowdfunding can become a vital instrument in the work to eliminate poverty and create shared prosperity if the Bank is brave enough to engage.

Notes

1. The CEPF case study was prepared by Isabel Nicholson.
2. To see a video of Executive Director Patricia Zurita discuss the CEPF: http://youtu .be/EPVSPa5gg3Q.
3. To see Patricia Zurita discuss regional implementation: http://youtu.be/fdRIqlw_-OE.

4. To see Patricia Zurita discuss how donors and partners work together: http://youtu .be/7lkqJO4A-UI.

5. The GTI case study was prepared by Alison Wescott, Global Tiger Initiative.

6. The GPO case study was prepared by Lelei TuiSamoa LeLaulu.

7. To see Lelei Lelaulu introduce the Global Partnership for Oceans: http://youtu.be /PVWSVQYtnKY.

8. To see Lelei Lelaulu discuss the role of the World Bank: http://youtu.be/M0pO1rqeckA.

9. To see Lelei Lelaulu discuss the foundations for partnership: http://youtu.be /PQ_6Q-Cfm1s.

10. http://www.theglobalfund.org/en. http://www.gavialliance.org. https://www.global partnershipforoceans.org.

11. To see Lelei Lelaulu discuss a sea change against business as usual: http://youtu.be /L1Cxf9uLFn8.

References

IEG (Independent Evaluation Group). 2010. *The World Bank's Involvement in Global and Regional Partnership Programs: An Independent Assessment.* Washington, DC: World Bank.

———. 2011. "The Forest Carbon Partnership Facility." *Global Program Review* 6 (3).

Kania, John, and Mark Kramer. 2011. "Collective Impact." *Stanford Social Innovation Review* 63 (Winter).

World Bank. 2012. "Global Tiger Recovery Program Implementation Report 2012." Global Tiger Initiative Secretariat, World Bank, Washington, D.C.

CHAPTER 10

Urban Sustainable Development: Re-envisioning the City of 2025

Julianne Baker Gallegos and Sintana Vergara

For better or worse, the development of contemporary societies will depend largely on understanding and managing the growth of cities. The city will increasingly become the test bed for the adequacy of political institutions, for the performance of government agencies, and for the effectiveness of programs to combat social exclusion, to protect and repair the environment and to promote human development. (Galea, Freudenberg, and Vlahov 2005)

Cities offer promise of economic opportunity, innovation, education, and culture (Bettencourt et al. 2007; World Bank 2012), as well as the challenge of providing for human and ecosystem needs—sustainably. This chapter considers the attributes that make a sustainable city, examines the forces that threaten it, and postulates how the World Bank might promote measures to ensure that cities act to conserve the global commons and promote of human health.

Why Youth?

Recent social movements, such as the Occupy Movement in Washington, DC, and the Arab Spring in multiple countries, have demonstrated that urban youth are not only numerous, but they have a voice and want things to change. Almost half the world's population today is under 25 (nearly 3 billion total), and nearly half of those (1.3 billion) are between 12 and 24 (UN-HABITAT 2013). The majority of youth are concentrated in towns and cities where they have opportunities, resources, and access to services not generally available in rural areas in the world.

Cities in the developing world, which also happen to concentrate the highest number of youth, account for more than 90 percent of global urban growth (UN-HABITAT 2013). This means that by 2025, 3 billion of current global residents (the majority residing in Asia and Africa) will be determining the fate of our planet. Furthermore, the youth voice is consistently undervalued in economic valuation methods, surveys, and policy making, which tend to be

To see Julianne Baker Gallegos and Sintana Vergara discuss nine priorities for the city of 2025: http://youtu.be/01viUk-9qyl

developed based on household and family information, leading to gaps in our understanding of the impacts of unemployment (and child labor), health, education, violence, gender, substance abuse, and poverty (among others) on youth.

At the same time, today's youth are being raised in a technological era in which cellular phones, the internet, and social media are viewed as natural parts of everyday life. They are accustomed to a rapidly changing world and are active members of a global community that gives them access to an abundance of information, allowing them to see, hear, learn, and experience the world in a variety of ways.

While many regions still have limited access to certain technologies, urban areas worldwide tend to have the highest access to communication media; even internet cafes and mobile cell phone coverage (and personal cell phones) can be found in the most unexpected and remote areas of the world. Increasingly, mobile technology is used as a means for accountability, the internet as an educational tool, and social media as a more reliable news source than some of the world's best-known news media. And the most active users of these technologies are usually young members of society.

Notwithstanding their communication abilities, urban youth are rarely included in consultations, planning, management, and decision-making processes around the world. The half of the world's population that has been most exposed to this recent outburst of technology, urbanization, and globalization is also the half that has the least say in how our planet will be managed in the future. Urban youth today have grown up in a much more complex and interconnected world than previous generations, yet they continue to play a secondary role in urban development. The initiative presented in this chapter first proposes that development institutions such as the World Bank start setting an example by involving youth in defining the sustainable city of 2025. Rather than pose the question to senior decision makers—those who are most often consulted—this initiative sought to hear from youth, the decision makers of 2025, about what they want their cities to look like.

Nine Priorities for the City of 2025

As the share of the global population living in cities soars beyond 50 percent, answering one question is central for sustainable development: "What attributes should your city to possess in 2025?" The question is also central to rethinking the role of the World Bank in catalyzing sustainable development in 2025. The authors ran a series of participatory workshops with professional and low-income youth, aged 15–30, to find out what they wanted in their cities. At least three workshops were held in each of four cities—Bangkok, Manila, Tokyo, and Washington, DC. The workshops asked participants to respond to the following:

1. **Describe your city:** A one-word answer. Participants shared a word or a phrase that described where they were from.

2. **Visualize your city:** A game. In the game, participants worked in pairs to answer four questions:
   a. What attributes do I want my city to possess in 2025?
   b. What actions can be taken to implement this vision?
   c. What barriers stand in the way of this vision?
   d. What can I do to implement this vision for my city?
3. **Picture your city:** A photo competition. Participants were invited to submit up to three or their own photos depicting their cities. In low-income areas, disposable cameras were distributed to workshop participants.

Pairs of participants would answer the first question, then pass their paper to another pair, who would then answer question 2 (actions to be taken) based on the previous group's response to question 1 (desired attributes) and so on through question 4. After all four questions were answered, lively discussion ensued.

Figure 10.1 Word Cloud for "Describe Your City in One Word"

Results of the Workshops

The words and phrases used by participants in Bangkok, Manila, Tokyo, and Washington, DC, to describe their city are shown in "word clouds" throughout this chapter. The size of a word corresponds to the number of times it came up during the introductory exercise.

This exercise demonstrated two characteristics of these youthful participants. First, they spoke eloquently and clearly about their cities and showed that they were empowered to affect change in their communities through the ideas they proposed for actions that could be taken to implement the vision for their city (questions 2b and 2d). While in general many found it easier to come up with barriers (question 2c) to the actions proposed in the game (question 2b), in a workshop for low-income youth in Manila, the participants came up with more individual actions than barriers to create the cities they desired.

Second, the experiences of youth in the same city can differ radically. Young professionals in Washington, DC, envisioned a city with better mobility; low-income youth in DC wanted a city with less gun violence. Young men in Tokyo wanted a more decentralized city; young women there wanted a city that could give them a better work-life balance.

While the diversity of experiences challenges a simple summary of the results, there were common attributes that were most important to youth across cities.

Figure 10.2 Proportion and Percentage of Responses for Specific Attributes in Youth Workshops

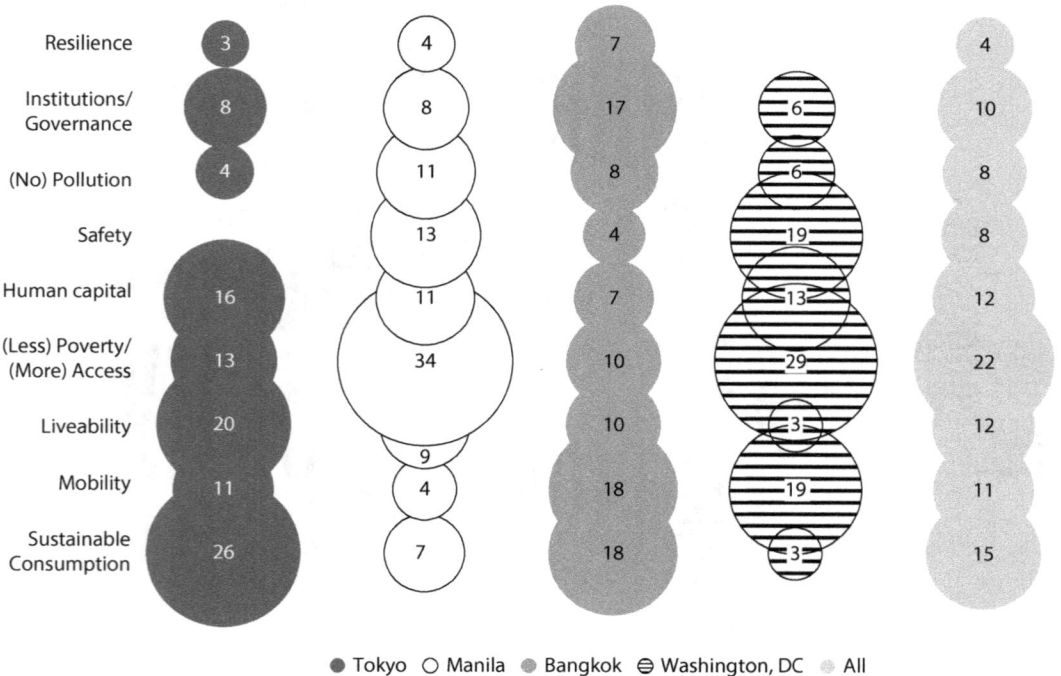

● Tokyo   ○ Manila   ● Bangkok   ◒ Washington, DC   All

Note: Bubble size is proportional to the number of responses, and percentage illustrates the frequency with which particular attributes came up during the workshops for each of the cities surveyed.

An analysis of the data showed clear trends that led to a natural grouping of attributes into nine categories. The youth wanted their city of the future to (1) provide access to basic needs and opportunities, (2) exhibit sustainable modes of consumption, (3) be livable, (4) possess human capital, (5) grant its citizens mobility, (6) exhibit good governance, (7) have low or no pollution, (8) be safe, and (9) be resilient to climate change. These attributes are largely in accordance with the scientific literature on sustainable cities (Kenworthy 2006).

Though there are differences between the attributes rated important in each city, access to basic needs and opportunities was cited as the most important attribute in Manila and Washington, but was not of urgent importance in Bangkok and Tokyo, However, all nine of the attributes were important across the cities. These nine priorities guide this chapter, which explores each with respect to its role in the city of the future and proposes how the World Bank can catalyze its attainment.

Sustainable Consumption

Cities as centers of consumption of renewable and nonrenewable resources (Howley, Scott, and Redmond 2009) have a tremendous impact on public and environmental health. The world is urbanizing rapidly at a scale never before seen; this urbanization is centered in smaller cities within low-income nations (Cohen 2004). Over the next decades, this urbanization will be centered in Africa (UN-HABITAT 2010b). Already majority urban, the world population is projected to be 75 percent urban by 2030 (Galea, Freudenberg, and Vlahov 2005).

These rapidly urbanizing places are also home to a billion "new consumers" in developing nations, who as a group have the spending capacity of all U.S. consumers (Myers and Kent 2003). This newly affluent population is dramatically

Figure 10.3 Word Cloud for "Sustainable Consumption"

increasing consumption of meat, electricity, cars (the number of cars owned in the developing world grew 89 percent during 1990–2000, with China's fleet increasing 445 percent and Colombia's 217 percent), and other consumer goods (Myers and Kent 2003).

The increase in population and consumption demands more extraction of natural resources and the production of more energy, resulting in increased greenhouse gas (GHG) emissions and more solid waste. Effective management of municipal solid waste poses "one of the biggest challenges [to] the urban world" (UN-HABITAT 2010a). In low-income countries, most cities collect less than half of the waste generated, of which only half is processed to minimum acceptable environmental and health standards.

The challenge is growing, and the waste is piling up. Along with rapid urbanization and population growth, municipal solid waste generation from the world's cities is increasing at unprecedented and alarming rates—from 1.3 billion tonnes in 2006 to a projected 2.2 billion tonnes by 2025. All of this growth is centered in developing country cities.

So these two dramatic demographic shifts—more people moving to cities and people consuming more—mean that cities drive global consumption and determine whether it is done sustainably. Thus they must become more efficient at handling their own by-products (from emissions to air, land, and water) to protect their citizens.

Not all consumption is created equal, and how cities consume has important environmental and health consequences. Bluefin tuna stocks—more than half of which is sold in Japan (and most of that in Tokyo)—are currently 96.4 percent below their historical abundance levels (Hoornweg et al. 2013).

A global public good (GPG), then—for example tuna stocks in the sea—is driven by the consumption of cities. And the consumption of a citizen in New York is far greater than the consumption of a citizen of Dhaka; Newman (2006) estimates that the environmental footprint of one Donald Trump is equal to that of several million low-income households in developing nations.

Increasing wealth and urbanization is not, however, a one-way street to destructive consumption. In fact, cities are recognized as "principal engines of innovation and economic growth" (Bettencourt et al. 2007, 7301), and the area of consumption is no exception. "Collaborative consumption" has emerged as a way in which citizens can save money, resources, and time. Its main principle is that people want services rather than things, and to meet that need, businesses in cities are beginning to offer car shares (for example, Zipcar), bike shares (for example, Capital Bikeshare), tie rentals, tool libraries, sheep rentals for lawn mowing, and even age-appropriate toys. Sharing extends to lifestyles too; young people in cities are increasingly choosing to live in intentional communities and cooperative houses, to share the labor and the possessions of city life (Vergara 2012a).

In a rapidly growing and urbanizing world, if greater numbers of urban residents chose to share or rent rather than own a car, the resulting improved air quality and reduced GHG emissions would be substantial. A tremendous amount of resources could be saved if citizens sold or exchanged clothes or electronics, rather than discarded them. Similarly, moving back to collective rather than individual living would reduce furniture production, energy consumption, and food waste. Cities—and their citizens—will be the main determinants of the global mode of consumption and its environmental consequences.

Multilateral institutions like the World Bank are uniquely qualified to nudge consumption and thus govern—or at least influence—the global commons. The Bank can encourage consumption changes in a number of ways: by effectively valuing natural resources as a source of wealth and heritage, by actively protecting natural resources (even before they are threatened), and by catalyzing international cooperation to govern global public goods. Box 10.1 gives example of actions and barriers from the participatory workshops related to the desired attribute "sustainable consumption."

Mobility

Within the realm of consumption, people and cities are shifting their modes of transportation, and they are shifting in the wrong direction. In 1988 Kristof (1988) wrote that 76 percent of road space in China's capital was taken up by bicycles—one in every two people owned a bicycle—which was 5.6 million bikes for 10 million people. But as of 2012, Beijing's traffic patterns are impressive for a very different reason. Cars now clog the streets, slowing down rush hour traffic to 9 miles per hour, and bicycles have all but disappeared. Chinese consumers have overwhelmingly embraced the car—whose number increased from 1.1 million to 6 million, between 1990 and 2000, a 445 percent leap.

Box 10.1 Sustainable Consumption (Workshop Responses)

Actions: Participants suggested government regulation and city-specific plans are extremely important, as is the need for international standards to regulate global industrial processes.

Barriers: Some of the barriers to sustainable consumption identified by participants include lack of education, the misconception that owning material objects constitutes well-being, governance challenges in both the public and private sectors, and the lack of accountability when public utilities are privatized.

My Actions: At the same time, the young workshop participants came up with multiple individual actions they could take to consume more sustainably in the future. Some of these actions include the following:

- "Practicing energy-saving actions."
- "Share my practices with others."
- "Share service provision with friends and neighbors (car-sharing, tool sharing, etc.)."
- "Start free shop and swap meets for recycling and reusing old items."

Too Global to Fail • http://dx.doi.org/10.1596/978-1-4648-0307-9

Figure 10.4 Word Cloud for "Mobility"

The hunger for cars is growing; China is now home to more than 78 million cars, 6.5 million of which are in Beijing alone.

The explosion of cars is not only China's doing; the world's citizens are driving 1 billion cars now. Car ownership is highest in the United States, where there are 1.3 people per vehicle, compared with China's 6.75. What is interesting about China is that its cities experienced a mode shift from bicycles to cars in 20 years, and now cities all over the world are aiming to do the opposite.

Many developing cities are now where developed cities are trying to be in terms of having high mode shares of public transit, walking, and cycling, though many of these cities lack a set of good alternatives, especially for poorer citizens (Sietchiping, Permezel, and Ngomsi 2012). In Sub-Saharan Africa, cycling and walking are the dominant forms of urban mobility, with bicycles and motorcycles growing in prevalence. While bicycling is understood to have a variety of health and environmental benefits, it often goes unacknowledged as an important mode of transit by planning authorities (UN-HABITAT 2010b).

If the goal is "providing fair, affordable, sustainable transit options in order to improve citizens' lives and their capacity to engage in economic and social opportunities and minimize negative environmental impacts" (Sietchiping, Permezel, and Ngomsi 2012, 183), then mass motorization is not the solution. At a global scale, road transportation is a large and growing source of GHG emissions: transport emits 25 percent of CO_2 from global energy use; 75 percent of such emissions come from roads, and vehicle emissions are a major source of black carbon, whose powerful global warming potential and public health risks are just beginning to be understood (Bond et al. 2013). At a city scale, mass motorization threatens public health and environment and creates unlivable cities. Car-centered cities have worse air pollution and higher asthma rates; recent work shows that urban residents' exposure to air pollutants in developing cities can be orders of magnitude higher than those for high-income countries. Cities built for cars in developed nations—especially those in the United States—are facing obesity epidemics directly linked to sedentary lifestyles. Cars are also dangerous: road traffic injuries are expected to be the third leading cause of death worldwide by 2020.

The risks incurred by cyclists and pedestrians depend on the city. Car-centered cities create a vicious cycle: they are more dangerous for bikes, so people drive more. In American cities, residents use cars for 66 percent of trips under 1 mile and 89 percent of trips 1–2 miles long; these trips could easily be taken by bicycle.

A virtuous cycle can be created by cities that encourage cycling and facilitate leaving the car behind. A few cities whose recent efforts to reimagine the role of the bicycle in transporting its citizens—through policy measures suggested here—highlight the wisdom of Beijing's boulevards of 20 years ago.

In developing countries, however, the bicycle, though the most commonly used form of transportation, is being rapidly replaced by the car. This shift is an active choice, by people and by cities, and is occurring whether we choose to seek inspiration from Beijing in the 1980s or Beijing in the 2010s, whether we build cities for 1 billion cars or 1 billion bicycles; these choices will profoundly shape the health of our citizens and life in our cities.

The World Bank is well positioned to encourage the development of people-centered cities, by both investing in pedestrian and bike-friendly development—bike lanes, bike share programs, pedestrian walkways, and traffic education—in addition to mass transit and by not promoting urban development centered on private motorized vehicles.

Box 10.2 describes example actions and barriers from the participatory workshops related to the desired attribute "mobility."

Livability

Livability emerged in the workshops as a desirable attribute in a number of forms, including the need for more recreational space, for green areas within the city, and for a better work-life balance.

Box 10.2 Mobility (Workshop Responses)

Actions: Some actions proposed by participants to increase efficiency in urban mobility included encouraging public transport usage among urban residents, developing better infrastructure (both roads and commuter lines), creating awareness about traffic rules and implementation of the rules, and building highways and parking lots when necessary.

Barriers: Participants identified a series of barriers to higher urban mobility, namely, how time-consuming the use of public transportation can be, the difficulties of using a flawed system (service disruptions, route changes, etc.), and lack of resources for proper development and maintenance of the transportation system.

My Actions: Workshop participants identified many individual actions they could take, including the following:

- "Using cars only when necessary."
- "Move to live near business area to reduce the amount of transportation needed (walk to work, etc.)."

Figure 10.5 Word Cloud for "Livability"

What makes a city livable? Most would agree that it is a desirable trait in a city, but it is difficult to define because it is a combination of the previously mentioned attributes—access to basic needs and opportunities, sustainable consumption, human capital, mobility, good governance, less pollution, safety, and resilience. By investing in the above attributes, the Bank would be actively creating sustainable, livable cities for the future.

Box 10.3 gives examples of actions and barriers from the participatory workshops related to the desired attribute "livability."

Box 10.3 Livability (Workshop Responses)

Actions: A proposed action in a couple of the cities was to move office areas to the suburbs or other cities, to decentralize action from a single urban center, and to create polycentric urban areas or even extend activities to other regions to reduce density in one city and attract youth and new workers to other cities as well.

Barriers: One of the principal barriers identified by the participants is lock-in, or the settling in of business and activities.

My Actions: Work-life balance emerged as a priority in some cities, particularly in Tokyo, where individuals identified the need to find a job with better balance than they have right now. Some of their suggestions included the following:

- "Find a job that has work-life balance."
- "Chose work based on work-life balance—not easy in Tokyo."
- "Secure budget for acquiring land for parks."
- "Formulate regulations for restricting density."

Access to Basic Needs and Opportunities

Since the early 1980s, cities have been considered *engines of economic growth*, producing greater prosperity and access to resources such as jobs, health care, and information (World Bank 2011). While cities may generate economic prosperity, the costs and benefits of this growth tend not to be distributed evenly across urban populations (UN-HABITAT 2013). Urban residents are required to spend significant portions of their income on goods and services that they might be able to produce themselves in rural settings, such as food, fuel, water, and shelter (Kuiper and van der Ree 2006).

In principle, urban agglomeration provides a more favorable setting to resolve social and environmental problems by delivering education, health care, and other services more efficiently in high-density areas and relieving the pressure on natural habitats produced through the extraction of natural resources (for example, deforestation to obtain fuel) (UNFPA 2007). In practice, urban poor have difficulty accessing adequate employment and income, housing, and basic infrastructure, as well as services, such as health care, education, and personal security (Kuiper and van der Ree 2006).

Between 2011 and 2013, the unemployed population grew globally by 4 million people, 75 percent of whom were in developing economies in Asia and Sub-Saharan Africa. Of these, nearly 200 million unemployed people, 37 percent were youth ages 15–24. Furthermore, unemployment rate trends were increasing, from a projection worldwide of an additional 1.1 million unemployed in to 3 million in 2014 (ILO 2013). While cities can foster economic development and provide opportunities, they must also enact appropriate policies to generate change and allow prosperity to be more evenly distributed, especially among the growing urban youth population (UN-HABITAT 2013).

Access to basic needs and opportunities involves a balanced mix of economic growth and policies that promote access to decent and productive job opportunities. Employment serves as a first step for the urban poor to gain better access to resources and benefit from the provision of services in urban areas.

Figure 10.6 Word Cloud for "Access to Basic Needs and Opportunities"

Thus, well-defined pro-poor and pro-job policies and programs must be developed by urban planners, managers, policy makers, and multilateral development agencies (Kuiper and van der Ree 2006). The city of the future needs an integrated design that enables it to absorb growing populations productively and to develop policies that generate enough decent jobs and address inequality so that informality, poverty, and insecurity can be reduced.

There is no doubt that new and improved macro-level policies are required to generate greater prosperity among urban populations, especially when it comes to youth unemployment. At the same time, macro-level policies require data that is not always readily available in developing countries and may not be fitting for their cities. Increasingly, examples of local-level economic productivity efforts have proven to be an important strategy to generate urban youth employment (UN-HABITAT 2013). Ghana's Youth Empowerment Synergy YouthWorks Project, for instance, provides solid waste management training and capacity-building for youth in a submetropolitan region of Accra. More than 150 youth have obtained full-time employment while contributing to improved sanitation in Accra's low-income submetropolitan areas, according to the Youth Employment Inventory (YEI 2013).

Box 10.4 gives examples of actions and barriers from the participatory workshops related to the desired attribute "Access to Basic Needs and Opportunity."

Box 10.4 Access to Basic Needs and Opportunity (Workshop Responses)

Actions: Some of the actions that can be taken to increase equality in access to opportunity include changes in policy or authority, making accessible and improved education systems available to those less privileged, and creating awareness of local population needs among policy makers.

Barriers: Workshop participants found this particular category very challenging. Some of the obstacles youth identified to achieve equal access to opportunity in the City of 2025 included, among many other obstacles, rich or powerful people who look down on underprivileged communities and are not willing to yield power; corrupt and immoral policy makers who develop regulations to benefit themselves, the valuing of money over moral principles prevalent among politicians and the privileged; the lack of transparency and use of social networks for job selection that limit the real opportunities youth have when looking for jobs and positions of power.

My Actions: While the barriers were abundant for this category, participants proposed a series of individual actions to achieve poverty reduction and decrease inequality. Examples included the following:

- "Educating my own children and people around us to give more than they take."
- "Donate to the less fortunate and engage in more community services and philanthropic activities (self and others)."
- "Be more considerate of others."
- "Encourage people to engage in community service."
- "Comply with laws and regulations for immigration."

Multilateral development agencies like the World Bank could change current trends by influencing urban development through policies and programs for pro-poor job creation that apply a "youth lens" and take youth skill sets, needs, and interests into consideration in the creation of jobs. Considering urban demographic structures in developing countries, there is a strong case for the Bank and others to address the vulnerabilities of the young population that the global economic crisis has exposed. Statistics show that youth who are not integrated into the workforce after leaving school have a much higher risk of becoming part of the urban poor and not going into formal employment. The Bank can catalyze funding for local civil society organizations that support efforts to empower youth through capacity building and access to credit.

> An unemployed youth represents a colossal waste of resource, a social hazard, and a burden on families or the government social support schemes, where any. Being forced into precarious livelihoods by intense poverty and lack of social protection is a lost opportunity, since these young people might otherwise attend school or college and acquire the skills and abilities that could raise their future. (UN-HABITAT 2013)

Human Capital

Traditionally cities have been considered a hub for human capital—a place where skilled labor, knowledge, myriad competencies, and creativity come together and interact in new ways. These interactions, in turn, produce tangible benefits, such as economic growth through the ability to perform and generate economic value. Other less tangible benefits include social cohesion and resilience—both crucial in times of distress, like illness, insecurity, or during natural disasters. A direct correlation has been established between human capital and skill or educational level. But even though human capital has been mentioned frequently by economists and urbanists as an asset, surprisingly few efforts have been made to examine its workings (Stolarick, Mellander, and Florida 2012).

Urban studies developed in the United States have demonstrated that places with higher levels of human capital have attracted more skilled people over the last three decades. This may be because local entrepreneurs might tend to start firms in their own city or the city where they attended university, creating demand for new skilled labor. Over the last 30 years, for instance, high-skill entrepreneurs have innovated in ways that have led to more employment for other skilled people (Berry and Glaeser 2005). Similarly, a recent study evaluating the distribution of human capital and its effect on economic performance found that human capital in center cities and suburbs of U.S. metropolitan areas has a positive effect on metro income levels and housing values across the board. As metros increase in size, human capital in the center city plays a bigger role, whereby the percentage of college grads in the center city plays a greater economic role in large metros (Stolarick, Mellander, and Florida 2012).

Increasingly, though, human capital is associated with qualities that extend beyond skill level—such as diversity, culture, and tolerance. Human capital

Figure 10.7 Word Cloud for "Human Capital"

development
generations health
ethnic diversity
considerate
cultural unity education
activities
generation
gender racial capital
musical multicultural

is built as a result of human interaction; thus having a diverse, cultured, and tolerant environment is key for creativity to flourish and innovation to occur. According to business and technology expert Soumitra Dutta (Manohar 2011), ideas that result from direct interaction between producer and consumer (or producer and producer) are highly valued in economies that are largely based on service provision. As such, he argues that there must be investment in human capital to enable an environment that supports a service economy by attracting competent people who understand global markets and are sensitive to other cultures. In order to do this, cities need to remain competitive by providing efficient basic infrastructure—both hard infrastructure (such as roads and transportation) and soft infrastructure (such as public spaces, museums, waterfronts, and green spaces).

As the world becomes increasingly urban, the need to have a better understanding of where and why human capital clusters (and of the different roles that those different kinds of clusters play in economic development) will become more and more important for urban planners, politicians, and developers. As this is an area that has not been studied in depth, international organizations with analytical capacity like the World Bank can gather lessons learned from successful "global" cities (such as London, New York, and Singapore) to support their clients in developing competitive urban areas.

Human and social capital[1] were valued by workshop participants as essential to building more unity among neighbors, for more positive actions at the community level, and for more disciplined urban dwellers who can take better care of common areas and urban infrastructure. Cultural openness, tolerance, and diversity were also mentioned as characteristics youth would like their city to have.

Box 10.5 gives examples of actions and barriers from the participatory workshops related to the desired attribute "Human Capital."

Box 10.5 Human Capital (Workshop Responses)

Actions: Some actions mentioned for strengthening social networks included creating more recreation centers, advertising activities in the community, having more clubs working around specific interests in the community, improving the educational system, imposing more severe penalties for law violations, and promoting the selection of good regulators who do not abuse their power.

Barriers: Participants believed there were multiple barriers to this vision, including the fact that most adults don't care or simply have too many responsibilities to be able to care; some children don't care because they just want to hang out on the street; and some cities don't have enough funding to develop communal activities, such as recreation centers.

My Actions: Nonetheless, young people proposed a series of measures that can be taken to strengthen social networks such as the following:

• "Start doing interesting (positive) activities with our free time and encourage our friends to do so too."

Security

In recent decades, urban violence has become a significant source of concern for local and national authorities. During the last decade alone, urban violence has unquestionably become the most serious form of lethal violence in the world. Its presence in transitional democracies and historically war-prone areas is a given, but it also prevails in non-conflict countries and regions that are generally considered "at peace." Around the world, Latin America and the Caribbean, South Africa, and a number of cities in the United States are recognized as "hubs" for urban violence (EUISS 2012).[2] In these cities, levels of lethal violence are much higher than the global national average. Further, registered lethal violence in some of these areas is even higher than in war-torn areas. Not to mention that specific intra-urban areas around the world (such as informal settlements in the developing world) or targeted groups of marginalized communities are exposed to much higher levels of violence than is captured in the national or urban average (EUISS 2012). Violence does not affect all members of society equally, and there are certain population groups that are clearly impacted more or differently by urban violence. Some variables that influence vulnerability to urban violence include but are not limited to gender, age, ethnicity, and race (Muggah 2012).

While urban violence is difficult to define due to the dynamic, evolving, and case-specific nature of the phenomenon, a series of drivers are considered key to the rising trend in urban violence—namely, population growth, density, and inequality; unemployment; lack of social cohesion; and governance failure. For instance, some academics, the United Nations, and the World Bank have connected rapid urban growth with a dramatic increase in violence levels (Muggah 2012).

Similarly, the "social disorder" associated with human agglomeration in a dense city has been historically associated with personal disorganization, mental

Figure 10.8 Word Cloud for "Need for Security"

breakdown, suicide, delinquency, crime, corruption, and disorder (Wirth 1938). While the association between density and violence is not always prevalent, UN-HABITAT has observed a tendency toward increased levels of violence (such as domestic violence and child abuse) when there is overcrowding in inadequate dwellings (UN-HABITAT 2007).

While traditionally, poverty has been linked with violence, it is increasingly obvious that inequality, rather than poverty, is more relevant in that it comprises a form of "structural" violence that triggers a reactionary form of violence on behalf of the marginalized individual or community. An example would be unemployed youth who might be limited in their options and therefore are vulnerable to organized crime groups (Muggah 2012).

A critical element that shapes urban violence is the ability (or inability) of state institutions to regulate and manage the use of force. In many cities in the developing world, law enforcement systems (ranging from police to penal systems) are dysfunctional or not trusted by the population due to corruption. In these circumstances, it is not uncommon for law enforcement agencies to be considered the worst offenders by civil society, sometimes due to inability or lack of resources and capacity and sometimes due to an existing culture of impunity (Muggah 2012).

Some of the proposed ways in which urban violence can be addressed are pacification processes and community policing, enhanced protection measures and reducing exposure of youth at risk, promoting social capital and urban cohesion, slum upgrading and urban safety, and addressing urban governance for the purpose of citizen security.

The World Bank already works on many of these initiatives, supporting national and local authorities in developing policing interventions and pacification processes and developing urban infrastructure that is more open and has better lighting to reduce gender-specific violence. However, there is much more to do, particularly when it comes to engaging youth at risk and promoting social capital and urban cohesion. Further, urban violence is a nascent field of study, and much more analytical work is needed to understand drivers and evaluate impacts of development interventions on incidence of urban violence—all of which the World Bank, with its extensive urban development portfolio, would be qualified to deliver.

The issue of urban security emerged as a theme in the workshops in the context of reducing gun violence, having more peaceful cities, and guaranteeing citizen safety. This attribute was a particularly relevant to youth in Manila and Washington, DC, demonstrating how urban violence transcends the traditional North-South divide, affecting developed and developing nations alike. Notably, violence was most relevant to Washington, DC, youth than to any other youth group consulted.

Box 10.6 gives examples of actions and barriers from the participatory workshops related to the desired attribute"Security."

Box 10.6 Security (Workshop Responses)

Actions: The actions proposed to enhance security include enforcing gun control and limiting gun permits, police enforcement, helping people find non-violent ways to express themselves (art), building and placing billboard ads on the negative effects of gun possession, making guns less accessible, doing more thorough background checks on those who apply for a firearm, requiring schools to get more strict with bullying, using to peer mediation, participating in and organizing peace rallies, improving lighting in dangerous areas, installing hidden cameras, enforcing criminal punishment, starting a neighborhood watch, and increasing the presence of police.

Barriers: Many obstacles were identified to increased security and safety, including cycles of violence within families and peer groups, people feeling the need to carry guns to protect themselves, bullies, people thinking it's cool to have a gun, social networking, people living in an environment that leads them to believe they need a gun, easy access to guns, apathy, the United States being is a bully, people's mindsets, thirst for power/domination, budget and income generation, lack of enforceability and transparency by responsible agencies, budget and labor supply, job conditions, public perception of police occupation, culture, fear, corruption, small institutional capacity, and limited jail space.

My Actions: The following measures were proposed as individual actions to increase safety:

- "Petition."
- "Lobby police department and public forums for safety."
- "Support peace-seeking groups."
- "Don't hang in the wrong crowd."
- "Sharing knowledge/technology."
- "Fund training for law enforcement/security personnel."
- "Invest in legal reform."
- "Stop supporting people who like/use guns for the wrong purposes."

Too Global to Fail • http://dx.doi.org/10.1596/978-1-4648-0307-9

Reduced Pollution

A necessary by-product of consumption is waste production, and as cities are centers of consumption, they are also factories of waste. Effluent from industrial, commercial, and residential activity pollutes the air, water, and land. Air pollution—the emission of byproducts of combustion (for example, particulate matter, carbon monoxide, and carbon dioxide, ozone, nitrogen dioxide, lead, and mercury, among others)—occurs parallel to urbanization, as fossil-based transportation, manufacturing, and power production ramp up to meet demand (Byrd and Joad 2006).

The urban environment, in turn, defines population health—the food that people eat, the air they breathe, where they work, and how they live (Galea, Freudenberg, and Vlahov 2005). Emissions from motor vehicle use are a major cause of morbidity and mortality in developing cities (Moore, Gould, and Keary 2003). The health risks from indoor air pollution are highest in developing country cities, where combustion of biomass for heating and cooking is prevalent (Zhang and Smith 2003). Black carbon, whose primary emission sources are motor vehicles and biomass combustion, is an important contributor to climate change (Bond et al. 2013). More than 1 billion people lack access to clean water, and 2.5 billion lack access to adequate sanitation (Nelson and Murray 2008), leading to a vicious cycle of waterborne morbidity and mortality. Finally, improper management of solid waste also directly impacts human health, as open burning and incineration emit air pollutants, untreated leachate contaminates water bodies, and waste attracts disease vectors (Giusti 2009; Vergara 2012b; Vergara and Tchobanoglous 2012).

Figure 10.9 Word Cloud for "Pollution Reduction"

Box 10.7 Reduced Pollution (Workshop Responses)

Actions: A series of actions were proposed to accomplish pollution reduction: conducting regular surveys and gathering data on pollution levels, holding public workshops to create awareness, establishing adequate penalties for polluting, planting more trees, increasing gas prices (stop subsidies), imposing higher taxes on cars, building more efficient and less polluting public transportation, and establishing disincentives for driving (penalizing driving during peak hours and rewarding driving during off-hours).

Barriers: The obstacles to successfully implementing this vision included unyielding behavior of urban populations, poor waste management practices, cars that are too large and highly inefficient, large factories unwilling to move, and people's attitude toward mass transit.

My Actions: Workshop participants proposed the following individual actions to reduce pollution:

- "Vote for a politician who can solve this problem to be government leader."
- "Propose a code for solving this problem and try to enact the code."
- "Encourage the use of public transportation systems."
- "Raise awareness of simple environmental protection measures among people close to me."
- "Act as check and balance to government's environmental protection measures."

The public health impacts of pollution are differential: the poor are disproportionately affected by pollution because of where they live and work (Wang'ombe 1995). Children and the elderly are also more susceptible to pollution (Byrd and Joad 2006).

While the World Bank has a very active portfolio in public health, its impact in cities could be more powerful if it moved away from investing in GHG-intensive transportation. Promoting human-powered and public transit would decrease both GHG emissions and exposure to air pollutants. Stepping up the decidedly un-sexy work of providing the world's poor with proper sanitation—sanitation that is dignified but locally appropriate and seeks to recycle nutrients, rather than dispose of them using clean water—to would provide great environmental and health benefits.

Box 10.7 describes example actions and barriers from the participatory workshops related to the desired attribute "reduced pollution."

Governance and Planning

Local governments play an essential role in urban sustainability. Not only are they responsible for development planning, but they are also in charge of the delivery of basic social services, energy and water supply and management, transport, land use planning, and waste management (Hoornweg et al. 2013). Local governments require sufficient governance capacity in order to fulfill these roles, but unfortunately, in many developing nations, this capacity is limited.

Too Global to Fail • http://dx.doi.org/10.1596/978-1-4648-0307-9

Some of the limiting factors include access to financing, municipal competencies, absence of a multi level governance framework, and transnational networks (Bulkeley et al. 2011). Pro-poor adaptation to the impacts of climate change is one area where, in general, city and municipal governments need greater capacity. Improved knowledge, competence, and accountability would increase the adaptive capacity of local bodies (Satterthwaite et al. 2009).

In order to deliver sustainable urban plans, cities require significant investments, new institutions, and financial instruments. Multiple instruments have been discussed at the international, national, and local scales, including carbon finance and carbon markets (Kamal-Chaoui and Robert 2009), specialized climate or environmental funds, socially responsible investment (Labatt and White 2007), and subsidized access to capital.

Similarly, many countries have decentralized their governments in recent decades, giving cities more power to raise and manage their own revenues (IEG 2008). Decentralization shifts authority, responsibility, and accountability for public functions from the national government to local governments, allowing municipalities to create and broaden their own sources of revenue in addition to receiving a share of national revenues and proceeds from the use of natural resources within their jurisdiction (Hoornweg et al. 2013).

However, limited financial resources place a strain on municipalities in developing countries where local governments are at times unable to provide even basic services, particularly to the urban poor. Access to financing—and the accountability measures that necessarily go hand-in-hand with the financing—will be crucial to building sustainable cities.

The most empowering forms of decentralization provide political space for local government action that derives from citizen participation, collaborates with civil society organizations, and benefits from public-private partnerships for effective service provision.

Figure 10.10 Word Cloud for "Governance"

International agencies such as the World Bank would most benefit urban development by providing tools, knowledge, and best practices to cities; building strong partnerships with transnational municipal networks (e.g., the C40 Climate Leadership Group; ICLEI—Local Governments for Sustainability; Metropolis' United Cities and Local Governments (UCLG); and training civil society organizations that fill important service provision gaps (Hoornweg et al. 2013).

It is increasingly obvious that quality of governance depends on participation and accountability, encouraging a shared vision and understanding of the tools necessary to achieve better governance and service provision (ASEAN 2010). Slowly, governance models are changing from the traditional technocratic model to a participatory approach that engages with civil society and with the private sector (UN-HABITAT 2010b). New technologies, such as mobile telecommunications, the internet, and social media have played a critical role in citizen participation, allowing mass collaboration by enabling connectivity at scale. Collaborative problem solving is slowly becoming an essential method to address the complex challenges our societies face today, particularly in the urban context (Hoornweg et al. 2013).

During the youth workshops, the role of institutions emerged as an essential component for more effective urban planning. This involved stronger, more capable institutions and a reduction in corruption, an area where social media and the internet are playing a critical role as of late (for example, youth mobilization to demand government accountability in the Middle East through social media).

Low-Carbon and Climate-Resilient Urban Development

As global populations have agglomerated in urban areas, cities have increasingly become a source of global GHG emissions. The World Energy Outlook estimated that approximately 70 percent of global GHG emissions are ultimately attributable to the residents of cities, and the proportion is expected to continue to rise in the upcoming decades (IEA 2008). Not only have cities contributed the largest share of the world's GHG emissions, they also concentrate many of the people most at risk from the effects of climate change and the businesses that generate most of the gross world product (Satterthwaite et al. 2009).

These patterns do not necessarily overlap, since most of the cities that face the highest risks are those with small GHG contributions. In developing countries, vulnerability is often increased due to informal settlements, lack of infrastructure, and limited institutional capacity. The urban poor are particularly vulnerable, as they tend to occupy locations that are more exposed to hazards and have limited adaptive capacity (Baker 2012). Estimates suggest that as much as 80 percent ($70–100 billion) of the projected annual costs of adaptation to climate change through 2050 are in urban sectors: water supply, coastal zones, and infrastructure (Hoornweg, Sugar, and Trejos Gomez 2011).

Box 10.8 gives examples of actions and barriers from the participatory workshops related to the desired attribute "Governance and Planning."

Box 10.8 Governance and Planning (Workshop Responses)

Actions: Proposed actions for this attribute included: creating a citizen report card for citizens to rate their government/services and request change, improving government accountability, creating public spaces for street vendors to conduct business, implementing stricter regulations and enforcing them, designing better zoning plans, requiring the government to lead by example and be honest, designing transportation systems, which result in an urban form that uses resources efficiently, building cities from scratch when they are locked-in in unsustainable urban forms and improving the quality of buses, bus driver behavior, the vehicle itself, and safety conditions for passengers.

Barriers: Some of obstacles to the development of stronger institutions are people's discipline, weak laws and law enforcement, outlaw groups, manipulative media and populations' vulnerability to it, lack of budget, and lack of technology. Also cited were politicians' lack of incentives to participate in the political system due to low salaries, the fact that politicians are feared rather than respected, perverse incentives that encourage politicians to make decisions to the detriment of urban residents, and tolerance for corruption. Some of the obstacles for better urban planning included infrastructural lock-in, an infrastructure built and centered around cars, corporate interests (car and oil companies), people's habits (used to driving), historical areas that make it impossible to redesign infrastructure/remodel urban form, incentive systems for using the bus, lack of faith in the political process, authority's ignorance, lack of decision-making capabilities to handle urban problems, street vendors that oppose stricter laws and law enforcement, and short-term vision by local decision makers regarding urban planning.

My Actions: Proposed individual actions workshop participants suggested included the following:

- "Start from ourselves."
- "Be honest."
- "Reject any bribery/lobbying."
- "Don't buy/support counterfeit products."
- "Report any inappropriate actions to authority (for example if your friend cheats, report to office)—police."
- "Use social media as a tool to pressure people who act unlawfully (in Bangkok, years ago when a video was televised and shared on Facebook about politicians engaged in bribery and they were fired)."
- "Use social media as whistleblower."
- "Vote for politicians that will fund better infrastructure/urban planning."
- "Use public transportation (to create demand)."
- "Send letters/call city officials to request more green space."
- "Encourage citizens to express their concern/voice."

Figure 10.11 Word Cloud for "Low-Carbon and Climate-Resilient Urban Development"

The need for climate action in cities is pressing, and delay is costly—particularly in the rapidly growing cities of developing countries, where most infrastructure will be built in the next few decades (Hoornweg et al. 2013). Going forward, plans to mitigate climate change through more efficient city systems need to be integrated with adaptation measures to build resilient urban areas. Managing for resilience and understanding that cities are exposed to uncertainty, rather than seeing them as static systems, increases the likelihood that development can be sustained under changing climatic and environmental conditions (Folke, Carpenter, and Elmqvist 2002).[3] Mitigation will not progress quickly enough to avoid significant climate change impacts, hence adaptation is necessary. Both approaches are not only necessary, but complementary (Wilbanks and Sathaye 2007). Linking mitigation and adaptation at the local government level is expected to enhance and strengthen the potential impacts of both types of climate action.

Urban infrastructure and buildings are long-lived and generally locked-in for decades or more. Once an urban form is chosen and locked-in, it will determine the pattern of a city's resource intensity for decades or even centuries. When densities are too low, bike lanes or subway schemes, for example, become too expensive. GHG reduction plans can drive efficiency and allow cities to reduce waste and cut costs (Hoornweg et al. 2013). Dense cities tend to have lower per capita emissions, provided that they are also served by good public transport systems (Hoornweg, Sugar, and Trejos Gomez 2011). Higher density also enables more energy-efficient heating and cooling in buildings and lower embedded energy demand for urban infrastructure. The savings in operating costs from shorter transport networks and less diffuse utility infrastructure can amount to thousands of dollars of annual savings for the average household (Litman 2013).

At the same time, urban planners and managers must now consider measures to adapt their cities' buildings, infrastructure, industry, institutions, and services to the impacts of climate change. There are many ways to do this, ranging from adjustments in building codes and land use regulations to the use of insurance to spread risk to effective, well-established emergency management services (Sattherthwaite et al. 2009).

There is consensus among climate change scientists that large-scale disasters are increasing in frequency worldwide, largely due to weather-related events. Many of the extreme weather events that have caused significant economic and human loss in the past 60 years have taken place in urban areas or have affected them indirectly (for example, through immigration from affected areas or interrupted service provision).

Most of the costs of adaptation will be borne by cities. Cost estimates are wide ranging, but the United Nations Framework Convention on Climate Change (UNFCCC) estimates a global cost of $49–171 billion per year by 2030 (Parry et al. 2009), and the World Bank (2010) estimates $80–100 billion per year. Currently, adaptation is financed mainly through private income, national and municipal revenues, grants from multilateral and bilateral institutions, and market-based mechanisms. There is room for cities to be creative in leveraging more funding from donors and collaborating with the private sector to help finance adaptation (World Bank 2011).

The World Bank (along with other multilateral development agencies) is uniquely poised to support cities in developing holistic climate action plans by providing technical assistance to strengthen local awareness and building local capacity on climate change impacts in urban areas. It can also leverage funding to ensure local governments have access to the resources they will need to develop coherent mitigation plans (starting with GHG emissions inventories and building toward low-carbon urban development) that contemplate long-term climate impacts.

Resilience was addressed in the workshops, both directly and indirectly, usually in the context of flood risk reduction. In Tokyo, the prevention of nuclear disasters and unexpected secondary impacts was discussed, while in Manila and Bangkok, the flood damage and the need to prevent future life and material loss from flooding seemed to be most relevant.

Photo Voice Project

In the low-income workshops held in Manila and Washington, DC, participants were given disposable cameras and told to document their city and their experience—for example, what they like about their city, what they would like to change about their city, their life in their city, and so on. Participants were asked to keep a log of their documentation and write a caption saying what each photo meant to them. This enabled the youth to present images of their city through their own eyes and see that their contributions were valued.

In the other workshops, participants were invited to take photos with their own cameras and submit their photos and captions. More than 150 photos were submitted, and 34 were featured in the *Visualizing My City* photo exhibit during

Box 10.9 Low-Carbon and Resilient Development (Workshop Responses)

Actions: Actions proposed by workshop participants for low-carbon and resilient development included long-term city planning, accepting the inevitability of flooding, spreading out economic resources, decentralizing and reducing density in urban area, cooperating and making low-carbon development a public problem nationally and internationally, doing more effective integrated water management, implementing better zoning laws, and building artificial land to be able to take refuge in emergencies.

Barriers: Multiple obstacles were identified for developing long-term urban resilience. These included the government itself, dependence on existing vulnerable infrastructure, settlements in at-risk areas (what to do with them?), groundwater withdrawal, people's resistance to change, and planning for water and disaster management and understanding political and economic interests influencing it.

My Actions: While being identified as one of the most challenging priorities, resilience was also perceived as an empowering attribute, where by individual and community action can play an important role. Some examples included the following:

- "Learn to swim/practice swimming."
- "Teach others how to swim."
- "Practice rowing."
- "Learn surviving skills for emergencies."
- "Raise my house."
- "Move to higher ground."
- "Raise awareness about the sinking/flooding."
- "Use social media (Facebook) to warn others and create awareness."
- "Elevate the issue to mainstream media so if more people know, then they will stop settling in at-risk areas."
- "Raise awareness within private sector as a multiplier of awareness."

the 6th Urban Research and Knowledge Symposium in Barcelona. Their photos and information about the youth that participated in these consultations can be found at the Visualizing My City Facebook group, https://www.facebook.com /groups/356225034456068/.

Box 10.9 gives examples of actions and barriers from the participatory workshops related to the desired attribute "Low-Carbon and Resilient Development."

Notes

1. See the section on security for further information on social capital.
2. Arguably this could be in part due to the deficit of research on homicidal violence in Southeast Europe and Asia (Muggah 2012).
3. Resilience is the capacity of a system to continually change and adapt yet remain within critical thresholds (SRC 2013).

References

ASEAN (Association of Southeast Asian Nations). 2010. "Urbanisation in Southeast Asian Countries." Institute for Southeast Asian Studies, Singapore.

Baker, J. 2012. *Climate Change, Disaster Risk, and the Urban Poor*. Washington, DC: World Bank.

Berry, C. R., and E. L. Glaeser. 2005. "The Divergence of Human Capital Levels across Cities." National Bureau of Economic Research Working Paper 11617, Cambridge, MA.

Bettencourt, L. M., J. Lobo, D. Helbing, C. Kühnert, and G. B. West. 2007. "Growth, Innovation, Scaling, and the Pace of Life in Cities." *Proceedings of the National Academy of Sciences* 104 (17): 7301–6. doi:10.1073/pnas.0610172104.

Bond, T. C., S. J. Doherty, D. W. Fahey, P. M. Forster, T. Berntsen, B. J. DeAngelo, M. G. Flanner, S. Ghan, B. Kärcher, D. Koch, S. Kinne, Y. Kondo, P. K. Quinn, M. C. Sarofim, M. G. Schultz, M. Schulz, C. Venkataraman, H. Zhang, S. Zhang, N. Bellouin, S. K. Guttikunda, P. K. Hopke, M. Z. Jacobson, J. W. Kaiser, Z. Klimont, U. Lohmann, J. P. Schwarz, D. Shindell, T. Storelvmo, S. G. Warren, and C. S. Zender. 2013. "Bounding the Role of Black Carbon in the Climate System: A Scientific Assessment." *Journal of Geophysical Research: Atmospheres* 118 (11): 5380–552. doi:10.1002/jgrd.50171.

Bulkeley, H., H. Schroeder, K. Janda, J. Zhao, A. Armstrong, S. Y. Chu, and S. Ghosh. 2011. "The Role of Institutions, Governance, and Urban Panning for Mitigation." In *Cities and Climate Change: Responding to an Urgent Agenda*, edited by D. Hoornweg, M. Freire, M. J. Lee, P. Bhada-Tata, and B. Yuen, 125–60. Washington, DC: World Bank.

Byrd, R. S., and J. R. Joad. 2006. "Urban Asthma." *Current Opinion in Pulmonary Medicine* 12 (1): 68–74. doi:10.1097/01.mcp.0000199001.68908.45.

Cohen, B. 2004. "Urban Growth in Developing Countries: A Review of Current Trends and a Caution Regarding Existing Forecasts." *World Development* 32 (1): 23–51.

Davis, S. J., and K. Caldeira. 2010. "Consumption-Based Accounting of CO_2 Emissions." *Proceedings of the National Academy of Sciences*. http://www.pnas.org/cgi/doi/10.1073/pnas.0906974107.

EUISS (European Union Institute for Security Studies). 2012. "Urban Violence and Humanitarian Challenges: Joint Report." Brussels: EUISS-ICRC Colloquium, January 19.

Folke, C., S. R. Carpenter, and T. Elmqvist. 2002. "Resilience and Sustainable Development: Building Adaptive Capacity in a World of Transformations." *Ambio* 31 (5): 437–40.

Galea, S., N. Freudenberg, and D. Vlahov. 2005. "Cities and Population Health." *Social Science and Medicine* 60 (5): 1017–33. doi:10.1016/j.socscimed.2004.06.036.

Giusti, L. 2009. "A Review of Waste Management Practices and Their Impact on Human Health." *Waste Management* 29 (8): 2227–39. doi:10.1016/j.wasman.2009.03.028.

Hoornweg, D., L. Sugar, and C. L. T. Gomez. 2011. "Cities and Greenhouse Gas Emissions: Moving Forward." *Environment and Urbanisation* 23 (1): 207–27.

Hoornweg, D., M. Freire, J. B. Gallegos, and A. Saldivar-Sali. 2013. *Building Sustainability in an Urbanizing World: A Partnership Report*. Washington, DC: World Bank.

Howley, P., M. Scott, and D. Redmond. 2009. "Sustainability versus Liveability: An Investigation of Neighbourhood Satisfaction." *Journal of Environmental Planning and Management* 52 (6): 847–64. doi:10.1080/09640560903083798.

IEA (International Energy Agency). 2008. *World Energy Outlook 2008*. Paris: OECD.

IEG (Independent Evaluation Group). 2008. *Decentralization in Client Countries: An Evaluation of World Bank Support 1990–2007*. Washington, DC: World Bank.

ILO (International Labour Organization). 2013. "Global Employment Trends 2013." http://www.ilo.org/global/about-the-ilo/newsroom/news/WCMS_202320/lang--en /index.htm.

Kamal-Chaoui, L., and A. Robert. eds. 2009. "Competitive Cities and Climate Change." OECD Regional Development Working Paper 2, Paris.

Kenworthy, J. R. 2006. "The Eco-City: Ten Key Transport and Planning Dimensions for Sustainable City Development." *Environment and Urbanization* 18 (1): 67–85. doi: 10.1177/0956247806063947.

Kristof, N. D. 1988. "Seeing Beijing from a Bicycle." *New York Times*, June 19. http://www .nytimes.com/1988/06/19/travel/seeing-beijing-from-a-bicycle.html?pagewanted =all&src=pm.

Kuiper, M., and K. van der Ree. 2006. "Growing Out of Poverty: Urban Job Creation and the Millennium Development Goals." *Global Urban Development Magazine* 2 (1). http://www.globalurban.org/GUDMag06Vol2Iss1/Kuiperpercent20&percent20van percent20derpercent20Ree.htm.

Labatt, S., and R. R. White. 2007. *Carbon Finance: The Financial Implications of Climate Change*. Hoboken, NJ: Wiley.

Litman, T. 2013. "Smart Growth Savings: What We Know about Public Infrastructure and Service Cost Savings, and How They Are Misrepresented by Critics." Victoria Transport Policy Institute, Victoria, BC, Canada.

Manohar, P. 2011. "Human Capital, Cities, Economic Growth: An Interview with Soumitra Dutta." *The Urban Vision: Expert Diary*, December 7. http://www.theurbanvision .com/blogs/?p=877.

Moore, M., P. Gould, and B. S. Keary. 2003. "Global Urbanization and Impact on Health." *International Journal of Hygiene and Environmental Health* 206 (4–5): 269–78. doi:10.1078/1438-4639-00223.

Muggah, R. 2012. "Researching the Urban Dilemma: Urbanization, Poverty and Violence." International Development Research Centre. Ottawa, ON, Canada.

Myers, N., and J. Kent. 2003. "New Consumers: The Influence of Affluence on the Environment." *Proceedings of the National Academies of Science* 100: 4963–68.

Nelson, K. L., and A. Murray. 2008. "Sanitation for Unserved Populations: Technologies, Implementation Challenges, and Opportunities." *Annual Review of Environment and Resources* 33 (1): 119–51. SSRN: http://ssrn.com/abstract=1319909.

Newman, P. 2006. "The Environmental Impact of Cities." *Environment and Urbanization* 18 (2): 275–95. doi:10.1177/0956247806069599.

Parry, M., N. Arnell, P. Berry, D. Dodman, S. Fankhauser, C. Hope, S. Kovats, R. Nicholls, D. Satterthwaite, R. Tiffin, and T. Wheeler. 2009. "Assessing the Costs of Adaptation to Climate Change: A Review of the UNFCCC and Other Recent Estimates." London: International Institute for Environment and Development.

Satterthwaite, D., S. Huq, H. Reid, M. Pelling, and P. R. Lankao. 2009. "Adapting to Climate Change in Urban Areas: The Possibilities and Constraints in Low- and Middle-Income Nations." London: International Institute for Environment and Development.

Sietchiping, R., M. J. Permezel, and C. Ngomsi. 2012. "Transport and Mobility in sub-Saharan African Cities: An Overview of Practices, Lessons and Options for Improvements." *Cities* 29 (3): 183–89. doi:10.1016/j.cities.2011.11.005.

SRC (Stockholm Resilience Centre). 2013. *What Is Resilience?* http://www.stockholm resilience.org/21/research/research-videos/12-1-2011-what-is-resilience-.html.

Stolarick, K., C. Mellander, and R. Florida. 2012. "Human Capital in Cities and Suburbs." Working Paper Series in Economics and Institutions of Innovation 264, Royal Institute of Technology, CESIS—Centre of Excellence for Science and Innovation Studies, Stockholm.

UNFPA (United Nations Population Fund). 2007. "State of the World Population 2007: Unleashing the Potential of Urban Growth." UNFPA, New York. https://www.unfpa.org/swp/2007/english/introduction.html.

UN-HABITAT. 2007. *Global Report on Human Settlements 2007: Enhancing Urban Safety and Security*. Nairobi: United Nations Human Settlements Programme.

———. 2010a. *Solid Waste Management in the World's Cities*. London: United Nations Human Settlements Programme.

———. 2010b. *State of the World's Cities 2010/2011: Bridging the Urban Divide*. London: Earthscan.

———. 2013. *State of Urban Youth Report 2012–2013: Youth in the Prosperity of Cities*. Nairobi: UN-HABITAT.

Vergara, S. E. 2012a. "Collaborative Consumption—A Trend for the Young, the Hip, and the Urban." *World Bank Sustainable Cities* (blog), World Bank, Washington, DC. http://blogs.worldbank.org/sustainablecities/node/591.

———. 2012b. "Global Youth Assert Their Visions for the City of 2025." World Bank, Washington, DC. http://blogs.worldbank.org/sustainablecities/manila-bangkok-tokyo-and-washington-dc-youth-assert-their-visions-for-the-city-of-2025.

Vergara, S. E., and G. Tchobanoglous. 2012. "Municipal Solid Waste and the Environment: A Global Perspective." *Annual Review of Environment and Resources* 37 (1): 277–309. doi: 10.1146/annurev-environ-050511-122532.

Wang'ombe, J. K. 1995. "Public Health Crises of Cities in Developing Countries." *Social Science and Medicine* 41 (6): 857–62. doi: 10.1016/0277-9536(95)00155-Z.

Wilbanks, T. J., and J. Sathaye. 2007. "Integrating Mitigation and Adaptation as Responses to Climate Change: A Synthesis." *Mitigation and Adaptation Strategies for Global Change* 12: 957–62.

Wirth, L. 1938. "Urbanism as a Way of Life." *American Journal of Sociology*, 44 (1): 1–24.

World Bank. 2010. *Natural Hazards, Unnatural Disasters: The Economics of Effective Prevention*. Washington, DC: World Bank.

———. 2011. *Cities and Climate Change: An Urgent Agenda*. Washington, DC: World Bank.

———. 2012. "Cities as Engines of Economic Growth." Webinar. http://einstitute.worldbank.org/ei/webinar/cities-engines-economic-growth.

YEI (Youth Employment Inventory). 2013. "National Youth Employment Programme (NYEP)." World Bank, Washington, DC. http://www.youth-employment-inventory.org/inventory/view/404/.

Zhang, J., and K. R. Smith. 2003. "Indoor Air Pollution: A Global Health Concern." *British Medical Bulletin* 68 (1): 209–25. doi:10.1093/bmb/ldg029.

CHAPTER 11

Managing Transitions to Sustainable Provision of Global Public Goods

Derk Loorbach, Roebin Lijnis Huffenreuter, Niki Frantzeskaki, and Jan Rotmans

This chapter focuses on transition management in the context of global sustainability challenges and their governance. The chapter comprises three interrelated components: (1) the transition perspective on achieving global sustainability, (2) the transition management approach and related challenges and tensions around governance of sustainability transitions, and (3) suggestions for implementation of transition management in a global context.

Global Systemic Change and Persistent Unsustainability

The challenges of achieving sustainable development and global public goods (GPGs) are highly complex, and the solutions require actions by multiple stakeholders over long time periods. It has been difficult for countries and multilateral organizations to develop and implement appropriate strategies for tackling challenges in this context. The difficulties are magnified by the numerous uncertainties that long-term actions face, whether political, economic, or environmental. But this means that a different kind of strategic planning, implementation, and monitoring is required. The transitions approach is a new planning method for long-term change that has been developed and tested and will be examined here.

Policy making itself has become highly complex in the context of a globalizing network society (Castells 1996), with persistent unsustainability problems and related uncertainties, as different actors, stakes, and perspectives need to be dealt with. Clear solutions or mechanisms to assess progress and success are lacking. It is clear that addressing global sustainability challenges through formalized institutional settings and mechanisms is not delivering effective solutions at the pace required. Examples, such as the international climate negotiations, UN sustainable development policies, and multilateral agreements, have so far not led to the major reorientation of societal change toward sustainable use of GPGs. Therefore, another form of governance is needed, one that complements current

---

To see J. Warren Evans discuss donors and aid architecture: http://youtu.be/QRoyJurEmpg

institutionalized forms, an approach that effectively empowers and facilitates desired developments and breaks down undesired ones.

The Transitions Approach does not seek to redefine sustainable development, but takes a different perspective. It considers sustainable development as a particular type of societal change that requires a new governance model built on knowledge of social, ecological, economic, and technological complexity and evolution, while also understanding how such processes unfold and can be steered (Rotmans et al. 2001).

Even though sustainability is popularly advocated as a desirable goal on local, regional, and international levels, current action is not enough, and, as such, society is in an era of unsustainability facing "concatenated global crises" (Biggs et al. 2011). Scientific and policy debates have shifted from "understanding sustainability" to "practicing and acting for sustainability." Acting for sustainability requires a new governance mode that builds on knowledge of social, ecological, economic, and technological complexity, while understanding how such uncertain processes can be triggered and steered toward cooperative and sustainable provision of the GPGs.

The Transitions Approach adds to this policy-science debate by focusing on understanding the drivers and processes that steer historical transformations. The Transitions Approach takes into consideration complex adaptive systems (such as societal sectors, regions, or cities) that go through fundamental nonlinear changes in cultures (attitudes, perceptions, and routines), structures (institutions, ways of organizing, hierarchical orderings), and practices (behavior, implementation procedures, and daily routines).

Such transitions in complex adaptive systems take a very long time to materialize, often more than 25 years. Transitions are the result of co-evolving processes in economy, society, ecology, and technology that progressively build toward revolutionary systemic change (Rotmans, Kemp, and van Asselt 2001; Frantzeskaki and de Haan 2009; Loorbach 2010). Because of this complexity, transitions are impossible to predict, fully comprehend, or steer directly, but they are seen as a pattern of change that can be anticipated. These processes can be adapted to in such a way that the inevitable nonlinear shifts and associated crises provide massive windows of opportunity for accelerated reorientation toward sustainability.

Directing the sustainability transition path toward 2050 will entail massive changes at multiple levels and in multiple domains on multiple time scales. Conflicts between individual interests will surface, but the meeting of mutual interests can advance collective solutions. The needed changes in socio-technological infrastructures, participatory actor engagement, and long-term partnerships will give rise to new forms of problems that will be hard to solve through existing governance approaches. It is reemphasized that aside from fundamental changes in economic development, changes in social-ecological development are critical for dealing with persistent unsustainability problems and for tipping the system's trajectory away from unsustainable lock-ins.

Unsustainable Lock-Ins

Unsustainable lock-ins are path-dependent trajectories in which (infra)structures, cultures, and practices in societal (sub)systems enforce patterns of unsustainability (Frantzeskaki and Loorbach 2010; Unruh 2002). In the context of sustainability challenges, such lock-ins are called persistent unsustainability problems (Rotmans, Kemp, and van Asselt 2001; Grin, Rotmans, and Schot 2010). Persistent problems are problems that are rooted in incumbent regimes, which are systemic and cultural patterns that in order to realign require fundamental systemic change in one or more societal (sub) systems.

A fundamental intervention in the organization of the societal system is needed in order to alter established patterns of organization and activity that produce global public bads. For persistent problems, treating symptoms (for example, emissions, biodiversity losses, poverty, and inequalities) and dealing with partial issues of a larger systemic problem are not enough. Marginal changes in organization and operation of systems by definition must be ineffective when facing persistent sustainability problems.

The Transitions Approach thus argues that for *persistent* problems to be tackled adequately, fundamental changes from totally unsustainable to more sustainable systems are required. When not dealt with effectively, complex problems tend to reproduce themselves, reinforce each other, and, as such, persist over relatively long periods of time (Schuitmaker 2012).

During the 21st century, the world's configuration of societal (sub) systems will change on an unprecedented scale. Development discrepancies between East and West and North and South are becoming less and less extreme. The growth potential of economies in eastern and southern parts of the globe is the largest at present (World Bank 2012).

By 2050 it is estimated that the total gross domestic product (GDP) of former developing countries will be twice that of industrial countries today. A realistic look at global trends reveals that after 2025, traditional developed countries will remain the wealthiest nations in terms of per capita income but will be overtaken as the dominant economies by much less developed countries (Dadush and Stancil 2010).

In terms of societal transitions, this means that the epicenter of sociotechnological progress will shift, not only geographically, but also demographically and culturally. Population growth, economic development, and technological progress in developing countries will change global demographics and global socioeconomic settlements.

The Complexity of Providing GPGs

A combination of certain persistent sustainability problems and unsustainable lock-in of societal (sub) systems causes insufficient provision of GPGs. Countries have not been able to come to terms on which GPGs should be provided or on how to share the burden of financing them. GPGs are inherently "non-excludable goods or services" (Karlsson-Vinkhuyzen, Jollands, and Staudt 2012: 12) that require careful governance that challenges global governance architectures and logic given that for the provision of GPGs "no single level of organization is appropriate for all social functions" (Trachtman 1992: 468, cited by Karlsso-Vinkhuyzen, Jollands, and Staudt 2012: 13).

Additionally, there is a vast overproduction of global public bads, broadly referring to negative externalities of goods and services that impede survival and have universal liabilities. Again, countries cannot come to terms on which global public bads should be countered or how to share the burden of financing disincentives. This leads to painstaking international policy problems because these

> issues that have traditionally been merely national are now global because they are beyond the grasp of any single nation. And crises endure perhaps because we lack the proper policy mechanisms to address such GPGs [and bads]. In addition, the pervasiveness of today's [economic, ecological, and social] crises suggests that they might all suffer from a common cause, such as a common flaw in policy-making, rather than from issue-specific problems. If so, issue-specific policy responses, typical to date, would be insufficient—allowing global crises to persist and even multiply (Kaul, Grunberg, and Stern 1999: 21).

At the end of the day, provision of clean energy, air, water, land, food, shelter, sanitation, healthcare, education, security, and other services that satisfy human needs requires collective solutions at an international level and new policy responses that transcend across multiple levels. For sustainable development it is of highest importance that people have equal access to goods and services crucial for survival, now and in the long term.

Need for Reflexive Management

Along the way to 2050, international relations will change in radical ways, making it more difficult to manage in an orderly way the complex dynamics of sustainable development and to counter existing bad practices. In response to increasingly complex dynamics in international relations, international institutions will start to reform their rigid governance structures to become more flexible, that is, equally accessible, transparent, and representative of the new economic, social, and ecological landscape that is emerging. This trend is already advocated by institutions such as the World Bank:

> In particular, the governance and functioning of the bedrock international institutions—the G20/G8, World Bank, IMF, WTO, Global Stability Board, and the UN—will have to be rethought. It is probably inevitable that, in seeking balance between legitimacy and effectiveness to deal with a wide range of complex international collaboration issues, a "flexible geometry" or plurilateral approach to the issues will become the norm. Illegitimate small clubs of the most powerful (G7), ineffectual universal assemblies (UN, WTO), and *overly complex and unaccountable constituency structures will likely be eschewed in favor of more flexible approaches involving a critical mass of players on a given issue or in a particular geographic region.* (Dadush and Stancil 2010: 17, author's emphasis)

Dealing with the eschewing of "overly complex and unaccountable constitu-ency structures" requires that international institutions preemptively start developing flexible transition strategies. This reflexive approach to formulating transition strategies requires very different mindsets, ways of operating, and means of forming "a critical mass of players" to be at the forefront of the transition.

Considering the economic rise of developed countries during the last century, all will have to adapt from a world with some countries holding "superpower status" to a more modest, collaborative leadership. At the same time, former developing countries have to change into innovative game changers of great influence. Eventually dealing with the global transition will require a more open-minded and collaborative outlook to tackle shared unsustainability problems on a given issue or in a particular geographic region (see also Loorbach and Lijnis Huffenreuter 2013). Thus, international institutions may be advised to prepare for the new distribution of economic, social, and ecological power and to start proactively to manage even more complex challenges of multilevel coordination for providing GPGs and countering global public bads beyond 2025.

The Transitions Approach to Global Sustainability Transitions

This section introduces the basic concepts of transitions as they have been devel-oped in the emerging field of transition science (Grin, Rotmans, and Schot 2010).

The Science of Transitions

The dynamics of transitions are driven by developments at different levels of scale, in multiple domains, and at different time intervals that in combination result in different types of systemic societal organization and behavior. Transitions are characterized by the relatively long periods or phases they take to develop, speed up, gain momentum, and pass a tipping point, after which a rapid, chaotic, and largely unmanageable acceleration takes place in which societal (sub)systems reconfigure (see figure 11.1).

Transition phases are time periods in which developments take place that irreversibly change the system. Hence the passages from one phase to the next signal different types of changes and processes. In the predevelopment phase, sustainable alternatives to dominant unsustainable systems are explored and further developed by pioneers, frontrunners, and other experts. Along the phases, existing structural subsystems of the societal system (values, institutions, regula-tions, markets, and so on) fade away while new ones emerge (Geels 2004; Loorbach, van der Brugge, and Taanman 2008). This fading away and rise of structural subsystems result in alternating phases of transition dynamics. "The dynamics of transitions in time can be described as altering phases of relatively fast and slow dynamics, which together form a strongly non-linear pattern where there is a shift from one dynamic state of equilibrium to the other" (Rotmans 2005: 23).

Transitions can be viewed as the outcomes of the continuous change of actor's practices and the interactions of practices and developments that take place at

Figure 11.1 Transition Phases

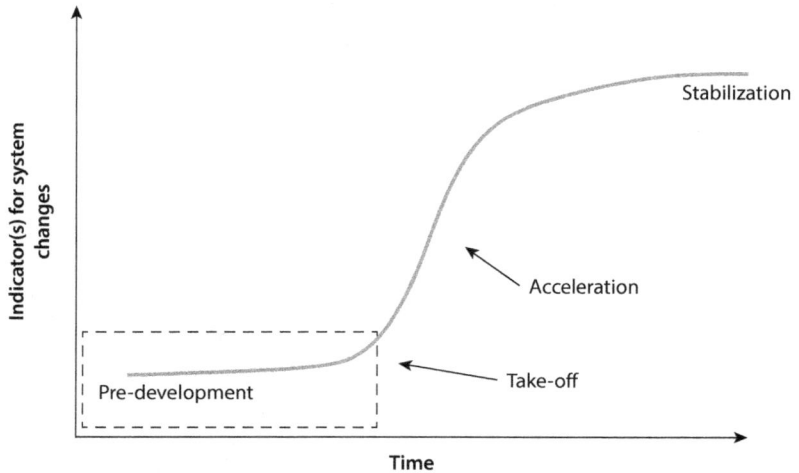

Source: Grin, Rotmans, and Schot 2010.

different levels. Changes at every level of interaction produce a convergent change that leads to a "new normal" or regime. In hindsight, such systemic revolution on the long term (decades) will be perceived as a system transition.

In the Transitions Approach, and especially in sociotechnological transitions writings, three levels are identified on which changes take place (Geels 2005, 2011; Geels and Schot 2007): the micro level, where niches are found; the meso level, where regimes are located; and the macro level, which hosts trends and developments, such as globalization (figure 11.2). These levels make up the so-called multilevel perspective (MLP), which generally focuses on the interplay between niche developments on the micro level, institutional developments at the meso level, and landscape developments at the macro level (Geels 2005, 2011).

Patterns of Transitions

A first step to explaining transitions is to classify transitions using the sigmoid curve as an initial mapping of the transition evolution. A "transition path" is one curve that maps the transitional evolution of a system (see figure 11.3). Since every system is viewed as a unique entity, its transition path differs from those of other systems. As stated by Rotmans, Kemp, and Van Asselt (2001: 18), "[I]t is possible to have different paths to the same equilibrium level as well as it is possible for the same transition pattern to be realized in different ways." Although transition paths lead the systems to their new state, characteristics of the end state of the systems can be used as foundations for a classification scheme.

History has witnessed numerous transitions in economy, agriculture, mobility, and energy, but also in areas such as education, health care, and social structure.

Figure 11.2 Multilevel Perspective of System Transition

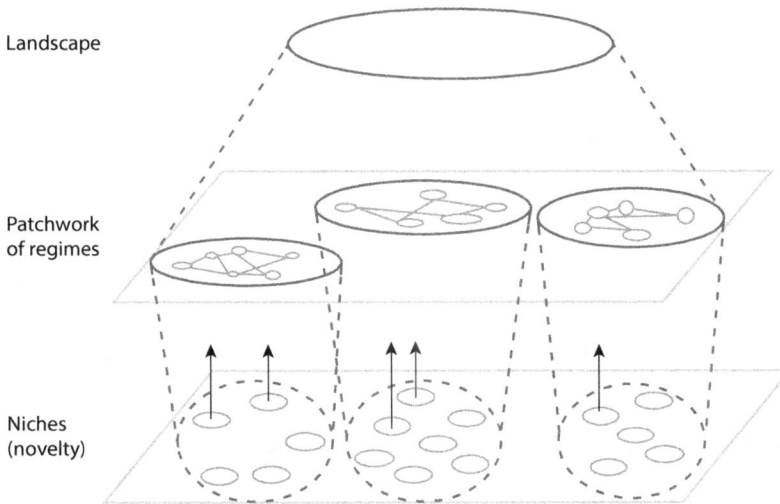

Landscape

Patchwork
of regimes

Niches
(novelty)

Source: Geels 2005.

In all instances, relatively long temporal stretches of stability alternated with relatively short periods of rapid social change. According to Rotmans (2005: 23–24), "the manifestation of alternating phases is the so-called S-curve: an aggregation of underlying curves" (see figure 11.3). However, other manifestations in time are also possible.

The S-curve represents an ideal transition, in which the system adjusts itself successfully to changing internal and external circumstances, while achieving a

Figure 11.3 Multiple Patterns of Transitions

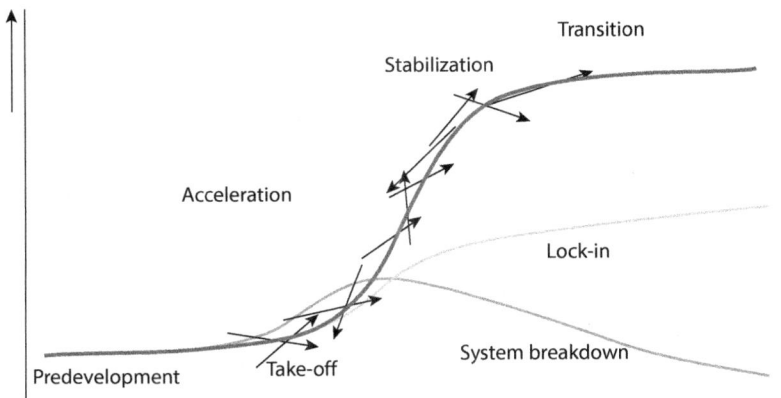

Transition

Stabilization

Acceleration

Lock-in

System breakdown

Predevelopment

Take-off

Source: Based on Rotmans, Kemp, and van Asselt 2001.

higher order of organization and complexity. However, such transitions do not necessarily lead to a more sustainable system. And alternative patterns are also possible, such as an enhanced lock-in or even a system breakdown.

Complex Adaptive Systems

The Transitions Approach conceptualizes societal systems as complex adaptive systems. Complex adaptive systems are considered to co-evolve, self-organize, and exert emergent behavior. Co-evolution refers to the mutual irreversible interchanges between the (sub) systems and their environment. Self-organization refers to the capability of (sub) systems to organize themselves without external involvement. Transitions studies show that over the last decades, societal (sub) systems have increasingly acquired technology, skills, knowledge, funds, and perhaps even the confidence to self-organize. This increasing influence of self-organization has not been sufficiently recognized, thus social actors are not in policy-making processes. The capability to self-organize is a form of emergent behavior, which refers to systemic processes that are not linearly related to the reconfiguration of (sub) systems. What transition studies reveal is that the dynamics of societal change are highly complex and adaptive, and governance processes are only a small piece of the puzzle of continuous co-evolving societal dynamics.

This complex transition process requires policy adaptations to allow institutions to be more flexible and reflexive toward social and technological changes and advancements. This requires understanding the transition dynamics that underlie both persistent sustainability problems and governance of unsustainable lock-in of entangled societal (sub) systems.

Multiple actors and subsystems establish processes and contribute to processes' emergence. A society, or the planet, is a complex and adaptive system in which such processes co-evolve resulting in system evolution and system innovations. Co-evolution also takes place between system metabolic processes (for example, demographic processes), problem processes (for example, problem-framing processes), and governance processes (for example, processes of collectively searching and creating solutions). This creates a complex co-evolutionary dynamic. A transitions approach requires a new perspective toward governance of planetary problems as follows:

- Action needs to tap into and be in confluence with ongoing dynamics in order to steer the system with incremental steps toward a new sustainable (system) state (co-evolution rather than revolution) (Rotmans, Kemp, and van Asselt 2001).
- Small-scale actions need to be directed to domains in which a small intervention can result in tipping toward larger changes or simply seek changes that can cascade toward broader system's innovation (tipping innovation's cascade) (Frantzeskaki, Loorbach, and Meadowcroft 2012; Loorbach, Frantzeskaki, and Thissen 2011).
- Actions need to also refer to processes that will couple with or reroute ongoing processes in a co-evolutionary continuum (feed in and onto co-evolutionary processes) (Loorbach 2010; Frantzeskaki and Grin 2012).

However, an in-depth analysis of the complex adaptive characteristics of societal transitions can inform policy makers only to a certain extent. They still have to translate the generic transition governance propositions into a specific context to actions that are responsive to societal complexity and uncertainty.

Characteristics of the Transitions Approach and Governance

The challenges for sustainable development beyond 2025 will be to address persistent sustainability problems, to escape and prevent unsustainable lock-in, and to drive the transition toward sustainability. The Transitions Approach offers a useful framework for analyzing and governing processes of change in complex adaptive societal (sub) systems. It provides a generic heuristic tool, along with knowledge programs and real world experiments for better governance of complex dynamics and for co-evolution of these (sub) systems over the course of a transition (Kemp, Rotmans, and Loorbach 2007; Grin, Rotmans, and Schot 2010).

Four general characteristics of transition governance require special attention:

1. Transition governance generally agrees with and supports the ends of sustainability while allowing for different means of pursuing these ends. Given that there are different approaches to dealing with transitions focused on different aspects of sustainability (for example, climate change, recycling, carbon emissions, pollution, biodiversity, and so forth), the Transitions Approach has a predetermined target with a flexible targeting (or strategy implementation) system. In line with this, the aim is to achieve as many interconnected aspects of sustainability as possible within the scope (Loorbach and Frantzeskaki 2012; Frantzeskaki, 2012; van Buuren and Loorbach 2009; Loorbach and Wijsman 2013).

2. Transition governance recognizes that current top-down modes of governance require intimate connections with bottom-up initiatives and horizontal orientation to allow for shifts toward inclusive sustainable development and more flexible organizations in its favor (Nevens et al. 2013; Frantzeskaki et al. 2012 (a)). The Transitions Approach supports values formulated in a multidisciplinary way by the international scientific community to be the determinants of general sustainability. They remain highly adaptive and reflexive to the contexts of regional and local particularities and concerns.

3. Experiences with transition governance show that a plurality of societal systems have different dynamics between different actors on different levels and in different domains. They partially have to put their personal interests and aspirations aside, or forward, when transition pathways to sustainability are drawn up and decided on. Actors have divergent backgrounds and interests, thus they seek different windows of opportunity in systemic societal change toward sustainability (Dirven, Rotmans, and Verkaik 2002; Brown, Farelly, and Loorbach 2013; Smith and Raven 2012). The Transitions Approach serves as a connection between structures, cultures, and practices of different

Too Global to Fail · http://dx.doi.org/10.1596/978-1-4648-0307-9

societal actors with several (conflicting) public and private interests to span multiple levels, domains, and terms (van Eijndhoven, Frantzeskaki, and Loorbach 2013).

4. Transition governance builds on the adaptive and transformative capabilities of societal systems. When in their transition new types of problems arise that increase uncertainty, adding to the level of the systems' complexity, new reflexive frameworks for their analysis are required (Loorbach and Frantzeskaki 2012). As earlier suggested by Brewer and deLeon (1983: 93),

> Because of their complexity, social systems are capable of producing problems neither expected nor results intended. Participants may perceive these surprises as occurring outside of their spheres of interest or responsibility; with increased complexity, beneficial and harmful externalities [...] seem to happen more often.

The Transition Governance Framework

Transitions are complex and nonlinear, multilevel, and multiactor. A new governance approach has been developed called transition management or governance (Loorbach 2007, 2010). Transition governance offers a prescriptive approach toward governance as a basis for operational policy models, and it is explicitly a normative model taking sustainable development as along-term goal. It starts from the premise that developed as well as developing societies have increasingly become interconnected, complex, and "hard to manage" in a traditional top-down manner. This is evident at the level of societies, the level of the problems facing our societies, and the level of dealing with these problems (governance).

Basic Tenets of Governance

Tenets for transition governance have been formulated from the literature (Loorbach 2007; Rotmans and Loorbach 2009; Frantzeskaki, Loorbach, and Meadowcroft 2012) as follows:

- The dynamics of the system create feasible and nonfeasible means for steering. This implies that content and process are inseparable. Process management on its own is not sufficient; insight into how the system works is an essential precondition for effective management.
- Long-term thinking (at least 25 years) is preferably used as a framework for shaping short-term policy in the context of persistent societal problems. This means reflection and forecasting: the setting of short-term goals based on long-term goals and reflection on future developments through the use of scenarios.
- Objectives should be flexible and adjustable at the system level. The complexity of the system is at odds with the desire to formulate specific objectives and blueprint plans. While being directed, the structure and order of the system are also changing, so the objectives set should change as well.

- The timing of the intervention is crucial. Immediate and effective intervention is possible in both desirable and undesirable crisis situations.
- Managing a complex, adaptive system means using disequilibria as well as equilibria. Relatively short periods of non-equilibrium therefore offer opportunities to direct the system in a desirable direction (toward a new attractor).
- Creating space for actors to build up alternative regimes is crucial for innovation. Actors at a certain distance from the regime can effectively create a new regime in a protected environment to permit investment of sufficient time, energy, and resources.
- Steering from "outside" a societal system is not effective. Structures, actors, and practices adapt and anticipate in such a manner that these should also be directed from "inside."
- A focus on (social) learning about different actor perspectives and a variety of options (which requires a wide playing field) is a necessary precondition for change.
- Participation of and interaction between stakeholders is a necessary basis for developing support for policies and to engage actors in reframing problems and solutions through social learning.

The challenge is to translate these relatively abstract governance tenets into a practical management framework without losing too much of the complexity involved and without becoming too prescriptive. This analysis attempts this by developing a framework for transition management. The framework emerged out of theoretical reasoning (following the line of reasoning and conceptual integration described earlier) combined with practical experiment and observation. In other words, it is based on "natural" processes of governance that can be observed in society (Kemp and van den Bosch 2006), but then structured and defined based on the characteristics of complex societal transitions. In this sense it is an analytical lens to assess how societal actors deal with complex societal issues at different levels, but consequently also to develop and implement strategies to influence these natural governance processes. In the transition management framework, four different types of governance activities (Van der Brugge and van Raak 2007) are identified that are relevant to societal transitions: strategic, tactical, operational, and reflexive (Loorbach 2007).

Governance Dimensions: Transition Management Cycle

In transition management, the governance process is a cyclical process of development phases at various scale levels (Loorbach 2007). The core idea is that four different types of governance activities can be distinguished when observing actor behavior in the context of societal transitions:

- **Strategic:** activities at the level of a societal system that take into account a long time horizon, relate to structuring a complex societal problem, and create alternative futures—often through opinion making, visioning, and politics.

- **Tactical:** activities at the level of subsystems that relate to build-up and break-down of system structures (institutions, regulation, physical infrastructures, financial infrastructures, and so on), often through negotiation, collaboration, lobbying, and so on.
- **Operational:** activities that relate to short-term and everyday decisions and actions. At this level, actors either re-create system structures or they choose to restructure or change them.
- **Reflexive:** activities that relate to evaluation of the existing situation at the various levels and their interrelation or misfit. Through debate, structured evaluation, assessment, and research, societal issues are continuously structured, reframed, and dealt with.

These activities exhibit specific characteristics (in terms of the types of actors involved, the types of process they are associated with, and the types of product they deliver) that make it possible to (experimentally and exploratively) develop specific instruments that have the potential to govern transition processes. The transition management cycle describes the different phases that occur during a transition management process being used in a project or public policy program.

More specifically, the transition management cycle consists of the following phases: (1) problem structuring, establishing and organizing the transition arena, and envisioning future states; (2) developing a transition agenda, a vision of sustainability development, and transition paths; (3) establishing and carrying out transition experiments and mobilizing the resulting transition networks; and (4) monitoring, evaluating, and learning lessons from the transition experiments and, based on these, making adjustments in the vision, agenda, and coalitions (Loorbach 2010; Loorbach and Rotmans 2006).

Every phase of the transition management cycle relates to different transition management instruments (see figure 11.4). The transition management instruments have been developed with practical experiences (and theoretical deduction). All the transition management instruments are participatory and have an explicit focus to stimulate or facilitate innovation (of different types, for example, technological innovations or governance innovations). According to transition management experiences so far (Loorbach and Rotmans 2010; van Buuren and Loorbach 2009), there is no fixed sequence of the phases, and the phases can differ in importance in any given cycle. In practice, the transition management activities are carried out partially and completely in sequence, in parallel, and in a random sequence.

The basic idea is that ongoing or emerging transitions in society can first be identified and analyzed through the transitions lens and, accordingly, a strategy can be developed using the transition management cycle. So far, practice has shown that the majority of transition management processes have started with the establishment of a transition arena, possibly because of the phase many transitions were in (predevelopment) and the fact that the initiative often came from entrepreneurial policy makers (de Graaf and van der Brugge 2010;

Figure 11.4 Transition Management Cycle and the Related Transition Management Tools

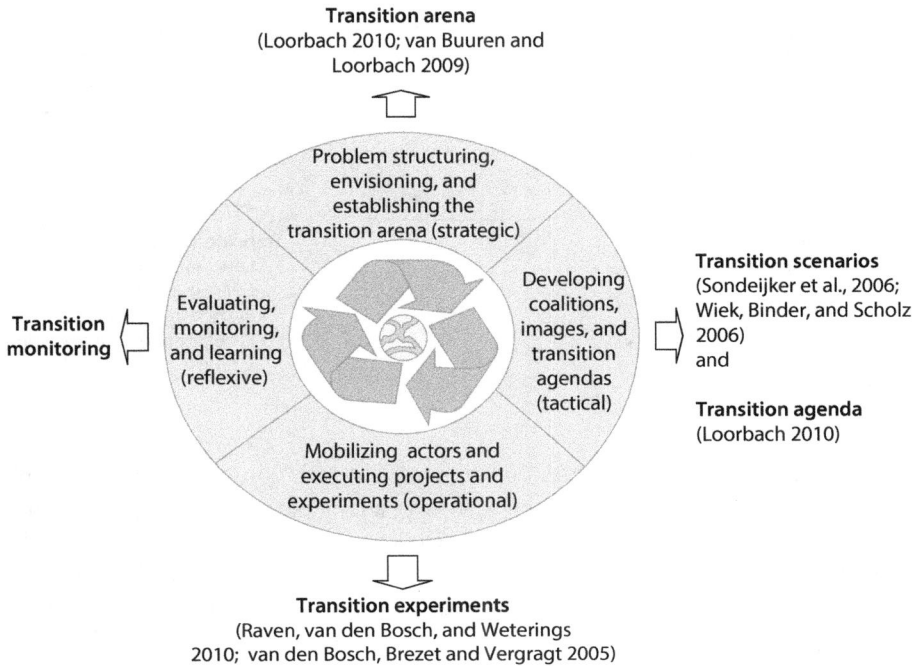

Transition arena
(Loorbach 2010; van Buuren and
Loorbach 2009)

Problem structuring,
envisioning, and
establishing the
transition arena (strategic)

Developing
coalitions,
images, and
transition
agendas
(tactical)

Transition scenarios
(Sondeijker et al., 2006;
Wiek, Binder, and Scholz
2006)
and

Transition agenda
(Loorbach 2010)

Transition
monitoring

Evaluating,
monitoring,
and learning
(reflexive)

Mobilizing actors and
executing projects and
experiments (operational)

Transition experiments
(Raven, van den Bosch, and Weterings
2010; van den Bosch, Brezet and Vergragt 2005)

Hendriks 2009; Loorbach and Rotmans 2010). Both cases imply that a small start of the processes is most feasible.

Transition Management for Sustainability Transitions

In practice, transition management comes down to a combination of developing around a common understanding of a transition challenge and a shared ambition to drive it toward sustainability. By using the transition perspective as a lens, transition teams develop an analysis of a particular persistent problem in a complex societal system. This could be a geographical area (from neighborhood to city, country, or region), sector, or societal issue. Based on the preliminary analysis, the transition team can identify regime and niche actors that are potential contributors to a desired transition and bring them together in so called transition arenas or experiments. In and around these arenas and experiments, a shared discourse, ambition, and agenda is developed in such a way that it empowers participants and enables them to translate it to their own daily environments. Through such a social learning process, individuals start to relate to a broader common context and ambition, creating the conditions for diffusion, self-organizational processes, and emergent innovation.

Transition management thus proposes to develop *informal networks* in which individuals and later, organizations, are provided the mental, social, and physical

Figure 11.5 Regular Policy Arena, Transition Team, and Transition Arena

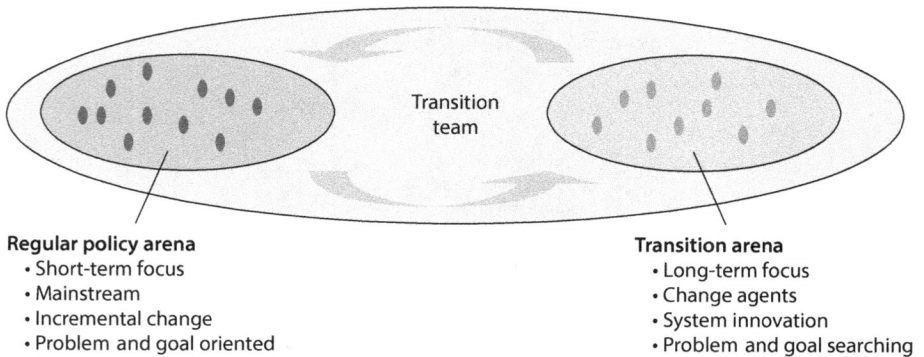

Regular policy arena
- Short-term focus
- Mainstream
- Incremental change
- Problem and goal oriented

Transition arena
- Long-term focus
- Change agents
- System innovation
- Problem and goal searching

Source: Loorbach 2007.

space to develop new ideas, common language, and ambitions, as well as new joint projects (see also figure 11.5). In doing so over a long period of time, participants will increasingly translate the transition perspective and ideas into their own daily context. These transition management processes therewith indirectly influence and change regular policies in government, business, research, and civil society.

Establishing a Transition Team

Transition management processes can be developed in any complex societal system in which individuals or organizations experience persistent both problems and the possibility of a transition, in other words, a context in which current common approaches and solutions do not suffice, future developments are highly uncertain, and major sustainability challenges are present. It therefore starts with people, individuals who seek more fundamental alternatives or are convinced these are necessary.

To actively engage with the emerging transition so as to influence its speed and direction, a transition team needs to be formed that can manage both content and participatory process. The transition team needs to include people with different backgrounds: a representative of an initiating organization or problem owner (often a governmental organization, but also increasingly businesses and nongovernmental organizations); experts in the particular transition arena; and transition management experts.

It is crucial that the transition team be allowed the necessary space for experimentation and learning—through funding as well as mandate. The transition team is in charge of bringing together the first, rough integrated analysis of the transition at hand, analyzing the governance and actor networks, identifying and selecting frontrunners, and managing the different phases and dimensions of the transition-management process. These include problem structuring and establishment of a transition arena; developing sustainability visions, images, and transition pathways; initiating and executing transition experiments; and transition monitoring and evaluation.

Problem Structuring and Establishment of a Transition Arena

Transition management boils down to creating space for frontrunners (niche-players and regime-players) in transition arenas. Formed in transition arenas for a specified issue are a vision, an agenda, and a social commitment to sustainability values. A transition arena can be also seen as a constellation of governance innovations toward sustainability. It is based on the promises of increased group-learning and effectiveness of small groups, and it agrees with the best practices indicated by the literature on small-group negotiations (De Dreu and West 2001; van Knippenberg, De Dreu, and Homan 2004) and social learning writings (Grin et al. 2004). In addition to these objectives, a transition arena aims at creating an advocacy coalition that identifies and reframes a persistent problem, and articulates and commits to a vision of sustainable development and to a shared agenda for moving in this direction.

The common perspective and terminology developed in the transition arena group relates to the shared belief in the possibility of transition in the near future and the need to develop strategies to guide this transition toward sustainability. Through the process of exchange of perspectives, framing societal complexity in terms of transitions, and developing a strategy of multiple pathways and experiments, transition arenas simultaneously develop a sensitivity for complexity and uncertainty inherent to societal change processes, as well as an action perspective related to insights about how (small-scale) strategic interventions might fundamentally alter system trajectories over time. In this way, a transition arena differs from a network of actors, since actors in a transition arena are tied by a common belief (even when having divergent interests), and it is not tied by common or complementary interests like a network of actors.

More specifically, the transition arena is a small group of actors characterized as frontrunners (for example innovative thinkers, practitioners, social entrepreneurs) with different backgrounds. Within the transition arena, various perceptions of a specific persistent problem (for example, congestion or climate change) and possible alternative solutions can be compared and integrated. The actors involved in the transition arena participate on a personal basis, not as delegates or representatives of their institutions, and they are selected based on necessary competencies.

The competencies of the transition arena participants include the ability to understand and reflect on complex problems; the ability to understand and learn from different disciplines; possession of a certain level of authority within various networks; the ability to establish, communicate, and explain visions of sustainable development within their own networks; and willingness to work in a group and to welcome innovative means and ways to deal with complex (persistent) problems—that is, they do not participate to advocate a pre-decided solution to the problem at hand (Loorbach 2010: 173–74). More particularly, the actors that participate in the transition arena need to have an understanding of the complexities of the persistent problems at hand and to reflect upon existing practices, existing cultures, and structures and how they relate to the persistent problems.

Developing Sustainability Visions, Pathways, and a Transition Agenda

Problem structuring and envisioning are very important processes for transition management. The actors involved in the envisioning process are stimulated and supported to reflect upon their everyday routines. What is actually realized is a deeper understanding from the actors of the complexity of the challenge (societal problem). The involved actors understand the challenge and realize that their small-scale, everyday actions do have a cumulative impact on the societal system. Throughout the envisioning process, actors shift from passively observing societal problems to realizing that their actions reinforce those societal phenomena. An outcome of the envisioning process is that actors who are involved in transition arenas change their daily routines after reflecting on them. What is thus realized is a change or reflection of short-term actions of actors that contemplate and align with the long-term vision that is a product of the envisioning process.

The outcomes of the first phase that take place in the transition arena are as follows:

1. The basic transition narrative—a mapping of the pathologies/flaws of the current system that answers the question" Why a transition?"
2. The sustainability criteria—the conditions under which the same societal function can be provided in the future in a sustainable way, for example, the energy system needs to include clean energy, the health care system needs to be oriented to the individual level and not to systems.
3. The formulation of areas that require changes expressed in the form of transition images—for example, if one considers the clean energy vision, biomass or wind energy can be included as transition images that link to such a transition vision.

The process itself of envisioning and the group dynamics it encompasses function as a selection environment. This means that the group dynamics may result in some actors exiting the transition arena, while other actors might be invited to join depending on their alignment to the vision and to the produced group dynamics. The transition vision depicts the common desires and beliefs of the transition arena group and is an outcome that has a guiding role for the following activities and outcomes of the transition process.

In the next phase, the transition agenda becomes the selection instrument. The actors who are involved already operate within the themes/images outlined in the transition agenda. In an attempt to develop an agenda for action, attention is paid by the transition managers to steering the actors in the transition arena so as to create a vision of the future desirable system. Deliberative processes are employed and enabled for involving niche actors and deriving a view from the niches and innovations that can contribute to an overarching vision. In this way, a marriage of a top-down system perspective (vision from a bird's eye view) and bottom-up innovations (vision from an earth's view) is attempted.

At this phase, people who can contribute to the realization or orientation toward the visions/images are invited. For these new entrants, the selection criteria differ from those previously presented. At this phase, the selection criteria for new entrants concerns the following:

1. The involvement or power of the actors in the different thematic areas specified in the transition images; and
2. The role of the actors in specific institutions and organizations (or in simple words, actors who are practicing or implementing policies/programs or developing technologies for specific problems/domains are invited and brought in, so as to translate the vision into a policy/program).

The Initiation and Execution of Transition Experiments

Transition experiments are high-risk experiments with a social-learning objective that are supposed to contribute to the sustainability goals at the systems level and should fit within the transition pathways (Kemp and van den Bosch 2006). It is important to formulate sound criteria for the selection of experiments and to make the experiments mutually coherent.

The crucial point is to measure the extent to which the experiments and projects contribute to the overall system sustainability goals and to assess in what way a particular experiment reinforces another experiment. Are there specific niches for experiments that can be identified? What is the attitude of the current regime toward these niche experiments? The aim is to create a portfolio of transition experiments that reinforce each other and contribute to the sustainability objectives in significant and measurable ways. Around and between these experiments all sorts of actors can be involved who not engage regularly in debates about long-term issues; these can be small business, consumers, citizens, or local groups, for example. Here as well, the emphasis is on involving frontrunners.

Monitoring and Evaluating the Transition Process

Continuous monitoring is a vital part of the search and learning process of transitions. Monitoring the transition process itself and monitoring transition management are distinct processes. Monitoring the transition process involves physical changes in the system in question, slowly changing macro developments, and fast niche developments—seeds of change as well as movements of individual and collective actors at the regime level. This provides the enriched context for transition management.

Monitoring of transition management involves different aspects and tasks in the following order:

1. The actors within the transition arena must be monitored in their behavior, networking activities, alliance forming, and responsibilities, and also in their activities, projects, and instruments.
2. Next, the transition agenda must be monitored in the actions, goals, projects, and instruments that have been agreed upon. Transition experiments need to be monitored regarding specific new knowledge and insight and how these are transferred, but also in aspects of social and institutional learning.

3. The transition process itself must be monitored with regard to the rate of progress, the barriers, and the points for improvement, and so on. Integration of monitoring and evaluation within each phase and at every level of transition management may stimulate a process of social learning that arises from the interaction and cooperation between different actors involved.

In each of the above activity clusters, coalition and network formation is of vital importance combined with the systemic structuring and synthesizing of discussions. The transition arena is meant to stimulate the formation of new coalitions, partnerships, and networks. Most often, coalitions emerge around transition pathways or experiments or around specific sub-themes, where arenas arise from arenas. The very idea behind transition management is to create some kind of societal movement through new coalitions, partnerships, and networks around arenas (and arenas from arenas) that allows for building continuous pressure on the political and market arena to safeguard the long-term orientation and goals of the transition process.

Transition Governance in a Global Context

The strength of the Transitions Approach is that it offers a generic framework and principles for developing specific management processes in each complex context. Implementation always depends heavily upon the particular problem, the people involved in the transition teams, the available support (political and/or financial), and the phase of the transition, among other things. The principles and methods, therefore, only provide guidelines, seeking to offer a basis for developing an alternative "glocal governance" strategy. This strategy must be one in which a more generic and shared insight into complex sustainability transitions and GPGs is combined with bottom-up, context-based insights and initiatives.

The academic literature and political debates present two types of solutions for the transition problem: one bottom-up and one top-down. The bottom-up alternative suggests that voluntary action, grassroots initiatives, and decentralized sustainable solutions should be stimulated.

In most of the literature on transitions, emergent innovations are examined in terms of niche management, (technological) innovation systems, and transition experiments. Top-down strategies include long-term sustainability policies, global agreements, and institutional solutions. In transition studies, this top-down management element is less prominent, but in related literatures on earth system governance (for example, Biermann 2007) this is a central focus.

Transition management suggests shifting the focus to actions and solutions that divert from existing business-as-usual scenarios or incremental, green-growth types of improvement strategies—in other words, looking for permanent, systemic solutions. Such alternatives cannot be categorized as merely global or local, thus the term "glocal" (Svensson 2001), which combines both. This has been used in multiple ways, often referring to the simultaneous process of globalization and regionalization. It is used here to refer to the phenomenon where in very different places, domains, and communities, similar patterns and alternatives are emerging. Glocal alternatives share common and generic characteristics, but otherwise have very specific forms in local contexts. Examples are food and energy cooperatives, mobility sharing, cooperative social services, as well as new public-private cooperatives and financial instruments. Interestingly, it seems that glocal alternatives share characteristics such as a focus on broader value definitions; self-organizational structures; and explicit links to local communities, sustainable technologies, and low-impact but high-quality lifestyles.

This in itself is not an entirely new analysis, let alone new practice. In fact, transition management as a theoretical concept and framework has been developed based on analysis of emerging and past systemic innovations, as well as by systematically experimenting with the approach. Since 2000 it has been adopted, applied, and further developed mainly in a small number of developed countries. The experiences suggest that it is most effective at a scale relatively close to the actors involved (a region, city, neighborhood organization, or urgent issue). However, translating it into other sociocultural and socioeconomic contexts requires novel forms, methods, and implementation strategies altogether. The formulated principles and basic elements of an implementation of transition management provide a certain basis for this, but it is also clear that in the context of GPGs debates, as well as implementation in lower- and middle-income countries, a number of fundamental tensions and challenges need to be taken into account.

Tensions in Transitions from a Global Perspective

Transition management in low- and middle-income countries will by definition differ from implementation in the context of developed countries. For one, the major challenge in developed countries is to open up locked-in systems in which high levels of consumption, technology, and welfare are the "norm," and the societal systems that produce these are highly optimized and therefore also inert. Creating space for more fundamental acknowledgement of the persistence of a problem, the sense of urgency around a necessary sustainability vision, and creating the (social) innovation spaces to work in this direction should be core goals of transition management in these contexts.

In low- and middle-income countries, the challenge much more is to deal with accelerating and arguably competing transitions—toward modernized, "western" systems and toward more sustainable futures. For example China—leading both in terms of accelerated growth and related unsustainability, as well as in terms of developing sustainable (energy) alternatives—struggles with the chaotic and nonlinear unmanageable dynamics of acceleration. The challenge in this context is more how to coordinate these dynamics in the direction of resilient and sustainable future regimes. While leapfrogging is an attractive idea, from a transition perspective a more fundamental challenge is this: In these contexts can the space for innovation and the turbulent dynamics in their socioeconomic, political, and cultural domains be played into so as to make a rapid systemic shift directly toward the desired level of "sustainability" in developed countries. Dealing with acceleration phases of transitions is poorly understood in transition management, and much can therefore be learned (and experimented with) in low- and middle-income countries.

Besides fundamental differences in transition contexts and related challenges between high-, middle-, and lower-income countries, a number of more fundamental challenges that face transition management (in theory and practice) need to be further addressed, explored, and (re)conceptualized when it comes to governance of sustainability transitioning in a global context. These challenges are as follows.

Inclusivity

The premise of transition management is that it is based on selective participation and involves frontrunners, especially in earlier stages of the process. So far, this has been argued as a legitimate strategy based on the need to break out of existing dominant paradigms and routines, but in practice this does not always lead to including marginalized perspectives and opinions.

Especially in countries with more authoritarian policy regimes, the danger lies in transition management being hijacked and used as another legitimization for dominant perspectives. Therefore the question is not only practical (how to involve outsider, marginalized, and less-articulated perspectives and interests in the process), but also fundamental (how and where transition management can be positioned so that it creates a protected space for such interests to freely and openly participate).

Democracy

Related to inclusivity, questions may arise regarding leadership of the transition management process. It can be challenged as undemocratic and the sources of its legitimacy questioned. In the experiences and literature so far, the main argument is that the "informal" status of the transition management process ensures that outcomes will only be adopted when supported by other actors inside the policy arena or society at large. It is argued that the approach seeks to offer a "supplementary democracy," that is, a semi-structured arena in which societal actors can collectively identify problems and solutions and discuss implementation. However, this presupposes an institutionalized, formal democratic system that is relatively open to such "shadow processes."

In lower- and middle-income countries, where democratic traditions are often relatively young, transition management could easily provide a mechanism to help build such a tradition and engage larger parts of civil society, but it could also easily lead to a too technocratic and functionalistic implementation with hardly any impact felt beyond the participants.

Diversity and Openness

In predevelopment phases of transition, there is a clear drive for more diversity and for exploring multiple pathways, but toward the acceleration stage there is a tendency toward homogenization of systems of provisioning, in part as a consequence of the mainstream proclivity toward uniformity, centralization, and standards setting.

Yet, diversity is arguably an important characteristic that needs to be maintained so that sustainability initiatives are embedded in—and sensitive and adapted to—local contexts, in a way that promotes their longevity and system reflexivity in the long term. The conditions to ensure diversity in the context of coupling and rescaling transition initiatives are yet to be explored, but seem critical given the importance of space and place in engendering acceleration. Especially when it comes to external initiation of transition management, the process is framed toward specific solutions/outcomes. In practice, the challenge is to provide throughout the transition management processes a context in which to reflect, open up, and explore variety.

Speed of Change

Transitions are defined as systemic changes in which economic, technological, social, cultural, and ecological changes co-evolve. While this has been true in historical transitions, in most sustainability transitions—especially in the context of lower- and middle-income countries where modernization and sustainability transitions emerge simultaneously—it can be questioned whether gradual co-evolution is possible, given the different paces of change in different dimensions. Sociocultural changes take place on a much longer time horizon than technological ones. The West African highway—on which pedestrians were often killed—is an example of leapfrogging in terms of mobility transition while the cultural routines are not yet adapted to it. In these contexts, transition management is challenged to play into the different speeds, identify the tensions they create, and try to address them.

Social Learning and Capacity Building

Transition management is mostly about social learning—collectively trying to understand systemic challenges and identify strategic actions that play into complex processes of social change in order to influence them in a certain direction. Often transition management is interpreted as instrumental; developing a vision and innovation networks is the end goal.

Using transition management tools to support and help guide social-learning processes requires skills and competencies, both among participants as well as within the transition team. In many countries, neither the expertise nor the knowledge and facilities to acquire such competencies may be available. Such competencies may be developed through experience, but a certain level of social entrepreneurship, scientific knowledge, and process/governance capacity are a prerequisite of successful transition management.

The Role of Multilateral Organizations

The World Bank and other multilateral institutions should be able to advise their partners and clients, representing national, regional, and local institutions, about the risks and opportunities of proactively managing global transitions beyond 2025. They also can play an important role, moving toward 2050, in the co-evolution of sociotechnological progress and collective solutions to sustainability problems in former developing and developed countries. As the World Bank stated in *The Road to 2050* (World Bank 2006: 2),

> Growing to a world economy of $135 trillion poses enormous risks to the natural environment, and the risks are greatest in developing countries. Investment decisions in the near future must factor in those risks and provide some insurance against undesirable surprises. Some of the most difficult issues will involve trade-offs between preserving natural systems and pressing forward with development. Truly global issues will require collective action on an unprecedented scale.

Current unsustainable trends, such as large-scale sociotechnological systems with high eco-footprints and short life cycles, have set the world on a path toward environmental catastrophe. If the risks today are not properly accounted for and met with viable solutions, they will present disasters beyond 2025. The ramifications of these climate disasters will be costly and even more difficult to solve than they are now.

Climate change is one telling example. The outcome is certainly highly uncertain, but is better understood and researched today than ever before (Perkins 2013). The international process toward climate mitigation is slow, although the emergence of national programs, regional strategies, and local initiatives is encouraging. Now a joint framework and collective strategy is much needed to scale up and speed up the sustainability transition.

The transition and transition management approach could provide such a framework, but obviously needs to be further developed, tested, and adapted in this context. Based on the analysis in this chapter and previous insights and tensions, a number of concrete suggestions can be made as follows:

- Develop a generic set of guiding governance principles for sustainability transitions. Drawing on the transition management principles, these should focus on a long-term sustainable transition, short-term diversity of solutions, representative participation of different interests and values, equal participation, and a focus on social learning.

- Formulate the basic conditions, boundaries, and values within which transition management should be implemented, for example, inclusivity, democratic accountability, and a focus on sustainability outcomes.

- Develop an open source pool of knowledge, experts, instruments, and skill sets. Bringing together and training transition professionals and teams that could develop and coordinate implementation of transition management in different countries, regions, and local contexts can make a powerful contribution to sustainability transitions worldwide and could also offer the possibility to guard over the previous two points.

- Develop a "world map of transition" from a multilateral perspective. Build on the work in this chapter and develop more encompassing and deeper insight into different transition dynamics in different areas. This could provide the basis for interventions, provide a powerful platform for exchange of knowledge and debate, and be the starting point for national or local transition management processes. Data and knowledge are available to accomplish this, but not directly in the form of integrated transition analyses.

- Fund and otherwise support transition management processes. Besides funding reforms and specific (sustainable) projects that are often infrastructure based, transition management could be funded and supported by providing knowledge and personnel in multiactor networks developed around specific innovations and projects and in which ambitious, broadly supported, and guiding sustainability visions and agendas are developed. These in turn could produce ideas for concrete projects that could accordingly be (financially) supported. This could also help create support and acceptance of certain interventions.

The World Bank will become engaged in many more partnerships among diverse actors. It will not always be feasible or desirable for the Bank to lead, but it should not retreat to a marginal role. It will need to be a substantial actor without always being in the driver's seat—something that has been a challenge for it to date under existing global and regional partnership programs.

The World Bank's partners are also likely to change in the coming years (World Bank 2012). For example, mayors or city administrations may become more important in partner networks than national or provincial ministries in tackling some critical GPG challenges that rely on shifts in production and consumption patterns. The new Global Partnership for Oceans (GPO) (see chapter 8) presents an excellent opportunity to explore the shape large-scale, long-term partnerships formed to address complex, global issues might take in the coming years.

Conclusion and Fundamental Reflections

The global challenges around the world's common goods and futures are massive—climate change, energy and resource scarcity, poverty, water quality and availability, and access to public services, like education and health—and may seem at this point too big to handle. Progress has been made in major attempts at addressing these and other global challenges, but arguably not at the speed necessary given the urgency and the expected increasing shocks and crises associated with so-called persistent unsustainability. The transition perspective and

Too Global to Fail · http://dx.doi.org/10.1596/978-1-4648-0307-9

historical case studies show that such systemic crises are not only a natural part of complex societal change, but also necessary to create space for more fundamental solutions. In other words, the major systemic crises the world now faces economically, ecologically, and socially also provide the windows of opportunity to reorient development pathways and shift to inherently more sustainable ones.

Nonlinear changes and shocks are thus a normal feature of social change in the long-term development of societies. Too often, however, governance systems and institutions focus on optimizing for the short term. Through specialization, efficiency, and control mechanisms and policy-centric thinking, the Transitions Approach suggests starting from the innovative power in actors and societies at large to empower and channel this energy toward more sustainable futures. The transitions perspective offers a way to anticipate, analyze, and adapt to broader complex societal changes, as well as providing a basis for collaborative intervention and experimentation.

The transitions governance framework is operationalized in a set of transition management tools of systemic instruments: a set of intervention strategies based on the transition approach that aims to guide and accelerate sustainability transitions.

Depending on the specific context, transition processes can be organized so that frontrunners, champions, and entrepreneurs with different backgrounds are brought together to develop society-based transition agendas. Over the past decade, a lot of experience has been built up with this approach, leading to substantial input into policy agendas. The transitions approach empowers, stimulates, and facilitates social innovation beyond policy. Its tools and instruments help to collectively set boundaries, develop deeper and shared understanding of challenges, share inspiring visions for the future, and create scenarios and pathways toward strategic innovation. Governments and policy-related institutions can find tools that support the different roles they can play in transitions: from facilitating to empowering, from regulating to enforcing, and from initiating to coordinating.

The transitions approach is based on the conviction that policy alone cannot solve the aforementioned complex societal issues. The awareness of similar problems in markets and civil society leads to emerging solutions: new technologies, networks, business models, practices, and so on, always in a decentralized and context-specific manner.

The argument made in this chapter is that these kinds of solutions should be taken as starting points for transition governance as they create resilience and sustainability at the local scale and start to contribute to solutions on a global scale. Transition governance in this sense is a "glocal approach," as it brings in the more generic and global issues as drivers and uses external challenge as a context to create space for bottom-up context-specific solutions. This in itself is a major transition challenge for governance institutions addressing global issues: they need to shift from seeking generic solutions to offering more generic frameworks that create space for and help to enable bottom-up social innovation.

Box 11.1 What Young Development Professionals Think About Complexity and Innovation

Benedikt Signer, Global Facility for Disaster Reduction and Recovery

The risks and challenges the world faces in the 21st century are increasingly global and interconnected- from climate change to food security, resource and energy scarcity to population trends, economic instability and unsustainable growth. Governance structures, however, remain largely national. We have to make decisions involving increasingly complex systems, yet within national decision-making frameworks.

As the gap between the need for joint action and the ability of governments to act together is widening, the need to strengthen the capacity of leaders in the international system to anticipate and plan for future changes becomes evident. Looking ahead to the next 10 years, embedding the long term back into decision making is crucial at all levels. We have to learn to take the long view.

Five broad principles should guide our decisions as we tackle the challenges of the 21st century and shape the world we will hand down to future generations.

Considering the **long-term** risks and effects of our actions has to be a guiding principle. In everything we do, we should ask ourselves what will be the impact on future generations? Yet even in areas where we clearly see the problems (think ecosystem destruction, climate change, or unplanned urban growth), we largely fail to act.

We need to accept that we live in **complex systems** and stop reducing intrinsically connected problems into individual parts. By considering challenges in isolation, we largely fail to see the complexity and dynamics of the ecological, social, and economic systems in which we are embedded. In complex systems, we have to consider aspects of connectedness, stocks and flows, the interactions of the individual parts, and systems behavior, such as nonlinearity, feedback loops, and inertia. Can we really claim that we understand, let alone act on, not only the immediate effects of our actions, but also the second- and third-order effects? The unpredictable and nonlinear? The financial crisis of 2008, climate change, pandemics, and the complex links between climate change and migration are all examples of such dynamics.

As we prepare for the increasing uncertainty, short-term shocks, and long-term pressures we can only begin to foresee, **risk management** becomes ever more crucial. For all the overuse (and abuse) of the concept of resilience—the long-term capacity of a system to absorb shocks and adapt to change—it provides a very useful guiding framework to help us prepare for future uncertainty. Integrating resilience into decision making allows countries endure and grow through shocks we fail to predict or prevent. This is especially important when faced with systemic risks such as regime shifts, cascading effects, thresholds, and tipping points.

The **science-policy interface** is of central importance, as planning for the future has to be based on the best science and knowledge available. An iterative process between decision makers and technical experts should help the former ask the right questions, while informing the work of the latter to provide the needed analysis. Technical analysis should provide decision makers with the tools to evaluate alternative paths, and decision makers should be looking to include these tools in their processes.

Science alone, however, can never tell us what we should do; we need a set of VALUES to provide a moral framework and give direction to our development. Values also allow leaders to make difficult decisions. The right values in society have to empower leaders to move beyond immediate benefits to achieve the collaboration of millions of people around the world to solve global, collective-action problems. At the same time, rapid changes test our moral frameworks to answer such questions as how much risk are we willing to take on as we face climate uncertainty and can genetic engineering provide the solutions to food insecurity?

Taken together, these five principles need to underwrite a new way of thinking. John Sterman of the System Dynamics group at the Massachusetts Institute of Technology provides an example by contrasting the dynamics complicating understanding systems, in this case climate change, to our "old" way of thinking: "The overwhelming majority of everyday experiences involves simple systems where cause and effect are closely related in time and space, time delays are short, and information cues are highly correlated. The water in the teakettle boils and the whistle sounds. Unfortunately, that doesn't apply to climate change and the consequences for this misunderstanding are high."

Ensuring sufficient supply of global public goods (GPG) in a highly complex environment requires foresight. More needs to be done to help governments and leaders enhance their strategic vision faced with an uncertain future. Looking toward 2025, the World Bank can grow into a new role, supporting comprehensive approaches to global challenges, planning for future changes, and developing a coherent approach for the provision of GPGs.

References

Biermann, F. 2007. "'Earth System Governance' as a Crosscutting Theme of Global Change Research." *Global Environmental Change* 17 (3–4): 326–37.

Biggs, D., R. Biggs, V. Dakos, R. J. Scholes, and M. Schoon. 2011. "Are We Entering an Era of Concatenated Global Crises?" *Ecology and Society* 16 (2): 27. http://www.ecologyandsociety.org/vol16/iss2/art27.

Brewer, G. D., and P. DeLeon. 1983. *The Foundations of Policy Analysis*. Belmont, CA: Dorsey Press.

Brown, R. R., M. A. Farrelly, and D. Loorbach. 2013. "Actors Working the Institutions in Sustainability Transitions: The Case of Melbourne's Stormwater Management." *Global Environmental Change* 23 (4): 701–18.

Castells, M. 1996. *The Rise of the Network Society*. Malden, MA: Blackwell Publishers.

Dadush, U., and B. Stancil. 2010. "The World Order in 2050." *Policy Outlook*, Carnegie Endowment for International Peace, Washington, DC. http://carnegieendowment.org/files/World_Order_in_2050.pdf.

De Dreu, C. K. W., and M. A. West. 2001. "Minority Dissent and Team Innovation: The Importance of Participation in Decision Making." *Journal of Applied Psychology* 86 (6): 1191–201.

De Graaf, R., and R. van der Brugge. 2010. "Transforming Water Infrastructure by Linking Water Management and Urban Renewal in Rotterdam." *Technological Forecasting and Social Change* 77 (8): 1282–91.

Dirven, J., J. Rotmans, and A. Verkaik. 2002. *Samenleving in transitie: Een vernieuwend gezichtspunt.* Den Haag: Innovatienetwerk Agrocluster en Groene Ruimte.

Frantzeskaki, F., and H. de Haan. 2009. "Transitions: Two Steps from Theory to Policy." *Futures* 41 (9): 593–606. http://dx.doi.org/10.1016/j.futures.2009.04.009.

Frantzeskaki, F., and J. Grin. 2012. "Drifting between Transitions: The Environmental Protection Transition in Greece." 3rd International Conference of Sustainability Transitions, Copenhagen, August 26–28.

Frantzeskaki, N., and D. Loorbach. 2010. "Towards Governing Infrasystem Transitions: Reinforcing Lock-In or Facilitating Change?" *Technological Forecasting and Social Change* 77 (8): 1292–301.

Frantzeskaki, N., D. Loorbach, and J. Meadowcroft. 2012. "Governing Transitions to Sustainability: Transition Management as a Governance Approach towards Pursuing Sustainability." *International Journal of Sustainable Development* 15 (1/2): 19–36.

Geels, F. W. 2004. "From Sectoral Systems of Innovation to Socio-Technical Systems: Insights about Dynamics and Change from Sociology and Institutional Theory." *Research Policy* 33 (6–7): 897–920.

———. 2005. "Processes and Patterns in Transitions and System Innovations: Refining the Co-Evolutionary Multi-Level Perspective." *Technological Forecasting and Social Change* 72 (6): 681–96.

———. 2011. "The Multi-Level Perspective on Sustainability Transitions: Responses to Seven Criticisms." *Environmental Innovation and Societal Transitions* 1 (1): 24–40.

Geels, F. W., and J. Schot. 2007. "Typology of Sociotechnical Transition Pathways." *Research Policy* 36 (3): 399–417.

Genus, A., and A. M. Coles. 2008. "Rethinking the Multi-Level Perspective of Technological Transitions." *Research Policy* 37 (9): 1436–45.

Grin, J., F. Felix, B. Bos, and S. Spoelstra. 2004. "Practices for Reflexive Design: Lessons from a Dutch Project on Sustainable Agriculture." *International Journal of Foresight and Innovation Policies* 1 (1–2): 126–48.

Grin, J., J. Rotmans, and J. Schot. 2010. *Transitions to Sustainable Development: New Directions in the Study of Long Term Transformative Change.* New York: Routledge.

Hendriks, C. M. 2009. "Policy Design without Democracy? Making Democratic Sense of Transition Management." *Policy Sciences* 42 (4): 341–68.

Karlsson-Vinkhuyzen, S. I., N. Jollands, and L. Staudt. 2012. "Global Governance for Sustainable Energy: The Contribution of a Global Public Goods Approach." *Ecological Economics* 83: 11–18.

Kaul, I., I. Grunberg, and M. A. Stern, eds. 1999. *Global Public Goods: International Cooperation in the 21st Century.* Oxford, U.K.: Oxford University Press.

Kemp, R., and S. van den Bosch. 2006. *Transitie-experimenten. Praktijkexperimenten met de potentie om bij te dragen aan transities.* Kenniscentrum voor duurzame systeeminnovaties en transities. Erasmus University, Rotterdam, Netherlands.

Kemp, R., J. Rotmans, and D. Loorbach. 2007. "Transition Management as a Model for Managing Processes of Co-Evolution Towards Sustainable Development." *International Journal of Sustainable Development and World Ecology* 14 (1): 78–91.

Loorbach, D. 2007. "Transition Management: New Mode of Governance for Sustainable Development." Ph.D. Thesis, Erasmus University, Rotterdam, Netherlands. http://repub.eur.nl/res/pub/10200/.

Loorbach, D. 2010. "Transition Management for Sustainable Development: A Prescriptive, Complexity-Based Governance Framework." *Governance* 23 (1): 161–83.

Loorbach, D., and F. Frantzeskaki. 2012. "Governing Societal Transitions to Sustainability." *International Journal of Sustainable Development* 15 (1): 19–36.

Loorbach, D., and K. Wijsman. 2013. "Business Transition Management: Exploring a New Role for Business in Sustainability Transitions." *Journal of Cleaner Production* 45: 20–28.

Loorbach, D., and N. Frantzeskaki. 2012. "Why Taking Complexity Seriously Implies a Paradigm Shift for Policy Studies." In *COMPACT I: Public Administration in Complexity*, edited by L. Gerrits and P. Marks, 327–45. Litchfield Park, AZ: Emergent Publications.

Loorbach, D., and R. Lijnis Huffenreuter. 2013. "Exploring the Economic Crisis from a Transition Management Perspective." *Environmental Innovation and Societal Transition* 6: 35–46.

Loorbach, D., and J. Rotmans 2006. "Managing Transitions for Sustainable Development." In *Understanding Industrial Transformation: Views from Different Disciplines*, edited by X. Olsthoorn and A. J. Wieczorek, 187–206. Amsterdam: Springer.

———. 2010. "The Practice of Transition Management: Examples and Lessons from Four Distinct Cases." *Futures* 42 (30): 237–46.

Loorbach, D., N. Frantzeskaki, and W. Thissen. 2011. "A Transition Research Perspective on Governance for Sustainability." In *European Research on Sustainable Development— 1: Transformative Science Approaches for Sustainability*, edited by C. C. Jaeger, D. J. Tàbara, and J. Jaeger, 73–89. Berlin: Springer.

Loorbach, D., R. van der Brugge, and M. Taanman. 2008. "Governance in the Energy Transition: Practice of Transition Management in the Netherlands." *International Journal of Environmental Technology and Management* 9 (2): 294–315.

Nevens, F., N. Frantzeskaki, L. Gorissen, and D. Loorbach. 2013. "Urban Transition Labs: Co-creating Transformative Action for Sustainable Cities." *Journal of Cleaner Production* 50: 111–22. doi: 10.1016/j.jclepro.2012.12.001.

Perkins, S. 2013. "Global Temperatures Are Close to 11,000-Year Peak." *Nature*, March 7.

Raven, R. P. J. M., S. van den Bosch, and R. Weterings. 2010. "Transitions and Strategic Niche Management: Towards a Competence Kit for Practitioners." *International Journal of Technology Management* 51 (1): 57–74.

Rotmans, J. 2005. "Societal Innovation: Between Dream and Reality Lies Complexity." DRIFT Research Working Paper, Erasmus University Rotterdam, Netherlands. http://ssrn.com/abstract=878564.

Rotmans, J., and D. Loorbach. 2009. "Complexity and Transition Management." *Journal of Industrial Ecology* 13 (2): 184–96.

Rotmans, J., R. Kemp, and M. van Asselt. 2001. "More Evolution than Revolution: Transition Management in Public Policy." *Foresight* 3 (1): 15–31.

Schuitmaker, T. J. 2012. "Identifying and Unravelling Persistent Problems." *Technological Forecasting and Social Change* 79 (6): 1021–31. http://dx.doi.org/10.1016/j.techfore.2011.11.008.

Smith, A., and R. Raven. 2012. "What Is Protective Space? Reconsidering Niches in Transitions to Sustainability." *Research Policy* 41: 1025–36.

Sondeijker, S., J. Geurts, J. Rotmans, and A. Tukker. 2006. "Imagining Sustainability: The Added Value of Transition Scenarios in Transition Management." *Foresight* 8 (5): 15–30.

Svensson, G. 2001. "'Glocalization' of Business Activities: A 'Glocal Strategy' Approach." *Management Decision* 39 (1): 6–18.

Trachtman, J. P. 1992. "L'etat, c'est nous: sovereignty, economic integration and subsidiarity." *Harvard International Law Journal* 33: 459–73.

Unruh, G. C. 2002. "Escaping Carbon Lock-In." *Energy Policy* 30 (4): 317–25.

Van Buuren, A., and D. Loorbach. 2009. "Policy Innovation in Isolation?" *Public Management Review* 11 (3): 375–92.

Van den Bosch, S., H. Brezet, and P. Vergragt. 2005. "Rotterdam Case Study of the Transition to a Fuel Cell Transport System." *Fuel Cells Bulletin* 2005 (6): 10–16.

Van der Brugge, R., and R. van Raak. 2007. "Facing the Adaptive Management Challenge: Insights from Transition Management." *Ecology and Society* 12 (2): 33. http://www.ecologyandsociety.org/vol12/iss2/art33/.

Van Eijndhoven, J., N. Frantzeskaki, and D. Loorbach. 2013. "Connecting Long and Short-Term via Envisioning in Transition Arenas." In *Connective Capacity in Water Governance*, edited by J. Edelenbos, N. Bressers, and P. Scholten, 172–190. London: Ashgate Publications.

Van Knippenberg, D., C. K. W. De Dreu, and A.C. Homan. 2004. "Work Group Diversity and Group Performance: An Integrative Model and Research Agenda." *Journal of Applied Psychology* 89 (6): 1008–22.

Wiek, A., C. Binder, and R. W. Scholz. 2006. "Functions of Scenarios in Transition Processes." *Futures* 38 (7): 740–66.

World Bank. 2006. *The Road to 2050: Sustainable Development for the 21st Century.* Washington, DC: World Bank.

———. 2012. *Food Prices, Nutrition, and the Millennium Development Goals.* Global Monitoring Report 2012. Washington, DC: World Bank.

PART 4

The Final Stretch:
High Road or Low?

CHAPTER 12

Conclusion

Robin Davies and J. Warren Evans

The international public goods discussed in this book are critical enablers of sustained poverty reduction, human well-being, and economic growth in all countries and regions, but particularly in developing countries. They are global public assets to which correspond some major global public liabilities—the medium- and long-term risks posed by the loss of biodiversity and the degradation of ecosystems and the services they provide; water scarcity; depleted or collapsed oceanic fisheries; and pandemics.

Any one of these liabilities is already worrisome enough individually to justify a new look at how all such liabilities are being addressed. Moreover, the rapid acceleration of urbanization will, under business as usual, drive corresponding increases in the consumption of natural resources and the production of harmful wastes. And then if one factors in the growing effects over the next 20 years of the great exacerbator, climate change, global risk profiles move into largely uncharted territory. While the impacts of climate change are difficult to predict with any certainty in particular locations, the world can expect, with unchecked carbon emissions, even greater shortages of resources, more frequent and severe storms and droughts, more widespread disease, the disruption of food and energy supplies, and perhaps in some cases inter- or intrastate conflict.

Set against this bleak catalogue of liabilities is the fact that major advances in economic growth and social development in many communities and countries, and strengthened cooperation within and across regions, have improved the resilience of people, communities and nations to these risks—but only so far. It can be argued that improvements in human welfare achieved over the last few decades have been attained at least in part on credit—that the welfare gains are largely illusory given the scale of the liabilities that we have.[1] On this view, building global public assets, and reducing the corresponding global public liabilities, is fundamental to the maintenance and improvement of human welfare. The development and dispersal of knowledge and innovation, the cooperative management of common-pool resources, the mobilization of large-scale private investment in low-carbon energy generation and energy efficiency, and well-managed and networked urbanization are all important elements in mitigating global risks.

To see Vice President Rachel Kyte discuss development aid financing: http://youtu.be/KhK5DALZh18

Global Risks and the World Bank

We have shown that global institutions such as the World Bank have in the past played a key role in identifying some key global risks and opportunities and in assisting countries to manage risks and seize opportunities. While the impacts achieved have been quite variable, the strong leadership role that the Bank has played in supporting countries' efforts to mitigate and adapt to climate change has been recognized by most constituencies. However, the critical question, if one takes a longer-term view, is whether these actions add up to enough—that is, whether they will ever lead to the delivery of the global public goods needed in the quantities required. In many cases, we do not have a ready answer because there is no easily quantifiable "solution" (though exceptions exist, such as the Global Tiger Initiative and the Montreal Protocol). In the cases of biodiversity conservation and climate change, however, the ready answer is most certainly "no."

As discussed in previous chapters, the Bank's strong country focus in the allocation of its own resources for public investment (through the International Bank for Reconstruction and Development and International Development Association [IDA]) leads to a bias toward short-term interventions and national public goods. With the impacts of both climate change and globalization, the Bank and development agencies increasingly find themselves helping governments to douse "Monday morning fires." Less and less time, energy and funding is available at the country level for longer-term, regional and global issues management. In addition, within institutions like the World Bank there are few incentives for country teams to work on such issues—even where additional, earmarked donor funding is made available to support the work.

This is not entirely a bad thing; it would not be desirable for Bank engagement with recipient countries to be strongly driven by the preferences of donors with special-purpose trust funds. However, often it is the country team that is best equipped to support client countries in tackling critical transnational and global challenges. They know the risks and opportunities and the financing, capacity, and governance problems that must be well understood in order to devise successful long-term solutions. They know where the entry points are and the locked doors. And of course the Bank's country teams are backed by an institution with unparalleled convening power, an impeccable fiduciary management track record, and a deep capacity for innovation and analysis. There should, in principle, be no question about the centrality of the World Bank's role in the provision of global public goods.

Bob Dylan sang "The times they are a-changin'."[2] Consider the following glimpse of a possible future.

- By 2025, the number of IDA-eligible countries is halved and today's emerging economies, and largest IBRD borrowers, are partners in funding the development of other developing countries.
- Official development assistance (ODA) remains flat at around present levels or declines, and a large share of it is used in support of global public goods,

including support for private sector–led green growth, with the balance allocated to a residual group of fragile and conflict-affected countries.

- ODA from traditional Organisation for Economic Co-operation and Development (OECD) sources is rivaled or even overtaken by contributions from emerging official donors, private foundations, or "direct giving" mechanisms.
- Action on global challenges is increasingly taken forward by coalitions of like-minded parties, incorporating sovereign states, cities, civil society organizations (CSOs), businesses, institutional investors, regional and international organizations, and youth movements, with coalition governance[3] geared toward achieving "collective impact" on large-scale challenges.
- The vehicles for dealing with such challenges are increasingly special-purpose, internationally coordinated, and long-term mega-programs designed to solve the problems, rather than put dents in them.

The scenario outlined above might look far-fetched. But aspects of it are already coming to pass—consider, for example, the emergence of the Global Fund to Fight AIDS, Tuberculosis and Malaria or the GAVI Alliance or the Global Partnership for Oceans (GPO).

Business as usual, under which incremental and essentially marginal efforts are put forward to deal with global challenges, while most national and international effort is focused on national challenges, will clearly lead us to a world that is unacceptable to most of its citizens by the middle of the century. It is quite fair to say that the multilateral "establishment" has done a mediocre job of leading the way to long-term sustainability and now faces the risk of fading into irrelevance. Its success stories add up to very little, and in fact suggest a dismal outlook for future generations. Certainly, the World Bank has often moved ahead of, or stepped outside, that establishment. It has pioneered new forms of partnership, like the Global Environment Facility (GEF), the Critical Ecosystems Partnership Fund, the Climate Investment Funds, and a stable of carbon funds. These are all steps in the right direction, but none at the scale or with the durability to achieve what is required over time.

The question now is whether the World Bank and similar organizations can adapt their ways of working so as to assure their long-term relevance. In order to do this, they will need to lead or play a central role in new forms of partnership that exhibit the vision, scale, resourcing, and durability required to match large and uncertain global challenges—including those of promoting healthy oceans, productive ecosystems, sufficient freshwater supply, and a stable and hospitable climate.

During the course of this study, and based on the experience of the last three decades, it was considered a given that the World Bank would ultimately play a fundamental role in most such large-scale, long-term partnerships. A number of brainstorming sessions and workshops highlighted the strong technical and financial knowledge and operational capabilities of the Bank as critical requirements for effective action on global challenges. However, some important barriers were identified at the institutional level.

First among these was the Bank's governance—the primary factor cited by the designers of the Green Climate Fund (GCF) when arguing for a limited role for the World Bank. The dominance of developed countries in the Bank's board was a major problem, even though many recognized the Bank would have been the logical place to house the Fund.

A second issue raised in the course of the study was the heavy reliance on external, special-purpose funding for regional and global initiatives. The Bank is currently not able to take such initiatives onto its own balance sheet and also for the most part feels unable to support them through mainstream country operations.

A third issue is that heavy and often risk-averse bureaucratic processes geared more toward large, loan-financed operations than toward partnership-based and grant-financed programs impede flexibility, innovation, and speed, and therefore limit impact.

A final issue identified by some is that the Bank is perceived as a serious, engaged partner only when in the lead and in control.

We think the Bank does have the capacity to deal with these issues and play a fundamental role in meeting global challenges and that its place in the institutional architecture would in fact be strengthened if it were to assume this role. However, in order for this to happen, the Bank will need to sharpen its priorities and change the mindset it brings to country operations. At the same time, the Bank's contributors will need to change their expectations and the way they make available funding for global public goods.

Below we highlight three key areas in which the Bank can and should give much greater priority to action on global public goods, which we have treated in depth in preceding chapters. We then proceed to reinforce the points we have made about the role of ODA in financing global public policy and the ways in which international development organizations—particularly the World Bank— might need to alter some fundamental aspects of the way they work.

Bank-Led Partnerships: Three Key Challenges

What might future partnerships to tackle the world's mega-challenges look like and what might be the role of the World Bank within those partnerships? We look at three mega-challenges below, each of which is being addressed by ongoing World Bank–led partnerships, namely, healthy oceans, climate-smart agriculture, and climate-smart, livable cities. Our purpose is not to criticize actions under way or to suggest detailed alternatives, but rather to reflect on how such long-term issues can most effectively be dealt with through collaboration between like-minded partners, including the World Bank.

The starting point in each case needs to be a vision of what success would look like and an understanding of what collective action is needed to get the world into that state. The challenges we face on urban growth, ocean degradation, and food security are as long-term and complex as they could be, but if we do not ask where we need to be, and agree on a framework for action that is commensurate with the challenge, then we are certainly destined to continue tinkering at the edges.

Oceans

A vision of what the GPO should strive for was described in Chapter 10. That vision may seem far-fetched to some, who will argue that it is too complicated and needs to be broken down into component parts with associated site- or objective-specific actions. But that is exactly what the fisheries, eco-tourism, coastal resources management, urban pollution, and other "communities" that have been working on oceans issues in the past have always done. Their successes do not add up to success: they add up to piecemeal and often temporary progress as the natural productivity of the oceans declines.

Whether a Bank-led GPO or an even broader coalition takes the reins, a new backbone institution will likely be required in the near future to take on a secretariat and management function: the challenge, number of actors, and need for fund-raising will justify an independent body for this purpose. One of the initial actions of such a body should be to engage in transition planning so that there is a clear understanding of the roles and responsibilities of all actors in dealing with the complexities and uncertainties that the partnership will face over time. A key challenge and opportunity will be to establish a leadership role for private sector stakeholders from the energy, shipping, extractive, and tourism industries as well as the fishing industry. Relationships will also need to be built with the major centers of consumption—cities. The GPO and the C40, and similar associations of mayors, could work together to identify opportunities to shift consumption trajectories toward a more sustainable use of ocean resources.

Finally, an appropriate level of funding will be required to get the level of collaborative action and impact at the scale and with the durability required to save the oceans and benefit from the economic opportunities they provide. Traditional sources of public sector funding are in short supply for such mega-programs. New approaches, such as the International Finance Facility for Immunisation (IFFIm) or the Blue Bonds suggested in Chapter 10, need to be considered. In addition, there is a clear opportunity to support ocean recovery with climate finance: climate change will wipe out the benefits of many past and current efforts to conserve living oceans and manage coastal resources owing to acidification, warming, storm surges, and sea level rise. The "oceans community" needs to play an aggressive advocacy role, pushing for reductions in greenhouse gas (GHG) emissions at the scale required to reduce these risks. But it should also tap a significant portion of climate finance in order to establish the foundation for a substantial source of dedicated funding, which could be augmented by traditional and non-traditional donors and private sector stakeholders, for the highest priority actions required over the next decades.

Climate-Smart Agriculture

The Bank and many other international and national organizations have been supporting the inclusion of a strong focus on climate-smart agriculture in the international climate negotiations and in agricultural development assistance to developing countries. Agricultural production needs to increase by at least 70 percent in the next 35 to 40 years to feed the world, meaning greater demand for water at a time when water shortages are already affecting production in many parts of the world. The climate impacts of higher temperatures and shifts in rainfall patterns will greatly exacerbate agricultural production challenges, no less than the growth of the population to be fed.

Supporters of climate-smart agriculture believe that a transition to proven techniques such as mulching, intercropping, conservation agriculture, crop rotation, integrated crop-livestock management, agro-forestry, improved grazing, and improved water management can all serve to strengthen food security, increase climate resilience, reduce GHG emissions, and sequester carbon. Climate-smart agriculture also includes improved weather forecasting, drought- and flood-tolerant crops, and risk insurance.

While all of these elements are important and will certainly improve the situation, is this approach big enough and bold enough to achieve a food-secure, climate-resilient agriculture sector in vulnerable areas? Is it as climate smart as will be required for agriculture to have a significant role in the mitigation of climate change? The international community, with leadership from the Bank, IFAD, FAO, the CGIAR, and other major sources of technical and financial support for commercial and subsistence farming, including both large operations and smallholders, should come together to develop a longer-term vision than has been achieved to date. Again, the challenge is too great to hope that the various actions now being taken are collectively adequate to achieve the long-term transition to sustainable, climate-smart agriculture that is required.

A key missing link is the need to shift where possible to production of perennial grains instead of annuals.[4] A tremendous level of progress has been achieved by a very small, underfunded group of researchers during the last ten years in the development of perennial grains. This research and development work needs to be scaled up rapidly with the objective of at least enabling cropping in some of the large tracts of degraded lands in some of the world's poorest countries. The climate benefits of perennials as opposed to annuals are well known: these result from reduced soil carbon loss, because land is not tilled on an annual basis, and from greater water use efficiency and soil moisture conservation, which provides greater resilience to weather variability. Other local benefits include less soil erosion and lower levels of chemical use, thus less agricultural pollution.

A second element of a climate-smart agriculture sector is the development of a new fertilizer regime that reduces the growing impact on coastal waters that is leading increasingly to the emergence of "dead zones." Achieving healthy and productive oceans in the face of climate impacts requires that non-climate ocean degraders, such as agricultural nutrient runoff, be quickly reduced on a massive scale.

Increasing attention to perennial grains development and replacing conventional agricultural inputs like today's commercial fertilizers are major challenges. They are achievable with the right kind and level of collective action, but will require determined effort in the face of strong opposition from a powerful international business community that has a significant commercial interest in the status quo.

A third element of a long-term view of climate-smart agriculture involves a reconsideration of the role and sustainability of smallholder agriculture. This very large part of the agriculture sector is by far the most vulnerable and least resilient to climate impacts. How will smallholder producers survive climate change, let alone contribute to local, national, or regional food security? Cooperatives of smallholders have been in existence for many decades. A new approach to the use of the cooperative concept should be explored that focuses on collective action to secure funds, improve productivity, access markets and add value, incorporating the climate-smart actions at scale discussed above. Experience from innovative funding mechanisms like the Bank's Biocarbon Fund can be built upon to explore how to tap climate finance as an important source of funding at the cooperative level.

Finally, as in the case of oceans, improving linkages with the consuming class in major cities can open up markets for certified products, increasing finance and technical support for cooperatives.

Reducing Greenhouse Gas Emissions from Cities

What we know now about the severity of the risks associated with uncontrolled climate change makes it crystal clear that massive efforts are required to bend the GHG emission curve. With luck, we might only have to deal with two degrees of warming by the end of the century, already a frightening prospect. One way or another, cities will play a large role in this drama. They will, under business as usual, contribute massively to the growth in global emissions. Or, with intelligent and concerted action, they will help to bend the curve.

We are seeing a large-scale population shift from rural to urban areas and from agriculture to the manufacturing and service industries, such that most future population growth will be in developing country cities. Asia, a major source of greenhouse emissions, is expected to have an urban population of about 2.2 billion by 2020, the largest of any region. This population includes an estimated 70 percent of the global poor. By 2030, it is estimated that 2.7 billion people, about 55 percent of the population in the Asia region, will live in urban areas; this will be an increase of more than 70 percent (1.1 billion) in the next 29 years. Sub-Saharan Africa has even higher urban growth rates but a very different starting point and, at present, limited GHG reduction opportunities. Other regions have mixed levels of urban growth and offer varying GHG reduction opportunities.

Cities and their inhabitants—families, businesses, institutions, factories—are already a significant source of GHG emissions. Poor investment decisions made now could lock the world into a future with limited opportunities to reduce GHG emissions at the scale required. Thus, the urban sector (including urban-based industry) presents perhaps the greatest opportunity to achieve decisive GHG emission reductions. How can this opportunity be realized? We believe the challenge needs to be viewed from the perspectives of both the global community, with its climate mitigation objective, and city mayors, concerned about their ability to provide the infrastructure and urban services that their constituents and future generations need. If only the global perspective is taken, it is unlikely that anything on the scale required will be achieved. If only the mayors' perspective is taken, a major increase in carbon emissions is guaranteed.

Why would a mayor give priority to low-carbon investments? Many of the existing cities in developing countries are already significantly under-provided with critical infrastructure, largely because of a lack of finance. The price tag for meeting today's needs has already risen significantly in many coastal and other cities vulnerable to climate impacts because of the need to build climate resilience into infrastructure designs. For a mayor in a developing country city to give priority to low-carbon development requires that it be integral to meeting wider urban infrastructure and services needs, at the present and into the future. Thus the price tag associated with achieving large-scale GHG reductions from cities is actually much much higher than that of stand-alone low-carbon investments. But by bringing low-carbon development incentives together with technical and financial support for meeting current and future needs, multilateral development banks (MDBs) can make a mayor's decision to "go low carbon" easier.

The urban challenge and opportunity also requires a new kind of partnership and commitment to long-term, large-scale action, including very significant commitments for technical and financial support. A new level of financial innovation aimed at drawing in partners from the private sector, in the form of institutional investors, will be required to mobilize the trillions of dollars required over the next decades. International public financing will be crucial to support cities to become creditworthy and to reduce financial and political risks so that private sector finance can be mobilized at the scale and within the timeframe required.

Having discussed some key global challenges from a sectoral perspective, we now proceed to underline some broader points made in preceding chapters about the role of ODA in financing global public policy and about the ways in the World Bank and other international development organizations should change direction.

The Concept and Supply of Aid

As argued in chapter 5, with stagnant or declining ODA levels, increasing pressure to apply ODA to growing global challenges, a dramatic thinning of the ranks of the low-income countries, and a still-dominant aid policy narrative that says ODA should be applied to the national challenges of the poorest countries, something has to give.

There is no realistic prospect that international public financing, additional to current levels of aid, will be mobilized on any significant scale by means of "innovative" financing mechanisms. In the absence of this, and without the kind of growth we saw in aid budgets over the decade to 2010, the obvious conclusion is that we must rely upon aid budgets, at approximately their current levels, to finance global public policy. As we have shown, this has been happening to an ever greater extent over the last two decades, but without recognition in the dominant aid policy narrative. That narrative needs to change with the times, or it will eventually be dangerously out of kilter with the reality of aid allocation. Such a disconnect, once recognized, could lead a serious loss of public and political support for aid.

In short, the purpose of aid must be reconceived to recognize the reality that aid is and needs to be used for financing global public policy. However, this reconception should disturb the existing, core rationale for aid as little as possible. That rationale is sound, even if incomplete, and has proven successful in rallying support for aid. It should not be abandoned, obscured, or in any way taken lightly. We have therefore advocated a relatively conservative modification of the rationale for aid that nevertheless carries implications for resource allocation, delivery mechanisms, the institutional and global governance of the relevant financial flows, and the measurement of those flows.

According to the rationale we have suggested, the purpose of aid is a simple but twofold one: to support national public goods and to support global public goods (taken here as including regional public goods). This rationale can be adopted without revisiting the fundamentals of the ODA concept. The existing ODA definition is capable of supporting a rationale or narrative that gives much greater prominence to the role of international development organizations as agents for the supply of global public goods, rather than merely as agents for the delivery of bilateral resources. An important feature of this rationale is that financing global public policy is essentially seen as the domain of global institutions. This is not just a matter of emphasis; it entails material changes in the way in which they conduct and present their operations, to which we come further below.

We have also outlined our thinking on how aid donors should make ODA available for use in the service of global public goods. Our core idea here is that a Global Financing Facility should be established at arm's length from any existing institution, while using existing administrative structures and financing channels. In addition to its financing function, this facility should be equipped with strong policy advisory and evaluation functions. It should be financed in several ways: by folding in resources from a range of existing funds (possibly including the GCF if it proves unable to mobilize sufficient funds—say $20 billion a year by 2020), by raising cash contributions from donors, and possibly also by raising funds in the capital markets through the issuance of "global x" bonds backed by long-term ODA pledges (where x represents one or another global challenge). The facility, we have argued, should be required to allocate a defined proportion of its resources to the mobilization of market-based investments in global public goods.

The governance arrangements for a Global Financing Facility would need to be very different from those of existing MDBs, which reflect an economic order that is receding into the past and are not fit for the facility's purpose—the financing of action on challenges in which very broad groupings of sovereign and non-sovereign actors all have stakes. Thus the facility's governing body would include both sovereign and non-sovereign representatives and would aim to give them voice in proportion to their exposure to global challenges, not in proportion to their cash contributions to the financing mechanism of the facility.

The Role of International Development Organizations

According to the aid policy narrative we favor, international development organizations would have a central and indeed privileged role in the supply of aid-financed global public goods. By the same token, those organizations would be expected truly to make that role central to their mandates, rather than seeing it as marginal and confined to the domain of special-purpose donor trust funds.

In order to meet the latter expectation, we have argued that international development organizations should adopt institutional strategies for contributing to the supply of global public goods through both country and global programs. These should as far as possible be linked across key institutions and certainly across the MDBs. They should be more than policy statements: they should be operational strategies that set goals, drive resource allocation, articulate implementation arrangements, and provide a basis for monitoring and evaluation.

Such strategies should lead to a consolidation and rationalization of the existing patchwork of arbitrarily sized and unreliably funded global and regional funding mechanisms operated by the World Bank and, to a lesser extent, other MDBs. In addition, the impact of approaches and instruments trialed to date—many of which hold promise but most of which exist as pilots with little hope of follow-up—needs to be more systematically assessed, so as to support decisions about which to replicate and scale up and which to discontinue.

We have pointed out that the G20, particularly since its transformation into a leaders' level forum in 2008, and its adoption of a development mandate in 2010, has a unique capacity to ensure that linked institutional strategies are developed, resourced, and implemented. It also has an obvious role in monitoring the supply of global public goods important for global stability and prosperity. This could well be the defining theme of its development agenda, as that agenda evolves further.

We have argued also for what might be termed a Copernican shift in the way that global problems are viewed within the MDBs. At present, they are viewed as important but outside the scope of the mainstream work of the banks—in short, as sidelines, almost "hobby shop" preoccupations. But, from a sustainability perspective, the most important global public goods are not those that can be supplied by means of relatively small funds and tight-knit coalitions of like-minded organizations. The most important global public goods will be supplied by governments and private actors through cumulative, large-scale action across multiple countries. It is therefore of paramount importance to create incentives for the pursuit of global public goods through mainstream country operations, rather than merely through global programs. Incentives are needed for both clients and for Bank staff, particularly in middle-income countries, which now have a much wider range of financing options than previously.

A weak formulation of the point above would be that MDBs should do more through their country operations to contribute to the supply of global public goods. A stronger formulation, reflecting the Copernican shift just mentioned, would be that MDBs should make this their primary job—to find and work at the intersection between national and global public policy priorities. The latter formulation is likely to seem increasingly relevant as developing countries, in this "age of choice" (Greenhill et al. 2013), increasingly turn to bilateral development financing institutions or other emerging sources of finance, such as the mooted BRICS bank, to support their national development priorities.

In light of the availability of non-concessional financing for development from an increasing variety of sources, MDBs should be enabled and indeed mandated to offer flexible financing packages to clients that provide sufficient incentives to undertake or modify investment intentions in favor of global public goods. These might blend concessional and non-concessional resources in various degrees, with the blend determined not by the characteristics of the borrower or the operation, but by the level of incentive required to reach agreement in a particular case. Consideration should be given to the development of a set of multilateral principles for responsible investment in areas related to the provision of global public goods with a view to avoiding unhealthy races to the bottom on financing terms.

Where the blending of "hard" and "soft" money in order to calibrate incentives results in the provision of concessional financing to a middle-income country, or indeed to any developing country, this should not be characterized as the provision of "aid." The package should be considered as official development finance of a piece with non-concessional lending, as the concessionality benefits all countries, not just the project host.

The Last Word

It is our firm conviction that decisive action needs to be taken now to strengthen international cooperation on global public goods important for development, particularly but not only the avoidance of dangerous climate change. International cooperation has a bad name right now, thanks to the frozen state of negotiations on international climate change and trade liberalization agreements, but international cooperation can and does work at a more practical level—provided resources are available and provided there are effective international institutions to support it. We may not have all the resources we need, particularly in the present, straitened times, but we have and are already using ODA heavily in the service of global public goods. This is appropriate, particularly at a time when new financing for national public goods is beginning to emerge from nontraditional sources. The use of aid for global public goods must be reflected explicitly in a new and broader aid policy narrative or we run the risk of losing public and political support for aid. This new narrative should underline the centrality of international development organizations in supplying global public goods. Much more than that, however, it should entail a rethinking of their mandates such that it becomes their primary purpose to ensure that national and global public policies are interlocked and mutually reinforcing.

Notes

1. For an argument that economic welfare has in fact decreased since 1978, see Kubiszewski et al. (2013).

2. http://www.youtube.com/watch?v=k2sYIIjS-cQ.

3. The National Intelligence Council, in *Global Trends 2030*, identifies as one possibility that the World Bank's governance will change to reflect modern practice and economic reality.

4. *Reaping the benefits: science and sustainable intensification of global agriculture*, The Royal Society, October 2009, highlights the need to scale up research on perennial grains since the conversion of annual crops into perennial plants could help sustain the health of cultivated soils. To date, there are no perennial species that produce adequate grain harvests. However, there are breeding programs aimed at developing perennial grain crops—wheat, sorghum, sunflower, intermediate wheatgrass, and other species. Perennial crops store more carbon and maintain better soil and water quality, manage nutrients more conservatively than conventional annual crops, and have greater biomass and resource management capacity. Given adequate support, these efforts could lead to the development of perennial crops within 10 years.

References

Kubiszewski, Ida, Robert Costanza, Carol Franco, Philip Lawn, John Talberth, Tim Jackson, Camille Aylmer. 2013. "Beyond GDP: Measuring and Achieving Global Genuine Progress." *Ecological Economics* 93: 57–68.

Romilly Greenhill, Annalisa Prizzon, and Andrew Rogerson. 2013. "The Age of Choice: Developing Countries in the New Aid Landscape." Working Paper 364, Overseas Development Institute.

Environmental Benefits Statement

The World Bank Group is committed to reducing its environmental footprint. In support of this commitment, the Publishing and Knowledge Division leverages electronic publishing options and print-on-demand technology, which is located in regional hubs worldwide. Together, these initiatives enable print runs to be lowered and shipping distances decreased, resulting in reduced paper consumption, chemical use, greenhouse gas emissions, and waste.

The Publishing and Knowledge Division follows the recommended standards for paper use set by the Green Press Initiative. Whenever possible, books are printed on 50 percent to 100 percent postconsumer recycled paper, and at least 50 percent of the fiber in our book paper is either unbleached or bleached using Totally Chlorine Free (TCF), Processed Chlorine Free (PCF), or Enhanced Elemental Chlorine Free (EECF) processes.

More information about the Bank's environmental philosophy can be found at http://crinfo.worldbank.org/wbcrinfo/node/4.

green
press
INITIATIVE

www.ingramcontent.com/pod-product-compliance
Lightning Source LLC
Chambersburg PA
CBHW080413270326
41929CB00018B/3010